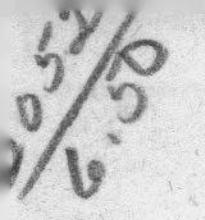

THE STORY OF FABIAN SOCIALISM

OTHER BOOKS BY

MARGARET COLE

Marriage Past and Present

Women of To-Day

Beatrice Webb

Makers of the Labour Movement

Robert Owen of New Lanark

Growing Up into Revolution

Servant of the County

EDITOR

Our Partnership

The Diaries of Beatrice Webb, 1912–24, and 1924–32

The Webbs and Their Work

Twelve Studies in Soviet Russia

Democratic Sweden

WITH G. D. H. COLE

The Condition of Britain

The Brooklyn Murders, and 29 other detective novels

The Fabian Window at Beatrice Webb House. Ordered by Shaw in 1910 and executed by Caroline Townshend. It shows Pease, Webb and Shaw (at the top) building a new world (the Fabian coat-of-arms, in the background, is depicted as a wolf in sheep's clothing) and leading members of the Fabian Executive: H. G. Wells, cocking a snook (a reminder of the 'Episode of Mr Wells'), Charles Charrington, Aylmer Maude, G. R. Stirling Taylor, Lawson Dodd, Mrs Pember Reeves, Mary Hankinson, Mabel Atkinson, Mrs Boyd Dawson, Caroline Townshend (creator of the window).

THE STORY OF FABIAN SOCIALISM

by

MARGARET COLE

STANFORD UNIVERSITY PRESS
STANFORD, CALIFORNIA

First Published 1961

Stanford University Press
Stanford, California

Library of Congress Catalog Card Number: 61–16949

Printed in Great Britain

Contents

PART THREE

Boom and Conflict, 1906–1914

PART FOUR

The Ways Divide, 1914–1938

List of Illustrations

Acknowledgements

MY thanks are due to the Passfield Trustees, the Fabian Society, and the Society of Authors and the Public Trustee for their permission to reproduce from letters and other documents from the Bernard Shaw Estate; also to the Webb Trustees for the reproduction of the stained-glass window at Beatrice Webb House which appears as the frontispiece, to Lady Allen of Hurtwood for the photographs of Clifford Allen, to Hubert Humphreys for photographs of the Fabian Summer School and to Low and Vicky for their cartoons.

I am especially grateful to the London School of Economics and to Sir Sydney Caine, for allowing me access to the Minute Books of the Hutchinson Trust, which were opened when this book was already in the press, and to Sir Sydney's own lecture on the Trust and the origins of the School, which will, I hope, be published. The Minute Books, naturally, contain much more detail than would be appropriate here; but they do not alter the main outline. Sir Sydney's considered opinion is that the 'shroud of secrecy'—Webb actually spread two different versions of the genesis of the School—'covers no action which reflects any discredit on Webb and his co-trustees'. If 'discredit' is strictly interpreted, I should not disagree, though the extraordinary precautions taken against any publicity—the Minute Books were not to be opened until *all* the Trustees were dead—do suggest that Webb was at least doubtful of what the public reaction might have been.

The whole of the manuscript was read by my son Humphrey Cole, and parts by my brother, Raymond Postgate, John Parker, M.P., and W. T. Rodgers, then General Secretary of the Fabian Society. To these, as to all others who helped me by answering questions and giving information, I offer my thanks. But my chief debt cannot now be personally acknowledged. As every reader will realise, without the work of the late President of the Society this book could not have been conceived, much less written; it is my deep regret, and the public's loss, that he did not live long enough to read more than the first draft of the opening chapters. For the rest, I have only to add the traditional Fabian disclaimer—that the book does not represent the opinions of the Society or of anyone else, 'but only the view of the individual who prepared it'. Errors and omissions are all my own.

MARGARET COLE
Finchley, 1961

Preface

ONE reason for writing this book must be obvious. The only history of the Fabian Society which exists was published by Edward Pease in 1916, written during the period of quiescence which followed the outbreak of the first world war, and reissued, with a concluding chapter added, in the year of the first Labour Government. Since then there has not been a straight history of the oldest Socialist society in the world, whose name has given an adjective, 'fabian', to English and foreign political terminology. This does not seem to have been for want of trying. There are, to my knowledge, several 'theses' on the Fabian Society or on various aspects of Fabianism existing in the libraries of universities, in this country and elsewhere, and if enquiries of the Fabian office are any indication, there must be others unknown to me; but so far none of them has seen the light in England, and it is therefore very difficult for any seeker to find out what the Fabian Society was, or was doing, at any time in its history after 1914.

I am here trying to fill that gap, as well as making the adjustments in Pease's very readable account from fuller information derived, for example, from Beatrice Webb's *Diaries* or from studies in the origins of the Labour Party and the London School of Economics—which were not available when he wrote. But the book aims at being a history, not of the Fabian Society in isolation, but of Fabian Socialism, because, as I came to study the period more closely, I found that the Fabian Society's own archives represented only a part of the whole. Many students of Socialist history believe that the drawing of the tortoise which adorns the covers of modern Fabian publications was happily, if not deliberately, chosen as a symbol for a society which was capable of hibernating inactively for many years at a time and then reviving, as the Fabian Society did in 1938–9. This picturesque approach is true enough if the Society alone is taken into account; after the stormy period which ended in 1915 with the possibility of its either splitting or finishing altogether it did sink, gradually, into an unimportant somnolence from which it was only aroused, by the process chronicled in Chapters XVI and XVII of this book, on the verge of a second world war. But 'Fabian Socialism' did not sink as the Fabian Society sank; those who believed in the principles of 1889 (the date of *Fabian Essays*) and in the reforms which the Fabians were trying to bring about, did not cease to do so, though they put their main effort into other bodies—into the new Labour Party of 1918, for example, into the Labour Research Department which grew thunderously out of the Fabian Society in 1915–17, and later into the Society for Socialist Inquiry and Propaganda and the New Fabian Research Bureau. Of these bodies, with the exception of the Labour Party, no history has ever been written, and one of them certainly in its beginnings expressed vehement dissociation with some of the old Fabian leaders, particularly the Webbs in their extreme 'collectivist' period. But once the records have been studied, it plainly emerges that the basic similarities were much greater than the differences, that the basic Fabian aims of the abolition of poverty, through legislation and administration; of the communal control of production and social life, and of the conversion of the British public and of the British governing class (or 'caste', according to date), by a barrage of facts and 'informed' propaganda, were pursued with unabated energy by people trained in Fabian traditions, whether at any moment of time they called themselves Fabians or loudly repudiated the name. The National Guilds League itself, the body created by the Guild Socialists, was, as S. G. Hobson shrewdly pointed out at the time, not much less 'Fabian' than the Fabians themselves, however violently it seemed to disagree with them on tactics, and this was even truer of the Labour Research Department. The fundamental likeness is attested by the fact that after the storms produced first by Syndicalism and then by the Russian Revolution in its early days had died down, those 'rebel Fabians' who had not joined the Communist Party (and the many who, having initially joined it, left in all haste), together with G. D. H. Cole's connections in the working-class education movement and his young disciples from Oxford of the 'twenties, found no mental difficulty in entering the revived Fabian Society of 1939—nor did the surviving faithful find any difficulty in collaborating with them to raise the Society to a size and activity not known before.

It is this tough tradition in British political life—comparable, as many have suggested, with that of the Utilitarians—that this book is endeavouring to put on record; but it does not, of course, intend to be a history of the British Labour movement or even of British Socialism as a whole, for which there are many other sources. It describes the British social scene in so far as is necessary for the understanding of its subject, and deals with other societies where they impinged on Fabianism; but it makes no attempt to tell the history or evaluate the contribution of, say, the Independent Labour Party or the Social-Democratic Federation, or, later, of the Labour Party itself or the Left Book Club, which gathered in so many young Socialists in the days before the last war. For this reason it can devote comparatively little attention to those leaders of Socialism who though in fact they were members of the Society, were best known for the work they did, not within but outside it—the names of Keir Hardie, George Lansbury, Arthur Henderson, Harold Laski spring to the mind immediately, and any reader who has lived through, or read through, the annals of the working-class movement will be able to supply others for himself. No disrespect is thereby implied; but this is the story of *Fabian* Socialism.

PART ONE

Early Days

1883–1894

'Britain as a whole was never more tranquil and happy. No class is at war with society or the government: there is no disaffection anywhere, the Treasury is fairly full, the accumulations of capital are vast.' *Spectator*, summer of 1882; quoted in E. R. Pease, *History of the Fabian Society*.

'For the right moment you must wait, as Fabius did most patiently, when warring against Hannibal, though many censured his delays; but when the time comes you must strike hard, as Fabius did, or your waiting will be in vain and fruitless.' Motto of the Fabian Society, as printed at the head of Fabian Tract No. 1.

The wording of the motto was supplied to the Society by Frank Podmore. No one has ever found any version of it in Latin texts; but lapse of time and long usage have given it the air of historical authenticity. An attempt was once made to get it altered; but the voting was even, and the discussion lapsed.

CHAPTER I

The Small Beginning

THE date is October 24th, 1883; the scene is one of a pair of rooms in number seventeen Osnaburgh Street, close to Great Portland Street Underground (a site now occupied by the large block of flats known as the White House), rented by Edward Pease, a young man of twenty-six, then a partner of sorts in a Stock Exchange firm, an occupation which he considered immoral, as he had become a devotee of William Morris and all his works. This serious-minded young man was much given to study and discussion and, according to his own recollections, was a frequent volunteer as secretary for the ephemeral groups which arose out of such discussion; it was therefore natural that he should lend his large sitting-room for sixteen persons, including the philosopher Havelock Ellis, to assemble and talk about a 'Fellowship of the New Life'. Another of those present was Frank Podmore, the future biographer of Robert Owen and a member of the Society for Psychical Research, whose acquaintance Pease had made while they were both watching (vainly) for a ghost to appear in a supposedly haunted house in Hampstead.[1]

The *raison d'être* of the group was a recent visit to London of Thomas Davidson, known as 'the wandering scholar'. Davidson was a Scottish schoolmaster who had emigrated to America, and in that land of cranks and Utopians had developed a cloudy idealistic philosophy which demanded that its votaries should pledge themselves to live according to high ideals of love and brotherhood, founding wherever possible communities in which such a life could be lived completely, but short of that putting their principles into practice while pursuing their ordinary avocations. Most of what Davidson wrote is confused and rather

[1] *For My Sons*; unpublished MS. by Edward R. Pease, begun in 1930. Later Pease showed gifts as a water-diviner; but he never concealed his opinion that spiritualism was arrant rubbish.

nonsensical; but he seems to have been a man of magnetic personality; he ran for several years summer camps in the States which were well attended, and he left in London some ardent disciples, one of whom, a civil servant named Percival Chubb, had brought together the little gathering in Osnaburgh Street.[1] What came of it can be found in the handwritten report at the beginning of a dilapidated quarto exercise book now in the archives of the Fabian Society.

The proceedings began, we are told, by the reading of a paper by Davidson himself on 'The New Life', after which there was a discussion, of which no details are given, on the possibility of founding a community for common living.

'It was suggested,' the record proceeds, '—and the suggestion was appropriately received—that undoubtedly the first thing to be done was for those present to become thoroughly acquainted with each other': the meeting then turned to general conversation and adjourned for a fortnight. At the resumption on November 7th (after some argument as to whether it was desirable to have any formal association at all) a resolution was carried announcing 'That an association be formed whose ultimate aim shall be the reconstruction of Society in accordance with the highest moral possibilities.' A month later, with Hubert Bland, the future treasurer of the Fabian Society, in the chair, a Dr Burns-Gibson produced a draft 'Plan for a Fellowship of the New Life', of which the first two clauses may be quoted:

Object—*The cultivation of a perfect character in each and all.*
Principle—*The subordination of material things to physical.*

The group reached no decision at the time; but it appears that to some of them, at any rate, the draft Plan appeared somewhat ambitious and imprecise, for at a later meeting, held on January 4th, 1884, there was a difference of opinion, and a vote. On the motion of Podmore, a resolution was carried by nine votes to two in the following terms:

1. The name of the new society shall be The Fabian Society [the name, and the motto previously quoted, being supplied by Podmore].

[1] See *Memorials of Thomas Davidson*, edited by William Knight (1907), and the account in Vol. I of G. D. H. Cole, *History of Socialist Thought*. Percival Chubb emigrated to America to found various Ethical Churches there, and died in 1960 at the age of 99—the last survivor of all the long-lived pioneers.

2. The resolution of 23rd November [demanding the instant 'reconstruction' of society as a whole] should be amended by the insertion of the words 'to help on' between the words 'shall be' and 'the reconstruction'.

3. The Society should proceed to take practical steps, e.g. by holding discussions among its own members, by sending delegates to meetings of other bodies, and by the collecting of articles and other forms of information, to further the purposes which it has agreed.[1]

The nine who had formed the majority[2] then proceeded to choose an Executive Committee of three, Hubert Bland, Frank Podmore, and Frederick Keddell, who became the first secretary.[3] Between them they subscribed thirteen shillings and sevenpence for current expenses, and decided to meet fortnightly. On January 25th, one of their number, J. G. Stapleton, delivered the first Fabian lecture under the title 'Social Conditions in England with a view to Social Reconstruction or Development'; on March 7th the Society solemnly appointed a 'Pamphlet Committee', of which Rosamund Dale Owen, Robert Owen's granddaughter and later the wife of the novelist Laurence Oliphant, was a member; and a fortnight later, approving the conduct of its Executive Committee, it re-elected all three of them.

In this remarkably unobtrusive manner the longest-lived of all Socialist societies sidled into the world. The perfectionists whom the Fabians had abandoned were not disheartened; they maintained themselves until 1898 as 'The Fellowship of the New Life', having in their ranks, besides Havelock Ellis and his wife, Edward Carpenter, the author of *Towards Democracy* and *England Arise!*, the song of so many Socialist meetings, Henry Salt, the founder of the Humanitarian League, and the Liberal M.P.

[1] Minute Book of the Fabian Society. There is a more detailed account in Pease, *History of the Fabian Society*.

[2] It is not quite certain whether the number of those who formed the new Society was nine or ten. Fifteen were present at the meeting and appended their signatures in the Minute Book (Thomas Davidson 'by letter from Italy'); but they certainly did not all become Fabians. Bland's obituary in *Fabian News* says he was 'one of the ten founders'; but this list apparently included Havelock Ellis, who was never a member, according to a letter from Pease to the present writer. Percival Chubb seems to have joined, though his chief interest obviously lay in the parent body.

[3] Keddell was a City clerk, a friend of Bland; not long afterwards he emigrated to Calcutta. Pease succeeded him, and, save for a three-year interval when he was in Newcastle and Olivier took his place, held the post until 1913.

Corrie Grant (father-in-law of Lord Slesser, the Fabian), publishing a quarterly journal called *Seedtime*, and displaying from time to time yearnings to found a 'community' of one sort or another. Some Fabians were members of the Fellowship as well; and for one year its secretary was James Ramsay MacDonald, the future Prime Minister of Britain.

A dispassionate observer in the spring of 1884 might, in fact, have been put to it to prophesy which, if either, of the two insignificant little bodies had any future whatsoever. The handful of 'founding Fabians' rose in the first few weeks to about twenty, and in April, on the report of the Pamphlet Committee, an order was given to print two thousand copies of the first 'Fabian Tract' *Why Are the Many Poor?*—the name (which is still in use today for many of the Society's publications) recalls the Dissenting and missionary ancestry of much early Socialist and Trade Union organisation. The Tract was a four-page leaflet written by W. L. Phillips, a house-painter who had embraced the Positivist philosophy of Auguste Comte and was long cherished by the Society as its 'exhibit' working-class member, the only one of his kind to join for some years.[1]

The Society was proud of its first pamphlet, and kept it in print for many years, selling over 100,000 copies. But it could hardly be called a typical Fabian publication, as a few extracts will show:

> Do economists, statesmen, and sociologists stand hopeless before this problem of Poverty? Must workers continue in their misery whilst professors and politicians split straws and wrangle over trifles?
>
> No! for the workers must and will shake off their blind faith in the Commercial god Competition, and realise the responsibility of their unused powers.
>
> If Capital be socialised, Labor will benefit by it fully, but while Capital is left in the hands of the few Poverty must be the lot of the many.
>
> Teach, preach and pray to all eternity in your schools and churches and it will avail you nothing until you have swept away this blind idol of Competition, this misuse of Capital in the hands of individuals.
>
> You who live dainty and pleasant lives, reflect that your ease and

[1] The next, so far as records tell, was Hines, the 'intellectual chimney-sweep' of Oxford, whose 'character' was vividly described in his obituary in *Fabian News* of May 1904. There were of course many more when 'Fabianism' spread to the provinces after 1889.

luxury are paid for by the misery and want of others! Your superfluities are the parents of poverty. Surely all humanity is not burnt out of you by the gold your fathers left you!

The exclamation marks are in the original; it might have been written by any eager and not very lettered radical from the Chartists onwards. Even at that, it was completely outshadowed by Robert Blatchford's *Merrie England* and his *Clarion* articles as soon as these began to appear.

The incident which settled the event, as between the Fabian Society and the Fellowship, happened on May 16th. The Minutes of that date have a pencilled side-note in a handwriting which afterwards became world-famous: 'This meeting was made memorable by the first appearance of Bernard Shaw'—and on this occasion the writer was not guilty of any over-statement. Shaw was twenty-eight years old, a struggling journalist living on subsidies from his mother, when he came to 'the Fabian'[1] after experimenting with a body calling itself the Zetetical Society, which was a kind of junior partner of a Dialectical Society formed to discuss the works of John Stuart Mill, and with the Democratic (later Social-Democratic) Federation, founded by the impressive bearded and silk-hatted Marxist, Henry Mayers Hyndman;[2] he was admitted to membership in September and elected to the Executive in the following January. Shortly afterwards appeared Tract 2, a two-page leaflet entitled *A Manifesto*, which had been discussed clause by clause by the membership in October. It was unsigned, but the style is as unmistakable as the handwriting in the Minutes; it ends with the unquestionably Shavian—and un-Marxist—remark that 'the established Government has no more right to call itself the State than the smoke of London has to call itself the weather'.

In March 1885 the second major event occurred; Shaw brought along his friend Sidney Webb, then a clerk in the Colonial Office, to read to the fortnightly meeting a paper on 'The Way Out'; and in May Webb and his Colonial Office colleague, Sydney (later Lord) Olivier, were admitted to membership. The 'Big Four' of Fabian thought was completed in the

[1] The Society, in its early years, was often known as 'The Fabian' simply.

[2] Shaw, *Sixteen Self-Sketches*, 1949. Shaw said Hyndman looked very like Jehovah. In a private letter to the present author he denied that he was ever more than a 'candidate-member' of the S.D.F., dropping his candidature as soon as he discovered the existence of 'the Fabian'.

following year by the admission of Graham Wallas. It may be mentioned that in those pioneering days—and for a long time afterwards—Fabian membership was not to be had simply for the asking. It was necessary to be proposed and seconded by a member before one's name was submitted to the Executive; and this was no formality. Lord Attlee has recalled that, as late as 1909, when he, then a social worker, with a young friend sought out the Fabian Society in Clement's Inn with a view to joining it, Pease put them through a severe verbal cross-examination and all but turned them from the door as insufficiently serious-minded. (And this when all hands were going to be needed for the Poor Law campaign!)[1] Later, conditions were relaxed; the General Secretary was 'deemed' to have countersigned all applications; and by the second world war all formalities had lapsed. It is a comment on the courage of their convictions possessed by the early Fabians—and also of the absence of McCarthyism in their country—that for many years the Society issued a printed list of all its members, complete with names and addresses; this was only discontinued after complaints that it attracted the attentions of advertising touts.

Shaw, Webb, Olivier, and Wallas, however famous they subsequently became, were unknown names in 1885–6; in the former year the infant Society made its most spectacular convert to date, Annie Besant, the brilliant colleague of Charles Bradlaugh the Freethinker, the finest woman orator and organiser of her day, who had actually crossed swords with the Law for public advocacy of birth-control. Her conversion was effected, according to his own account, by Bernard Shaw; and she naturally became a propaganda asset. In the same year, during which, in Tract 3, the Society for the first time publicly announced that it was Socialist, it received what should have proved quite an advertisement through a Mr Miller, an Edinburgh industrialist, who provided the then enormous sum of a thousand pounds to finance a Conference on Industrial Remuneration to which the Society sent delegates, and which was to discuss which classes in the community had benefited most, and in what proportion, from the increases in productivity during the century. The conference duly met in London, and talked for three days. Arthur Balfour, the future Prime Minister, contributed a paper in which he paid somewhat unexpected tribute to the intellectual powers of

[1] See Chapter XIII.

Karl Marx, who had died shortly before, contrasting him with the Single-Taxer Henry George; Shaw delivered a fine *apologia* for burglars as compared with landowners and shareholders. The addresses were taken down and preserved in a fat volume; they are certainly no worse than a great many of the millions of words delivered at such conferences, but for some reason they attracted little attention and produced no effect. Mr Miller's thousand pounds might as well have been thrown into the Thames. Nor was a large conference in 1886, which the Society, then numbering some forty members and trying to make up its mind whether it was anarchist or collectivist, Parliamentary or catastrophic,[1] decided to run on its own, any more effective, in spite of being reported in *The Times*;[2] and though in 1887 one of the most important and characteristic of Fabian publications, *Facts for Socialists* (Tract 5, of which more hereafter), was issued, it took time to make any impression. By the winter of 1888 the Society had still less than a hundred members; and it is fairly safe to say that scarcely anyone of importance (including, at that date, Miss Beatrice Potter) had ever heard of it. It was a seedling which might easily have perished in a hostile soil.

[1] See pp. 19–20.

[2] It was shortly after this that members began to complain, according to Pease, that the Society had 'passed its prime', and the Executive decided (May 6th, 1887) to issue a Circular on 'Apathy'—whose text has not survived.

CHAPTER II

The Seed-Bed

IT did not perish, however; nor did the many of its kin that had their birthdays more or less simultaneously. It has often been observed, and observed correctly, that the 'eighties and 'nineties were the seeding-time for Socialist organisations in Britain. Hyndman's Democratic Federation adopted the name Social-Democratic in 1883, and at the end of 1884 hived off William Morris's semi-anarchist Socialist League; the Fabian Society had been founded earlier in the year. In 1891, Robert Blatchford left his job with Hulton's *Sunday Chronicle* to start the *Clarion* weekly, and Clarion organisations of many kinds sprang up in its wake; in the same year John Trevor, the Unitarian minister, set up the first Labour Church in Manchester. In 1893 Keir Hardie persuaded a collection of Labour and Socialist groups from all over the kingdom to join hands to form the Independent Labour Party, Socialist in its policy though not, for practical reasons, in its name; and in the same year the Trades Union Congress carried resolutions demanding the collective ownership of the means of production: it is true that about half the delegates cast no votes on that occasion, but such indifference on large and distant issues was not unknown at important gatherings either then or later. Socialism was not yet a force of which much account need be taken; no one had to read Marx, whose International Working Men's Association was dead in New York; but the forms of propaganda were coming into being, and it seems that the soil was not hostile.

There has been a very great deal of discussion on the nature of that soil; but there seems no doubt that its main constituent was economic *surprise*—surprise at the failure of Progress. Up to the early 'eighties, the quotation which opens this book might seem fairly correct. The desperate class battles of the first half of the century, the struggles of the Political Unions, the Owenite

Trade Unions, and the Chartists, had died down not merely by reason of the defeat or destruction of the organisations which had fought them but also because of the increasing prosperity and security brought by the railways, the stabilisation of bread prices, the expansion of industry and export trade, and all that was summed up in the words 'The Great Exhibition'. Workers could breathe again, and look forward a little to the future; even if their organisations still inserted clauses about 'community living' into their rule books, as did the Rochdale Pioneers and the 'New Model' Amalgamated Society of Engineers, it was as a long-distance hope rather than an immediate objective. Wages rose and employment steadied; Trade Unions were formed or re-formed; Trade Unionism even spread to low-paid groups such as Joseph Arch's agricultural labourers. At the same time, governments of both political complexions were moved to do something in the way of passing down some of the surplus wealth that was being generated—mainly in the field of public health, although much more could have been done there had the Local Government Board created in 1871 been given into the hands of enlightened experts such as Sir John Simon rather than those of the mandarins of the Poor Law. Even the Poor Law itself, however, came to be mitigated in its application after the scandals of the Hendon and Andover workhouses; and there was actually a timid attempt, in the Cross and Torrens Acts, to do something about the frightful state of working-class housing so vividly described in Engels' *Condition of the English Working Classes in 1844*. Other improvements were made, by private philanthropy and by public authority, in some of the larger towns, notably Birmingham, where Joseph Chamberlain's mayoralty (1873–5) was the high-water-mark of mid-century reform. Someone has said that the only chain which the official of the New Model Union had to lose was the gold albert across his stomach; this is of course a wild exaggeration, but security of a sort, for the skilled worker at all events, was a real fact in the 'seventies, and 'the inevitability of gradualness' was born then, and not in any Fabian study.

'Security', however, is the key word. Living conditions improved mainly because employment was steadier, and even improved conditions were only a layer over a foundation of squalor and poverty which anyone could realise who read Mayhew's *London* as more than a guide-book of entertaining tit-bits about the lives of common sewermen and the like.[1] 'Security' was for the better-off among the working class; and at the end of the 'seventies 'security' suddenly came to an end. What was later called the Great Depression—in reality two or three trade recessions coming on the heels of one another in a comprehensive trough—began a long period of fluctuations, and confidence in 'security' vanished almost overnight. It was not so much an actual drop in incomes. Money wages came down, it is true, but not by very much; and the curve of real wages in fact rose, as steel ships and steel rails brought in cheap American corn—later, with cold storage, cheap New World meat as well—to break prices and ruin farmers. Food could be bought when work was available; it was the return of heavy unemployment which created despair. In the black winter of 1879, 11 per cent of those organised in Trade Unions—the 'better-off' of the working class—found themselves out of work, without wages, and once their small savings and union benefits were exhausted dependent on charity or the cold rigidities of the Poor Law. (It may be noted that in the 'prosperous' days of 1869 the Charity Organisation Society had been formed to deal with the 'scandals' produced by unorganised private almsgiving; whatever 'scandals' there may have been, the attitude of some of the officials of the C.O.S., who seemed determined to beat the Poor Law officers at their own game,[2] was hardly likely to be sympathetic when leaner times came.)

The skilled trades were hard hit. Harder still was the lot of those in less fortunate positions—dockers living always on a basis of casual labour, unorganised groups like Beatrice Potter's 'trouser-hands' or Annie Besant's match-girls, agricultural labourers discharged from the ruined farms, of whom nearly 100,000, according to the Census returns, migrated to the cities in the ten years between 1871 and 1881. These last, it may be noted, had come from country districts where, however much repression and arbitrary treatment of individuals there might be, there was nevertheless a tradition of some personal contact

[1] Though in 1883 the Rev. Andrew Mearns' pamphlet, *The Bitter Cry of Outcast London*, had a wide circulation and reached the eyes of Queen Victoria, thereby causing the appointment in the following year of a Royal Commission on Housing, which looked impressive on paper but produced nothing.

[2] See *My Apprenticeship*, by Beatrice Webb, who tried working with the C.O.S.

between the farmer (and occasionally the landowner) and his men, to a city life in which there was none. Nor was this 'depersonalisation' confined to ex-rural workers. Sir Robert Ensor has well stressed[1] the importance of limited liability in the Companies Acts—very much used after 1872—in replacing the old personal nexus between employer and employee by an abstract relationship with a Board of Directors, and Beatrice Webb's autobiography underlines this from her own early experience. 'Coupled mysteriously with its mate capital, this abstract term "labour" was always turning up in my father's conversation, and it occurred and re-occurred in the technical journals and reports of companies which lay on his table. "Water plentiful and labour docile", "the wages of labour are falling to their natural level", etc.' [2] In this atmosphere of abstraction and friendlessness the young Unions which had grown up in the years of security collapsed or shrank to skeletons; their seniors shook themselves angrily and began to wonder—as did some members of the middle classes—whether there was not something wrong with the beneficent system of *laissez-faire* which had so cruelly let them down. It was not surprising that 'well-paid artisans' horrified the respectable by making common cause with the 'riff-raff' who demonstrated in Trafalgar Square and broke shop and club windows in Pall Mall.

At the same time, the stream of social legislation showed signs of drying up, and it appeared that the impetus of the parties, particularly the Liberal Party, towards social reform was coming to an end. There was some political reform to come—the Municipal Corporations Act of 1882, and the more far-reaching Local Government Acts of 1884, 1888, and 1894, which together with the 1883 Corrupt Practices Act did a good deal both to end the blatant power of wealth in elections and to open the possibility of representation to the working classes. But the pace of social reform which cost money was markedly slowed down, and that not merely because Gladstone had embroiled himself with an Irish Coercion Bill immediately after his re-election in 1880, and before and afterwards with imperialistic adventure in Egypt. It was, of course, only to be expected in a time of bad trade. 'Deficit spending' as an idea was half a century and more away; members of the upper classes, however philanthropic and kindly, who were faced with an unexpected decline in their own incomes,

[1] Ensor, *England, 1871–1914*, p. 112. [2] *My Apprenticeship*, p. 3.

were not likely to look tolerantly at public 'extravagance', whether tax- or rate-borne.

Joseph Chamberlain, it is true, did not share that attitude; he excoriated the Marquess of Salisbury and his class in terms more abusively demagogic than were to be heard in public from a Minister of the Crown until the days of Lloyd George and Limehouse, and he made a great endeavour, throughout 1885, to save the soul of the Liberal Party by preaching on public platforms an 'Unauthorised Programme' based on the idea that owners of private property owed society a 'ransom' for their enjoyment of it, which should take the form of ever-increasing contributions to social welfare. Free education, public housing, compulsory land purchase, payment of members and higher taxation, all found place in that programme which, mild as it reads today, caused the Earl of Iddesleigh to call its author another Jack Cade.[1] The Unauthorised Programme undoubtedly helped the Liberals in the election of 1885—in which many miners voted for the first time; but that it was *unauthorised* was heavily underlined almost immediately afterwards, when its framer broke with his leader over Home Rule, and turned from social reform at home to those wider issues which brought him in the end to the sordid adventure of the Jameson Raid. With him—and with Dilke—went out the hope of large reforms from the Liberals,[2] as their leader and their party fell into the Irish bog.

If social reform was dying down, there were others than Chamberlain to regret it. There was a third strain of thought which contributed to the emergence of Socialism, for which the best term is J. L. Hammond's 'The Conscience of the Rich' [3]—and of the near-rich. The mid-Victorian may have had a sense of

[1] It also contributed to early Fabian programmes—a contribution never acknowledged at all. But the Fabians were always unwilling to give any credit to Chamberlain. 'Why,' wrote Shaw in the first chapter of *The Webbs and Their Work*, 'refer to Chamberlain any more than to Balfour or Randolph Churchill or any other of the pre-Marxist figureheads?' It may be that they disliked him for the same kind of reason as prevented the Webbs from ever getting on terms with Lloyd George; possibly his loudly expressed hostility to the London County Council contributed to their attitude.

[2] For the 'window-dressing' episode of the Newcastle Programme, see p. 45.

[3] Hammond, *The Town Labourer*, Chapter X. Hammond was referring to an earlier period; but the feeling is the same.

security in matters material, but on the non-material side of life much of the evidence goes to show that he was very far from feeling secure. As a Christian he was uncertain, after Newman, whether he was doing right by God and his own soul, and (after Darwin) whether he was believing what he ought to believe about himself, his descent, and the history of the world; and to these uncertainties was added the clamour of people always ready to abuse him for the immorality and ugliness of his values and the works of his hands. To take only the most obvious examples, Carlyle and Ruskin had thundered at him for years from their personal pulpits; Matthew Arnold was lecturing him, as G. K. Chesterton said, 'with a smile of heart-broken forbearance, as of the teacher in an idiot school' [1] for being a Barbarian or a Philistine; John Stuart Mill, philosopher of liberty and son of the great lieutenant of Utilitarianism, was suggesting that 'the greatest good of the greatest number' seemed, in modern society, to mean some form of Socialism. These might possibly have been discounted as generalised sermons, cries of recurrent Savonarolas; it seems nevertheless the case that, as social reform died down, more and more people became actively conscious, not of the generalisations, but of the *facts* of squalor and poverty, of the disease, the dirt, the foul smells and foul language which were all around them, as soon as they began to use their eyes, ears, and noses—especially in London, the rich capital city of the richest country in the world, which now began to look as if its social foundations were as filthy and unstable as the mud-flats of Chicago. Charles Booth's monumental *Life and Labour of the People of London* did not begin to appear until 1889; but when it did, it told a much more serious and documented story than Mayhew's: *thirty per cent* of London's people living in 'poverty'—and 'poverty' in Booth's sense did not mean just pinching and scraping, but a poverty which enforced a degrading and disgusting existence. This fact, earlier discovered and announced, though not in statistical terms, by George R. Sims and the Salvation Army, forced itself into the consciousness of men and women grown more sensitive than their forebears.

Economic insecurity—the slackening of reform—a sense of social shame; all these played their part in creating the mental atmosphere in which the Socialist societies were born. To these three might be added a fourth factor—fear. For a feeling that

[1] Chesterton, *The Victorian Age in English Literature*.

the social system might stand in need of serious revision was reinforced by a less strong but nevertheless real feeling that worse things might come about if revision were not attempted, or postponed too long. Whatever may be said about 'increasing misery', as a matter of fact it is not the hopelessly downtrodden, but those who have known happier days, who tend to react angrily to worsening conditions, and it was the anger of the 'respectable' working man which frightened his betters, and caused the subscriptions to the Lord Mayor's fund for the relief of distress to take an instant leap upwards after the Pall Mall riots—an instinctive insurance against the social revolution which Hyndman and his friends were confidently predicting for 1889, the centenary of the fall of the Bastille. The historically romantic choice of date might have suggested to the fearful that revolution was not in fact all that imminent; practical revolutionaries, practical plotters, do not, as we now know, obligingly announce the date of their uprising some years in advance. Yet it *might* be true; memories of the Commune of Paris were not all that far away; there were assassinations in Ireland; and one of Hyndman's supporters, the ex-artillery officer H. H. Champion, was actually drilling unemployed members of the S.D.F. in readiness for The Day. It is not surprising that a handful of members of all classes, moved by shame and anger at the state of things in Britain and the apparent impotence, or unwillingness, of available governments under the existing system to alter it, should be willing to look at proposals for a new and nobler deal, more especially if they could promise change without bloodshed.

Walter Crane's cover design for the first edition of *Fabian Essays*, published 1889 under the title *Socialism*.

Camera Press

Bernard Shaw

Graham Wallas

William Clarke

Sydney Olivier

THE SEVEN ESSAYISTS (i)

CHAPTER III

The Earliest Years

EVEN the handful, however, did not immediately flock to join the Fabian Society, which for some years was still much of a hole-and-corner affair—a 'silly business' as Shaw characterised it in *The Webbs and Their Work*. Its first two Tracts have already been described; the third—the one which contained the first mention of Socialism—was another Shavian leaflet, and the fourth, called *What Socialism Means*, a discussion between the Anarchist and Collectivist elements in the Society. These two strains, appearing in so small a group, reflected the fierce debate which went on for many years in the counsels of European Socialists[1] and were hardly resolved until the end of the century; in the Fabian Society, as will be seen, the issue was early decided against the Anarchists, who did not, however, sever connections. William Morris remained a Fabian. The next published document was a report on *Government Organisation of Unemployed Labour*. This, the product of a committee of five—Hubert Bland, F. C. Hughes, Frank Podmore, J. G. Stapleton, and Sidney Webb (who, it may be presumed, actually wrote it)—was the first attempt of the Society to put forward 'practical' proposals. It was not well received by the membership. Its merits, in fact, are not great; it suggested a form of national conscription—anathema then and for generations to the English working classes—and the establishment of government-subsidised tobacco-growing in England, which was merely silly. The Society agreed to publish it, but, to mark its disapproval, published it as a report by the authors only, which was tantamount to a disclaimer.[2] Next, however, came *Facts for Socialists*.

Facts for Socialists is important because it first expresses the

[1] See G. D. H. Cole, *History of Socialist Thought*, Vol. III, Chapter I.

[2] Later, many of the Society's specialised publications appeared under their authors' name or names; but most of the early ones were supposed to be communal productions, even if the authorship was obvious.

conviction, which became one of the most important parts of the Fabian creed, that no reasonable person *who knows the facts* can fail to become a Socialist, or, at the very least, to be converted to the Socialist policy on any subject or problem presently under discussion—that out of their own mouths, or rather out of their published material, the defenders of capitalism can be made to prove that it is inefficient, brutal and idiotic. There was nothing particularly original in the idea. Marx had made devastating use, in the historical chapters of *Das Kapital*, of material gathered from the official reports of H.M. Inspectors of Factories; and there is no reason to doubt the statement of Shaw (who alone among the Fabians had studied Marx)[1] that he propounded the idea to Webb. But there is this difference. *Das Kapital*, Vol. I, was a large formidable tome: *Facts for Socialists* was a penny pamphlet intended for a wide circulation.

The first edition of *Facts for Socialists*—there were 16 revisions in all, the last published in 1956—was not in itself a very large or impressive document. There were 16 pages of it; it included, with some tables and simple diagrams, information about national income, production, and occupations, rents, profits and salaries, a comparison of the conditions of the 'Two Nations', and some facts about infant deaths, industrial accidents, pauperism, and other ills which affected the poor. It provided material for speeches; but was very slight compared with *Facts for Londoners* (Tract 8, 1889) in whose 55 pages, priced at sixpence,[2] Sidney Webb showed what he could really do in the way of collecting telling statistics for popular consumption. *Facts for Londoners* was produced as ammunition for the reformers in the elections for the first London County Council, and must certainly have contributed to their handsome majority—said to be two-thirds,[3] though party lines were not then strictly drawn. The Tract contains suggestions for policy as well as facts; but policy was much more clearly laid down in *The Fabian Municipal Programme* (Tracts 30–37)[4] issued for the second L.C.C.

[1] Webb, according to Pease, once read the first volume of *Das Kapital*, but was not impressed.

[2] The 1956 edition of *Facts for Socialists* had 49 pages; but it cost two shillings.

[3] Gibbon and Bell, *History of the London County Council*, p. 77.

[4] Webb's Tract was the modest forerunner of the L.C.C.'s comprehensive publication, *London Statistics*.

election in 1892, when Webb was himself a candidate, and elected for Deptford.

The sixth Tract was a very brief *Radical Programme*, presented as an alternative to the election programmes of the Liberal Party; the seventh, entitled *Capital and Land*, was a longer and more closely reasoned argument addressed to the Single-Taxers and the advocates of land nationalisation, inviting them to support the nationalisation of capital as well. With the ninth, which is a fairly precise and detailed draft of a possible Eight Hours Bill, we reach a form of activity, the presentation of practical proposals for consideration by interested and informed persons, which the Society was to make peculiarly its own. The Tract was drafted in November 1889; and the foreword to the edition announced as 'Twentieth Thousand' states that its proposals have been approved in general by the London Liberal and Radical Union, the Metropolitan Radical Federation,[1] the London Trades Council and most of the London Working Men's Clubs, as well as by the first large May Day Labour demonstration (1890). By producing this Tract, the Society showed itself well in the front of current Socialist thought. For the eight-hour day, as is not always remembered, in the late nineteenth century was not just an item in a programme of social reform, comparable, say, with a better provision of public baths or libraries; it was a fundamental demand of the radicals among the working classes and, because of the arguments of the anti-Factory Act type of economist that all the employer's profits were earned in the last hour of the working day, it was considered to be a demand which struck at the roots of capitalism. Even Marx believed that the eight-hour day was not a 'palliative' but a real step towards revolution.

During these years, the Society began, in a small way, to take definite shape. At the beginning of 1886 the Executive Committee was enlarged to seven members, of whom Annie Besant was one; and in September of that year the Fabians finally made up their minds on the question of Anarchism *versus* Parliamentarianism. At a meeting at Anderton's Hotel, Bland and Mrs Besant brought this question to a head by respectively moving and seconding the following resolution.[2]

[1] Possibly the London Municipal Reform League, founded in 1881 by John Lloyd (Gibbon and Bell, *op. cit.*).

[2] Shaw, *Early History of the Fabian Society*. Tract 41.

> That it is advisable that Socialists should organise themselves as a political party for the purpose of transferring into the hands of the whole working community full control over the soil and the means of production, as well as over the production and distribution of wealth.

To this a rider was moved by William Morris as follows:

> But whereas the first duty of Socialists is to educate the people to understand what their present position is and what their future might be, and to keep the principle of Socialism steadily before them; and whereas no Parliamentary party can exist without compromise and concession, which would hinder that education and obscure those principles, it would be a false step for Socialists to attempt to take part in the Parliamentary contest.

I shall not attempt to describe the debate, in which Morris, Mrs Wilson [the leading Fabian Anarchist], Davis and Tochatti did battle with [John] Burns, Mrs Besant, Bland, Shaw, Donald, and Rossiter—that is with Fabian and S.D.F. combined. Suffice it to say that the minutes of the meeting close with the following significant note by the secretary:

> Subsequently to the meeting, the secretary received notice from the manager of Anderton's Hotel that the Society could not be accommodated there for any future meetings.[1]

Everybody voted, whether Fabian or not; and Mrs Besant and Bland carried their resolution by 47 to 19. Morris's rider being subsequently [*sic*] rejected by 40 to 27.

After this rather noisy clarification of its views the Society characteristically tempered the wind to the minority—and thus avoided any split—by forming the *majority* into a Fabian Parliamentary League with a separate existence and a separate committee. This device of not forcing the issue, of allowing the longest rope possible to differences of opinion within the membership, was the very opposite of the practice of the majority of Socialist and other doctrinal societies, and largely accounts for the fact that the Society endured for three-quarters of a century without ever splitting its ranks. This was not mainly because its membership was, and has remained, small; all who have participated in politics, particularly left-wing politics, know that, as a general

[1] According to a note in Shaw's writing in the Fabian Minute Book, this was caused by a tinsmith called Graham, an Anarchist follower of Morris, who 'came drunk and comported himself with unseemly heat'.

rule, the smaller the organisation the stronger its fissile tendencies. Nor was the reason that there was no Fabian 'discipline'; the seriousness of would-be entrants was, as we have seen, carefully scrutinised, and there was undoubtedly a definite difference between being a Fabian member and being an outside sympathiser on whom Fabian members could work. But it was not a difference which was pressed home in detail or in matters which common sense would later show to be inessential.

The Parliamentary League produced the sixth Tract, which has already been mentioned, and a few leaflets; but the case for Parliamentary action having now been accepted, the vocal opposition gradually faded away, and the League, as a body, became imperceptibly merged in the Society itself. The most important result of the incident was the formulation, in 1887, of the 'Fabian Basis', the document to which all members were asked to subscribe before being admitted to the Society, and which, with a single addition, endured unchanged until 1919.

The Basis, with the 'women's rights' amendment added in 1907, is printed in Appendix I. It is not, in itself, one of the Society's better literary efforts; it is verbose and vague. As Pease says in his *History*, nobody was satisfied with it for long, and it would have been revised many times had the would-be revisionists been able to agree on an alternative form of wording which would have satisfied enough of them to bring it into effect without driving others out of the Society. It never amounted to more than a consensus of opinion—not even so much as a confession of faith—and some of its clauses were, by common consent, disregarded from the first. As, however, it was for so many years the only statement of principle which was ever nominally binding on all Fabians—*Fabian Essays*, of course, committed nobody but the Essayists themselves—it is worth observing that in its short compass it twice affirms the principle of gradualism—achieving Socialism by persuasion and the dissemination of information—and that it hedges on the question of compensation for those who lose property rights as a result of 'socialisation'. This ambiguity seems to have been deliberate, for a year previously the Executive had carried a resolution against all 'interest', an amendment moved by Webb to add 'for the benefit of individuals' being lost by a narrow majority. The attitude of the Society, as expressed in the Basis, remained undefined, though as the years went by it became steadily clearer that compensation rather than confiscation represented the majority view.[1]

In June 1886 Sydney Olivier had taken over the secretaryship, to be succeeded in 1890 by Pease upon the latter's return from Newcastle; this was the beginning of Pease's long term of uninterrupted and faithful service. In April 1888 the elected Executive consisted of Annie Besant, Hubert Bland, William Clarke, Sydney Olivier, Bernard Shaw, Graham Wallas, and Sidney Webb; these were the seven who wrote *Fabian Essays.* The number of Fabians whom they guided through their regular meetings is unknown, since the first Annual Report—four pages issued in 1889—gives no membership figures. Shaw speaks of the Society, as 'passing rich on forty pounds a year' and 'holding meetings in one another's drawing-rooms'.[2] This, he argues, effectively if not explicitly excluded working men; it must also have limited the number who could conveniently assemble for regular discussion, though there were, of course, other and larger gatherings besides the one in Anderton's Hotel. Other phrases in Shaw's account, however, suggest a subtler limitation.

I was guided [he says, explaining why he chose the Society as the proper field for his efforts] by an instinctive feeling that the Fabian and not the Federation [S.D.F.] would attract *the men of my own bias and intellectual habits* [my italics] who were then ripening for the work that lay before us . . . it was at this period that we contracted the invaluable habit of freely laughing at ourselves which always distinguished us, and which saved us from becoming hampered by the gushing enthusiasts who mistake their emotions for public movements. From the first, such people fled after one glance at us, declaring that we were not serious. Our preference for practical suggestions and criticisms, and our impatience of all general expressions of sympathy with working-class aspirations, not to mention our way of chaffing

[1] In 1909 Webb, in a lecture summarised in the January *Fabian News,* endeavoured to explain that 'compensation', in the Socialist sense, was a *solatium* paid to those 'injuriously affected by changes made for the public interest'—including workmen; but that it should not be regarded as a right. No compensation, for example, had been paid in 1806 to the slave-traders. It does not appear, however, that this definition ever became official. See also a rather muddled discussion by Pease in Tract 147, *Capital and Compensation* (1909).

[2] Shaw, *Early History.* In 1886 the Treasurer told a meeting of an income of £35 19*s.* and expenditure of £27 6*s.* 6*d.*; so Shaw was probably not very wide of the mark.

our opponents in preference to denouncing them as enemies of the human race, repelled from us some warm-hearted and eloquent Socialists, to whom it seemed callous and cynical to be even commonly self-possessed in the presence of the sufferings upon which Socialists make war.

More will be said in later chapters of the norm, the image, of a typical Fabian member—who certainly was not Shaw—and of the risks inherent in the attitude to political emotion shown in the above quotation; but it is clear that the society described is a restricted one, restricted to persons of a certain economic and still more educational equality. 'Freely laughing at ourselves', however invaluable, is a habit which can take root only in circles whose members understand one another's jokes—which implies a minimum of education and acquaintance with middle-class culture; so does 'chaffing opponents' without turning them into bitter enemies.[1] This attitude, rather than any conscious restriction on entry, explains why the membership of the Society was less than a hundred at the end of 1888, while that of the more dogmatic, but less class-conditioned, S.D.F. ran into four figures. But it is clear that the tiny roll earned its keep many times over in addressing meetings less socially restricted. Shaw's own picturesque account of 'training for public life' is too vivid not to be reproduced here.[2]

My own experience may be taken as typical. For some years I attended the Hampstead Historic Club [an association founded to study Marx and Proudhon] once a fortnight, and spent a night in the alternative weeks at a private circle of economists which has since blossomed into the British Economic Association. . . . I made all my acquaintances think me madder than usual by the pertinacity with which I attended debating societies and haunted all sorts of hole-and-corner debates and public meetings and made speeches at them. . . . Every Sunday I lectured on some subject which I wanted to teach to myself; and it was not until I had come to the point of being able to deliver separate lectures, without notes, on Rent, Interest, Profits,

[1] The 'chaffing' was real—and harsh—enough. *The Radical* of March 1888, for example, reported under the title 'Butchered to make a Fabian Holiday', a meeting at which R. B. Haldane, M.P., the friend of the Webbs, was torn to pieces by Shaw, Webb and Mrs Besant. This did not turn Haldane into an enemy of the Society (though he did not join it until 1925); had he been a working-class orator the result might well have been different.

[2] Shaw, *Early History*.

Wages, Toryism, Liberalism, Socialism, Communism, Anarchism, Trade Unionism, Co-operation, Democracy, the Division of Society into Classes, and the Suitability of Human Nature to Systems of Just Distribution, that I was able to handle Social-Democracy as it must be handled before it can be preached in such a way as to present itself to every sort of man from his own particular point of view. . . .

A man's Socialistic acquisitiveness must be keen enough to make him actually prefer spending two or three nights a week in speaking and debating, or in picking up social information even in the most dingy and scrappy way, to going to the theatre, or dancing or drinking, or even sweethearting, if he is to become a really competent propagandist—unless, of course, his daily work is of such a nature as to be itself a training for political life; and that, we know, is the case with very few of us indeed. It is at such lecturing and debating work, and on squalid little committees and ridiculous little delegations to conferences of the three tailors of Tooley Street, with perhaps a deputation to the Mayor thrown in once in a blue moon or so, that the ordinary Fabian workman or clerk must qualify for his future seat on the Town Council, the School Board, or perhaps the Cabinet.

It is possible that Shaw's audience—the Conference of Fabian provincial delegates described in Chapter VII—did not fully relish being called 'squalid little committees'; but of the essential truth of that account of early Socialist propaganda work there is no doubt. Every memoir of those who grew up in the late nineteenth century bears it out; William Morris broke his heart struggling with stupid and intransigent little groups, and Shaw himself was at times prouder of what he did, or tried to do, as Vestryman of St Pancras, than of all his plays and prefaces put together. The few score of Fabians did their duty no less faithfully than members of other classes; in a single year—apart from the other interventions mentioned by Shaw—they gave 721 public lectures to organisations of various kinds. These were organised, partly, by a Lecture Sub-Committee which, at some point in 1888, decided that the time had come for an organised attempt to present Socialism to the intelligent British public, and that accordingly, at the fortnightly members' meetings (to which visitors were admitted), the formal business should be followed by lectures, given by members of the Executive, on the case for and the meaning of Socialism. The first lecture was given by Sidney Webb at Willis's Rooms on September 21st; when the series was completed it was found that it had excited sufficient interest to be repeated by request in a room lent by King's College, Cambridge, and at Leicester.[1] (The London lecture which followed the series, Edward Carpenter's discourse on *Civilisation, its Cause and Cure*, actually excited more immediate interest than any one of the series individually.)

The response, therefore, seemed hardly startling, but the Executive Committee decided to issue the lectures in book form. Shaw was appointed editor, made or suggested some alterations to the several contributions, and added another of his own.[2] After a very prolonged period of gestation, and what turned out to be a fortunate dispute with the outside publisher first approached, the Fabian Society, which had not hitherto taken on anything larger than a pamphlet, ventured to produce them at its own risk as a six-shilling book, with frontispiece drawn by the artist Fabian, Walter Crane.[3]

The response surprised the Society. The first thousand copies sold out within a month; within a year reprints and cheap editions had been called for to the number of 25,000; American editions and translations burgeoned. Suddenly, Socialism became a best-seller.

[1] Pease, *History*, p. 77.

[2] *The Transition to Social Democracy*. Originally delivered to the Economic Section of the British Association at Bristol.

[3] A very early Fabian member. In July 1886 he had taken the chair for Morris's moving lecture on 'The Aims of Art', subsequently reprinted in the book *Signs of Change*.

CHAPTER IV

'Fabian Essays in Socialism'

TODAY'S reader of *Fabian Essays* may find this excitement hard to understand. Reading from the angle of the mid-twentieth century he will observe that the book is of very uneven quality, both in style and thought: he will note that the chapter by Olivier on *The Moral Basis of Socialism* is as dull and as obscure as (according to Pease) it was on the day it was written; that Wallas's essay on *Property* is slight and unworthy of its author; that Annie Besant's contribution on *Industry under Socialism*, after stating defiantly that it is 'non-Utopian', proceeds to sketch out a scheme for establishing socialism by County Councils taxing land values, taking over local industries and services, employing the unemployed in productive enterprises which would gradually squeeze out private competition and running them by democratic sub-committees—no mention at all of Trade Unions, which is curious in one who had just successfully organised the match-girls' strike that paved the way for the great victory of the dockers—which cannot be called anything less than Utopian;[1] that the final essay, *The Outlook*, by Hubert Bland, is for the most part cynically different in tone and wording from the others, suggesting, in contrast to the plain hope of his collaborators that the Liberals may be driven into Socialism, that there is precious little to be hoped for from either of the dominant parties. He will comment that there is a fair amount of repetition, which Shaw's editing seems not to have succeeded in removing; that Sidney Webb's *Historic Basis of Socialism* chapter reads more like an enlarged *Facts for Socialists*, and can scarcely have been delivered in its printed form even to the most long-

[1] The editor, at least, had an inkling, even before the book was published, that the County Councils, even had they been willing, would not be permitted to do anything of the kind. See rueful footnote on p. 188 of *Fabian Essays*.

suffering audience;[1] and finally that most of the essays (even Bland's) conclude with perorations on the beauties of Socialism which seem rather to have been stuck in as an afterthought or a concession to the S.D.F.

All this is true enough. But it is also true that, even in the slighter essays, and eminently in the contributions of Shaw himself, Webb (catalogues notwithstanding), and William Clarke, the Fabians of 1889 laid down an exposition of Socialist thought that was sufficiently definite without being dogmatic—'The Essayists', said the Preface, 'make no claim to be more than communicative learners'—and above all sufficiently British to hold the field for a very long time, and to continue to sell for over seventy years.

The main characteristics of Fabian thinking, as expressed in the *Essays*, are, first, that it is eclectic, following no single leader, but taking ideas from several and adapting or developing them on its own lines. Thus Shaw in the first of his contributions, *The Economic Basis of Socialism*, takes much from Ricardo and Jevons, but also a good deal from Marx. He argues that both land and capital produce for their owners 'rent' which is essentially anti-social, and which should either be added to the remuneration of labour or taken over by the community for public purposes. This 'rent',[2] he says, is what Marx called 'surplus value'; and the assumption, implied though not explicitly stated, is that when this surplus has been sequestered, and the waste of competitive capitalism and the kind of luxury spending exposed by economists like Thorstein Veblen removed, the result will be to provide

[1] See, for example, this magnificent sentence—only one of four catalogues which appear in swift succession: 'In addition to births, marriages, deaths and electors, the State registers all solicitors, barristers, notaries, patent agents, brokers, newspaper proprietors, playing-card makers, brewers, bankers, seamen, captains, mates, doctors, cabmen, hawkers, pawnbrokers, tobacconists, distillers, plate dealers, game dealers, all insurance companies, friendly societies, endowed schools and charities, limited companies, lands, houses, deeds, bills of sale, corporations, ships, arms, dogs, cabs, omnibuses, books, plays, pamphlets, newspapers, raw cotton movements, trade-marks and patents; lodging-houses, public-houses, refreshment-houses, theatres, music-halls, places of worship, elementary schools, and dancing-rooms.' *Fabian Essays*, p. 49. Five pages further on the same essay quotes, for two pages of small type, a Radical election programme reproduced verbatim from the *Star*.

[2] Shaw drew a distinction between 'economic rent', arising from differences in the fertility or the situation of land, which he said should be used solely for public purposes, and other 'rent'; but other Fabians did not follow this up.

for everyone in the community what the Webbs were later to call 'A Minimum Standard of Civilised Life'. 'The economic problem of Society is thus solved,' says Shaw, 'and Economics is no longer Dismal but Hopeful.' Calculations of this order were common, of course, in the writings of other early Socialists, from Robert Owen to Edward Bellamy,[1] who one and all both underestimated the enormous extent to which the poorer classes in the most 'civilised' communities—to say nothing of the rest of the world—fell below *any* standard of living which could be regarded as even moderately civilised, and failed entirely to anticipate the immense increase in popular demand for commodities once regarded as pure luxuries, which emerged as soon as mass-production made it possible to provide them.

In the two essays following, Sidney Webb and William Clarke similarly take what they want from the teachings of Marx and the Utilitarians. Webb, as was only to be expected, his father having been one of John Stuart Mill's committee-men in Westminster, derives strongly from Bentham. 'The greatest happiness of the greatest number' is a good enough principle for him; he is simply concerned to show that the greatest happiness can only be attained by means of the communal use of the resources of production. As to Marx, both he and Clarke accept that half of the materialist conception of history which declares that economics (the 'powers of production') determines the political conditions of society; Clarke describes the growth of manufacturing industry and its ensuing trustification in perfect Marxian manner (though not in Marxist terminology); and Webb regards the economic progress of the century as leading directly to Socialism.

But not leading *via* catastrophe: at this point the Fabians part company with Marx, the Dialectic, the theory of class-war leading to revolution and the dictatorship of the proletariat. The second characteristic of Fabian thought was that it was democratic, that it believed that alongside and equally important with the economic influences, 'the main stream which has borne

[1] *Looking Backward* (1887)—an extreme case of economic optimism. Yet optimism is not even now dead. As recently as 1960, Soviet academicians were prophesying that within twenty years hours of labour in the Soviet Union would have been reduced to four a day, the main necessities of life supplied free of charge to all, and the remainder of the day given to cultural activity of the highest type.

European society towards Socialism during the past hundred years is the *irresistible* [my italics] progress of Democracy'.[1] Using De Tocqueville as their guide, and studying the political history of their own country, which so plainly justified the mournful prophecy attributed to the Duke of Wellington, that 'if I say A I must say B, and so go on to C and D', they concluded that the Socialist measures demanded by economic necessity would be forced upon the rulers by the pressure of popular opinion. They did not regard the State, as nearly all European Socialists (*pace* De Tocqueville) regarded it, as the paid gaoler of the possessing classes, locking the doors of the prison upon the workers, but rather as a Supreme Court which, in the words of Mr Dooley, eventually 'followed th' illiction returns'; and subsequent British history surely proves that they were correct as far as their own country was concerned, even though the cautious Webb did observe that if Tories such as Sir Henry Maine proved to be right and the course of democracy was turned back, nobody could prophesy what might happen.[2]

This belief in democracy produced the third Fabian characteristic, that they were conscious, as the Trade Unions were unconscious, gradualists. We have already noted the gradualism in the Basis: Webb puts it explicitly:

> All students of society who are abreast of their time, Socialists as well as individualists, realise that important organic changes can only be (1) democratic and thus acceptable to a majority of the people and prepared for in the minds of all; (2) gradual, and thus causing no dislocation, however rapid may be the rate of progress; (3) not regarded as immoral by the mass of the people, and thus not subjectively demoralising to them; and (4) in this country at any rate, constitutional and peaceful.[3]

And Shaw, more picturesquely:

> You cannot convince any man that it is impossible to tear down a government in a day [as indeed it is not]; but everybody is convinced already that you cannot convert first and third class carriages into second class; rookeries and palaces into comfortable dwellings; and jewellers and dressmakers into bakers and builders, merely by singing the 'Marseillaise'.[4]

They were democratic, then, in the sense that they believed

[1] *Fabian Essays,* p. 33.
[2] *Ibid.*, p. 61.
[3] *Ibid.*, p. 35.
[4] *Ibid.*, p. 183.

that democracy would be the political agent of Socialism, that the central machinery of the state would eventually be captured by democratic forces, and that socialised production would be democratically run. But by this they did not mean 'run by the Central State'. Universal nationalisation was certainly not the ideal of the early Fabians, though twenty years later Fabians like Emil Davies and Leo Chiozza Money—and to some extent, Webb himself—greatly expanded the scope of nationalisation.[1] Some enterprises, particularly the railways,[2] they thought should obviously be run on national lines like the Post Office, and they toyed with the idea of new national experiments to be financed by the State out of the produce of 'surplus value'.

But for the most part they envisaged the 'surplus value' going to local units—they called them Communes, a term which recalls Owen and the Christian Socialists, but to the Fabians meant cities and the newly created County Councils. Of course the project of turning County Councils into agents of socialisation was a chimera, as already noticed. Apart from the political complexion of practically all of them—a complexion which in 1960 was still prevalent in the majority—the central government immediately made it quite clear that County Councils existed to perform the functions laid down for them by statute, and no others. There was to be no question of County Councils entering into any field which might make them competitive with private industry. This proposal, therefore, fell dead almost from the start, and nowhere more dead than on the London County Council, which had been a high hope of the radicals. Town and other Councils, as later history shows, were just as heavily fettered by the law, and the interpretation of the law, in making socialistic experiments. Nevertheless, the impetus which *Fabian Essays* lent to the idea of municipal and local enterprise gave considerable help and ammunition to local groupings of Socialists and was of marked assistance to the I.L.P. after its foundation.

It should be noticed, also, that by 'democratic management' the Essayists meant, unequivocally, 'management by the democratically elected representatives of the community'—whatever that community was. They had no use whatever for 'interests' of any sort or shape; they would have violently disliked the present-day practice of inviting nomination from various 'interests'

[1] See pp. 145 and 172, and Cole, *History of Socialist Thought*, Vol. III, p. 214.
[2] The Society took over the Railway Nationalisation League in 1903.

to the governing bodies of, for example, technical colleges, and this prejudice applied to working-class organisations as much as to any others.[1] Trade Unionism, as we have seen, they ignored even in 1889, though the events of that year soon convinced them that they had made a mistake; as to co-operation, they seem to have accepted William Morris's view that it was little more than a method of turning working men into petty capitalists,[2] and therefore not worthy of recognition. 'Workers' control', i.e. any suggestion that the men actually engaged on the job should have any voice in the policy of industry, or in the appointment of those who controlled their conditions, they rejected out of hand.[3]

Their desire to see socialised undertakings controlled by democratically chosen committees did not mean, however, that they were unaware of the need to attract men of ability to do the actual running of them. William Clarke's essay points out the distinction which trustification of industry was already producing between the salaried manager and the *rentier* owner, and Shaw and Annie Besant both agree that in the transitional stage the socialist undertaking will have to be prepared to bid for its managers against the salaries which private industry is prepared to pay them—a suggestion which would have scandalised the type of Trade Union which wished to pay its general secretary no more than the day-wage of the man at the bench.[4] Shaw, in his second essay,[5] appears to envisage paying a competent manager at the rate of £800 a year, which must then have been quite a competence, if one is to judge from the motion of one of the Progressive members of the first L.C.C. to reduce the salaries of that body's senior officers, with the argument that 'in private concerns men of great ability can be obtained for four or five hundred a year'.[6]

The Fabians were certainly not doctrinaire equalitarians, at all events in the transitional stage, though it must be remembered

[1] Wallas, in particular, was a passionate opponent of 'interests'; and became even more so as he advanced in years. See his book, *Our Social Heritage* (1921). But Webb, when devising the Technical Education Board of the London County Council in the 'nineties, included on it a number of representatives of educational 'interests'—with excellent results.

[2] *Fabian Essays*, pp. 88–9. [3] *Ibid.*, p. 158.

[4] See Raymond Postgate, *The Builders' History*.

[5] *Fabian Essays*, p. 197.

[6] William Saunders, *The First London County Council* (1892).

that they hoped that, as the abundance looked for from Socialism and the increase of communal good came into being, the need for great differences in money incomes could gradually disappear. Meantime, they had no illusions that 'good' Socialism, however much it chimed in with the march of events, would come of itself without any human aid.

> The Zeitgeist [says Webb] is potent; but it does not pass Acts of Parliament without legislators, or erect municipal libraries without town councillors. Though our decisions are moulded by the circumstances of our time, and the environment at least roughhews our ends, shape them as we will, yet each generation decides for itself. It still rests with the individual to resist or promote the social revolution, consciously or unconsciously, according to his character and information.[1]

This recalls Webb's oft-quoted remark that 'the work of the Fabian Society consists of the work of individual Fabians', and the constant endeavours of the leaders of the Society to see that that work was competent, that the propaganda statements were honest and accurate, and that the detailed proposals which were made would, as far as was humanly possible, stand up to criticism by their opponents. If that were so, the Essayists and their fellows earnestly believed, the walls of Jericho would be so subtly and gradually undermined that Webb's *Zeitgeist* could blow them down even without a trumpet, and the greatest happiness of the greatest number would be assured.

For the final characteristic of the early Fabians is that they were both optimists and enthusiasts. They believed that the march of events was going their way, and they were as convinced as ever was Robert Owen that it only needed patient explanation of facts to persuade others of the truths of Socialism and the desirability of socialistic reforms—though as later chapters will show, they were more discriminating than Owen in their selection of persons to be the first objects of persuasion. And though they deliberately eschewed appeals of the more emotional and oratorical type—which, indeed, they were not well-equipped to make—their disinterested faith in humanity was none the less strong for that. 'They thought of the advance of Socialism', writes G. D. H. Cole,[2] 'in terms mainly not of

[1] *Fabian Essays*, p. 50.

[2] *History of Socialist Thought*, Vol. II, p. 114.

Times Hulton Picture Library

Sidney Webb

Radio Times Hulton Picture Library

Annie Besant

Hubert Bland

THE SEVEN ESSAYISTS (ii)

Shaw talking to Mrs Charlotte Wilson (Anarchist leader)

FABIAN SUMMER SCHOOL, PENLEE, 1908

Left to right:
Aylmer Maude,
Emil Davies,
Shaw, Olivier

power alone, but of power animated by rational conviction, and inspired by the ethical impulse to achieve social justice'; and to themselves they often put their end in terms not quite so dry.

When Wallas wrote,

> Socialism hangs above them as the crown hung in Bunyan's story above the man raking the muck heap—ready for them if they will but lift their eyes. And even to the few who seem to escape and even profit by the misery of our century, Socialism offers a new and nobler life, when full sympathy with those about them, springing from full knowledge of their condition, shall be the source of happiness and not, as now, of constant sorrow—when it shall no longer seem either folly or hypocrisy for a man to work openly for his highest ideal.

he was not being hypocritical or talking to the groundlings. Idealism, in the eighties, was not confined to William Morris and his Socialist League; and *Fabian Essays*, at least up to the appearance of *Merrie England*, held the field to an extent it may be difficult nowadays to credit.

CHAPTER V

The First Blooming

THE success of *Fabian Essays* showed clearly how great was the potential demand for a clear statement of a Socialist programme. The timing—in part accidental—was exactly right. After the black years of the mid-'eighties, trade and employment had taken an upward turn, to the advantage of labour. The successful strike of Bryant and May's match-girls, supported and organised by Annie Besant, was followed by the great London Dock Strike of 1889, which drew public attention not only to Trade Unionism but to the shocking conditions of the workers in low-paid and seasonal occupations; and the startling success of the young Dockers' Union in winning the 'dockers' tanner' (sixpence an hour) against the embattled might of the employers in the Port of London, which was extremely well publicised, had more than a propagandist effect; it contributed to the well-known growth of 'New Unionism' amongst the unskilled and the semi-skilled, which soon began to make inroads into the domination of the older craft Unions over the Trades Union Congress and—possibly in the long run the more important result—to change gradually the attitude of the members and officers of those craft unions so as to make them rather more 'class-conscious' of working-class aspirations as a whole, less sectional in their outlook, and more critical of what was offered them politically by the established parties. The process was of course gradual; the ebb and flow of Trade Union opinion, symbolised by the continued struggle between Henry Broadhurst and Keir Hardie to gain the support of Congress, can be read in any standard history of the 'nineties. But by and large the mass was in motion, and its impetus was increased by the publication, in the year of the Dock Strike, of the first volume of Booth's *Life and Labour of the People of London*[1]—to which the future Mrs

[1] Originally undertaken, it is said, in order to refute angry generalisations about London squalor made by S.D.F. speakers; the result was to prove them up to the hilt.

Sidney Webb, working as a 'plain trouser-hand' in the service of sweating employers, had made her contribution.[1] The ground was ready for the harvest.

The Fabian Society, as such, played no part in the Dock Strike, which was led mainly by members of the S.D.F., though a few of the militants such as Tom Mann, John Burns, and Ben Tillett, were already Fabians or joined the Society within a few months. It did, however, realise quickly that the neglect of Trade Unionism by the Essayists had been a serious error, and within a couple of years Shaw was explaining to a delegate conference of Fabians from the provinces that the enlightened Fabian propagandist would urge the members of his audience to join the appropriate Union branch or lodge and convert it to a Socialist outlook.[2] The said branches and lodges, or many of them, were looking eagerly for a Socialist policy expressed simply in terms of British conditions, without the tough and arid Marxism on which the S.D.F. insisted; and *Fabian Essays*, and those who expounded them, appeared at exactly the right moment to fill the need.

The demand began almost immediately. But it seems to have been some time before the London-based Executive realised that anything out of the common was happening. The Minutes, throughout 1890, show little sign of excitement, though it is noted that at the mid-July meeting Shaw delivered a very long paper on a dramatist called Henrik Ibsen, so long that, as the reporter complains, there was no time left for discussion—this paper, re-written at greater length, became world-famous as *The Quintessence of Ibsenism*. By September the membership roll began to increase, and some of the names of November entrants seem to have been hurriedly scribbled in pencil at the close of the meeting. More significant is the news, on October 20th, of the formation of a Fabian Society in Birmingham with *seventy-five members*, set up in accordance with a resolution of 1886 which permitted the foundation of Fabian Societies outside London with a membership of not less than ten, 'subject to the proviso

[1] Beatrice Webb, *My Apprenticeship*.

[2] The earlier attitude, however, did not die away immediately. As late as December 1890, Sidney Webb, in the lecture reprinted as Tract 15, was still parroting orthodox economics to the effect that 'belief in universal Trade Unionism as a means of permanently raising wages all round must be dismissed as a logical fallacy'—because one group of wage-earners could only lift themselves at the expense of another.

that no rule shall be made which conflicts with the basis and aims of the Central Society'. This ruling had resulted in the formation of a society at Edinburgh, and the example was now followed by many towns; such societies should not, however, be confused with the Fabian 'groups' in the metropolitan area, which were generally composed of full Society members, and upon occasion received small grants from central funds to help them with their postage bills. Of one such group, Shaw related that it collected an audience of five persons to listen to Samuel Butler discoursing upon the authorship of the *Odyssey*.[1]

The growth, however, was unmistakable. By February 1891 the secretary announced a 'red letter day', with a long list of aspirants and new Societies formed in Bristol, Plymouth, and Wolverhampton; and by the time of the Annual Meeting in April there were 361 full members (more than double the previous year's total), of whom 122 were resident outside London, and twelve local Societies with an estimated membership of 300–400, including one in Bombay which gave lectures to 'educated natives'.[2] The income had jumped from £40 to £860, and the total print of Fabian Tracts during the past year had been 335,000, nearly five times the total number printed during the seven preceding years.

The nature of these new Tracts is of some interest. Five were propaganda leaflets of three or four pages, with titles such as *What the Farm Labourer Wants* (Tract 19) and *What Socialism Is* (Tract 13); but the majority were much more solid reading. *Facts for Londoners* was followed by a similar, though shorter, *Facts for Bristol* (Tract 18); it was intended to produce a *Facts* series for the principal towns, but the venture proved too unremunerative and was dropped. Tract 15, *English Progress Towards Social Democracy*, was a long reprint of a lecture by Sidney Webb, which, as we have seen, was economically a trifle behind the times; three others, Tracts 11, 14, and 17, dealt at some length with current political problems. The first, *The Workers' Political Programme*, set out a fairly detailed policy which, besides advocating ownership of land and local industry by public bodies, as

[1] *Fabian News*, May 1891, and Pease, *History*, p. 105.

[2] The records of the time did not chronicle the foundation in 1892 of a Fabian Society in Vienna, of whose existence the parent Society was apparently unaware until, early in 1929, Michael Hainisch, the President of the Austrian Republic, proclaimed his membership of it.

in *Fabian Essays*, included nationalisation of railways, canals, and mining royalties; the second was *A New Reform Bill*, and the third, the first of many of its kind, proposed various reforms of the Poor Law. These three show the Society pursuing the task, already begun in the Tract on the Eight Hours Bill, of preparing blue-prints for possible radical legislation; but they bear no obvious relationship to the public events of the year.

By this time, the growth of the Society was at last causing its Executive to sit up and take notice. Though the provincial Societies were in no sense 'branches' and the central Society took no financial or any other responsibility for them,[1] the mere fact of their appearance in such rapidly increasing numbers, and the questions and requests for advice which they and the growing membership roll of the Society itself sent in almost daily to the secretary—to say nothing of the demand for speakers and lecturers—convinced even the most cautious that some modest expansion was desirable. Accordingly, the Executive Committee—to whose members the secretary was wont to refer a great deal of the incoming correspondence—was enlarged to fifteen members,[2] and was soon meeting every week, with various standing or special committees meeting also; in the first contested election Webb headed the list with 103 out of 117 votes, with Shaw and Wallas tieing two votes behind him—the postal ballot was not introduced until 1894. The generosity of a member, D'Arcy Reeve, made possible the removal of the Society's files from the secretary's private abode to a regular office in the Strand; and a further daring decision gave the said secretary a salary of one pound a week. This was hardly princely; but, as Pease relates,[3] another pound accrued to him as part-time secretary to Sidney Webb.

> But [he adds], I did not feel then, and I do not think now, that the work I did had any value to him or anybody else. I think he made the plan in order to help the Fabian Society out of a difficulty. They could

[1] 'It is to be hoped', said the Annual Report for 1892, rationalising this attitude, 'that, forced to rely on themselves, they will prove more permanent and effective centres of activity.'

[2] In November, however, the Executive lost its then best-known member, Annie Besant, who abruptly embraced theosophy, and entered upon the new phase which eventually made her, until her death in 1933, the patron saint of Indian nationalism.

[3] *The Webbs and Their Work* (ed. Margaret Cole), p. 19.

hardly engage me for half-time unless I had work for the other half, and I think the £50 Webb paid me was actually a gift to the Fabian Society.

The dilemma is so typical of the Fabian Society, and the expedient so typically Webbian that the guess is probably correct; if so, the manœuvre was successful, for before the year was out the Society had nerved itself to risk £100 a year for a full-time appointment, and no subsequent financial crisis ever produced the suggestion that the secretary's salary should be saved. At the time, however, the proposal to pay anything at all did not pass unquestioned. An anonymous pencilled grumble in the original Minute Book says 'We shall hear more of these beginnings of tyranny—a Chairman and a Code' !; and a definite opposition was led by Mrs Hubert Bland ('E. Nesbit' of the children's books). No more was heard of this until years afterwards when H. G. Wells (who was not at the earlier date a member of the Society and had long ceased his first toyings with Socialism) managed to persuade himself that this was due to a desire of Bland to become secretary himself, and in his own reminiscences produced a mythical running feud between Bland the treasurer and Pease the secretary.[1] It is quite inconceivable that Bland, a journalist with expensive tastes, should ever have coveted the humdrum job of running the Fabian office for £100 a year; the only plausible explanation of the story is that Wells's fury with the Fabian 'Establishment' on the occasion of his defeat in 1907–8,[2] coloured his recollections for many years afterwards.

Finally, the Society decided that it was time to have a regular means of printed communication with its membership. *Fabian News*, 'For Members Only', started its long life in March 1891, as a four-page quarto printed in double column with a headpiece 'after' Walter Crane which continued to decorate it until 1943, when the format was changed; it is an indication of growing Fabian activity that the very first issue contained the announcement that the office desired the services of a Smart Boy.

For the boom did not come to an end in 1891; it continued in full swing for another two years. By April 1893 the full membership was over 500, the income £1,270; and there were, in addi-

[1] Wells, *Experiment in Autobiography*, p. 602 ff., and Pease, in *The Webbs and Their Work*.

[2] See Chapter XII.

tion to the metropolitan groups, over seventy local Societies with a membership which was of course not recorded in detail, but which was probably not short of 2,000—a figure not reached again for over twenty years. 'There is scarcely an important town in the kingdom', boasted the Annual Report, 'which does not contain a local Fabian Society.' The full list of provincial Societies at the peak is given in Appendix III, and goes far to bear out the claim; it also shows, from the names of the places in which they were functioning, that they were real local Socialist Societies, with a membership which must have been far less narrow, far more representative of working men, than the picture drawn by Shaw in his *Early History*. Their foundation was, of course, due directly to *Fabian Essays* and to the demand these created for Fabian speakers to come over into Macedonia and tell groups of the discontented and aspiring about Socialism for Britain.

The Fabians answered the call. In London the annual Fabian Lectures, inaugurated by the Essayists, continued year by year down to the time these words were written; and for the provinces ninety travelling lecturers, according to Fabian publications of 1891–3, were available. In a single year the total of recorded lectures (and there must have been many more unlisted) reached 3,400;[1] and where a Fabian lecturer went he tended, as often as not, to leave behind him an embryo Fabian Society. Lecturing, in fact, was as cheap a form of propagandist activity as the Society could find, for the vast majority of the lecturers gave their services free or for 'expenses' only; and the Society did its level best to ensure that inevitable 'expenses' were met, in part at least, by the body responsible for calling the meeting—in this, of course, it was following the English radical tradition which (in contrast to the American) has always endeavoured to make peripatetic propagandist lecturing a financially unattractive pursuit. As they lectured, so the Fabians took trouble to provide their new members with appropriate ammunition which they could use, particularly in local elections, to harry candidates with questions and demands for specific pledges on policy.

Between 1891 and 1894 the Society issued ten Tracts in the form of searching *Questions* to be put to members of or candidates for different representative bodies—Poor Law Guardians,

[1] Some of these, particularly in Lancashire, were financed by Henry Hutchinson, whom we shall meet again.

Vestrymen, Parliamentary Candidates, School Board Candidates, County Councillors, Town Councillors, London County Councillors[1]—the list is formidable, and the questions, set out in column form over four pages, with blank spaces provided for the recipient's written replies, were formidable too. One specimen, the *Questions for Town Councillors* (Tract 27), contains no fewer than forty-seven items, ranging from 'the construction and maintenance by the Council of an adequate number of cottages and common lodging-houses', to 'the provision of waterproof coats for outdoor labourers'. The others are scarcely less searching, and one feels that any prospective Councillor who answered these examination papers creditably deserved any seat to which he was aspiring. Nor was their use to be left to chance; an instruction in *Fabian News* of June 1892 has a distinctly modern ring about it.

HECKLING CANDIDATES [it runs]. In order to facilitate the asking of questions at candidates' public meetings a set of three printed slips has been prepared, each containing one question, with space for the signature of the questioner. These ought to be *judiciously distributed* [my italics] to persons who will attend meetings and use them. A supply will be sent free of charge to any member or local Society applying for them.

The most spectacular result of such probing and canvassing was undoubtedly to be seen in the 1892 elections to the London County Council, when, aided by Webb's *London Programme* (which was also published under eight separate headings as Tracts 30–37), the Fabian candidates, all standing as Progressives, all romped home by majorities ranging from 600 to 1,500, and succeeded also in getting Ben Tillett of the Dockers on to the aldermanic bench, while the solitary S.D.F. candidate polled 76 votes only. London was of course the Fabians' particular battlefield: but the appropriate *Questions* were available for use by members of provincial Societies and later, of course, by the I.L.P.

Some who read the *Questions* today may feel that they were rather elaborate and must have made heavy demands on the knowledge and intelligence of those who were invited to put them. This is certainly true; though the *Questions* were intended to be of practical use, the main emphasis of the Fabian campaigns of the early 'nineties was educational rather than political, and

[1] Later, Metropolitan Borough Councillors were added to the collection.

one of the lecturers in the north, W. H. Utley, actually sent back to headquarters a complaining report that the membership seemed to be more interested in immediate political problems than in 'improving their minds by listening to lectures'. The lectures were supposed to be educational; they were supplemented by correspondence courses (first mentioned in *Fabian News* of September 1892), by boxes of books supplied on loan, from about the same date, to Societies in so far as funds permitted (a book-box cost about £3 to provide), and by elaborate—for that period—bibliographies such as *What to Read, a List of Books for Social Reformers* (Tract 29, first issued in November 1891)—and, of course, by numerous queries answered by the secretary either out of his own knowledge or by reference to one of the members of the Executive. It seems probable that the Executive still believed, like Owen, that extensive education and information would do the trick; at all events, they made no attempt to issue any organisational directives to the upsurgent Fabian Societies. They regarded them with surprise and some pleasure, as evidence of the growing interest in Socialism and the effect of *Fabian Essays*, but to transform them into a disciplined army of political assault was far from their thought. For direct political action they looked rather to national bodies—the Socialist Societies and political parties; the next chapter tells of their relations with both.

CHAPTER VI

Politics and the I.L.P.

IT is not the case, of course, that the sudden growth of Fabian membership was made entirely, or even mainly, at the expense of other Socialist Societies. As already mentioned, the growth was indicative of an absolute increase in the number of Socialists, and while accurate figures of membership are impossible to obtain—they were exaggerated alike by friends and foes—there is no reason to suppose that the membership of the S.D.F., for example, was not also increasing.[1] There was also a fair amount of overlapping. Socialist Societies were not, then, mutually exclusive organisations; and though the Fabian leaders found it difficult to put up with Hyndman's temper and disliked his tactics,[2] there was a good deal of sympathy among the rank and file of both organisations. Clashes, however, were not infrequent; and early in 1893, on the initiative of the Hammersmith Socialist Society—all that remained of Morris's following after the Socialist League had turned him down and gone over to pure Anarchism—an attempt was made to bring together the three Societies, in the London area at least. There was a joint conference, which set up a joint committee with Morris as chairman; and a manifesto was drafted by Shaw, Morris, and Hyndman, and accepted by the Fabian Society after being read aloud by Shaw to a members' meeting. It was published in May as a *Manifesto of English Socialists*, with eighteen signatories, bound in 'exquisite

[1] It was claimed to be 4,500 in 1894.

[2] Particularly in relation to the 'Tory gold' incident in the 1885 election, when the S.D.F. ran 'Socialist' candidates with the aid of money from Conservative funds. The candidates polled derisory votes, and the whole Labour movement felt it to be a scandal, though it should be noted that the comparatively mild Fabian resolution of condemnation led to the first recorded resignation, that of Keddell, whose place on the Executive was taken by Sidney Webb.

red covers';[1] but as Shaw said long afterwards, it was the only published work of any of the three authors which was not worth a halfpenny, and it fell completely flat. Not long afterwards temperamental differences between the Fabians and the S.D.F. particularly reached such a pitch that the Fabian representatives withdrew for the sake of peace and quiet; it was not the last time they retired for similar reasons.

Before this, however, another challenge had arisen with the foundation of the Independent Labour Party.

The 120 who met at Bradford in January 1893 comprised delegates from a great variety of 'Socialist' and 'Labour' groups, including both the S.D.F. and the Fabian Society; the two Fabians were Shaw and W. S. De Mattos, the latter one of the Society's most assiduous lecturers but not the most popular of personalities.[2] (Eleven other Fabian Societies were represented, and the Executive had asked the Bradford Society to convene a preliminary meeting of Fabian delegates to the conference, apparently without result.) Neither the S.D.F. nor the Society had any intention of merging itself in the new body, and Shaw's blunt statement to that effect, coupled with his opposition to any enforced severance of individuals from connection with older parties—'he himself was on the Executive of a Liberal Association, and he had taken some trouble to get the position in order to push Labour interests there. He intended to stick to it, and most of the energetic men he knew in London had done the same things, and had found there was a good deal to be gained thereby'[3]—came near, at one moment, to getting the two Fabians slung out of the conference hall; but they stayed in, and played their part. At the Fabian members' meeting in July 'Bernard

[1] *Fabian News*, May 1893. The covers may have been the contribution of a mysterious Fabian 'Committee on Taste', which made a single fleeting appearance in the Executive Minutes of December 1892; it was never mentioned again.

[2] 'I hear from Oxford', Shaw wrote to Webb in a private letter, 'that De Mattos is ravishing every maiden in the country. York Powell [the historian] writes to me urging the importance of disassociating ourselves.' There was much trouble in Bristol and Bradford over his 'free love' propaganda. (Letters in Fabian archives.)

[3] *I.L.P. Conference Report*. 'London' is the important word, for in London Liberalism was 'permeable' by Fabian and Radical effort; but provincial Socialists found that Webb's L.C.C. association with Rosebery stuck badly in their throats.

Shaw gave a long account of the Conference . . . and of his work as delegate to it'. It is a loss both to history and the gaiety of nations that this account was not preserved; in later years Shaw was liable to summarise the proceedings more briefly, saying for example, 'I met Keir Hardie on the stairs, and in two minutes told him what to do'—a piece of Shavian impudence which has been thought worthy of serious refutation by some historians. It is recorded elsewhere, however, that he persuaded the Conference to include in its objects the abolition of indirect taxation and the taxation to extinction of unearned income; and his eloquence certainly helped Hardie to defeat, albeit with a substantial minority, the foolish proposal known to history as the Manchester Fourth Clause, under which Socialists would have been forbidden to vote at election time for any but Socialist candidates—thereby disfranchising, in any foreseeable future, the bulk of Socialists in the country.[1]

The Fabian Executive, on the return of the delegates, formally welcomed the new Society without great enthusiasm or, it seems, anticipation that it would before long quickly absorb the bulk of its own provincial membership. When it did, there was no real rivalry or bickering such as went on continually between the S.D.F. and the I.L.P.; Fabian Tracts and *Questions* continued to provide I.L.P. branches with ammunition for their fight for reform against local reactionaries;[2] and though Fabian tactics in the capital sometimes provoked Hardie (maybe in momentary exasperation with the Webbs) to denounce the London Fabians and the L.C.C. as a menace to Socialism, the I.L.P. in the metropolitan area was too weak for this to be more than a passing cloud. The subsequent relations of Fabian and I.L.P. leaders must be deferred to a later chapter.

So much for the Society's relationship with its fellows in the movement; we turn now to the wider political scene.

The Fabians, as Socialists, were always prepared to participate in conference with other organisations, as in the May Day demonstrations, meetings on the Eight Hour Day and international gatherings such as those at Brussels (1891), Paris (1886

[1] This clause was the peculiar pet of Robert Blatchford of the *Clarion*; it resembles other 'Spoil Your Vote' campaigns. But the size of the minority showed that such ideas had a considerable appeal at the time.

[2] The outstanding example being the long and gallant struggle of Fred Jowett in Bradford itself.

and 1889), Zurich (1893), and London (1896).[1] But the proceedings at all such gatherings tended to be either theoretical or declamatory; they seldom gave a definite lead for positive action, least of all in Britain. The Fabians, the least internationally conscious of any radical group (as Shaw told them time and again), wanted action in Britain, and wanted it within their own lifetimes. It is probable, also, that they were to some small extent deluded by the immediate success of their own propaganda, in *Fabian Essays* particularly, and thought that they were in a position to influence the social development of their country more rapidly than was in fact the case. In any event, what they had to decide was whether the best tactic was to concentrate in forcing the existing parties, playing on their fear of the ballot and the growing power of an increasingly educated and organised democracy, to put parts of the Socialist programme 'gradually' into effect, or to try to form a new 'workers' ' party independent of both Tory and Liberal. Fabian policy, as will be seen, vacillated between these two courses; but at the end of the 'eighties, when the only members of the working classes sitting in Parliament were sitting on Liberal sufferance, and when Progressive policies, largely indistinguishable in content from Fabianism, seemed to be triumphing on the L.C.C., it was natural to think first of capturing the Liberals.

At its Newcastle Conference in 1891, the Liberal Party, to most people's astonishment, accepted a statement of policy (the Newcastle Programme) which was a fine hotch-potch of radical nostrums. It included, besides Home Rule, disestablishment of the Church in Wales and Scotland, 'full powers' for the L.C.C. and all other municipalities, including taxation of ground values, and compulsory powers to local authorities to acquire land for allotments, smallholdings, village halls, and labourers' cottages; shorter Parliaments, simultaneous elections, the abolition of plural voting, and the recognition of the need to pay M.P.s; the establishment of District and Parish Councils—as the County Councils were already proving inadequate; free schooling for all, leasehold enfranchisement; local veto on liquor licensing; taxation of mining royalties; 'mending or ending' the House of Lords;

[1] An exception was their refusal, in 1890, to send a delegate to the memorial celebrations for the martyrs of the Commune of Paris. This was a reversal of previous practice, and the reason for it is unknown; it may have been political, or simply economy.

etc.[1] It was, in fact, a rather weaker version of the Unauthorised Programme now given Conference authorisation.

There is not anything very Socialistic about the programme; but it is certainly radical—too radical for many years to come—and if implemented would have made the 'next step' a good deal nearer. Opinions differ as to the extent to which the delegates at Newcastle, alarmed no doubt by 'industrial unrest' and looking forward with apprehension to the general election of 1892, were stampeded by a combination of reformers from London. Shaw had no doubt at all that they were. In a letter to Pease[2] he wrote:

> The exact facts of the launching of the Newcastle Program are these. Webb gave me the Program in his own hand as a string of resolutions. I, being then a permeative Fabian on the Executive of the St Pancras Liberal and Radical Association (I had coolly walked in and demanded to be elected to the Association and Executive, which was done on the spot by the astonished Association—ten strong or thereabouts) took them down to a meeting in Percy Hall, Percy Street, Tottenham Court Road, where the late Mr Beale, then Liberal candidate and milch cow of the constituency (without the ghost of a chance) was to address as many of the ten as might turn up under the impression that he was addressing a public meeting. There were certainly not 20 present, possibly not 10. He said they looked complicated, and that if I would move them he would second them. I moved them, turning over Webb's pages by batches and not reading most of them. Mr Beale seconded. Passed unanimously. That night they went down to the *Star* with a report of an admirable speech which Mr Beale was supposed to have delivered. Next day he found the National Liberal Club in an uproar at his revolutionary breakaway. But he played up; buttoned his coat determinedly; said we lived in progressive times and must move with them; and carried it off.

Later, in the grand philippic against the 1892 Liberal Government published in the *Fortnightly Review*,[3] Shaw said of the election programme and the election,

> it is not for the Fabians to spoil a stirring page of political history by bringing the public behind the scenes to see those eagle-eyed statesmen carried to the platform, kicking and screaming and protesting,

[1] Condensed from Liberal Leaflet, No. 1. 589, 1892.

[2] Reproduced in Pease, *History*, p. 112. See also Tract 41.

[3] 'To Your Tents, O Israel', article in *Fortnightly Review*, November 1893.

in the arms of the collectivist radicals of London, who offered them the alternative of saying what they were told or spending another seven years in opposition.

Discount as we may Shaw's picturesque detail of Mr Beale and his coat-buttons, it is clear that a paper victory was scored at Newcastle by smart rush tactics working upon fear of the electorate; and that it was no more than a paper victory and meant nothing to the leaders was apparent almost immediately after the election. Even at the time at which they were playing their 'bewildering tricks with the Liberal thimbles and the Fabian peas' (Shaw), the Fabians seemed to realise that the manœuvre might not come off, and in June 1892 the Society mounted the second of the alternative horses and issued its own *Election Manifesto* (Tract 40). In this, while still advising working men to vote for whichever candidate promised to meet most of their needs rather than not vote at all (the 'Fourth Clause' policy), the Fabians made it clear that this was a *pis aller* until the working class cared enough about working-class political interests to pay for a party of its own.

The existence of this pamphlet made it possible for the Fabians to cry loudly 'We told you so!' when the Liberals got their majority, and the Newcastle Programme, with the exception of Home Rule and (later) District and Parish Councils, vanished without trace; and when, further, Gladstone's last Government showed its unconcern for social reforms by rating as 'low-grade' ministries such departments as the Board of Trade, the Local Government Board, and the Council for Education, from which social reform proposals, if any, might have been expected to emerge.[1] The Socialists, up and down the country, were furious at the 'betrayal', and before the end of the year the Fabian Executive was discussing a request that the Society, then still in its boom period, should found a new 'United Socialist Party'. Wisely, the Executive decided that 'no United Socialist Party formed by the Fabian Society is possible'.[2] It was still, however, contemplating following up its election manifesto by a Tract on a Labour Party; and in April 1893—three months after the Bradford Conference—it ordered the production of a pamphlet

[1] R. C. K. Ensor, *England 1870–1914*, p. 293. The creation, under A. J. Mundella, of the Labour Department of the Board of Trade, was useful to the Collectivists; but it was not a very spectacular gain for radicalism.

[2] Executive Minutes, November 1892, and *Fabian News* of December.

on 'The Perfidy of the Government'. This document, prepared by Shaw with Webb's assistance, and approved by the membership after discussion, became the *Fortnightly* article already referred to; it was subsequently published by the Society, with considerable additional material, under the title of *Plan of Campaign for Labour* (Tract 49, January 1894).

The 'Manifesto', as it was called before it became a pamphlet, is a hearty piece of polemic; it attacks the Ministers collectively and severally, and has only a patronisingly kind word to spare for those of them as had collectivist leanings, such as Acland, Bryce, Haldane, and Mundella, who were said to be helpless prisoners of seasoned Whigs like 'We-are-all-Socialists-now' Harcourt. But denunciation takes up only the first part of the Manifesto and the Tract; thereafter Shaw turns to the future and argues that the only right course is to turn the Reform Act of 1885 (the Redistribution Act) to its proper use by putting up at least fifty Labour candidates for the next general election, and for the Trade Unions to foot the bill.

The Radicals [he said, quoting a few sentences from his own Tract 41] are at least conscious that the leaders are obstructing them; and they are now looking for a lead in attacking the obstruction. They say in effect 'Your policy of permeation has been successful; we *are* permeated; and the result is that we find all the money and all the official power of our leaders who are not permeated, and cannot be permeated, arrayed against us. Now show us how to get rid of these leaders or to fight them.'

But the Fabian Society's function [he continues] ceases when the permeation has been carried to saturation point. That point was indicated by the election last September [1893] of a Collectivist parliamentary committee by the Trades Union Congress. The trade unions must do the rest. . . .

The money difficulty, which is the great bar to parliamentary representation of the working class, does not exist for bodies which can raise a thousand pounds by a large levy of from a penny to sixpence per member. A subscription of a penny a week from every member of a trade union of this country would produce at least upwards of £300,000; and, *though such a subscription is not completely practicable* [my italics] the calculation shows how easily the larger unions alone, with their membership of a million, could provide £30,000 to finance fifty labor candidates at £600 apiece, and to force forward the long-deferred legislation for payment of members and election expenses.

On the whole, then, we may take it that the representation of the working-classes at the general election will depend on the great national trade unions, and not on the Socialist societies. Neither the Fabian Society nor the Social Democratic Federation, nor the Society known as the Independent Labour Party, has the slightest prospect of mustering enough money to carry through three serious candidates, much less fifty. Their part will be to provide the agitation which will enable the trade union leaders to obtain the support of the rank and file in rising to the occasion.

After this optimistic outline—which nevertheless was essentially the plan adopted in much emasculated form at the L.R.C. foundation conference in 1900[1]—the *Plan of Campaign* goes on to make a number of sensible suggestions for practical working. It opposes 'pocket boroughs' for trade unions:

the candidate must be the candidate of the whole working class in the constituency, and not of a section only, however powerful. . . . But the Engineers may quite properly say to Newcastle, 'If you will run a Labor candidate who, as member of our union, would represent us as well as you, we will come to your rescue if you cannot find the requisite funds'.

It suggests, therefore, that the local Trades Councils—which were then affiliated members of the Trades Union Congress—should, when well organised, be put in control; should collect a thousand names of recognised electors prior to running a campaign, and set up an election fund 'with trustees to whom all monies should be paid' (it would have saved the Labour movement a great deal of trouble if that suggestion had been put into effect). It advises, further, that 'compact towns', where the electorate is not widely scattered, should be chosen for the first attempt, that sensible candidates should be selected who would not quarrel with their own side—'a man who cannot pick up one working-man's vote without dropping another's should confine himself to agitating', and that, while the candidates should be Socialistic, they should fight on a programme calculated to appeal practically to the division for which they are standing, and should not shout 'Abolish Capitalism' in answer to all questions. Finally, Shaw observes that, as in any event Labour will long be in a minority, its thoughts should be directed to home affairs, since 'there can be no question of foreign policy

[1] Even to the number—50—of candidates who in 1906 stood under Labour Party auspices.

E

and imperial statesmanship being thrown into the hands of the Labor Party yet awhile'—a statement which was unfortunately too long remembered.

Here, then, appeared a slashing attack on the Liberals coupled with the most precise plan for an independent Labour Party financed by Trade Unions that had yet been made. It is not surprising that it caused a hullabaloo in the right wing of the Fabian Society. Haldane, the personal friend of the Webbs, and his friends in the Government were not unnaturally hurt at the poor view taken of their efforts—they might justifiably have pleaded that they had not been given much time to try; a few members, including the political theorist D. G. Ritchie, author of *Darwinism and Politics*, resigned; and H. W. Massingham, the brilliant and hot-tempered political editor of the *Daily Chronicle*, exploded at the 'absurd and ill-timed reference to the Trade Unions', and walked out in a huff, though he seems to have been back again within the year. Even Graham Wallas is reported to have had doubts, 'feeling that we were rushed into it by fear of being thought complacent, and apathetic by the Independent Labour Party'.[1]

If that statement is at all true, it shows that members of the Society were still not decided which political horse it was right to back. But before we take the story further and follow the political life of the Society through to the formation of the Labour Representation Committee, it would be as well to take a look at the nature of the Society, itself, as it appeared at its first 'peak'.

[1] Beatrice Webb, *Our Partnership*, p. 110. But Beatrice's strong dislike, at that time, of both Keir Hardie and the I.L.P. makes it necessary to receive her evidence with caution. Her opinion of the former was shared by Shaw, who in a letter to Sidney written in 1892, said, 'My estimate of K.H. is that he is a Scotchman with alternate intervals of second sight (during which he does not see anything, but is suffused with afflatus) and common incapacity.'

CHAPTER VII

Fabians and Fabianism in the 'Nineties

THE Fabian Society, by 1894, had grown into something very different from the 'silly business' about which Shaw had been so patronising ten years earlier, and that not in membership alone. It was made up of two main elements; the leadership, which was the Executive Committee, and the hand-picked national membership. To these should be added, in order to estimate its effectiveness, the much larger body of sympathisers or semi-adherents, which included both the two thousand or so who had joined local Fabian Societies, and a smaller number, mostly living in London, who, while not prepared to sign the Fabian Basis, had sympathy with the Fabian analysis and were prepared to go along with a good many of the practical proposals made by Fabians. The non-Fabian members of the Progressive Party on the L.C.C. provided many examples in the last category.

The Fabian Executive was, by all accounts, one of the most effective and hard-working groups of its kind ever known. Out of many possible tributes I select one from S. G. Hobson, which, as its author finally resigned from the Executive after a public quarrel, may be considered reasonably unbiased.[1]

> While we were loyal colleagues we emphatically refused to be 'comrades', either in speech or writing. We shook hands in January, for the rest of the year we damned each other's eyes with impunity. There were two essentials: loyalty and intellectual honesty. Sidney Webb had his tentacles in various official circles, and never hesitated to tell us what he knew, however confidential.[2] He was never betrayed, advertently or inadvertently. Nor were there any intellectual

[1] S. G. Hobson, *Pilgrim To The Left* (1938), Chapter 8. Hobson did not join the Executive until 1900; but his account has all the marks of a well-established routine.

[2] But see next chapter.

reservations. We might sharply disagree—we disagreed on almost everything—but we opened our minds to each other. If . . . I lost my immortal soul, it was worth it to meet in weekly conference men like Bernard Shaw, Sidney Webb, Edward Pease, H. W. Macrosty, and Sydney Olivier, Graham Wallas, Stewart Headlam, Hubert Bland and others. . . .

Our Executive meetings always resolved themselves into two main divisions: first any urgent domestic matter, followed by political questions; then, secondly, consideration of Tracts . . . the Tract remains the Society's contribution to the social science of the times. Even the earliest are still worth reading. The procedure was thorough and searching. We would each have a draft in ample time to read and consider. Then we gave it corporate examination. Always there was somebody with the requisite special or expert knowledge; Shaw and Bland naturally saw to the literary quality. For all these Tracts the formula was light without heat.

This, then, was the procedure and tone of the Fabian Executive at its regular meetings—of busy adults, it must be remembered, engaged in earning their own livings, who between committee meetings fulfilled their Fabian job of lecturing as requested and also giving advice upon the matters referred to them by the secretary—the Fabian files indicate only a fraction of the volume of these, since in those far-off days letters tended to be answered in long-hand[1] by the member giving the information. By any standards, this is a remarkable record of industry.

The membership of the Fabian Executive was, for a voluntary society, unusually stable, as Shaw once pointed out, comparing it unkindly with the wild fluctuations which afflicted the S.D.F. The ten years following its enlargement to fifteen record only forty-five names, which, allowing for deaths, removals, and pressure of business, is a fairly low total. But, as in the case of all such bodies, however great their homogeneity and apparent equality, the chief weight fell upon half a dozen leaders, and on the Fabian Executive Shaw and Webb stood out above all others.

The fame of the great Webb Partnership, increasing since the publication of Beatrice Webb's *Diaries*, and its effectiveness over fifty years in spheres outside the scope of this book, has given the impression, in many quarters, that the Partnership was itself the Fabian Society, and that Beatrice Webb, though not one of

[1] In Webb's case, often on the back of the enquirer's original letter.

the founding fathers, was from the moment of her marriage as important as Sidney in its control. This is quite untrue, as Chapter IX will show; in the Fabian Society for many years the Partnership was not one of Beatrice and Sidney, but of Sidney and Bernard; and in some ways it is even more remarkable and surprising, while it endured, than the other.

'No two men', said Hobson, 'could be farther apart, spiritually and temperamentally'; and it seems, on the face of it, astonishing that there should ever have developed a close alliance between the irrepressible wielder of paradox and the indefatigable memoriser and master of facts, between the most brilliant stylist of his day and the man whose natural form of expression resembles nothing so much as the slow passing of an infinitely long, laden freight train.[1] But let Shaw speak for himself—and speak with greater modesty than he sometimes employed.

> Quite the wisest thing I ever did [he wrote][2] was to force my friendship on him and to keep it; for from that time I was not merely a futile Shaw but a committee of Webb and Shaw. . . . The difference between Shaw with Webb's brains, knowledge and official experience and Shaw by himself was enormous. But as I was and am an incorrigible histrionic and mountebank and Webb was the simplest of geniuses, I was often in the centre of the stage while he was invisible in the prompter's box.

And—extending his appreciation to embrace others of his colleagues—

> The repeatedly brilliant and extraordinary Shaw was in fact brilliant and extraordinary because he had in the Fabian Society an incomparable critical threshing machine for his ideas. When I seemed most original and fantastic, I was often simply an amanuensis and a mouthpiece with a rather exceptional literary and dramatic knack cultivated by dogged practice. My colleagues knocked much nonsense, ignorance and vulgar provinciality out of me.

Thus Shaw on Webb and his Fabian colleagues. Webb on Shaw seems not to have been set down in writing; but Shaw was one of his oldest friends, and the fact that he took the friendship

[1] See Chapter IV, p. 27, and the Webb *corpus* for innumerable other examples.

[2] *Sixteen Self Sketches*, Chapter XI.

unimpaired into marriage with a lady of strong views who could not make head or tail of Shaw[1] should be proof of the value he attached to it.

There is no need to spend much space in assessing the value of Webb to the infant Society; it has been often described and, even if it had not, the assets which he brought to it are obvious—his prodigious photographic memory, his ability in a very short space of time to tear the heart out of any document presented to him, his phenomenal gift for quick drafting of resolutions, amendments, reports, his power to grasp, almost simultaneously, the essence of any disagreement and the way in which a compromise could be effected—be it added, his knowledge of public and semi-public affairs, and (as mentioned by Hobson) his complete unscrupulousness in making use of confidential information in furtherance of 'good' causes, his general imperturbability and lack of personal rancour—the importance of all these is unquestionable. But what they needed, and what Shaw gave them, was above all translation into the spoken or written word. 'An amanuensis and a mouthpiece', Shaw called himself; but that is a very belittling phrase. Lacking their amanuensis, the Fabian thinkers might well have found their thoughts as dead and as boring to their audiences as the majority of sermons since the world began; Shaw put across, in the course of what he did not call his 'apprenticeship', the statistics they had garnered and the proposals they made in phrases which could not be ignored or forgotten; even today, no history of the Society can hope to be one half as readable as the brilliant summary which he gave to the delegates to the Fabian Conference of 1892. Webb built the Society's propaganda on a firm basis of fact; Shaw made the discussion of it an intellectual delight. Working together, as H. G. Wells found to his cost, they were one of the most devastating combinations ever known.

Webb-*cum*-Shaw, however, was not, as Shaw made clear, the

[1] She wrote of Shaw on early acquaintance (*Diaries*, September 17th, 1893) that 'he has not yet a personality; he is a pleasant but somewhat incongruous group of qualities'—a remarkably inadequate description: a little later that 'Sidney insinuates the ideas and organises the organisers. Bernard Shaw leads off the men of straw, the men with light heads.' Though she learned to endure and even to like him, and to be grateful for the trouble he took, unasked, to improve the style of the Webb output, one feels that the second judgment expresses the view she retained all her life of the relative importance, in the serious world, of her husband and his greatest friend.

Fabian Executive. Of the other leaders, after the departure of Mrs Besant, Graham Wallas was probably the most attractive —'a lovable man', Beatrice Webb called him when she was recording her early and not over-enthusiastic assessment of Sidney's Fabian colleagues. He was a very old friend of Sidney's, who in the early 'eighties wrote him long letters full of a rather surprising *Weltschmerz*, which are preserved in the Webb Collection. Among social historians Wallas will be longest remembered for his *Life of Francis Place*, since he failed to follow up the questions propounded—and still unanswered—in that extraordinarily suggestive book, *Human Nature in Politics* (1908). 'When a man dies for his country,' Wallas asked, 'what does he die for?'—with nationalism rampant over three-quarters of the world, we are yet not really certain of the answer. Wallas, a schoolmaster by training, gave up schoolmastering in 1885 'on a question of religious conformity', and took to University Extension lecturing. He was a Fabian from 1886 to 1904, when he resigned as a result of long-continued differences over policy.[1] His dislike of professional organisations—and of organised religion—which increased greatly in his later years, would in all probability have in the long run estranged him from the Fabians in any event; but as lecturer, and subsequently professor, at the London School of Economics, he had an immense influence, not to be measured by his published work, upon a generation of students; and in the formative years of the Fabian Society, his contribution, delivered in shaggy clothes and with awkward gestures, was unquestionable.

Sydney Olivier, afterwards Lord Olivier, was generally held to be the fourth of the 'big four', though he played a lesser part than any of the three foregoing, and his personality is less easy to re-create. Like Webb, he was a civil servant in the Colonial Office, but unlike him he remained in colonial affairs, and in 1899 left the Fabian Executive to become, first, Secretary and eventually Governor of Jamaica. (Much later, he was Secretary of State for India in the first Labour Government.) He was, perhaps, more simple and moral in his Socialism than some of his more sophisticated colleagues; his anti-imperialist publications, especially *White Capital and Colour Labour* (1910), were forthright in their expression, and he was the only one of the Old Guard to support S. G. Hobson against the other leaders over

[1] See below, p. 108.

the South African War.[1] The worst that could be said of him was that, though upright, an excellent administrator and a good man, he was inclined to be dull.

The two officers of the Society, Hubert Bland and Edward Pease, were very different types. Bland was a curious character, not one whom one would have expected to find enrolled in the Fabian Society at all, let alone holding the office of treasurer for over twenty years. He was a journalist, a star man on the *Sunday Chronicle*, a flamboyant personage with a black-ribboned monocle and a liking for sexual adventure; he and his wife, Edith Nesbit, had a large house at Well Hall, near Dymchurch, run on more or less Bohemian principles, where a number of up-and-coming young *littérateurs* (including in the new century H. G. Wells) ran in and out, and generally amused themselves.[2] He alone of the 'founding fathers' had no natural affinity with Liberalism; like Wilfred Scawen Blunt, he called himself a Tory democrat and had about as much sympathy with Liberal politicians as he would have had with a nest of snakes. That being so, one would have expected him to find Fabianism and Fabians generally uncongenial; yet he remained for that long period in office as treasurer, having little to do with the accounts, if Pease is to be trusted, except to sign the necessary cheques, but reading and revising Tracts and contributing one himself on the public feeding of schoolchildren (Tract 120). He was a pillar, with Stewart Headlam and Cecil Chesterton, of the Anti-Puritan League, which fought battles with the L.C.C.—and with others—over music-halls, etc.; and the very existence of himself and his household must have served to remind Socialists that Fabianism was not entirely the drab, narrow, public-service existence which some caricaturists had made of it.

Pease, the faithful guardian and watch-dog, has suffered somewhat in public reputation both because Beatrice Webb did not like him and thought him a bore and a nuisance—'worthy' was the damning word she used—and partly because his lifelong devotion to Sidney Webb made him regard with gruff suspicion anyone who criticised Webb or Shaw, or even—in the days of disputes within the Society—any would-be entrant who seemed

[1] See Chapter XI.

[2] See further in H. G. Wells, *Experiment in Autobiography*; Doris Langley Moore, *E. Nesbit* (1933). 'The Blands had a little Fabian circle of their own', Pease wrote in review of the latter book.

likely to turn into a critic. 'I cannot think', he wrote after Webb's death,[1] 'of any natural fault or weakness which can be attributed to him. I knew him for sixty years, and for much of that period had constant dealings with him, and if anyone says that I seem to regard him as a perfect character, I will not gainsay it.' A heartfelt tribute; but it is not to be expected that everyone would share that view; and Pease's hero-worship, which makes the words 'So the Old Gang triumphed' run as a *leitmotiv* through his Fabian History, irritated many people and obscured his own merits, for he was an admirable secretary to a fairly difficult team.

Of other members of the Executive at the time less need be said at this point. Massingham, the future editor of the *Nation*, Robert Dell, the international journalist, the Reverend Stewart Headlam, and Halliday Sparling, Morris's son-in-law, were the best known, though Miss Emma Brooke was a novelist of some fame in her day, and Constance Garnett, Tolstoy's translator, Tom Mann, and Henry Macrosty, the economist, who wrote on trusts and combines, joined the Executive soon afterwards. The membership roll of the Fabian Society, over the years, has contained many names distinguished in politics, literature, art, and even the Churches; but it is a mistaken belief that the Fabians enrolled the *élite* of English society.[2] It made no effort to do so; it let them come in if they wanted to, if they could pass the scrutiny of the Executive, and if they were willing to work hard in the Society's service—for which most of the *élite* would have had neither the time nor the inclination. It is true that not many Fabians would have gone the lengths suggested by Shaw in his account of his own training as a Socialist; but the earliest editions of the Basis state quite categorically that members *are pledged* to take part according to their abilities and opportunities in the general work of the Society, and this was no paper pledge. The Fabian member was required to supply the Executive with a list of his qualifications and specialities; he was expected to be

[1] *The Webbs and Their Work*, p. 26. In the Fabian files, Webb's letters, and Webb's only, are preserved *en masse*, which perhaps indicates the General Secretary's estimate of their importance.

[2] A very large number, however, of persons distinguished in their day were at one time or another members of the Society. Some of them figure in later chapters of this book; there is, unfortunately, no space for a full 'roll of honour', which would occupy many pages. But see *Index of Persons*.

ready to answer questions and prepare notes on his subject, and to lecture and write (if he could and were good enough; the standard was high). If he could not, he might type, address envelopes and fold circulars. He was to heckle, to canvass, to speak at street corners, to sell Tracts and other literature (being given, on Webb's suggestion, a modest discount for his trouble),[1] to volunteer for public service such as that of managers under the School Boards, and to contribute what he could reasonably afford to the Society's funds. Furthermore, he was expected to attend meetings regularly—we have already seen that he could be struck off if he did not, and Executive records show that the rule was taken seriously—and to discuss in detail the text of proposed publications, even though these had already been through the sieve of the Executive.[2] This could be, and upon occasion certainly was, a fairly heavy assignment, especially as the publication was quite often *read aloud* by the author, in order to save the expense of circulating proofs. It is on record that *Facts for Londoners*—not, one trusts, all the statistical tables—was so read; but we do learn that sometimes members made effective silent protest. *Fabian News* of August 1891, reporting a meeting called to pass or amend two drafts, one of which, *A Democratic Budget* (Tract 39), contained a full discussion of possible reforms in public finance, remarks reproachfully that 'the important business of discussing Tracts seemed to be regarded by most of those present as peculiarly dull, and before the meeting was over the hall was nearly as empty as the House of Commons on an Indian Budget night'. On another occasion, however, over 130 members came with suggested amendments to a Tract of which proofs had been sent out, so possibly the earlier apathy may be attributable to the subject.

The Fabian member was thus expected to take his Society and his obligations very seriously; if he had not done so the volume

[1] 'How to Be a Member for Nothing', was the heading which *Fabian News* later gave to this expedient.

[2] John Burns's 1893 Tract on *The Unemployed* was ordered to be printed without having been previously discussed, probably because that eminent personage would not have been likely to receive criticism with equanimity. But it was explicitly stated that this was not a precedent; and in 1899 the Executive, being anxious to hurry through a Tract on the nationalisation of Irish railways and unwilling either to await the ordinary monthly meeting or to spend 2*s.* 6*d.* per head (estimated) on the calling of a special one, propounded in the *News* a device for getting round the difficulty.

of work and its influence would have been very much less than it was. What sort of person was he, aside from his work? The answer to this is to be found mainly in the columns of *Fabian News*, supplemented by scraps of information from the minutes of members' and Executive meetings. *Fabian News* announced that its purpose was to summarise papers read at meetings, to chronicle the doings of members, groups, and local societies, to print reviews of books—'by members who have read them', a later issue reassuringly added—to publish facts useful for Socialist propaganda, and to provide a diary of lectures by Fabians. In practice, the promise to give Socialist 'facts' was not kept, other publications fulfilling that function; and book reviews were very scanty during the early years. In the next century, when the *News* was enlarged, reviews came to occupy a great deal of space, particularly reviews by Pease, who had an unexpectedly trenchant style and delighted to jump with both feet on any book favouring Syndicalism, Co-partnership, Guild Socialism, Utopian communities, or anything else other than the pure milk of the collectivist faith. Lists of lectures, however, were regularly printed, and the pledge to report important lectures at some length was fully implemented. Members' meetings—though not those of the Executive—were also reported, sometimes briefly, sometimes extending over a page or two; decisions of the Executive were mentioned very succinctly; names of proposed new members (and sometimes of those resigning) were printed; and a column headed 'What Members Are Doing' provided personal news. It is this last item, more than any other, which, with its faint parish-magazine quality, invests the files of the *News* with a lingering dusty fragrance all their own. The voluminous writings of the leaders do not, for reasons of space, appear in them, nor—except on rare occasions—the battles of principle within the Labour movement; it is the small beer which finds room.

Questions of ceremony and formality—or the reverse—upon social occasions seem much to have exercised the minds of members. In March 1890 they severely decided in conclave that 'the social occasion [of the Annual Meeting] must *not* conclude with a dance'; the *News* of February 1892, in giving particulars of the arrangements for the forthcoming Conference of all Fabian Societies, announced that 'all ceremonial business, including votes of thanks, is to be dispensed with', and two years later the

Executive decided 'to have no Conference, Soirée, Conversazione, Party, or other Frivolity'. The reason for this unusual outburst of austerity is unknown; and by 1897 the Society had relented to the extent of arranging 'Toasts' for its Annual Dinner. As to public ceremony, for the wedding of the Duke of York in 1893 the Society agreed to close the Strand office and let the windows to sightseers at the highest possible price, advertising in the *Morning Post*; but when the Executive decided to contribute to the general fund for illuminating the Strand at the Diamond Jubilee a republican revolt at the members' meeting reversed the decision in spite of the speeches of Shaw and Webb—one of the very few occasions on which that formidable combination was defeated.

Smoking worried the Society a good deal, as did the correct way in which to describe members and their personal activities. Smoking was several times forbidden at Executive meetings, 'cigarettes only' being allowed (after 6 p.m.) in 1896, though it was to be 'permitted and even encouraged' at the Dinner with the Toasts; the debate was still continuing at the time of the South African War.[1] 'Mrs' and 'Miss' were not to be used in announcements in *Fabian News*; this rule was rescinded, reimposed, and rescinded again. In July 1891 'What Members Are Doing' contained the rather surprising statement that 'Frank Podmore has married Miss E. O. Bramwell and *vice versa*'; in the May following, this formula was amended to 'F. E. Green and Miss Gertrude Beane have married one another', and later still it was simplified to 'Walter Edwards has married Ethel Samuel'—the most famous of all these entries being, of course, the line in the issue of August 1892, which says laconically 'Sidney Webb was married on 23rd *ult.* to Beatrice Potter'.

Other occupations and preoccupations make their appearance from time to time. There is a Fabian Challenge Swimming Shield and some Fabian Scouts—long before Baden-Powell; there is a Civic Shirt business run by a Fabian; there are the usual appeals for congenial spirits to come and share houses or apartments. Mr Edgar Bottle has a Large Cool House near Croydon which will accommodate Fabians and give them vegetarian meals if they desire it; there is a Fabian Spinster in search of a half-day engagement. The highlight of these, though it did

[1] As late as 1912, the Fabian Summer School refused to hold a 'smoking concert', because 'the number of dissidents was too high'.

not appear until the new century, was the 'Tolstoy Settlement for ladies, recently formed in Sussex with the object of providing a place where a simple life can be lived, and "slumming" carried on in agreeable surroundings [*sic*]. Vegetarian diet and no servants are provided for one guinea a week.' [1] What is most notably lacking is any reference to music, art, or even 'pure' literature. Bernard Shaw once ruefully observed that of the early Fabians only he and Bland had the faintest interest in art of any kind (he must have forgotten Walter Crane), and that it was no wonder that Morris was uncomfortable in so determinedly philistine an atmosphere; it was not until the second Fabian blooming was well under way that literary and artistic groups began to make their appearance.

It was people of this kind—hard-working, intelligent, earnest, but definitely of the bourgeoisie, and mostly of the London bourgeoisie at that—whom the leaders of the Society brought into contact with the Socialists from the provinces at the first and for nearly twenty years the only delegate conference of the Fabian Society, held in February 1892: with the boom in the Society it was the obvious thing to do. The Conference was held in the Essex Hall in the Strand; it was remarkably well attended, only about 300 of the extra-London membership being unrepresented, and was reported as an immense success.

The first item was a wonderful virtuoso performance, the long and brilliant discourse of Shaw on 'The Fabian Society: What it Is and What it Has Done': this was reprinted as *The Early History of the Fabian Society* (Tract 41).[2] It reads as well today as ever it did, and is still one of the Society's main historical sources. But, considered as an address to working-class delegates from the provinces, it must be accounted a beautifully spiced dish and no more. It is the work of a Londoner, a highly intellectual Londoner in touch with the intricacies of public affairs, and its account of political intrigues in the metropolis, however amusing, must have been so complicated for the delegates from Lancashire or Yorkshire to follow that we are not as surprised as the reporter was to learn that it 'so exhausted the brains of delegates

[1] *Fabian News*, June 1905.

[2] It was reprinted also in Shaw, *Essays in Fabian Socialism* (1932). It called forth an angry letter from Blatchford (September 17th) which is preserved in the Fabian files with the annotation 'the author gave Mr Blatchford a very large piece of his mind'.

that, after a few feeble attempts at raising debate by questions, the chairman fell in with the evident wishes of members and declared the sitting at an end'.

The 'exhausted brains' had not greatly revived by the Sunday morning, when some rather desultory reports of activities were produced and 'useful suggestions' made—a common euphemism for a scattered discussion which leads nowhere. After this the Conference turned to two political resolutions—we are not told whence they emanated.

The first suggested

that, in the opinion of this Conference it is desirable that the Fabian Society issue a leaflet for the General Election which, without laying down a hard and fast line for all constituencies, should name certain proposals to be brought forward on test questions, and recommend electors, in general, not to vote for any candidate who will not pledge himself to press them forward. The leaflet should also urge the running of Labor[1] and Socialist candidates where possible.

This resolution was lost by a small majority. The second, which was decisively rejected, proposed to make officials (not members) of the existing major political parties ineligible for Fabian membership. The Conference, having passed nothing at all, then went on, with some inconsistency, to welcome the possible formation of an independent labour political party—and adjourned for a soirée.

'Several delegates expressed the wish that the Conference should be an annual one'; and no doubt they had spent an agreeable week-end. But it is quite clear, to anyone reading the record, that the Conference had not been organised so as to produce anything of permanent value, and that its organisers had never thought out any plans for doing so. 'Difficulties', we are told, prevented arrangements being made for another conference in 1893; but the main difficulty must surely have been the negotiations for the Bradford Conference at which the I.L.P. took upon itself the job, which the Fabian Society had in effect refused, of providing a continuing direction, by means of branch organisation, for local groups of Socialists. For a time, while the I.L.P. was finding its feet, the number of local Fabian Societies

[1] Always so spelt in early Fabian literature; it was not an Americanism, but a personal fad of Shaw's. In April 1916 the Executive solemnly decided to use English spelling in future.

continued to grow; but by the end of 1893 it was clear that they were turning over to the fostering care of the new organisation, and the Fabian Executive saw them disappear with scarcely a pang. The 'boom' had proved a boom in Socialism, but not in what the Fabian Executive regarded as serious Fabian membership. In 1895 the Annual Report—influenced, possibly, by the development described in the next chapter—records without tears the disappearance of many local Societies, but hails with enthusiasm the formation of a Fabian group in the University of Oxford, with about thirty members, 'consisting of men who in a few years will be scattered throughout the country, *occupying in many cases posts of influence and importance*' (italics mine).

PART TWO

Interregnum

1894–1906

F

CHAPTER VIII

The Hutchinson Trust and the London School of Economics

HENRY HUTCHINSON of Derby had joined the Society in June 1890. According to Beatrice Webb, he was an elderly cantankerous creature who 'lived a penurious life and stinted his wife and by no means spoilt his children'.[1] He wrote voluminous letters to the members of the Executive, particularly to Shaw, who, he complained, refused to answer even on a post-card. Shaw was, however, forced by his colleagues to be more communicative, for Hutchinson was a very valuable financial asset. Among other gifts we find him putting up £100 for the first Fabian lecture tour in Lancashire,[2] and offering to guarantee the lease of the Fabian office. After 1893–4, with falling revenue, it would have been very urgent to keep Hutchinson in good mood; but in the end that proved not to be necessary. For in the summer of 1894, being in failing health, he committed suicide, and in September the Executive were informed that his will, after providing an annuity of £100 for the widow and some minor legacies, left the residue of the estate, amounting after payment of duty to nine or ten thousand pounds, in the hands of five trustees—his daughter Caroline, William Clarke, Pease, De Mattos, and Webb, of whom Webb was to be president for the first year—to be expended within ten years on 'the propaganda and other purposes of the said Fabian Society and its Socialism and towards advancing the objects in any other way they deem advisable'. In giving the Executive this information Webb added that the will appeared informally and hurriedly drafted, and might under the circumstances be contested by the disinherited family on the grounds of unsoundness

[1] *Our Partnership*, p. 84. Hearsay evidence, however.

[2] Executive Minutes, August 1890. The lecturer was W. H. Utley; he was paid five guineas a time.

of mind; to forestall this, on his advice the Trustees had decided to double the widow's allowance. There was no contest; and when Caroline Hutchinson died a year and a half later the bread thus prudently cast upon the waters returned in the form of a legacy to the Trust, which pretty nearly made up the difference.

This was not the only decision made before the Executive had heard of the legacy. Before it met, before even the five Trustees had met, one of their number had already settled their main business for them.

On a certain day in August, 1894 [wrote Graham Wallas],[1] Mr and Mrs Webb, Mr G. B. Shaw and I were staying at the little farm [Borough Farm, near Godalming]. . . . *The day before Mr Webb learnt that, by the will of Mr Henry Hutchinson, he had been given the duty of directing the expenditure of a sum of money. He and Mrs Webb woke early, had a long discussion, and at breakfast told us* that part of the money would be used to found a School in London on the lines of the École Libre des Sciences Politiques in Paris.

The italics in the passage are mine. Wallas made no comment; possibly, even in 1925, he did not know the whole story, which the researches of the late Lady Beveridge have recently made available;[2] if he had, he would have observed that on this occasion Mr and Mrs Webb had woken very early indeed. For it is plain from records and correspondence that for some time past—at least since his creation in 1893 of the Technical Education Board of the L.C.C.[3]—Sidney had been yearning to set up an institution of that kind, and had even discussed possibilities with people who might be interested. He may indeed have have had some idea of the provisions of Hutchinson's will before his death —though there is no evidence that he had; but the death, and the definite news of the legacy, came as manna from heaven. Nevertheless, though the will provided that Webb should be the first chairman of the Trust, it did not specifically enjoin that he should personally 'direct the expenditure'—even if Hutchinson would have been content that he should, he had omitted to say so; and the omission had to be remedied.

The Fabian Basis contained the statement that included in the work of the Society was 'the further investigation of economic

[1] London School of Economics, *Student's Handbook*, 1925.

[2] Janet Beveridge, *An Epic of Clare Market* (1960).

[3] For this ingenious piece of manœuvring, see *Our Partnership*, pp. 78 ff.

problems, and the collection of facts contributing to their elucidation'; but it did not say in so many words that it was the Society itself that should do the investigating. Webb, accordingly, wrote out, as a kind of appendage to the Hutchinson will, a paper of his own[1] stating what he considered its provisions could mean in practice, including

the promotion . . . of *all or any* of the objects for the time being of the said Society, or in or towards the promotion of the study of Socialism, *Economics or of any other branch or branches of Social Science or Political Science* or in or towards the propagation or advocacy whether by lectures pamphlets books or otherwise of socialistic or economic or political teaching *or in or towards the promotion of any educational social or philanthropic object* [italics mine];

and to fortify himself against possible criticism enquired of R. B. Haldane, Q.C., whether this seemed all right to him. Haldane, it seems, asked Webb whether he was still a Socialist and whether he thought his proposed new foundation would really strengthen the case for Socialism; receiving the answer 'Yes' to both queries he gave 'counsel's opinion' in favour of going ahead. Webb, however, had made up his mind well in advance of the consultation with Haldane—whose name was never mentioned in any discussion with the Fabian Executive—and had decided that at least half was to go to the foundation of the L.S.E., on whose behalf its first Director promised to the London Chamber of Commerce that 'the School would not deal with political matters and *nothing of a socialistic tendency* would be introduced';[2] furthermore, that whatever part the Fabian Society itself might be permitted to retain of the money left for its 'propaganda and other purposes' was not to be casually spent. A passage in Beatrice's *Diary* makes it perfectly clear that the Fabian Executive was not on any account to receive a large increase in its regular income, nor was the money to be frittered away on political activity in the ordinary sense.

If it is mainly used for ordinary work [she wrote],[3] then it will merely save the pockets of ordinary subscribers or inflate the common work of the organisation for a few years beyond its normal growth.

[1] Now in L.S.E. archives. See Beveridge, *loc. cit.*, pp. 27 ff.

[2] Minutes of the Chamber's Commercial Education Committee, quoted in Beveridge, *loc. cit.* My italics.

[3] *Diary*, September 21st, 1894.

Moreover, mere propaganda of the shibboleths [*sic*] of collectivism is going on at a rapid rate through the I.L.P.—the wheel has been set running and it is rolling downhill at a rapid pace. It looks as though the bulk of the working-men will be collectivist by the end of the century [!] But reform will not be brought about by shouting. What is needed is *hard thinking*. And the same objection applies to sending nondescript Socialists into Parliament. . . . Last evening we sat by the fire and jotted down a list of subjects which wanted elucidating: issues of fact which needed clearing up. Above all, we wanted the ordinary citizen to feel that reforming society is not a light matter, and must be taken by experts specially trained for the purpose.

All this, be it noted, was decided upon by the Webbs themselves, with the barest possible consultation with anybody. The attitude towards Socialists indicated in the above passage was underlined, and the Fabians were startled when, before the end of the year, the Webbs approached the expert whom they proposed to put in charge of the venture which would 'advance the objects of the Society'.[1] This was a young Oxford man named W. A. S. Hewins who had been of service and showed sympathy to the Webbs when they were writing the *History of Trade Unionism*. He had no leanings towards democracy or collectivism; later he became an ardent Tariff Reformer and joined the Roman Catholic Church—when he resigned in 1903 to become a campaign servant of Joseph Chamberlain he was succeeded as Director by the geographer Sir Halford Mackinder, later to stand for Parliament as a Liberal Unionist. Hewins was attracted by the idea of the School, and as an added inducement Sidney promised him that the L.C.C. Technical Education Board, of which he was chairman, would give an additional subvention out of the rates; a promise which was duly fulfilled, the T.E.B. giving £500 in the first year and £1,200 in the second—no inconsiderable contribution.[2] In the first two or three years of the School's existence the T.E.B. and the Hutchinson Trust gave it approximately equal amounts. But 'socialistic' it certainly was not; a selection of the 'eminent specialists' who shared the

[1] Graham Wallas was apparently designated at first; but eventually declined. Sir Sidney Caine has suggested that his appointment was merely 'gap-filling'.

[2] Beveridge, p. 87. The L.S.E. was not, of course, the sole body so to benefit. Other branches of university work—and the London Polytechnics—also received assistance.

teaching during the first three years includes many known for their Tory or Liberal views, but apart from Webb himself the only Socialist mentioned is Graham Wallas—Bertrand Russell, who had given his Trinity Fellowship to the School, being reckoned as a Liberal at the time. The fact that the Fabian Harry Snell was appointed to the then lowly post of Secretary to the School does not really alter the picture; and it is not surprising that Shaw, who had taken no apparent objection to the original proposition, exploded in a long and angry letter to Beatrice.[1]

The general impression left [he wrote], was that the Hutchinson Trustees are prepared to bribe the Fabians by subsidies for country lectures and the like to allow them to commit an atrocious malversation of the rest of the bequest; and that as the executive is powerless the best thing to do is to take the bribe, and warn future Hutchinsons to be careful how they leave any money they may have to place at the disposal of the Socialists. This won't do. First, Hewins must be told flatly that he must, in talking to the Guild of St Matthew and the other Oxford Socialists, speak as a Collectivist, and make it clear that the School of Economics will have a Collectivist bias. . . . Secondly, Hewins must be told that he MUST get somebody else than Acworth and Foxwell to put in the bill. It is easy to say where are the men; the answer is that that is precisely what Hewins is being paid out of Hutchinson's money to find out. Third, the Collectivist flag must be waved, and the Marseillaise played if necessary in order to attract fresh bequests. If the enemy complains, it must be told that the School has important endowments the conditions of which are specifically Socialist, and that if the enemy wants specifically individualist lectures, he must endow them. . . .

You see we must be in a position at any moment to show that faith has been kept with Hutchinson. If Webb is ever publicly convicted of having served up the County Council and the Chamber of Commerce on toast to the ghost of Hutchinson, everyone will laugh and think it is an uncommonly smart thing. But if he is ever suspected of having tampered with a trust of ten thousand pounds from a private benefactor, then we shall lose our character for being straight in money matters; and none of us can afford to do that.

Please show him this letter and allow it to rankle.

Presumably Sidney was shown the letter. But, as we know since the *Diaries* were made available, Beatrice was in fact the more anti-propagandist partner of the two, and Shaw seems to

[1] Webb Collection. July 1st, 1895.

have realised that it would be no use pressing the matter further. The School of Economics went ahead. Its foundation and establishment, on so slender a financial basis, was certainly an astonishing feat of 'social engineering'; its subsequent history, and any discussion of what contribution it may or may not have made to 'furthering the objects of the Fabian Society', fall outside the scope of this book. The manner of its founding, on the other hand, however abundantly Webb may have felt himself to be wise and justified—and there is little doubt that he did[1]—is another question; those critics of the Webbs who have accused them of sharp practice, of complete lack of squeamishness about the means they employed to further projects of whose rightness they had convinced themselves, will find a very handsome example in the foundation of the L.S.E.

The L.S.E.'s share in the Hutchinson legacy was quietly removed from Fabian ken. But, as we have seen, this did not mean that the Fabian Executive was to have the disposal of the rest of it.

In the December *News* members whose hopes might have risen were warned that the Executive had no say in the spending of the Trust money and that the need for the membership to pay their subscriptions remained as acute as ever. (The Society, like most of its kin, was more or less permanently 'in the red'.) In March came the first piece of good news. The Society was to receive £200, presumably as an annual grant, since on the strength of it the secretary's salary was raised by £50 to £150,[2]

[1] 'I envy Sidney his robust conscience,' Beatrice on one occasion confided to her *Diary*—but not in connection with the Hutchinson Trust.

[2] It must be admitted that the record of the Society, as an employer, was for many years one of strict economy, not to say cheese-paring. We have already noted the resistance to paying the secretary anything at all; Pease's salary was slowly and painfully squeezed up to £300 a year after twenty years, when he inherited a legacy and became honorary secretary, his successor, previously organiser, receiving £40 less. The Smart Boy was paid ten shillings a week, raised to fifteen at the end of the year. Two years later he got a pound, it being stated that he could receive overtime for any hours worked over 48 ('which means none', commented Pease); after seventeen years' service he had reached 45*s*., and in 1911, the year of the extensive Poor Law campaign, he was given a present of £5 'with intimation that his salary would not be raised'. A typist engaged in 1892 to operate a secondhand Barlock machine (still in use in 1917), was paid 25*s*. with permission to undertake paid work in the evenings; Julius West, later historian of Chartism, was taken on at the same figure in 1908, until adverse criticism by members

and the Executive set up a committee, under the chairmanship of J. R. MacDonald, to consider 'what new means can be adopted for increasing the usefulness of the Society': after a good many meetings the main result of the committee's labours seems to have been the provision of a Scheme of Lantern Slides for the assistance of lecturers—useful, but scarcely sensational.

In June the scheme for the School of Economics was for the first time 'fully explained' to the Executive—by Sidney Webb, who added the characteristic small bribe that Fabian members would be allowed to attend its lectures at half-price, the Hutchinson Trust paying the difference; about a dozen and a half availed themselves of the offer—one of these, at a later date, was Sir Frederick Osborn, now Chairman of the Town and Country Planning Association. At the same time a much more important decision was announced: to appoint 'Hutchinson Lecturers', who would carry Fabian education into the provinces. The Society would arrange the lectures; the Trust would pay their salaries and maintenance. Of the two full-time lecturers first appointed, one was MacDonald.

During the next half-dozen years the Hutchinson Lectures accounted for a very large proportion of Fabian activities. These lectures were very different from the efforts of casual propagandists. The lecturers were carefully selected for their competence; their subjects covered a wide range of social and political subjects, and the syllabuses (often for a series of meetings in a single town) were carefully prepared and supervised; and with the classes and correspondence arising from them and the book-boxes —partly paid for by the Trust—which were sent out all over the country, they certainly promoted a solid and extensive education in the principles and practical proposals of British reformist

forced a rise; as late as 1914, the woman attendant on the newly established Fabian Commonroom, had a room, fire, and light, and 14*s*. a week, an amendment to give her 15*s*. being defeated in Committee. This outrageous parsimony, which seriously inconvenienced the Society in later years, was directly due to Shaw and the Webbs, who believed in buying in the cheapest market, the *History of Trade Unionism* notwithstanding. It is only fair to add that the Executive could correctly claim that its stinginess lost it nothing; people did remain for long years in its service at very low pay (as they did in the service of the Webbs themselves). The episode of the clerk who, on his departure for war service, was found to have pocketed by stages more than £160, was exceptional and due to lax supervision; the original Smart Boy, E. J. Howell, retired in *1939* on a pension of £120 per annum.

Socialism the like of which had not been seen before,[1] and kept the name Fabian and Fabian Socialism alive in people's minds long after the local Fabian Societies had faded away or been merged.[2] In 1896, the Society's 'general grant' from the Hutchinson Trust was raised to £300 a year; and there can be no doubt that, under the firm guidance of Webb and his faithful Pease, the Society got as much, if not more, in cash than it would have received had Hutchinson lived on, and that the subvention was very well invested—better, possibly, than if the Executive had had the free spending of the capital sum.[3] Taking the Trust as a whole, it can safely be said that never since has £9,000 been spent with such remarkable results, and that Hutchinson, had he lived to see it, would surely have been astounded.

One member of the Executive, however, remained deeply dissatisfied; and this is perhaps a suitable point at which to deal with MacDonald's early relations with the Fabian Society, which are not without bearing on the history of the Labour Governments of which he was Prime Minister.

MacDonald was an early member of the Society—in 1892, when Pease fell seriously ill, there was talk of appointing him as temporary secretary, but nothing came of it. In 1894 he was elected to the Executive. There is no record of his raising any objections to the original proposals for the Trust—no resolution was proposed at the meeting of the Executive; and in 1895, while chairman of a committee for increasing the usefulness of the Society, he accepted employment as a Hutchinson lecturer. But his views of the functions of a Hutchinson lecturer clearly differed

[1] In 1901, the Society proposed to run a series of 'instructional lectures' for convicts at Princetown Prison. The Home Office was horrified, and it was not until 1944 that the London County Council succeeded in persuading the authorities that prisoners might be encouraged to study.

[2] The last of the 1892 foundations (the Ramsbottom Society) died in 1900; a Society at Liverpool, however, formed early in 1893, lived for nearly forty years.

[3] In 1904 the Trust was formally wound up. The remainder of the funds were divided with approximate equality between the School and the Fabian Society. £1,332 was the share of the latter, whose Executive Committee seized the opportunity to express its approval of the manner in which 'the Trustees have administered the Hutchinson Trust Fund'. This money the Society put into a Trust Fund of its own, to be spent on lectures, book-boxes, and distribution of Tracts; in 1923, the small remainder of this sum was handed over to the Fabian Local Government Bureau (see p. 201).

from those of the Webbs; and by April 1896 he was already writing 'furious letters' to the Webbs on their 'abuse' of the Hutchinson money by contributing a capital sum for the L.S.E.'s library, demanding that the Trustees should present 'detailed accounts' every six weeks to the Fabian Executive, and telling Pease that 'if the Trustees have practically mortgaged the Trust to [*sic*] £150 a year to the Fabian and the rest to the School of Economics I shall certainly oppose them and carry through the opposition to an appeal to the Society if need be' [1]—a threat which he did not carry out.

Beatrice, in her *Diary*, unkindly suggests that this attitude was due to his having failed to get a staff appointment on the new L.S.E. 'He is not good enough for that work; he has never had the time to do original work, or even to learn to do the old stuff well.' [2] There may be something in the accusation; MacDonald's vanity may have felt that he was being fobbed off with an unimportant job; he had already, in March, written to Pease that he was doubtful about standing for the Executive, saying that if he served again it would be 'more for the purpose of watching development than from any hope that the Society is going to do any useful work'.[3] But it is clear that he was trying to use his Hutchinson lectureship to 'advance the objects of the Society' by trying to refound Fabian Socialist Societies in the provinces—and the Webbs would have none of it. 'The truth is', wrote Beatrice, 'that we and MacDonald are opposed on a radical issue of policy. To bring about a maximum amount of public control in public administration, do we want to organise the unthinking persons into Socialistic Societies, or to make the thinking persons socialistic? We believe in the latter process.' Here was a clear clash of policy, though it should not be assumed that Mrs Webb's private diary necessarily reflected the general opinion of the Fabian Society, of which she was only a 'fringe' member.

MacDonald did stand for election, and remained on the Executive for four years longer. Sidney soothingly promised to make a report on the Trust to the Annual Meeting—there is no record of what he said; but, unappeased, MacDonald in May demanded to be shown the articles of the Trust and counsel's

[1] Letter to Pease, in Fabian Society files.

[2] *Diary*, April 18th, 1896.

[3] Letter to Pease, in Fabian Society files.

opinion thereon (a request which was presumably refused), opposed the autumn scheme for Hutchinson lectures and resigned from the lecture-directing committee on the ground that he had no power and no responsibility. Simultaneously, he pressed upon the Executive a plan for the 'expansion' of the Society to the tune of £500–£600 per annum, as it was now 'dropping out of the public eye'. The Executive, following its policy of conciliating dissidents and not fighting them, accepted the project 'in general', but refused to publish it in the *News*; and MacDonald seems to have dropped it. Shortly afterwards he was complaining about the non-appearance of a Tract on *Women*; and he objected violently to the publication of the Society's policy in Tract 70,[1] took his objection to a members' meeting which 'drew the largest audience recorded to date', and was soundly beaten. He did not, however, leave the Executive; and was even entrusted with the task of editing a second volume of *Fabian Essays*;[2] though in view of his expressed opinions and his increasing association with the I.L.P., it is not surprising that, notwithstanding Shaw's promise to contribute, the project was eventually adjourned *sine die*. His name was twice proposed as Fabian delegate to the discussions with the I.L.P. on the possible formation of a Labour Party, and as often rejected—which must have rankled; and he was obviously getting more and more out of sympathy. He opposed publication of the Tract on State education,[3] and finally left the Society, which, as he wrote in a letter to a friend, had got 'hopelessly reactionary and *petty*', on the issue of the South African War.

The whole story resembles very much the noisier, more public, though briefer battle of H. G. Wells with the Fabian leaders ten years later, and like the latter left an enduring resentment in the mind of the defeated party, and a mistrust in those of the victors, which is clearly visible in many entries in the Webb *Diaries*. In the matter of the Hutchinson Trust, MacDonald had certainly met an instance of Machiavellianism far more pronounced than ever Wells came across; but this does not seem to have been his

[1] See p. 92.

[2] A proposal frequently made, but never carried out until 1952.

[3] See p. 102. Previously, in 1898, while the Webbs were out of England on their transatlantic tour, he had made a great effort, assisted by Will Crooks, to get the L.C.C. grant to the School of Economics cut by two-thirds. Hewins managed to rally reserves to defeat him (J. Beveridge, *loc. cit.*, p. 91).

main criticism, which was more personal.[1] As late as 1933, in a preface to Arthur Compton-Rickett's autobiography, *I Look Back*, he described his quondam comrades as 'smart people who held weekly meetings, published pamphlets, and drafted resolutions the passing of which by a list of societies and Liberal Associations was to transform politics and the world'—a remarkable travesty of the facts as he must have known them.

[1] There was a belittling review (not by Pease) of his *Socialism and Government* in *Fabian News* of March 1910; several members, however, wrote letters of protest, and in any event it can scarcely have been a major cause of quarrel.

CHAPTER IX

Beatrice Webb and 'Permeation'

THE preceding chapter has introduced Beatrice Webb into the Fabian picture in characteristically definite fashion, and this therefore seems the appropriate moment at which to consider the role of Sidney's wife in the second decade of the Society's existence: with particular reference to the policy of 'permeation' with which she was especially associated.

'Our Partnership' began officially in July 1892; in fact, as the engagement was kept a secret until after Richard Potter's death, it had already been in operation for a year or two, and Sidney may be presumed to have been to some extent 'under the influence', at least after the Glasgow Conference at Whitsun 1890, where, according to *My Apprenticeship*, 'two socialists came to a working compact'. But their compact had nothing to do with the Fabian Society, as I have already said, though Shaw helped to foster illusion by sedulously spreading a myth that Beatrice carefully inspected the leaders of the Society with a view to matrimony and finally selected Sidney. No one will ever know why Shaw invented this story; psychologists may draw what conclusion they choose from the patent fact that Shaw slightly resented Beatrice's failure to succumb to his own charms; but the whole final chapters of *My Apprenticeship* show that it was completely untrue.

So far from Beatrice hunting for a Fabian to marry, it was Sidney, who, from the moment he was introduced to the beautiful Miss Potter as someone who 'literally pours out information', himself laid siege to her, and was accepted only after a prolonged and patient courtship. The reasons for her doubts and delays are evident enough. Sidney was not beautiful; he was short and scruffy, and it was not until long afterwards that his wife decided that his profile would look magnificent on a coin;[1] he came from

[1] *Our Partnership*, p. 5. Shaw said he resembled Napoleon III—a rather less flattering description.

a quite different stratum of society, far enough below her own to cause one of her sisters' sons to cry out in anguish, 'Aunt Bo is going to marry *that cad*!" He was not, of course, 'dragged up from the gutter', but he had risen from the ranks by his own efforts; and it was quite clear that, vulgar snobbishness apart, whatever he might become in the future, the *immediate* effect of their marriage would be the stepping down of Beatrice from the high life of Society, of 'those who gave *orders*', and from the dinner-tables at which she had shone and had enjoyed shining. Sidney was a civil servant with a practical interest in government and Socialism, not an adept at 'brilliant' talk; 'he dislikes unnecessary conversation', she wrote rather wistfully, 'even with his wife'; and no reader of *Our Partnership* can fail to note the pleasure she felt when, in the course of Sidney's adventures in public and university education, they began to have dinner parties with Society personalities like Arthur Balfour and the 'Souls', and she could enjoy again the scintillating table-talk which she had always appreciated so much more highly than she did the food and wine. Moreover, it must be remembered that Sidney's first advances came not many years after the abrupt ending of her abortive romance with Joseph Chamberlain. However right she and Chamberlain were in their mutual decision,[1] if she had married him she must have been at once in the front ranks of the 'political hostesses' in Society. This was not a prospect to be lightheartedly renounced; and it is absurd to suggest that she went grubbing about in an obscure office in the Strand to find consolation.

If there were any doubt, the confirmation is to be found in her own writings. She joined the Society after her engagement, because Sidney was a Fabian; she attended at least one meeting

[1] 'The little word No finished it.' Appendix to *Beatrice Webb's Diaries, 1924–32* (ed. Margaret Cole). It is not, however, necessary to leap to the conclusion, as some have done since the text of the *Diaries* was made accessible, that Beatrice pined after Chamberlain for the rest of her life, and that Sidney was a second-best; this is as much a myth as the Shaw story. It is true that the wound went deep; it may be that the youthful excitement which she felt over Chamberlain never returned, and that she recalled again and again, as many of us would, the pain and disillusion of their break. But those who doubt that her love for Sidney became the most important thing in her life should look again at the published record—see, for example, *Our Partnership*, pp. 11, 28, 144, 244; and many other references in later volumes of the *Diaries*.

as representative of the Sowerby Bridge Fabian Society, and later contributed a pamphlet (Tract 67, *Women and the Factory Acts*, 1896). But 'it was with some misgivings' that she joined it.

> To discover the process of social organisation, to observe and record the behaviour of men in society, had been my primary object in life; and it seemed to my cautious [*sic*] temperament that any pronounced views about social changes to be aimed at, might hamper those researches; partly because it might bias my own selection of facts and hypotheses, but also because the way of discovery might be blocked by those who held contrary opinions.[1]

And though, in that same passage (written, of course, many years afterwards) she admits that this was an error of judgment, it was nevertheless her opinion at the time, and she did not play any active part in the governance of the Fabian Society, nor, indeed, take it really seriously until after 1911, when the failure of the campaign to abolish the Poor Law had finally convinced her that 'permeation' of the older political parties was a blind alley. She was also, as her *Diaries* show, lukewarm in her appreciation of Sidney's colleagues, Shaw included; and had no part in the teamwork of the Fabian Executive which Hobson found so exciting. The episode of the Hutchinson Trust persuaded her that the Society might become a useful means of educating that part of the public which was educable in the facts of Fabian Socialism; but she still looked to the School of Economics rather than the Fabians to provide the leaders who would gradually transform Britain into a collectivist or semi-collectivist society—'we do not believe in more than a limited application of the collectivist principle', she wrote in July 1894.

She was, in fact, a much more complex character than Sidney; and while at periods of her life—the Wells who wrote *The New Machiavelli* would have said for practically the whole of it—her chief interest seemed to be in high-level social intrigue, in the manipulation of men and groups to serve collectivist ends, there is, in her diaries and her published writings, some indication that her most disinterested love, her real passion, lay in the collection and discovery of facts about the history and nature of society and social organisation and their gradual assemblage into a satisfying pattern. It was Herbert Spencer, in her lonely girlhood, who infected her with this enthusiasm; she had started on the col-

[1] *Our Partnership*, p. 107.

Edward Pease

John Parker, M.P.

Margaret Cole

Universal Pictorial Press

W. T. Rodgers

Some Officers of the Fabian Society

For details see Appendix II

London Express News and Feature Services

H. G. Wells (1907–8).
From a cartoon by Low

G. D. H. Cole (1912–15)

Clifford Allen (1911 and 1912–15)

Daily Herald

William Mellor (1912–15)

Some Leaders of Revolt

lection of facts about co-operation and Trade Unions before she met Sidney or became a Socialist; she employed her lover, as she herself sometimes said, as a superior secretary or amanuensis to enable her to get the facts more quickly and effectively sorted; and in *Methods of Social Study*, the most personal of all her works except the *Diaries*, she wrote of the joys of the investigator's life in terms more heart-felt than ever she used in describing Socialism, even the Socialism she thought to have found in the U.S.S.R.

To spend hour after hour in the chancel of an old parish church, in the veiled light of an ancient monument, in the hard little office of a solicitor, in the ugly and bare anteroom of the council chamber of a local authority, or even in a dungeon without ventilation or daylight (which was once our lot) with a stack of manuscripts, or a pile of printed volumes, to get through in a given time, induces an indescribably stimulated state of mind. The illusion arises that one has not one brain but several, each enjoying a life of its own. There is, first, the curiously concentrated satisfaction of the rapid rush through manuscript and printed paper, brain and hand combining to detect and to record, from among the 'common form' with which the records are filled, new features in the constitutions or activities of the organisation, or unexpected reactions between it and its environment. This interest in social structure is enlivened by an exciting chase after the human factor; the discovery of the leader or leaders; the play of the hand of this man or that; the emergence in the dry annals of pecuniary self-interest, personal ambition or personal vanity as well as of some continuously expressed policy or ideal. Meanwhile another active part of the brain is alert for indication of additional sources of information. Is there a collection of pamphlets? Is there a local news-sheet of old date, and where are the files to be found? What are the relevant biographies, autobiographies, travels, diaries, legal text-books, or other technical treatises? . . . Meanwhile, between all this intense but lovely automatic activity of the intellectual craftsman, there runs the more tranquil and deeper current of philosophic brooding: the underlying but continuously running controversy between the ego that affirms and the ego that denies. Apart from the satisfaction of scientific curiosity, has the product social value? Will the discovery of the past help the conduct of the present? Assuming that we have discovered and identified the poison secreted by the decaying vocational organisations of the eighteenth century, will this knowledge enable the modern man to find the antidote for similar poisons at work today in the life of a Trade Union or a professional association?

Such loving excitement her partner found less in research than in his striving to improve the conditions of life in the London which he cared for above all places on earth; but the passage quoted—which has parallels elsewhere—makes it clear why Beatrice felt that absorption in Fabian collectivist propaganda might dim her own light for her. Her immediate contribution to 'the Fabian' was therefore indirect, hesitant, and even negative; it was none the less important for history. Its main effect was to keep Sidney out of national politics, and to give a new twist to the theory of 'permeation'.

Sir Robert Ensor, in a very penetrating essay,[1] has pointed out that Sidney Webb, at the time of his marriage, would have been expected to proceed to a career in Parliament, leading to Cabinet office. He was, in those days, a good speaker and debater—very much better than when he actually entered Parliament thirty years later; his knowledge and memory were prodigious; and he had administrative experience in the Civil Service, which was shortly to be increased by service on the largest local governing authority in the world. With Beatrice's thousand pounds a year behind him, he could have afforded both to stand for Parliament and (in those leisured days) to pursue any other occupation and preoccupation he might choose; and he had a declared and definite policy and programme which required legislation to put them into effect. Under his guidance the Fabian Society had already published a number of detailed drafts for Parliamentary Bills; and the natural expectation was that he would proceed to put himself in a position to get them translated into Acts. He did, in fact, receive several invitations to stand under the Liberal flag; and if he had accepted the offer from Deptford (his safe L.C.C. constituency) he might quite easily have been elected, if not in 1895, then at the first available opportunity.

But he did not accept, partly, no doubt, because he had so many other irons in the fire, but partly because Beatrice set her face strongly against it, for both personal and other reasons. The personal reasons are obvious; as she quite candidly admitted to herself, 'a parliamentary career would destroy our united life',[2]

[1] Ensor, in *The Webbs and Their Work*, Chapter V. 'I naturally want to get into Parliament if I can', Webb had written to Haldane in 1891.

[2] *Diary*, March 12th, 1894. See also October 8th, 1895, and May 15th, 1899. The pattern was broken in 1922, and more fully in 1924, when Sidney became a Cabinet Minister; the *Diaries* show how much she disliked the prospect.

which even by 1894 had settled into the pleasant semi-routine which has so often been described and which they preserved for so long. But, that apart, she realised that a Parliamentary candidate must come out into the open; he must carry the label of one party or another—or if standing as an independent must make his own policy plain; he cannot stay in the background, pulling wires of different thicknesses connected with different persons and differing groups. But that sort of manœuvring was what interested Beatrice politically at the time.

> The trouble is [she wrote in a revealing passage][1] that *we want the things done*, and we don't much care what persons or which party gets the credit; we are pretty confident that, if it came to a fight, we know the arts of war as well as our enemies, but, between the battles, our cause may be advanced by diplomacy—even by a frank alliance with our former enemies if they be willing to take one little step forward in our direction.

These being her opinions, it is not surprising that when in January 1895 she and Sidney, at the request of MacDonald and Frank Smith of the I.L.P., who had been for some time 'harping' (the choice of verb is significant) on the desirability of a *rapprochement* between the two societies, gave a dinner for those two with Pease, Shaw, Hardie, and Tom Mann in attendance, the gathering all but broke up in disorder, Hardie accusing the Webbs of being the worst enemies of the social revolution.[2]

It may be pertinently pointed out that the 'confidence' which Mrs Webb expressed in her *Diary* was not at all well founded. The Webbs were remarkably inept at what she calls 'the arts of war' and others might term the realities of politics. This is very apparent in their repeated failure to come to terms with, or even to 'spot' the political leaders of their day. Among the Liberals, they could not get on with either Asquith or Lloyd George, and they despised Campbell-Bannerman;[3] they laid their bets rather on the spineless Rosebery or Haldane the arch-intriguer—Beatrice actually preferred Balfour the Tory to anyone else except possibly Haldane. On the Labour side, they alienated John Burns, the strongest leading personality at the time of their

[1] *Diary*, December 1894. [2] *Diary*, January 23rd and 25th, 1895.

[3] It is said that Winston Churchill, on being offered the Local Government Board under the Asquith Government, replied, 'I won't be shut up in a soup-kitchen with Mrs Sidney Webb!' The Webbs are hardly to be blamed for not having foreseen Churchill's career; but the comment is illuminating.

marriage, by trying to 'governess' him; their opinions of Hardie and MacDonald have already been quoted, and much later they thought George Lansbury a good deal of a fool. (These opinions of politicians are, of course, mainly drawn from the writings of Beatrice; Sidney kept no diary and might have expressed himself more tolerantly, but there is no reason to suppose that there was any great difference in outlook.)

In so far, therefore, as the Webbs had influence on the preferences of the Fabian Society, they led it to back the wrong political horses. More important, however, is that by turning their backs on Parliament they tended to minimise the necessity of getting control of the national machinery itself, of having Ministers—not merely civil servants or Ministers' private secretaries—who were committed to collectivist policies and would try to carry them out.

'The L.C.C.', wrote Beatrice, 'is a better platform from which to bring about collectivism than Parliament.' This is wishful thinking with a vengeance; the great achievements of the L.C.C. have been in the realm of social and civic services, not of 'municipal enterprise'. This reflects no discredit on the L.C.C., whose hands were largely tied by the almost continuous suspicion and hostility of successive Parliaments and Ministers to the thought of a powerful authority entrenched around the Palace of Westminster; but the fact should have demonstrated to the Fabians—as had already been indicated by the failure of the County Councils in general to become collectivist 'platforms'—that the best municipal programmes would not get very far without changes at national level. Fabians stood for Parliament from time to time, as they did for local governing bodies; and other Fabians were turned out to work and canvass for them; but apart from the New Heptarchy proposals for regionalisation of national government[1] the Fabian Society did not take Parliament really seriously till towards the end of the first world war. In the last Liberal Government their counsels were missing—Haldane's post at the War Office being one with which, 'having no interest in Peace and War' (Tract 70), the Fabian Society was not concerned.

What Mrs Webb wished to be concerned with was 'diplomacy . . . one little step forward', in a word 'permeation'.

'Permeation' is a peculiarly Fabian term, with a very long

[1] See p. 119.

history. It is first found in print in Hubert Bland's *Fabian Essay*—curiously enough Bland was not there advocating but warning the Society against it; but the casual reference shows that it was already in common use. Occasionally it seems to mean no more than what the Americans have taught us to call 'pressure groups'—persons organised with the purpose of forcing a particular measure, a particular interest, or a particular point of view upon those in power. Beatrice Webb in 1910–11, formed, with the Fabian Society as nucleus, a group of this nature, which was called the National Committee for the Prevention of Destitution,[1] in order to force the adoption of the Webb proposals for the abolition of the Poor Law; it failed. The Labour Representation Committee itself at its foundation came near to making itself a 'pressure group' merely; the wording of the initial resolution, 'to co-operate with any party which for the time being may be engaged in promoting legislation in the direct interest of Labour, and . . . to associate themselves with any party in opposing measures having an opposite tendency', left the possibility of such an attitude open until in 1903 the Committee definitely decided to separate its membership from that of the established parties and in 1904 put together what might be called a sort of programme of its own.

The Fabians would probably have approved this tactic for adoption by a comparatively large organisation supported by the Trade Unions—it is explicitly advocated in the *Plan of Campaign for Labour*. But the Fabian membership was not numerous or disciplined enough—or sufficiently one-idea'd—to be a pressure group of that kind. What Fabian permeation meant was primarily 'honeycombing', converting either to Socialism or to parts of the immediate Fabian programme, as set out in the continuous stream of Tracts and lectures, key persons, or groups of persons, who were in a position either to take action themselves or to influence others, not merely in getting a resolution passed, or (say) inducing a Town Council to accept one of the clauses of the Adoptive Acts, but in 'following up', in making sure that the resolution or whatever it was did not remain on paper but was put into effect. It was not necessary that these 'key persons' should be members of the Fabian Society; often it was as well they should not; what was essential was that they should at first or even second-hand be instructed and advised by Fabians.

[1] See p. 139.

Hence Shaw's insistence, at the Bradford Conference, that Fabians should be free to join Liberal and Radical associations where they could push the Fabian point of view; hence the Fabian delight over the formation of the Oxford University Fabian Society, full of potential rulers of England. One gets, sometimes, an impression of a Fabian vision of Britain in which every Important Person, Cabinet Minister, senior civil servant, leading industrialist, University Vice-Chancellor, Church dignitary, or what-not, would have an anonymous Fabian at his elbow or in his entourage who, trained very thoroughly (maybe in the Webbs' ideal School of Economics) in information, draughtsmanship, and the sense of what was immediately possible, would ensure that the Important Person moved cautiously but steadily in the right direction. This vision was never fulfilled, of course; but the influence of hard-working, educated, burrowing Fabians was sufficiently strong and persuasive to receive handsome tribute from historians like G. M. Trevelyan and Sir Ernest Barker, whose book on *Political Thought in England from Herbert Spencer to the Present Day* (1915) prophesied that 'the historian of the future will emphasise Fabianism in much the same way as the historian of today emphasises Benthamism.'

'Permeation', with the existing party system, ought logically to be carried to the extent of actually converting party leaders to Socialist policy. The obvious candidate for permeation, in the 'nineties, was the Liberal Party. Already, in London, the Progressive Party[1] was as near as no matter Fabian in its approach. The attempt at 'open permeation', if the phrase be permissible, made at Newcastle had been a failure; but attempts at capture of Liberal associations on a lesser scale were going on continuously, and the Webbs, in particular, assiduously worked on such Liberal politicians as seemed likely to subserve Fabian ends. But there were two major parties in the State, and wholehearted 'permeators' could not fail to observe that it might be possible to play one off against the other, to secure from Tory administrators 'little steps forward' refused by the Liberals. There was historical justification for this view. During the nineteenth century measures of social and political reform had been carried by Conservative as well as Liberal governments; and it

[1] The London Progressives, however, were much more radical than the Liberals as a whole; the Progressive Party was not really identified with the Liberals until after 1906. Ensor, *op. cit.*, p. 296.

is not surprising that the Webbs, especially Beatrice, with her strong intellectual and social affinity with Balfour,[1] should have sought to influence both sides and tried to push their Fabian colleagues in that direction. Their most outstanding success—over the Education Act of 1902–3—is described in Chapter XI.

But 'two-way permeation' involved a double risk. First, that 'permeating' the rival party—which means working with and making friends with its leaders—inevitably creates suspicion among the loyal members of the party of your first choice. Secondly, whatever the historical justification for regarding the Conservative Party as a potential vehicle of social reform, the working class *as a whole* certainly did not believe it. The L.R.C., of course, was founded partly as a result of the illiberalism of the Liberal Party as regards both social reform and in the selection of candidates for Parliamentary seats, and there were some Socialists and some Trade Unionists who were ready to cry that there was not a pin to choose between the two parties of capitalism. But these were few and for the most part of an intransigent temper which would not have made them natural recruits for the Fabian Society in any event; and MacDonald, at least, was well aware that Parliamentary success for Labour could be obtained only with Liberal acquiescence.[2]

The Webbs—and the Fabian Society in so far as it followed their lead—in the long run lost on both counts. 'Straight' party Liberals like Asquith regarded them with suspicion as persons who would not hesitate to change sides whenever it suited them, and who therefore offered no *quid pro quo* in exchange for socialistic measures; while the ordinary Labour supporter, if he knew what they were doing, thought of them as spiders without principle, spinning webs of intrigue which could entrap honest Socialists, and entirely without understanding of 'the great heart of the movement'.

Mrs Webb, in the late 'nineties, was completely oblivious to

[1] The frankest accounts of Beatrice's 'permeating' activities—at-dinner-parties and the like—are contained in her own letters to her sister Mary Playne, preserved in the Webb Collection. But it may be doubted whether Balfour took her much into his confidence on his own high-policy intrigues.

[2] He did not disclose this explicitly at the time and this not only because of his innate secretiveness.

these risks. On the eve of departing, with Sidney, for a tour of America and Australasia, she confided to her *Diary*:[1]

Our book [*Industrial Democracy*] has been extraordinarily well received; our party has recovered a good working majority on the L.C.C.; the London School of Economics is growing silently though surely into a centre of collectivist-tempered research, and establishing itself as *the* English school of economics and political science. We can now feel assured that with the School as a teacher body, the Fabian Society as a propagandist organisation, the L.C.C. Progressives as an object lesson in electoral success, our books as the only elaborate and original work in economic fact and theory [*sic*], no young man or woman who is anxious to study or to work in public affairs can fail to come under our influence.

'An hubristic passage', she commented long afterwards when reproducing it for publication. And so it proved.

[1] *Our Partnership*, p. 145. (*Diary*, March 1898.)

CHAPTER X

The Labour Representation Committee and Tract 70

NOTWITHSTANDING the doubts of Mrs Webb, and the educational bias given by the Hutchinson money, the Fabian Society did not divorce itself from Labour politics in the years following 1894; it might even be said to have underlined its connection by taking part in the formation of the Labour Representation Committee which became the Labour Party. None the less, the decade shows evidence of what later generations would have termed 'split personality', or at least an ambivalent attitude of the leaders which is worth study not only in itself but because it conditioned the opinion formed of the Society in Labour circles for a long time to come.

At the start, the Fabian Executive appeared to be pursuing, as far as possible, the course set out in the *Plan of Campaign.* In May of 1896, it agreed to join with the I.L.P. in calling a conference of Socialists and Trade Unionists with a view to founding a 'workers' political party'—this venture seems to have been abortive; and during the years immediately following it took part in more than one 'co-operative discussion'. One of these was concerned with a proposed 'Court of Honour', designed to prevent Socialist candidates from fighting one another at elections (which seems a sensible idea); but this project, like others already described, foundered eventually on the rock of S.D.F. refusal to sit in committee with Fabian delegates. Another, which was for a while much more effective, was a Conference of Elected Persons on various public authorities; this met several times, and usefully, if not spectacularly, exchanged experience and information. Finally, in June 1899, the Executive Committee, without showing marked enthusiasm—in view of past history this was not particularly surprising—replied to an enquiry from Keir Hardie that, 'if asked', it would send delegates to a conference of Socialist and Trade Union representatives to discuss the formation of a working-class political party. The invitation was in due course issued and accepted, and Pease and Shaw were appointed delegates without specific instructions. When the historic Conference met at the Memorial Hall, however, Pease attended by himself.

This fact is not without importance in the history of Labour–Fabian relations. If Shaw had gone to the Conference, he would certainly not have kept his mouth shut. He would have played at least as large a part as he had played previously at Bradford; he would very probably have quarrelled openly with MacDonald, and might have ensured the acceptance of the suggestion made by Harry Quelch of the S.D.F. that a Society with only 800 members had no claim to a seat on the Committee. But nobody wished to quarrel with Pease, who was known as a good committeeman, and—as trained by Webb—an excellent drafter of resolutions; and the services of the Fabian Society to Socialism, whatever its method of self-expression,[1] were well appreciated. So the Society was accepted as a constituent of the Labour Representation Committee; Pease appointed himself as representative, paid the affiliation fees, and duly received the approval and endorsement of his Executive, telling it for its comfort that the Memorial Hall meeting had passed a 'typically Fabian' resolution on the nature and purposes of the new organisation,[2] and commenting somewhat smugly on the 'development' in the minds of the I.L.P. and the S.D.F. which its acceptance showed. The resolution was, of course, the famous one already quoted which pledged the new body to co-operation under suitable circumstances with members of other parties; 'Fabian' is a quite fair characterisation of it.

Thereafter, Pease sat on the executive of the L.R.C. and subsequently of the Labour Party for many years unmolested and unopposed, reporting quietly to his own Executive at suitable intervals. Only once, on the occasion mentioned below,[3] is the Fabian Executive recorded as having concerned itself or its representative with questions of party policy; such influence as Pease had was exercised on organisation, and that was not inconsiderable. He seems to have been able to work with Mac-

[1] See below, p. 92. [2] *Fabian News*, April 1900.

[3] Chapter XI, p. 105. More typical is the instruction that the secretary 'do act in all matters, according to his own discretion'.

Donald, and would certainly have backed the latter in any proposals for arrangements with the Liberals had he been consulted; only MacDonald's own papers, when available, will be able to tell us whether he was. He sat on several sub-committees, including one on the organisation of the party, and drafted several resolutions. The most important service, however, which the Fabians rendered directly to the new body was to keep up continuous pressure for a maintenance fund for the support of Labour 'elected persons', and, as an essential corollary, for the fixing of L.R.C. subscriptions at a reasonable level. The Society had made these obvious suggestions long before 1900; it sent in its first official memorandum in June, when the L.R.C. was only four months old;[1] it reiterated its proposals again and again—at first against I.L.P. opposition—until in 1903 they were at last taken up by an affiliated Union, the Gasworkers, and a regular affiliation fee approved, though fixed, notwithstanding the efforts of Arthur Henderson the treasurer, at a miserably low level. If his advice, and the Fabian memorandum, had been accepted by the Trade Unions, the Labour Party would have been saved much squalid struggle, then and thereafter. The connection of the Society with the Party, though unspectacular, should not be minimised; while the Party was 'growing for six years in obscurity' (MacDonald), the secretary of the Society, in accordance with Fabian discipline, was doing his donkey-work in the shadows. But Shaw would probably have classed it with the three tailors of Tooley Street, and the majority of the Executive, including Webb, paid it very little attention.

It is indicative of a certain tolerance and common sense in the bulk of the Labour movement that the Fabian Society remained acceptable after 1896. For in the spring of that year, when discussions on the formation of a working-class party were actually in progress, the Society delivered itself of a manifesto calculated, one would have thought, to put an end to the possibility of any collaboration with anyone.

An enormous International Conference was being called in London in the autumn, and all the various societies were invited to present, as well as resolutions, statements of their own organisation and purposes. The Fabian Society seized the opportunity to do both. The resolutions, though they occupied several columns of *Fabian News*, need not detain us; they only dealt in

[1] Published in full in *Fabian News*, August 1900.

detail with the normal subjects of Fabian discussion. The policy statement, however, is more startling; the style is Shavian.[1]

Beginning with the explicit declaration that 'The object of the Fabian Society is to persuade the English people to make their constitution thoroughly democratic and to socialise their industries sufficiently to make the livelihood of the people entirely independent of private Capitalism,' it goes on to add (under the heading 'Fabian Integrity') that 'it does not ask the English people to join the Fabian Society. It does not propose that the practical steps towards Social-Democracy should be carried out by itself, *or by any other specially organised Socialist society or party*'—a phrase well calculated to annoy the I.L.P.; and under the same heading it announces that 'it has no distinctive opinion on Peace or War, the Marriage Question, Religion, Art, abstract Economics, Historic Evolution, Currency, or any other subject than its own special business of practical Democracy and Socialism.' This restrictive outburst was aimed at those who thought that a Socialist creed ought to prescribe correct beliefs for Socialists on all current controversies; it is a middle-class parallel to John Burns's near-contemporary denunciation of people who persistently talked about 'working-class housing, working-class boots, working-class margarine'; but its exclusions, even for Victorian days, are rather extreme.

On democracy generally, and electoral tactics, the statement expresses a desire to influence constituencies to select Socialists as candidates, though 'no person can obtain support of the Fabian Society, *or escape its opposition*, by merely repeating a few shibboleths and calling himself a Socialist or Social-Democrat'. Fabians are encouraged to join any and every organisation in which Fabian ideas can be spread, and the Fabian Society supports 'the ordinary man's desire for gradual peaceful changes', and therefore 'begs those Socialists who are looking forward to a sensational historical crisis, to join some other Society'. It regards the British House of Commons, when delivered from the Lords' veto and thrown open to all classes by the establishment of payment of members, as a 'first-rate practical instrument of democratic government', repudiating the referendum or any other device for direct popular decision. Socialism it defines as 'the organisation and conduct of *the necessary industries of the*

[1] The full text is too long for quotation here, however tempting; it will be found in Tract 70. The italics are mine.

country, and the appropriation of all forms of economic rent of land and capital, by the nation as a whole, through the co-ordinated agency of the *most suitable public authorities, parochial, municipal, local, national (Irish, Scotch, or Welsh), and central*', thus ruling out any general State monopoly of industry. 'The freedom of individuals', it says specifically, 'to engage in industry independently of the State, *and even in competition with it*, is . . . as highly valued by the Fabian Society as Freedom of the Press, Freedom of Speech, or any other article in the charter of popular liberties.'

Warming up, it condemns such phrases as 'the abolition of wages' as nonsense, wishing rather to establish standard allowances 'for the maintenance of all workers', and it 'resolutely opposes all pretensions to *hamper the socialisation of industry with equal wages, equal hours of labor, equal official status, or equal authority for everyone*. Such conditions are not only impracticable, but incompatible with the equality of individual rights, which is fundamental in modern Democracy, and the equality of subordination to the common interest which is fundamental in modern Socialism.' [1] It is equally opposed to 'the establishment of Socialism by private enterprise'—i.e. the foundation of 'utopian communities in South America, Africa, and other eligible localities'; it envisages Socialism not as a panacea, but as a specific remedy for the ills produced by bad organisation of industry and bad distribution of wealth.

Finally, after making some pointed remarks about the necessity of criticising 'obsolete and erroneous ideas' preached by Socialist 'authorities' like Marx and Lassalle, declaring the Fabian preference for newspapers with the largest circulations rather than milk-of-the-word journals as vehicles for Socialist propaganda, and patting Marx and the Society together on the back for their practice of collecting damning facts and statistics, the first draft of the statement delivered itself of the following calculated insult (expunged, after deliberation, before publication): 'The Fabian Society is fully alive to the social value of what

[1] It might be thought to be just as 'incompatible' with Shaw's frequently expressed opinion that *absolute equality* of incomes was the only true Socialism. Shaw would probably have countered with the reply that there was no incompatibility, because a fully Socialist society was one thing and 'gradual socialisation' quite another—or with any other argument which happened to occur to him. The passage shows, however, why many have thought him incurably frivolous as an economist.

is called "brain work", and deeply regrets that it cannot include under that description many of the speeches and articles produced at present in England either for or against Socialism'—and, a cheerful martyr, explained that the Society is accustomed to being violently denounced by Socialists and non-Socialists alike, until, in emergency, the former come running to beg its expert assistance.

This ebullient piece of propaganda was debated, and enthusiastically accepted for printing, as already related, by a large majority in an exceptionally crowded members' meeting, from which it may be concluded that the members enjoyed their fun; and the Tract was kept in print until 1918. What purpose it was supposed to serve is difficult to see. Its genesis may have been due to a fit of impatience with the other two Socialist societies and their miserable performance in the 1895 general election—or with MacDonald alone—and a desire to seize the opportunity of publicly lecturing them before the eyes of the International; if that was so, the attempt misfired. There is no evidence that the manifesto was discussed, or even mentioned, during the International Conference; and it is exceedingly unlikely that the foreign Socialists, if they read it at all, would pay attention to so very insular a document. In Britain it was, in effect, ignored; nevertheless, its tone, even more than its content, goes a long way to explain why the very word 'Fabian' long caused many an honest Socialist and Trade Unionist to writhe and foam at the mouth—even forty years later there were Divisional Labour Parties and party agents for whom 'Fabian' connoted simply 'superior snob'. It showed how silly the very intelligent could be, even though, in itself, it was a fire-cracker which fizzled out almost at once.

CHAPTER XI

Fabian 'Aberrances'

IN the previous chapter reference was made to aberrant political views of the Fabians; this chapter will describe them under their three headings—the South African War, the Education Acts, and the Tariff Reform campaign. On all these three the Society, during the four years between 1899 and 1903, took up, though not without considerable discussion, a line so widely at variance with the general consensus of radical and Socialist feeling that, had political groupings been as sharply defined as they were fifty or even thirty years later, it would certainly have been expelled from the organised Labour movement or forced into resignation or dissolution. After the passage of sixty years, it is more possible to judge dispassionately what the Fabian leaders were trying to advocate at the time, how far they were justified, and how far successful.

The South African War

In 1885 the British electorate, enlarged by the Liberal Government in the Reform Act of the preceding year, repaid the boon by turning it out of office, as in 1868 the newly enfranchised townsmen had similarly rewarded Disraeli; thereafter, except for the interlude of the weak Gladstone–Rosebery administration of 1892–5, it retained the Tories in office until the landslide of 1906. Some have seen in this an indication that the Seeley–Dilke–Chamberlain propaganda was taking hold, and that that portion of the great heart of Britain which enjoyed the parliamentary vote was becoming more imperial-minded, and this may be partly true; in London at any rate there appeared a growing chauvinism, particularly after the slaughter at Omdurman (1898) and Kitchener's proposal to use the skull of the exhumed Mahdi as a private house ornament—which was too much for even the none-too-sensitive Queen to stomach.[1] The chief

[1] See Sir Philip Magnus, *Life of Kitchener*.

development, however, after the defeat of the Home Rule Bill, was the shock of the South African War, an adventure which secured for this country an adverse foreign Press the like of which no country incurred save in a great war until the Soviet attack on Hungary more than fifty years later.

There is no need to re-tell in detail the events which led up to the war. All that has been written since, save for making manifest, after forty years of concealment, the complicity of Chamberlain in the plot of the Jameson Raid, has done nothing to alter the main lines of the story as they were apparent in 1899—that the Big Englanders, such as Rhodes, Milner and his circle, encouraged by the Colonial Secretary, united with the financial and mining magnates of the Rand in an attempt to force 'modern development', with all that that implied, on a community of obstinate Dutch farmers led by an intransigent and cunning Calvinist; that the war into which Kruger was not unwillingly manœuvred and which was expected to be a punitive police operation lasting a few weeks or months at most turned into a humiliating exposé of British incompetence and lack of foresight, followed by a long and expensive struggle with people who did not know when they were beaten, scandals of concentration camps and Chinese labour, and a final settlement which enfranchised and entrenched the gold-diggers, indeed, but at the cost of giving heavy compensation to the vanquished,[1] and of sowing the seeds, as we now know too well, of much trouble to come. Whatever the details, the war certainly came as a violent jolt to liberal and radical opinion in Britain, crystallising into one fierce reaction all the vague discontents with British society which had been growing during the past fifteen years and which the Fabian Society, along with others, had been concerned to express; the attitude eventually taken up by the Society was therefore only a little less of a shock to its supporters.

It is possible that this malaise partly accounted for the violence and irrationality of the passions let loose by the war, which are difficult to re-create today. It would almost seem, indeed, that

[1] Cf. Rudyard Kipling's *Piet*, published in *The Five Nations*, with its final lines:

> 'Ah, there, Piet, with your brand-new English plough,
> Your gratis tents an' cattle, an' your most ungrateful frow,
> You've made the British taxpayer rebuild your country seat—
> I've known some pet battalions charge a dam' sight less than Piet.'

Times Hulton Picture Library

Beatrice Webb (1939–41)

Radio Times Hulton Picture Library

Sir Stafford Cripps (1951–52)

G. D. H. Cole (1952–59)

PRESIDENTS OF THE SOCIETY

G. Bell & Sons Ltd

Labour's Medical Advisers by Will Dyson. Frontispiece to *The World of Labour* by G. D. H. Cole (1913). Lying on the couch is the Labour Giant, being anaesthetised by hot air from the House of Commons pumped by Ramsay MacDonald. Among those in attendance are (standing left to right): Hubert Bland (with eyeglass), C. W. Saleeby, Beatrice Webb, Ethel Snowden, Sidney Webb (with surgical instrument), Pease, Lloyd George, Will Crooks, C. F. G. Masterman, R. McKenna, Philip Snowden (behind). *Among audience, in front row, seated*: Shaw, Ben Tillett (with hat), G. K. Chesterton, George Lansbury. *Back row*: Hilaire Belloc (with sprouting hair and pear-shaped head), R. B. Cunninghame Graham (with homburg and imperial).

pro-war fury, among the British public, varies inversely with the actual perils of modern war. Even after the 'black week' of Stormberg, Magersfontein, and Colenso Britain risked no more than a serious loss of face, but pro-Boers were vilified, personally mobbed, and in some cases all but lynched; in the 1914–18 war, notwithstanding the handing out of white feathers, the treatment of some conscientious objectors and the turning out of Bertrand Russell from his Cambridge fellowship, the atmosphere was appreciably more tolerant, even at the dangerous moment of the last German break-through; in 1940, in the summer of Dunkirk, Communists were allowed to continue their anti-war propaganda almost without suffering, and there were immediate protests against the wholesale internment of aliens and even of suspects under Regulation 18b. The violent behaviour and language of the patriots of 1900, who talked, like Professor Cramb of King's College, London, of Englishmen riding 'the white steed of destiny' all over South Africa and made 'Mafficking' into a new word for a disgusting public exhibition, were proclaimed to the world and remained long in people's memories; but their opponents were not guiltless of talking sentimental nonsense at times and of seeing the issues in over-simplified terms, Milner as a plotter and no more, the mining companies as naked exploiters, Chamberlain as just an egomaniac, the Boers as simple, pure-living, God-fearing farmers. Keir Hardie even went so far as to talk of Kruger as if that narrow-minded nigger-driver were something only less than Jesus Christ; and there was an ugly strain of anti-semitism in some of the Liberal propaganda.[1] Neither side, in that struggle which, coinciding with the end of the century and the death of the Queen, seemed to mark so clearly the watershed between the old world and the new, appeared to give more than a passing thought to the bulk of the indigenous inhabitants of the territories over which they were quarrelling.[2] It had not always been so. In 1881, immediately after the Majuba Hill disaster, the Government, in conceding

[1] e.g. Hilaire Belloc's *Verses to a Lord who, in the House of Lords, Said that those who Opposed the South African Adventure Confused Soldiers with Money-Grubbers.* Reprinted in Belloc's *Verses* (1910).

[2] Chamberlain, indeed, held out to the British people the prospect of emigration to South Africa helping not merely to cure unemployment here but to produce a white majority there—a vision rapidly dispelled when the Rand mineowners closed their shop to expensive white labour and manned it with indentured coolies imported from China.

'self-government' to the Transvaal, had retained elements of trusteeship; but the Treaty of Vereeniging in 1902 left the question of native enfranchisement to be settled after the new Republics should have gained the right to do as they chose. Beatrice Webb, in *Our Partnership* (p. 192), drew attention to this; but that passage was written thirty years and more after the event.

All the same, the immediate reaction of all that was most generous in British public life to the Boers' declaration of war on October 11th, 1899, was that a big and rich society was trying to bully a small and poor one at the behest of politicians and capitalists whose motives were at the least highly suspect, that talk of 'trusteeship', as J. A. Hobson wrote in his *Imperialism*, was nauseating hypocrisy veiling a concert of interests for exploitation, and that British behaviour was morally disgraceful and would be rightly condemned by the world at large. On this assumption a member of the Fabian Society proposed that at the members' meeting due to be held on October 13th a resolution of sympathy with the Boers should be moved as 'urgent business'.

The Fabian leaders appear to have been taken by surprise. It is hardly likely that any one of them would have come out as supporting the Government's policy during the months preceding the war; some, in fact, had made individual protests. But once war had broken out they were prepared to accept the fact—and that the Government would fight it out—and *in their Fabian capacity* to ignore it, while continuing to work for Socialism at home. They regarded it, in effect, as a monstrous irrelevance to Fabian work, and did not wish to be drawn into discussion of its rights and wrongs. The Executive Committee, therefore, decided by seven votes to five to oppose any motion of 'urgency'; and the members' meeting—to which details of the E.C. voting were not disclosed[1]—acquiesced by twenty-six to nineteen. (The names of those voting are not recorded; E.C. members, if present, voted as they pleased.) Obviously, however, the matter could not be left there. Feeling was beginning to grow; Sydney Olivier, on the verge of leaving to govern Jamaica, wrote angrily that if the Society kept silence on this issue it would

[1] The Executive decided by six votes to five to keep the figures dark; the records do not give the names of those voting on either issue. Not until 1907 was it decided that names of those voting in the Committee could be published, and then only if a specific request was made by the dissentients.

proclaim itself nothing more than a 'Hutchinson Trust annexe'; and a week later demanded that the Society issue a leaflet on the war. The Executive refused the request, by one vote only; but, following its usual practice of endeavouring to calm opposition, decided that the Publications Committee should report on the possible production of a Tract on 'Imperialism'. Meantime a special members' meeting was fixed for December 8th, at which S. G. Hobson would endeavour to define by resolution the Fabian attitude to the war, and the subject of a Fabian lecture to be given on November 24th by Frederick Whelen, Executive member and founder of the Stage Society, was hurriedly changed from 'England in the Mediterranean' to 'England and South Africa'.

By the date of the special meeting attitudes were stiffening. Early defeats had inflamed both imperialist and pro-Boer passions, and made it likely that any debate would be heated; at the same time, there began to be heard an argument to the effect that small nations, especially small nations which did not seem able to manage their own internal difficulties, were not nations at all and should properly be policed in the interests of world prosperity.[1] If the report in *Fabian News* is to be trusted, Whelen's lecture, when it was delivered to a crowded audience, said that both war and annexation were inevitable. Bernard Shaw, taking somewhat the same view, was frankly irritated that the Society should be asked to occupy itself with a matter which, in his opinion, came within the 'prohibited degrees' of Tract 70, and concerned the Society no more than Home Rule, on which it had never taken sides; Webb, it would seem, was busy with the educational activities described later in this chapter and did not want to be bothered.

Hobson's resolution endeavoured to meet the criticism of 'no business of ours', by declaring that the war arose principally out of the character and tendencies of the British governing classes, that therefore it was essential 'for the furtherance of its own special aims' for the Society to make its attitude on the war plain, to dissociate itself formally from 'the Imperialism of Capitalism and vainglorious Nationalism' and to support the expansion of the Empire 'only in so far as that may be compatible with the expansion of that higher social organisation which this Society was founded to promote'. To this rather muted clarion-call

[1] In 1920, at the time of the Irish war, the ex-Socialist Karl Pearson voiced the same opinion in a letter to the present writer.

Shaw replied on behalf of the Executive with a poorly drafted amendment to the effect that the lack of a parliamentary vote (the main ostensible grievance of the settlers on the Rand) was too foolish an issue to fight over, but that since war had been joined the Government, when it was won, should either nationalise the gold mines or extract a swingeing royalty from them, and should enact legal protection for the mineworkers. This amendment, which of course entirely missed the point of the anti-imperialists, was defeated by a two-to-one majority, and the meeting proceeded, after a lengthy debate, to pass by fifty-nine to fifty 'the previous question'. This masterly exhibition of inaction (which was widely reported) by a body claiming to be the intellectual leaders of the constructive left wing of British opinion, moved the Press to such hilarious contempt that the Executive agreed by a small majority to rescind an earlier decision, and, on the motion of MacDonald, voted to 'take the sense' of the membership by a postal referendum—the question to be put being not 'Is the War right or wrong?' but 'Are you in favour of an official pronouncement being made by the Fabian Society on Imperialism in relation to the War?' Ballot-papers were printed and issued, with statements for and against, the former arguing, in summary, that the war was a glaring example of imperialist and capitalist aggression, would eat up funds urgently required for social reform, and was condemned by all international Socialists, with whom the Fabian Society ought to remain constantly in line, the latter that any pronouncement would deeply divide the Society, and would not, being merely the expression of opinion of a handful and not the result of any serious study, carry any weight whatsoever or have any effect on public opinion until the war was over.

When, after some weeks, the referendum was concluded, it was announced that 476 members (out of a total of something over 800) had voted, 217 in favour of a 'pronouncement'—which, it may be assumed, would have been of an anti-war character—and 259 against. The postal ballot thus, in effect, repeated the verdict of the members' meeting and voted 'next business'. Immediately, eighteen members, according to the list given in the *News*, gave in their resignations, including MacDonald and his wife, Emmeline Pankhurst, Walter Crane, Henry Salt, and the Trade Unionists G. N. Barnes and Pete Curran—not Keir Hardie; this, though small, is the largest number of resignations from the Society recorded on any one issue, and there may of course have been others who merely allowed their membership to lapse. Pease, in his *History*, regards the whole episode (including the low figure of resignations) as indicative of the good sense of the Society, since any positive action would have split it from top to bottom;[1] it may be observed that this is an assumption, since no one can tell, if the voting had gone the other way, whether any substantial number of those who favoured silence would have been moved to the length of severing connections. It is at least doubtful whether Shaw and Webb would have brought themselves to kill their Society altogether; and it will be recalled that the 'khaki' election held at the end of 1900, so far from being the landslide which those who remember only 1918 associate with the word, gave the Tories a plurality of only 300,000 in a vote of over four and a half millions. It may be that the Fabian caution, on this occasion, was unnecessary as well as pusillanimous; one argument of the majority, however, was sound and well taken to heart—that a small society does not *do* anything, or gain influence, merely by passing resolutions. 'The work of the Fabian Society', to quote Webb again, 'is the *work* [with emphasis on the word] *of individual Fabians*.'

Later in the year, with the approach of the general election, the Society decided to produce the manifesto on imperialism which the Publications Committee had been ordered to consider. Shaw drafted it, and it appeared as a shilling booklet with the title *Fabianism and the Empire*. Only a small part of the document is concerned with South Africa; that part lays down that 'a Great Power, consciously or unconsciously, must govern in the interests of civilisation as a whole, and it is not to those interests that such mighty forces as goldfields, and the formidable armaments that can be built on them, should be wielded irresponsibly by small communities of frontiersmen', and demands that when the war is concluded imperial officials, 'not subject to local Parliamentary authority', should enforce fair standards of life in the mines for white and coloured alike. For the rest, in so far as

[1] An attempt was made, by Hobson and one or two of his friends, to run an 'anti-imperialist' ticket for the Executive elections, to which Webb ran a counter-ticket. Neither effort met with full success; all Webb's list were elected save one, but Hobson and three or four of his got on as well. (Correspondence in the Society's files.) This is the only instance of direct lobbying in Fabian elections which I have been able to discover. The poll, on this occasion, was 62 per cent of the Society's membership.

external policy is concerned, it in effect accepts imperial domination by one or other Power as a modern necessity and only asks that the domination shall be efficient and sensible, and though Beatrice Webb later characterised it as 'the most prescient and permanently instructive publication of its date',[1] and Rosebery admired it, the modern reader will probably find it dangerous special pleading. At the time, also, the argument of the majority advanced during the special ballot proved correct; the pamphlet had no perceptible influence either on the election, or, as regards protection for mining labour, on the Treaty of Vereeniging; and though it secured favourable reviews, the public was so little interested that it was remaindered at a fairly early date.

The Education Acts

It has been mentioned that Sidney Webb was not interested in Fabian discussion about South Africa;[2] one of the main reasons for this was that he was deeply occupied, both before and after the outbreak of war, with ploys on the domestic front; particularly in education. Of two of the aspects of his educational activity—the reform of the University of London, and the School of Economics—nothing need be chronicled here; but the third, the reform of public education, very much concerned the Fabian Society, and provides, also, the most classical example of 'Fabian', 'permeative' tactics in successful operation.

As the century drew to its close it was clear that the public education system in England and Wales had reached one of its recurrent 'crisis points' at which something had to be done urgently to clear up the muddle, which affected elementary and secondary education alike. As is well known, elementary education at that time was provided either in 'denominational schools' run by the Churches—mostly, of course, by Anglicans—where the quality of teachers, and even more of buildings, was on the whole inferior and growing worse from year to year, or by specially elected School Boards whose size and efficiency ranged from the great London School Board, on which many Fabians

[1] *Our Partnership*, p. 194. The Press regarded it as a pronouncement in favour of the Government—an imputation which Pease strove to refute (*Fabian News*, February 1902).

[2] 'Sidney is pro-Boer in sentiment; he agrees with Asquith and Haldane who were pro-war by reason; but he has not thought out the question, has paid little or no attention to it. It suits him infinitely better to keep out of the whole affair.' Beatrice Webb's *Diary*, July 9th, 1901.

sat and whose 'three-decker' buildings were models of their day, to tiny district Boards whose members were often ignorant and occupied in sectarian quarrels—all Boards alike, however, providing 'undenominational' religious teaching under the Cowper–Temple clause in the 1870 Education Act. The quarrels between the sects, and between all sects and the secularists, bedevilled, as they had bedevilled for generations, all 'top-level' discussion upon education, and therefore all attempts at rational reform, however little apostolic blows and knocks seemed to matter in the schools themselves. Secondary education, desperately needed as literacy spread and as Britain's industrial competitors such as Germany vastly improved their own systems, was in an even worse muddle; in fact, it is almost true to say that no layman knew what bodies, and on what terms, were entitled to instruct children in subjects which went beyond the rigid Standards of the Elementary Code. The sensible thought-out recommendations of the Bryce Commission (1894–5), for which Michael Sadler did such excellent work, for a county system of secondary education, were largely forgotten when the Conservative Government, itself, of course, deeply connected with the Church and in general lacking in sympathy with School Boards and other publicly elected authorities,[1] came into office. There was, it should be added, no Ministry of Education or other central authority to co-ordinate any of the work.

So great was the confusion, so many the conflicting policies and voices, that the first discussions of the Fabian Executive on educational policy, held in 1896, seem to have broken up in disorder; at all events, they were not continued. But three years later the impending attack on the London School Board,[2] engineered by Robert Morant, contributed to a reawakening of

[1] Neither the distinguished membership nor the energetic experimentation of the London School Board saved it from sharing the almost pathological hatred felt by Ministers for the L.C.C. See my *Servant of the County,* Chapter III, and many other sources. These paragraphs are, of course, a very summary simplification of the story of public education, which can be read fully in many books, one of the best being G. A. N. Lowndes, *The Silent Social Revolution* (1937).

[2] This was the famous Cockerton Judgment, which forbade the London School Board from continuing to provide teaching in any but 'elementary' subjects. The fact that the Board must have long been aware that it was treading on very shaky legal ground did not make the blow to working-class higher education any less severe.

interest. In May 1899, a special members' meeting was held to discuss 'The Education Muddle and the Way Out'. To this meeting the Executive submitted a strong list of sixteen resolutions, drafted, presumably, by Webb, of which six dealt with general principles, and the remainder with 'Practical Proposals'. Discussions on the latter, after strong opposition by Graham Wallas, who, with Stewart Headlam, represented the Fabians on the London School Board, were adjourned *sine die*; the general resolutions, which were all carried, though not without considerable opposition, demanded that a single government department should be responsible for all education except the universities (and presumably also the private and endowed schools), and that in each local area there should be a single authority in charge which should not be specially elected, but should be the local council itself, acting through a committee or committees. Thus, at the outset, the Society declared itself definitely against the School Boards, thereby making sure of opposition from ardent educationists who feared, and by no means without cause, that members of local councils, with electors to placate on many issues, would not be single-minded in their devotion to education; at this stage, however, the Society felt that the largest School Boards, including of course the London School Board, would be too strong to kill, and therefore envisaged their survival as exceptions in some areas: this may partly have accounted for the defeat of the opposition.

In November, just before the South African debate, the draft of a Tract was submitted containing detailed proposals; but the discussion was so long and so heated that no conclusions were reached, and the draft was sent back to the Executive, which appointed Wallas and H. W. Macrosty to revise it. Revision took over a year, and the proofs of the revision were not discussed until December 1900, when a 'poorly-attended members' meeting'—previous ones had been crowded—accepted the draft with a few amendments. Stewart Headlam moved to substitute School Boards for local authorities throughout, but only collected one vote besides his own. The Tract[1] was published in January, and *Fabian News*, announcing it, remarked, 'It is a pronouncement of no small importance, and has already attracted much curiosity in influential quarters. *It is probable* [my italics] *that a Government measure on the subject will shortly be announced.*'

[1] No. 106: *The Education Muddle and the Way Out.*

It was not only probable; by then it was certain, and the form of the measure, moreover, was all but settled. When Morant began working against the School Boards, it was clearer than ever that something had to be done; but it seems very doubtful whether the Government had any idea what that something should be, and the confusion and disputes within the Privy Council Committee on Education, between the Duke of Devonshire, its sleepy chief, Sir John Gorst, the Vice-President, and Sir George Kekewich, its permanent head, have often been described. Morant was on terms with the Webbs, and Balfour the Prime Minister an old friend of Beatrice—and it 'happened' that Sir John Gorst asked for sufficient copies of the proofs of Tract 106 before it was published to circulate among the officials of his department. When the Government's Bill appeared a few months later it bore a remarkable resemblance to the Fabian proposals.

The Fabian opposition had concentrated mainly on the destruction of the School Boards. When the Bill (and the Fabian Tract) were published, however, the Liberals took violent objection to the clauses giving assistance out of the rates to denominational schools,[1] and a large number of Socialist and Trade Union leaders, the majority of whom were either Nonconformists or secularists and certainly no friends of the Church of England, were only less indignant. (Webb's strongly put defence was that it was impossible to destroy the denominational schools, in which more than a half of the children were being presently educated, and that those who would refuse them aid were in fact, for dogma's sake, voting to condemn Anglican and Catholic children to permanent ignorance.) The Labour Representation Committee wished to oppose the Bill, and the Fabian Society protested, the Executive Committee sending in a hortatory resolution to the effect that the L.R.C. was acting *ultra vires* in poking its inexpert nose into questions of education, and that 'the Committee's practice of travelling beyond the purpose for which it was appointed by passing and publishing general political resolutions was likely to lead to the withdrawal of constituent bodies and the disruption of the Committee'. This is the only recorded occasion on which the Fabian Executive took

[1] The opposition was particularly strong in the 'single-school' areas in country districts, where the only available school was almost always Anglican, sometimes aggressively so.

any but the mildest interest in the actions of the L.R.C.; it may be conjectured that Pease conveyed its views in a non-truculent manner, for there was no further recrimination, and the Bill, incorporating several further suggestions made by the Society, became law at the end of 1902, notwithstanding L.R.C. opposition.

The fight was quite as stiff, if not stiffer, within the Society over the separate Education Act for London, passed the following year. Leading Fabians had believed that the London School Board, with its great record of work and pioneering, its distinguished membership, in which women, debarred by legal interpretation from serving on the L.C.C., had been prominent, and its remarkably solid school buildings, the glory of their time, many of which still stand firmly to present a problem to an age which wishes to send its children to school in something less formidable than 'three-deckers', would be allowed to survive the Government's axe; they did not realise that the stronger, the more illustrious, and the more experimental the institution the less inclined was Morant to let it continue outside the pattern on which he had decided. The School Board was doomed, and the London denominational schools, of which there were many, were to receive their subsidies out of the rates,[1] whatever Webb's Nonconformist colleagues in the Progressive majority might say. Webb was, of course, the leading protagonist of the Bill—and therefore in effect the creator of the London school system of today; and he lost no opportunity of putting it through. The Fabian Society discussed the Bill often and in great detail; and both Beatrice Webb's *Diaries* and the Webb correspondence throw much amusing light on the *minutiae* of comprehensive wire-pulling[2]—including Sidney's part-editorship, for a week, of Northcliffe's *Daily Mail*—in order to secure these two points and to prevent the Metropolitan Boroughs (created in 1900 for the declared purpose of hampering the L.C.C.) from having any share in the control of education. There was opposition. Webb's influence with the Progressives practically vanished over the

[1] The number of these 'aided' schools, in the secondary field, greatly complicated the problems of the London School Plan of 1947.

[2] 'Dear Mrs Webb,' wrote R. P. Scott of Parmiter's School, 'I have done all your bidding, *including pressure on Mr Milvain*'; and Sir R. M. Beachcroft said, 'The man to get hold of is Balfour's private secretary.' (Letters—only two of many—in Webb Collection.)

question of the Church schools. There is little evidence of any very strong support for the claims of the Borough Councils, of whose personnel the Government, according to a letter of Haldane's marked 'Strictly Secret', had a poor opinion. But MacDonald, now on the L.C.C., worked hard and bitterly against Webb; Wallas was at best acquiescent—and later in a long angry private letter practically accused Webb of double-crossing him; and Headlam led an opposition, in favour of the London School Board, which was decisively defeated. Headlam, however, did not resign, either from the Society or the Executive.[1] No other resignations are recorded save Wallas's (see below).

In this case also, the Act as finally passed incorporated many amendments suggested by the Society and pressed, after careful coaching, by supporters in many quarters; and there is no doubt that the story of the Education Acts is very nearly the dream of Fabian 'permeators' come to life—proposals drafted by intelligent and hard-working Fabians, conveyed to puzzled or sympathetic administrators, and carried into effect by a Conservative Government. It is also a clear instance of the advantage of patient effort and research as compared with passing resolutions; but it certainly was not 'Labour' policy, though Labour opposition was less vocal and unrelenting than that of the Liberals.

Fiscal Policy

The third main item of disagreement—the question of tariffs—need not detain us so long. 'Tariff Reform', including taxes on food and preferential duty systems, was first proposed by Chamberlain in May 1903; and was received with howls of execration by the Liberals, the L.R.C., the I.L.P., etc. The Fabians felt that there was an element of shibboleth or Sacred Cow about this reaction; and Webb urged a members' meeting not to treat it as pure electioneering, nor to dismiss its arguments as having nothing in them. 'Free Trade' in commodities, Shaw pointed out in subsequent discussions, could not logically be divorced from 'free trade' in human labour, i.e. employing men and women at the lowest possible rates and in the worst possible conditions, against which Socialists had always set their faces.

[1] Nor did even that sturdy leader of Nonconformity, Dr John Clifford, who as a 'Passive Resister' saw his household goods regularly sold up to pay the education rate which he had refused on principle.

Eventually, he drafted Tract 116, *Fabianism and the Fiscal Question*, a longish argument which endeavoured to cry Plague on both houses, and to formulate a programme of action, including nationalisation of the railways,[1] improved technical education and consular services, and free ocean transport within the Empire—a curious selection of proposals which was, however, accepted after a long and meticulous discussion in January 1904. Graham Wallas moved that it be not published, and having secured only a handful of supporters, resigned from the Society with a letter[2] which, though written in polite language, shows quite clearly that he had for some time been bored and impatient of Fabian discussions—and not on education alone.[3]

Today, the feeling of the Fabians that neither 'Free Trade' nor 'Tariff Reform' made a policy for Socialists would seem obvious, but in 1904 they were ahead of their time; they had not thought out their alternative, and merely to say, as Shaw did, that 'a Labour Party, whatever its views may be as to Free Imports, must necessarily be uncompromisingly Protectionist as regards the laborer's standard of life', but that the L.R.C. has not tried to make any demands whatever, is to be unhelpfully abusive. He and his colleagues greatly underrated the appeal of cheap food to the British worker, and the 1906 election, with pictures of the Big and the Little Loaf on thousands of posters, blew Tract 116 away to the winds. Not until 1930, after years of heavy unemployment, did the British Labour movement begin to think seriously about Protection.

This chronicle of disputes and resignations and disagreements with Labour may have caused the reader to wonder how the Society managed to maintain its membership during so apparently argumentative a period. For maintained it was, though not increased. In the ten years from 1895 to 1905, it fluctuated round about the 800 mark, the decreases, other than

[1] Which, he said, should not be expected to pay their way. 'Nobody is now so foolish as to expect the Bath Road to show a profit on the cost of surveying and mending it; and there is even less reason for demanding a dividend from the Great Western Railway'—an argument which is certainly not without force today.

[2] *Fabian News*, February 1904.

[3] Wells (who had only just become a member) also proffered his resignation, but subsequently agreed to withdraw it.

the South African War resignations, being due to periodic 'purges' of those who persistently failed to pay up or keep contact. (One member so purged had contributed one shilling four years previously; one, resident in China, paid his debt in silk, and was allowed to continue.)

The main reason, of course, is the volume of non-spectacular activities which was continually going on. During those ten years, for example, the Society published fifty-eight Tracts, as well as *Fabianism and the Empire*; and comparatively few of these were leaflets, as in the earlier period. The others were pamphlets of some size. Twenty-two dealt with local government and its problems in one form or another, eight of these forming a full 'municipal programme', and four with education and the feeding of schoolchildren. Nine were reprints of lectures delivered elsewhere, among them Bernard Shaw's famous *Socialism for Millionaires* (Tract 107), the talk by William Morris on *Communism* (Tract 103), published long after his death, and a lecture by Sir Oliver Lodge, the scientist and spiritualist, on *Public Service versus Private Expenditure* (Tract 121). Eight were 'informatory' mainly; these included an unexpected best-seller, *The Workmen's Compensation Act* (Tract 82), which sold some 200,000, mostly to Trade Unions. The others covered a variety of subjects, some making practical proposals, e.g. on State pensions, direct labour, Irish railway nationalisation, the control of trusts, working-class housing, rural reconstruction, liquor licensing (Pease's pet subject), etc., a few discussing important questions without propounding conclusions. These were new publications; a good number of the earlier ones, notably *Facts for Socialists* and *What to Read*, of course continued to sell and to be revised as necessary. There were also from time to time special committees set up to deal with special problems, of which the most notable is the committee—known as the 'Baby' Committee—which conducted by questionnaire an elaborate enquiry into birth-control, etc. among members of the Society;[1] in this case the results were not made into a Tract, but written up by Webb in a series of articles in *The Times*. Add to these the continuous provision of London lectures and members' discussion meetings—and whatever the Hutchinson Trust lecturers included of Fabianism, which was fairly considerable—and the circulating

[1] An accountant bearing the appropriate name of Sweetlove is reported as being willing to give assistance.

book-boxes;[1] and it will be seen that the membership had good value for its money, if it chose to take it. True, no more than a minority made active contributions to Fabian policy. The Executive, at the end of 1899, was making an effort to increase 'participation' by deputing some of its members to lead discussion groups in different parts of London; this was unsuccessful at the time, the members, it would seem, preferring to journey to a hall in the centre and have a real go at the leaders. But the figures given from time to time of the number of amendments sent in for some of the draft Tracts, and the 62 per cent vote in the Executive elections of 1900, do not bear out the accusations of flagging enthusiasm and lack of interest which H. G. Wells and his supporters made in the following years.

[1] Correspondence courses were discontinued in 1900, after the foundation of Ruskin College, the Executive sensibly deciding, as it did on some other occasions, that there was no point in the Fabian Society trying to do what other organisations could do more effectively.

PART THREE

Boom and Conflict

1906–1914

CHAPTER XII

The Second Blooming

AT the end of March 1904, the Fabian Executive received with pleased surprise the news that the Society had no debt and £150 in hand, 'a situation without parallel since 1894'. True, £100 of the surplus was accounted for by a gift from Joseph Fels, the naphtha king;[1] nevertheless, the signs seemed hopeful. In December 1905 *Fabian News* announced a 'red-letter day', twenty members, more than for many years past, having applied for admission during the previous month; by January many more had come in. The Society itself seemed scarcely to be noticing the signs of the times, for the members' meeting, guided, presumably, by the Executive Committee, in December saw no need to consider the general election as having any 'urgency'. In the previous July there had been a 'vague discussion' on the Executive on the possibility of a Fabian election manifesto, which Bland and Macrosty were to draft; but so lukewarm was the interest that nothing was done, and at the beginning of December it was decided to forget all about it. Then came the election, and with the Liberal triumph the membership of the Fabian Society began to soar, and within a very brief while was between three and four times what it had been at any time in the preceding dozen years.

The Election of 1906 and its meaning

Of late it has become the fashion among social historians to play down the election of 1906, to suggest that there was nothing really radical about it, to endorse, in fact, the opinion of Bernard Shaw (who thought little or nothing of Liberal politicians) that it was a 'striking indication of the conservatism of the

[1] 'Fels-Naphtha Soap' on hoardings will be within the recollection of anyone born in the last century. Joseph Fels himself was a considerable contributor to 'good causes'; he was often tapped by George Lansbury, and he contributed to the help of the Russian Bolsheviks in exile.

electorate'. It is difficult for anyone who was alive and conscious in 1906 to hold that opinion. It is true, of course, that there was nothing of the definiteness of Labour's 1945 programme presented to the electors, and that the 'issues of the election', as seen in speeches and on posters, were a fine mixed bag—no Taxes on Food, No Chinese Labour on the Rand, No Money for Church Schools (in many districts), No Local Option (in some), Repeal the Taff Vale Judgment, Old Age Pensions (advocated by all Labour candidates), Votes for Women (by a few), End Imperialist Adventures. A few of these cries, particularly on the education issue, may fairly be described as conservative with a small C; and before the days of Gallup polls and psephologists it is not possible to decide which of the issues contributed most to the atmosphere of wrath and derision in which Balfour received the second most startling defeat in English parliamentary history. Those who followed the three-weeks course of the election day by day on the coloured battle flags stuck into large-scale wall maps had no doubt that a radical tide was pouring in and that oppression, negligence, and complacency were taking a beating, an impression heightened by the change in the personnel of Parliament. Not only had the Labour Representation Committee—helped, as is now more fully known,[1] by the rather over-apprehensive machine of the Liberal Party—brought well over half of its fifty candidates, practically all manual workers in origin, safely home; the swollen ranks of the Liberals themselves contained a large number of men so small in fortune as to be objects of contempt to the governing families, and in the Cabinet itself was Lloyd George, the pro-Boer, the demagogue, the son of an elementary teacher brought up by a village cobbler.

> Radicalism and Socialism alike [says Sir Robert Ensor,[2] himself a Fabian and soon to join the Executive], released from the suppression of two decades, were radiant with sudden hopes of a new heaven and a new earth. No leader not alive to that morning glory could have carried the House with him, and that was where Campbell-Bannerman in his kindly and generous old age gave the parliament an incomparably better start than . . . Asquith could have done.

The Fabian Society, accepting this, realised nevertheless that radicalism was not the same as Socialism, and that the dawn was not nearly so roseate as it appeared.

[1] See Bealey and Pelling, *Labour in Politics*.

[2] *England, 1870–1914*, p. 391.

At the present moment [it said in a Tract published in May 1906, outlining a series of immediate legislative suggestions which the Parliamentary Labour Party was urged to press], the Labor Party fills a place in the public mind out of all proportion to its actual electoral achievement, notable though that is . . . it looks like becoming the spoiled darling of Parliament. So far as the government is concerned it would seem as though the Labor members have only to ask, to have. All goes as merrily as a marriage bell. . . .

But

. . . The Labor Party in the House of Commons is as yet not disliked because it is not feared. Until it has made itself both disliked and feared it will be far short of having fulfilled the objects of its very existence. . . . Inasmuch as nothing short of an economic revolution can vitally or permanently improve the wage-earner's condition, it is at an economic revolution that a Labor Party must aim, and a revolution is none the less a revolution because it takes years or even decades in the accomplishing. Years and decades of hard work, of tireless activity, of small triumphs and dismaying defeats lie before the Labor Party inside and outside the walls of parliament, and they must be years and decades of revolutionary activity and of nothing less than that. In the course of a revolution somebody must needs suffer in mind, body or estate. Thanks to our constitutional system and to our widely extended franchise Labor can work out its own salvation without injury either to the sanity or to the skins of those who seek to hinder it. But the estates must be attacked, and attacked with vigor and despatch. A Labor policy which hurts no one will benefit no one.[1]

The Webbs had no opinion of Campbell-Bannerman; they did not anticipate the election results (which put an end to some intrigue-spinning by Haldane, Grey, and others of the Liberal-Imperialists, or 'Limps', in which they had been interested), and the 'radiant morning glory' left them quite cold. But even Beatrice noticed eventually the sudden growth in Fabian membership, though she attributed it to causes more rational than the general radical flush.

The little boom in the Fabian Society continues [she wrote rather

[1] *Socialism and the Labor Party*, Tract 127. This Tract shows that other members of the Society besides Shaw could write strong appeals to stand by Socialist principles, and indicates that 'gradualism' did not, to the Fabians of 1906, connote 'stagnation'. Its fears for the future were only too well fulfilled.

patronisingly in her *Diary*],[1] . . . and Sidney and I, G.B.S., and H.G.W. [Wells] sometimes ask ourselves, and each other, whether there is a bare possibility that it represents a larger wave than we think—are we, by our constructive thought, likely to attract considerable numbers of followers in the near future?

She probably had in mind something resembling the boom in thought and membership which had followed *Fabian Essays*; but the conditions were not quite parallel, and the developments were different.

The influx of members was, as we have seen, considerable, not only in London, but all over the country. Provincial Fabian Societies were formed—or revived—in many towns, and a feature almost wholly new was the creation of Fabian, or Fabian-Socialist Societies in nearly all the universities;[2] but the new membership differed from that of 1892 in at least three important respects.

First, it had come in intending, so far as it could foresee, to stay. It was joining, not an obscure little group of which nothing was known except that it had issued a handful of Tracts and one Socialist best-seller, but a body which had been twenty years in existence and whose name and practice were established. It had joined the Fabian Society and not the I.L.P. or any other body because it thought it saw in the former a means of bringing into being a Socialist society in Britain; accordingly, it was much concerned with the day-to-day running of the Society, and was not content to leave such matters entirely to the wisdom of the Executive; hence stemmed a number of constitutional discussions and arguments which we shall have to describe in due course. Second, the new membership, particularly the university membership, had a much wider intellectual interest than that of a generation earlier; it had read Shaw's plays and prefaces; it was more literary in its tastes, more fundamentalist in its discussions, more anxious to *argue* about the philosophy of Socialism and formulation of policy 'for the working class', but with less experience, especially among its younger members, of the realities of politics and administration, of 'permeative' cam-

[1] May 3rd, 1907. *Our Partnership*, p. 380.

[2] These, in 1912, were federated into a body called the University Socialist Federation, which had a loose, but definite connection with the Fabian Society. It maintained a vigorous life until the outbreak of war and a skeleton existence thereafter.

paigns such as that which brought the Education Acts into being. It was therefore much more ready to fight ideological battles and to carry these into open conference.

Third, and possibly most important, the Fabian membership, like all thinking persons who became adult in that legendary time 'before the wars', felt the spiritual distress and discomfort which preceded the mass slaughter. Disappointment, so soon to come, with the achievements of the Liberal Government, dissatisfaction with the inequalities and oppressions in society, with the condition of women, the old, the unemployed and the underpaid, which existing institutions, by whomsoever administered, seemed powerless to amend, led to 'unrest' (a frequent Edwardian phrase) unappeasable, apparently, by traditional methods of discussion and negotiation, and eventually to outbreaks of physical violence even among those who, in a nursery phrase, had been brought up to know better. The great strikes of 1910–13, the preaching of Syndicalism and Industrial Unionism among miners, railwaymen, builders, dockers, and on the other side, the mutiny openly prescribed to the Army in Northern Ireland—all these, so well described in George Dangerfield's *Strange Death of Liberal England*, gave a feverish quality to the disputes inside as well as outside the Fabian Society. The published output was no less; in fact, it was increased and widened, and the activity was intense. But there were strains set up which were unresolved at the outbreak of war.

The Episode of Mr Wells

The struggles began, even before the general election, with the Fabian Society's most distinguished recruit. H. G. Wells had just graduated from being a writer of 'science fiction' more compelling than anything produced today to a prophet of the future with an influence on youth as great as Shaw's. As he tells us in his discursive *Experiment in Autobiography*, which incidentally contains some vivid if not wholly reliable sketches of early Fabian leaders, he had in his youth played about with meetings and gatherings of Fabians and other Socialists and had not thought much of them, regarding them as 'pre-scientific' and unpractical. Thereafter, he seems to have forgotten them for quite a while, until his early brilliant sociological books forced them to take notice of him. One of his biographers recounts a story of 'Mr and Mrs Sidney Webb arriving suddenly on bicycles' at his door, and endeavouring to recruit him. It is certain that his *Discovery of the Future* was enthusiastically reviewed in *Fabian News* of June 1902 (and by Pease, which is surprising), *Anticipations* by the late Lord Haden-Guest in March, and *Mankind in the Making* by Bland in December. *Anticipations*, in particular, caught the attention of Beatrice Webb, who described it as 'the most remarkable book of the year' [1]—a well-justified encomium, as anyone can see who re-reads it today; and in February 1903 Mr Wells, on the proposition of Shaw and Wallas, was admitted to the ranks of the Society.[2]

At once he started to lecture to it—but not at once on the fundamentals of Socialism. When buying a house at Sandgate, he had lost his temper with what he considered to be fiddling little building regulations made by fiddling little local Councils; and in March he read to a members' meeting a paper with the unappetising (one would almost say Webbian) title of *The Question of Scientific Administrative Areas in Relation to Municipal Undertakings*. Pease says that hardly anyone present heard the lecture, because the lecturer delivered it in a mumble directed to one corner of the hall; but one member certainly noticed it. Beatrice (who had talked over the subject with Wells at a meeting of a club called the Co-Efficients) was immediately thrilled with the idea of rearranging the local government of England on 'scientific' lines, according to the several services performed, and despite a snub from the Director of the School of Economics,[3] brooded at intervals upon her plan until in the end it saw the light as part of the Webbs' *Constitution for the Socialist Commonwealth of Great Britain* (1920). It may have been partly her enthusiasm which made Wells, in the following year, member of

[1] *Our Partnership*, p. 226.

[2] 'The Webbs', he had written to Pease in 1902, 'are wonderful people. They leave me ashamed of my laziness.' (Letter in Fabian files.)

[3] 'I was much interested in your plan,' wrote Hewins, 'but if I were running Local Government affairs I could not at present accept it as an ideal. . . . Practically, we should not be at all likely to begin with a reform of the electoral unit [Beatrice had proposed that the whole country should be divided into small "Wards", which would be grouped differently for different services] but at the other end, by stripping existing authorities of the functions they now discharge. . . . Existing authorities would therefore tend to become mere electoral colleges, and their active functions would be limited to the miserable residuum of the dustbin.' April 14th, 1906. (Letter in Webb Collection.)

a Committee on the Reform of Local Government. This was only one of several set up at that time to discuss and make proposals for the better governance of the country, on which the Society eventually produced four Tracts,[1] called the 'New Heptarchy' Series, because the third of them, that in which Wells had a hand, suggested the regionalisation of government into areas which might perhaps correspond with those of the Saxon Heptarchy before the Norman conquest.

Wells, however, was not likely to be content with reforming local government areas. At the end of 1905 he offered to the Society two lectures. Both were delivered; the first, discussing the shoe trade and subsequently published as *This Misery of Boots*, was one of the most brilliant and successful indictments of private enterprise ever issued by the Fabians or by anyone else. With the second, *Faults of the Fabian*, read to a crowded audience on February 9th, the fat was well in the fire, and a battle began which was to last for over a year.

> The criticisms made by Mr Wells [said a pained note prefacing the printed copy which was distributed privately to all members] while perfectly legitimate in the intimacy of our society and its friends, are not of the sort that it is desirable to publish indiscriminately. . . . His comments are, it is considered, part of a private discussion of our policy and plans, conceived in a vein of frankness that the outsider might easily misunderstand.

He might, indeed.

The faults of the Fabian Society, as seen by Wells, were comprehensive. 'It is small, it is shabbily poor, it is collectively inactive.' It lives in a miserable cellar,[2] and has an insufficient staff. It is 'remarkably unbusinesslike, inadaptable, and uninventive in its ways'. It does not welcome members; it puts them through a stern test, makes them sign a Basis which is ill-written and old-fashioned, harsh and assertive, and when they have joined orders them to do fantastic things—lecture, write letters to the local paper, give away tracts, hold meetings, riot, rebel.

[1] Tracts 119, *Public Control of Electric Power and Transit*; 123, *The Revival of Agriculture*; 125, *Municipalisation by Provinces*; 126, *The Abolition of Poor Law Guardians*. Two or three more were projected but never appeared.

[2] In fact, a semi-basement office in Clement's Inn, Strand, which Webb in 1900 had secured for the Society at a low rent, after some characteristic manœuvring, traces of which can be found in the archives of the London County Council.

Most irritating of all its defects and 'little pettinesses' is the tendency of its members to have private jokes; their supreme delight is to *giggle*, and they permeate English society with their reputed Socialism about as much as a mouse may be said to permeate a cat. 'Fabian' it may be, but it is like Fabius in his obstructive old age, when all he could do was to try and prevent the young men joining Scipio in order to give the finishing blow to Carthage.

Measure with your eye [he cried] this little meeting, this little hall; look at that little stall of not very powerful tracts, think of the scattered members, one here, one there. Then go out into the Strand. Note the size of the buildings and business palaces, note the glare of the advertisements, note the abundance of traffic and the multitude of people, take a casual estimate of the site values as you go along. That is the world you are attempting to change. How does this little dribble of activities look then?

What to do? Wake up and expand. Take in members without any fuss and without a Basis; reorganise the Executive; publish plenty of new bright Tracts. Raise a thousand pounds to start with; tax subscribers in relation to their income (say one per cent per thousand pounds); get a 'light, beautiful and hopeful' office, engage a large and increasingly numerous paid staff, and organise a vast number of branches. 'Unless I am the most unsubstantial of dreamers,' Wells concluded, 'such a propaganda as I am now putting before you ought to carry our numbers up to the thousand mark within a year or two of its commencement.' It was the first, but not the last time that the Fabian Society was urged to make a splash in the world; on this occasion the membership roll was beginning, though Wells did not know it, to rise so quickly that a thousand pounds spent on an advertising campaign might well, for a time, have produced the result he prophesied.

The members' meeting was to be asked to recommend a committee to discuss ways and means of increasing 'the scope, influence, income, and activities of the Society'. The Executive indicated approval of the idea, and suggested deferring the election due in the spring until this special committee should have reported; they were willing to abolish some of the formalities of entrance, to set up a class of 'associates', who, without signing the Basis, paid to enjoy the Society's meetings and publications; and themselves stole a small piece of Wells's thunder by giving

Rosamund Bland[1] permission to form an association of 'junior Fabians'—the famous 'Fabian Nursery' in which so many of the second generation of Fabian leaders cut their political teeth.

Any impartial reader of the records of the struggle will have to admit that the Fabian Executive behaved with moderation and tolerance and Wells with remarkable ineptitude. The Executive began by inviting Wells to nominate anyone he chose 'up to a reasonable number' to sit with them on the special committee; Wells insisted on himself choosing both Executive and non-Executive members, and the Executive gave way. Wells demanded that his address should be printed verbatim in *Fabian News*; the Executive, for the reasons given in the preamble, refused, but offered to print it for private circulation. Wells declined—and changed his mind by telegram; a week later he wrote angrily complaining that a report of the discussion—which the Executive said was unauthorised and inadequate—had not been included.

Wells then, leaving the special committee discussing *in vacuo*, departed to America, returning, in his own words, 'to begin a confused, tedious, ill-conceived and ineffectual attempt to turn the little Fabian Society, wizened already though not old, into the beginnings of an order, akin to those Samurai in *A Modern Utopia*, which should embody for mankind a sense of the State';[2] on his return he found the Executive asking him to delete from *This Misery of Boots* a rude passage about the Society. He refused; the Executive in effect said he was a pig, but acquiesced.

By October the special committee had managed to finish its report, which repeated, though in much less vivid language, much of Wells's indictment; it called for new and handsome offices, a fixed minimum subscription payable on a fixed date in every year, *Fabian News* to be turned into a weekly with a wide circulation, a large production of brightly written pamphlets, a new Basis (draft provided), a change of name to 'British Socialist Party', the establishment of a fund to run Fabian Parliamentary candidates—a proposal which Wells himself did not particularly fancy. This report was issued with a reply written by Shaw for the Executive, which in effect cheerfully chaffed the special

[1] Adopted daughter of Edith and Hubert; she later married Clifford Sharp, first editor of the *New Statesman*.

[2] *Experiment in Autobiography*, p. 660. *A Modern Utopia* appeared just before the row began.

committee, saying that of course the Executive would delight to publish numbers of brilliant new Tracts as soon as the brilliant authors came forward to write them, and would like nothing better than handsome offices and a handsome journal as soon as the income to run the one and the capital to finance the other were forthcoming, that they had no objection to making the Executive more efficient, or indeed to revising the Basis, if revision seemed worth the time and trouble it would cost; but that they were unalterably opposed to a change of name. They were grateful, so the reply said, to receive the frank criticism for which they had been asking for years; but they felt that some of the critics lacked knowledge of the 'facts of life'. In December began a long series of discussions on the two reports, in the course of which Wells wrote to Pease (December 28th) saying he was 'sick of your Fabian politics', and then an angry letter to the *News*[1] accusing the Executive and Shaw of misrepresentation, personal attack, and distortion; in January, just before Wells's election to the fourth place on the Executive—Webb, Pease, and Shaw being above him—the report of the special committee was finally rejected so far as its main recommendations were concerned.[2]

As a member of the Executive Wells accepted nomination to one or two of its committees, but did not attend much, and in October resigned from them all in a letter which a somewhat perplexed meeting of the Executive interpreted as indicating (*a*) that the distance from his home was too great, (*b*) that the committees were all too large. In April 1908, while standing for re-election, he created a storm by supporting a non-Socialist Parliamentary candidate (Winston Churchill) in Manchester; the Executive declined to take any action or to accept a motion of 'urgency'. Subsequently he endeavoured without success (*a*) to reduce all committees to two members only, (*b*) to appoint all paid officers (except Pease) for one year only and from Fabian members under twenty-eight years old, (*c*) to banish all book reviews from *Fabian News*; in September he resigned altogether from the Society in a long letter[3] in which he unexpectedly announced that his chief objection to the Fabian Basis was that it 'proposed to leave mother and child economically dependent

[1] February 1907, for text and replies from Shaw and the E.C.

[2] A report of this meeting was sent to the *Sun* by a member privately—'a breach of confidence all the more disgraceful', fulminated the *News*, 'as such reports are presumably paid for'.

[3] *Fabian News*, October 1908.

on the father', which was not Socialism at all; and added that he had 'lost any hope of the Fabian Society contributing effectively to the education of the movement'. The final summing-up of his opinion of the Society may be found in the angry pages of *The New Machiavelli* (1911), the long political novel which contains the biting description of the Webbs as 'Oscar and Altiora Bailey' spinning their narrow semi-conspiratorial intrigues in their 'hard little house' on the Embankment.[1]

In the 'Episode of Mr Wells', as Pease calls it in his history, the immediate issue was one of personality not of principle—Wells *versus* the Old Guard, with Shaw as its chief spokesman. It is at least probable that a majority of the membership, both new and old, sympathised with what Wells was trying to do; two of the signatories of the special committee's report, Mrs Shaw and Headlam, announced that they agreed also with the reply of the Executive, which they could hardly have done had there been any fundamental difference of policy. In the 1907 elections 78 per cent of the members, an astonishingly high proportion, voted Wells into office, and a lesser vote retained him in the following year, while the membership was finally rejecting his proposals; and there is no doubt that, of the younger generation which was entering the Society, a great many regarded him as their inspiration. But their leader he could not be; his practical suggestions were absurd, and the gifted writer had the minimal capacity for putting them across in public meeting against Shaw's trained and practised virtuosity. In after years he confessed his own defects,[2] 'speaking haltingly on the verge of the inaudible, addressing my tie through a cascade of moustache that was no help at all, making ill-judged departures into parenthesis, correcting myself as though I were a manuscript under treatment'; and Shaw summarised the story briefly by saying that the Old Gang did not extinguish Mr Wells, he annihilated himself.[3]

[1] Relations had been further strained, after Wells's resignation, as a result of the first of his extra-marital experiments and of the publication of his novel *Ann Veronica*. This episode made Beatrice extremely angry, as unpublished passages in her *Diary* show, but the breach was subsequently healed after a fashion.

[2] *Experiment in Autobiography*, p. 661.

[3] The Fabian Society was not the only organisation to be abandoned in a fury by that most anarchistic of men, who called continually for planning in human affairs, but was constitutionally unable to abide human planners. The Labour Party, the League of Nations, the U.S.S.R.—all came in their turn under his angry ban.

But it was Wells the incompetent debater, and not Wells the man of ideas, who had been defeated; and his influence remained.

Constitutional change and new groups

In the realm of organisation, in fact, the enlarged[1] Executive of 1907 put into effect a good number of the less spectacular suggestions of the special committee. Standing orders of some length were adopted. Standing committees—for Finance and General Purposes, Organisation and Propaganda, Publications—were appointed, and presented typed reports to Executive meetings—a change which, incidentally, made Executive minutes less pleasing reading, since the occasional light-hearted and spiced comment[2] no longer appeared. The E.C. speeded up the admission of new members and carried a rule allowing the admission of Associates who were in general sympathy with the Society's aims, without giving voting rights—or requiring them to sign the Basis. They set up a social committee, including members from outside their own membership, to arrange entertainments, etc.,[3] and an 'Acquaintance Corner' to pick up new entrants and make them feel at home. They did not substantially alter *Fabian News* or take new offices (though the salaries of staff were slightly improved); but they worked out comparatively elaborate plans for the formation of provincial Societies, local groups (mostly in London), and special groups, all eventually to be covered by bye-laws.

Provincial Societies, almost non-existent during the previous dozen years, had begun to revive, and new ones to be formed, almost from the moment of the election. In 1912–13, the peak year, there were in existence 34 of them, with 6 local groups, and 11 university societies—the total membership of the Society was 2,807. Anticipating the development, the Executive convened in July 1907 the second Delegate Conference of the Society—the first had been held in 1892. This Conference, meeting under rules formulated in 1909, continued to meet annually until 1915, by which time practically all its constituent bodies had dis-

[1] Wells had demanded 25 instead of 15 members; the E.C. settled for 21.

[2] e.g. 'Wallas reported Mr Herbert Batley to be a distinguished Indian official, and a peculiarly pestilent crank.' Minutes, December 15th, 1891.

[3] For the Fabian Summer School (started in 1907) see Appendix.

appeared under stress of war.[1] It had extremely lively debates, which were fully reported in *Fabian News*; but it was not an Annual Conference, a final authority like the Conferences of the Labour Party or the I.L.P. Fabian Societies were autonomous bodies, not branches; the Executive, having once recognised a Society as 'Fabian', made no claim to control or discipline it, and, conversely, the Societies, as such, had no voice in the government of the centre. The supreme authority in the Fabian Society remained the members' meeting, at which individual members—including, however, all those on the rolls of provincial or university Societies—had individual votes.

'I've been a Fabian for forty years,' an outraged member is reported to have protested at one of the stormy meetings held just before the war, 'and never attended an Annual Meeting—and now these young men make me come up *all the way from Streatham* to vote against them!' As regards the university Societies, his complaint was not entirely without justification; they contributed ideas (and heat!) but not much solid support to the Society. Their members were supposed to pay a shilling a year for full membership rights, collected not by head office but by the university Society itself. This practice was not enshrined in any rule; it was a concession made some time previously by the Executive, in order to attract 'poor students', who were then expected to be few in numbers. As it turned out, in 1912 that category accounted for over a fifth of the Society's membership, many of whom could certainly have afforded a good deal more. The largest, and at first the most vigorous, was the Cambridge Society, led by such obviously 'coming' figures as Hugh Dalton, Clifford Allen (later chairman of the I.L.P. and still later Lord Allen of Hurtwood), and Rupert Brooke; a slightly later, but more obstreperous arrival was the Oxford Society, with the Cole–Mellor partnership as its spearhead; but smaller Societies sent no less vocal representatives to public gatherings. Obviously, a shilling a year was a derisory contribution to receive from people of that standing—who often continued in membership when they had ceased to be undergraduates and obtained paid university posts—even if it had been paid; but it was not. Early in 1915 the Executive, feeling that it had been patient long enough under

[1] A similar Conference, of Northern Fabian Societies, met first in 1909. It was 'officered' by the organiser, W. S. Sanders; but its debates seem to have been comparatively calm.

efforts to control policy made by persons with so exiguous a stake in the Society, conducted a survey and pointed out that *all* university Societies were heavily in arrears with their payments due, in some cases for three years, and that the *average* annual income to the Society from all its university contingents was £14 10*s*., less than half their actual cost on the lowest computation. They asked the Societies to pay up: Oxford, complaining that they could not, received the well-deserved rebuke, 'The Committee cannot believe that there can be any insuperable difficulty for a Society of 205 members and associates, few of whom can be so pressed for money that they have to ponder over every shilling of expenditure, to collect or borrow an amount per head which hundreds of thousands of workmen pay *weekly* to their Trade Unions.' [1] After this revelation the conditions for university membership were made more stringent, but the stable-door was closed too late. The horse had gone to the war.

The special groups were a new development which ran merrily, and shows that the 'new Fabians' had rather wider interests than the earlier ones. The single year 1907 saw the foundation of the Fabian Art Group, the Biology Group, the Education Group, and the Local Government Group[2]—also one called the Lyceum Club Group, which presumably catered for members of that selective women's club in Piccadilly. These all produced from time to time reports for the *News*. In the following year was announced a Socialist Medical League—mainly Fabian in its membership, though not a group of the Society; but in January, somewhat surprisingly, the Executive (with Shaw in the chair!) declared that 'The Executive cannot consent to the use of the word Fabian by a Dramatic Group.' [3] Later, Sidney Webb expressed the view that a Law Group was not practicable. Alongside those subject groups were the Fabian Nursery already mentioned, and the Women's Group, which, though not founded until March 1908, merits special attention.

[1] Minutes, February 12th and March 12th, 1915. Oxford was shamed into paying up about £8; the others paid scarcely anything. It was estimated that of the 500 'university members' only some 300 were actually *in statu pupillari*.

[2] Not to be confused with the Local Government Enquiry Bureau, started some years earlier and run jointly by the Society and the I.L.P. The new group was for discussion of principles and possible reform.

[3] There was, however, a dramatic society, which Fabians were invited to join, whose secretary was St John Ervine, the playwright and biographer of Shaw (*News*, February 1908).

The Fabian Society, unlike most of its contemporaries such as the I.L.P., had what might reasonably be called a lukewarm attitude to the Woman's Question. Some have ascribed this to the fact that Beatrice Webb was no suffragist, was bored and irritated by suffrage propaganda, and had actually, in 1889, signed Mrs Humphry Ward's manifesto against Votes for Women —an action which she later admitted to be ill-advised.[1] As Beatrice played so little part in the counsels of the early Society this can hardly be the case; the records suggest that the male direction of the Society was uninterested in the subject, and regarded it, like Home Rule, as something on which Fabians did not need to make pronouncements. As early as 1892 the Executive decided to answer an enquiry with the rather off-hand reply that 'universal suffrage has always been favoured in socialist societies';[2] in 1896 a committee which had been set up to consider a Tract on *Women* dissolved without reaching any conclusion, and in 1898, during one of the abortive discussions on New Fabian Essays, it was decided not to include an essay on Women. Few 'women of note', after the departure of Annie Besant, were active members of the Society—this contrasts sharply with their position in the I.L.P.; Mrs Pankhurst, who would certainly have forced the issue, resigned over the South African War. But at the end of 1906 the Executive was roughly awakened.

Wells had proposed the revision of the Basis, and the Executive, after conferring with him and his friends, had decided by six votes to five that no revision was called for,[3] when it was suddenly reported that the women members of the Society were strongly in favour of an amendment supporting votes for women. Shaw was appointed to negotiate with their spokesman, Mrs Pember Reeves,[4] and came off distinctly the worse, reporting to the next meeting that the women would vote for the special committee's report in a body 'unless the E.C. consent to recommend

[1] *Our Partnership*, p. 360.

[2] It had, in fact, in Tracts 6 and 11 (1887 and 1890), indicated its view that 'adult suffrage' must obviously include women; but this referred to voting rights purely.

[3] Executive Minutes, March 23rd, October 10th, November 30th, December 6th, 1906.

[4] Wife of the Hon. Pember Reeves, High Commissioner for New Zealand and Director of the London School of Economics from 1908 to 1919; author of the Fabian best-seller, *Round About a Pound a Week*.

the alteration of the Basis on the lines they desire'. The Executive hastily capitulated; Mrs Reeves was invited to move the amendment to include in the Objects of the Society 'the establishment of equal citizenship between men and women', which was carried—the only amendment made to the Basis before 1919.

So, at pistol-point, was the Fabian Society converted, rather late in the day, to overt support of women's suffrage. The point once gained, the Women's Group was formed, with Mrs Charlotte Wilson, the former Anarchist leader, as secretary, and went from strength to strength. It took part in Trafalgar Square and other demonstrations; over a score of its members went to gaol; it forced the Society to pass 'urgent resolutions on the treatment of suffragettes in prison' [1] and on the cat-and-mouse procedure of the Government; it put Edward (later Sir Edward) Troup of the Home Office in a terrible temper by giving publicity to the case of Lady Constance Lytton, when, having courted arrest under an undistinguished *alias*, she was forcibly fed in prison and fell seriously ill. All these were things which might have been done by any women's society of that date, anywhere; the Fabian Women's Group, however, undertook more serious 'Fabian' work,[2] holding education conferences, preparing Tracts, etc., for issue under its own special imprint; its first major effort was a study, published in book form, of the conditions of *Women Workers in Seven Professions*. It had its own Annual Reports, and its own funds; its secretary received, at a later date, a modest wage and a 'room of her own' in the office; it was affiliated, on its own, to the Standing Joint Committee of Labour Women's Organisations; it sometimes got rapped over the knuckles by the Executive for exceeding the powers to which that august body thought it should be confined;[3] and it alone, of all the groups, survived both world wars—during the doldrums of the 'thirties, in fact, it showed more life than any other. It is true that at times its Annual Dinner to current celebrities appeared to be the most important of its activities—as early as 1923 the report in

[1] 'Provided there is no debate', said the Executive in giving permission.

[2] In 1909 its members triumphantly defeated Webb (though not the Progressive Party) over the retention of the 'marriage bar' for teachers employed by the L.C.C.

[3] Minutes, July 7th, 1911. 'Not for the first time', the entry menacingly observed.

the *News* laments that the attention paid to the 'guests of honour' (ten of them, on that occasion!) overshadowed any other business. But it ran classes and conferences, and at intervals series of lectures on current women's and other problems; in the 'twenties one of its members established a Poor Persons' Legal Advice Bureau at the Fabian office; it was represented on other associations of women, such as the important Women's International League, and within the counsels of the Labour Party. As late as 1946, when the Royal Commission on Equal Pay was set up, it financed a research enquiry and presented evidence which was later published in summary.[1] Only gradually did it sink into oblivion as it became apparent that the newest generation of Fabian males was even less interested than their predecessors in women's problems, and that those Fabian females who were, preferred to pursue their causes along more sympathetic channels.

The main immediate issue left undecided after the special committee discussions was that of Parliamentary candidatures and relations with political parties. On this question an inconclusive and somewhat confusing debate went on for the next eight years—confusing partly because some of the more vocal participants seemed at times not to be at all clear in their own minds what exactly they did want, but even more because these were the years of indecision and uncertainty, when the policy of 'permeation' was coming and going, when no one knew quite what was the future of the little Labour Party, whether it was a potential spearhead of Socialism or a weak hanger-on to the coat-tails of a Liberalism fast losing its 1906 fervour,[2] and—more distant and less often canvassed—what was the future for the International, the only world organisation of the working classes.

[1] *The Rate for the Job*, by Margaret Cole. Fabian Research Series, 110. The argument of this pamphlet owed a good deal to Beatrice Webb's classic, *The Wages of Men and Women: Should They Be Equal?* (1919), which was a reprint of an earlier 'minority report' to an earlier government committee. It is a comment on British social policy that the argument needed restating, with fresh facts, nearly thirty years later.

[2] 'The Labour Party has lost its enthusiasm', wrote Blatchford to Jowett (*Clarion*, October 9th, 1908). 'It has grown too fast—the fire has died out of their hands and the light out of their eyes.' Blatchford was, as ever, in a hurry; he may have been thinking of the leaders' repudiation of Victor Grayson in the famous Colne Valley by-election; but after 1910 his words were certainly true. For the 'reappraisements' within the International see Cole, *History of Socialist Thought*, Vol. III, Chapter 2.

Already, in January 1907, a member of the Society had offered £50 to start a fund in support of Fabian candidates for Parliament, and in the following year the Executive sent out a circular inviting contributions to be put in a Trust fund. Promises to the amount of £2,650 were received, and a few candidates, including Will Crooks (already in Parliament for Woolwich), Harry Snell (later Lord Snell and long a Hutchinson Trust lecturer), and W. Stephen Sanders, the organising secretary, received support from it, until the fund was closed when payment of members was introduced in 1911. The support given to these few excited no controversy in itself; but the Society argued about what should be required of candidates as though it had tens of thousands of pounds to spend, for though many Fabians were Liberals and some Tories, the opinion of the vocal membership was beginning to set against them. In that same January, Percy Alden, a Fabian and a Liberal candidate, enquired of the Executive if he should stand for it, and that cautious body told him he had better not. Two months later R. C. K. (later Sir Robert) Ensor at a members' meeting proposed that the Society should run no candidates of its own, and that only I.L.P. candidates should be supported: this restrictive motion was mocked by Shaw, and referred to a committee of enquiry, but the attempt to deny support to any but Labour Party and Socialist candidates, and to forbid Fabians to stand under the auspices of any other body, was made again and again, and always defeated on a vote. The Executive temporised, begging members in effect not to stand against one another or to behave as tactlessly as did a Mr Chancellor, who in January 1910 stood against Herbert Burrows of the I.L.P., displaying a poster saying 'Socialism is a Dream'—being challenged, he put up the remarkably weak defence that it was a noble dream of the future. It is clear that the Executive felt fairly certain that no orders of that kind issued to members would be obeyed; and meantime they observed, on the opposite side, the resolution moved in January 1909 by S. G. Hobson,[1] that the Society disaffiliate from the Labour Party on the ground that the latter was not Socialist, which was true enough. Shaw suggested that if it were not, the solution was not to leave it, but to permeate it with

[1] One of the principal propagandists, a few years later, of Guild Socialism: author of *National Guilds*, and founder, after the war, of the National Building Guild.

Socialism; but Hobson was not to be put off; and when Shaw's amendment was carried demanded a referendum of the whole Society; the Executive refused, and he resigned in a long and pained letter.[1] In February 1912, at a business meeting of members, the Executive endeavoured to define the proper attitude of the Society to the Labour Party, suggesting that 'while treating with due respect expressions of opinion passed by the Labour Party Conference, it is not in any way bound to modify its attitude or alter its policy in accordance with the views of the Federation of which it forms a part'; privately, it refused a suggestion that it should consult the Party about the amount of 'private judgment and action' allowed to Fabians[2] and later in the same year the Annual Meeting agreed to a resolution from the Executive encouraging members and Societies to co-operate with the Labour Party. A further unsuccessful attempt to disaffiliate was made in March 1913, on the motion of H. J. Gillespie of the Oxford University Society, secretary of the newly created Fabian Research Committee; but this belongs properly to the Guild Socialist revolt described on a later page. Meantime, moves towards 'Socialist Unity' proceeded in a rather half-hearted way. The S.D.F. (which in 1911 took the name of British Socialist Party) from time to time made approaches—the latest in October 1914, when war had already broken out—which were either declined, or, if not declined immediately, came to nothing in the end;[3] all efforts of the International Socialist Bureau to induce the three English Socialist Societies to agree on their representation at international conferences foundered upon the inability of Marxists and non-Marxists to co-operate.

In the course of the argument about Fabian attitudes to the Labour Party, it was agreed in 1912 to embark upon informal discussions with Keir Hardie and Arthur Henderson (both Fabians). Nothing much seems to have resulted, the Executive being told that Henderson was willing but Hardie 'could not

[1] *Fabian News*, March 1909. There were rules governing the taking of a referendum; but the opinion of the Society was generally against it—not merely on the score of expense; and the only referendum ever taken (except for a ballot on a change in the Rules, held in 1949) was the vote on the South African War.

[2] *Fabian News*, March 1912. Executive Minutes, June 6th.

[3] Executive Minutes, May 27th, 1908; July 1st, October 7th and 20th, 1910; June 6th, 1911; June 27th, 1913; October 23rd and November 27th, 1914.

make up his mind';[1] with the I.L.P., however, rather more progress was made. The two non-Marxist bodies, notwithstanding rude remarks made from time to time, had really a good deal in common, and in 1911, having conferred together without the Marxists, their two Executives agreed to set up a standing joint committee, and to run (not without some misgivings on the Fabian side) a joint series of London lectures in the autumn. This committee continued in being, owing a good deal to W. C. Anderson, who became chairman in 1913; it organised, as well as lectures, classes in London and the provinces, public conferences, demonstrations, particularly in connection with the campaign for the break-up of the Poor Law (see below), and a week of discussion at the 1913 Fabian Summer School, presided over by Hardie. In April 1913 there were some proposals for a much wider Labour Propaganda Committee, to be formed by the Fabian Society, the I.L.P., the Women's Labour League, the Labour Party, the Parliamentary Labour Party, and (possibly) the Parliamentary Committee of the Trades Union Congress; but nothing had come of these by the outbreak of war.

[1] Minutes, June 26th and July 5th, 1912.

CHAPTER XIII

Conflict

THE pre-war Fabian Society never achieved the handsome offices or the ten thousand membership which Wells had urged on it; at the peak of its 'second blooming' it rose, as we have seen, to a total of something less than three thousand, which nobody could have considered enormous. But the total of work and output by this handful was remarkable. To begin with a few figures.

In the eight and a half years between the 1906 election and the outbreak of war the Society published fifty Tracts, nearly half as many as those it had issued during the twenty-two years of its previous history; and in bulk of print, this amounted to a good deal more than the bare figures indicate, because none of these were leaflets, as in the earlier period, but all pamphlets of considerable size. The range of subject was wide, and so was the range of authorship, which can now be precisely determined, since from 1907 onwards it became the practice for Tracts to be signed, and published by decision of the Executive, without scrutiny at proof stage by a members' meeting. One new line may be particularly noticed—the Fabian Biographical Series: this had been under discussion for some years previously, but only came to life in 1912, with the issue of Tract 165, *Francis Place*, by St John Ervine.

By 1916 six Biographical Tracts had been published,[1] and the Socialist movement thus instructed in its past (which until the last decade the official organisations have been very prone to neglect) as well as its present.

Concurrently, a longer and more solid series was started, the

[1] The others were *Robert Owen*, by B. L. Hutchins (166); *William Morris*, by Emily Townshend (167); *John Stuart Mill*, by Julius West (168); *Charles Kingsley*, by C. E. Vulliamy (174); *John Ruskin*, by Edith Morley (179). The series was continued, though intermittently, in later years.

Socialist Sixpennies, published on behalf of the Society by A. C. Fifield, of which the most widely known was Shaw's best-seller, *The Commonsense of Municipal Trading*. On the lighter side, possibly under the influence of Cecil Sharp, who was an active Fabian member and organiser of musical entertainment at many gatherings, the Society proposed to compile a book of songs suitable for Fabian and other Socialist meetings. This project was taken very seriously; the entire Executive studied the proofs. One song, by a member of the Committee, was 'hotly' discussed —and the book finally emerged as *Songs for Socialists*, competing for many years with E. Nesbit's *Ballads and Lyrics of Socialism*, which went out of print in 1919. 'I believe *you* know about *poetry*,' said Pease to the author of this book in 1918, '—can you tell me if these are *out of date*?' Of other specific Fabian achievements in the arts little is recorded, though a stained-glass window (by a member of the Women's Group) in Burne-Jones's 'greenery-yallery' style, in which Wells is depicted playing pan-pipes to various recognisable members of the Executive dressed in robes and wreaths, may still be seen by the faithful at Beatrice Webb House on Leith Hill in Surrey. In drama, besides the greatest of his day,[1] the Fabians had Harley Granville Barker and St John Ervine; and achievement of a minor kind is at least indicated by the following extract taken verbatim from the 'Personal Notes' column in the *News* of July 1911:

> On November 13th, the Gaiety Theatre, Manchester, is to produce 'Our Little Fancies', by Miss Margaret Macnamara. *Though not didactic, this play answers the question, Given good management, what is wrong with the General Mixed Workhouse?* [italics mine].

So much for publications, etc. The general stream of Fabian lectures, of course, continued at full speed; by the middle of 1907 the demand for Fabian lectures all over the country had become so large that Stephen Sanders was appointed Organising Secretary to cope with it.[2] The majority of these lectures, of course, were free to all comers, or rated only a modest charge or a collection for expenses; but already the Society was beginning to

[1] So recognised after the 1906 Shaw season at the Royal Court Theatre.

[2] Replaced Pease as General Secretary at the end of 1913 until he joined the army two years later; after demobilisation he returned for a year, at the end of which he took a post in the International Labour Office, and was succeeded by F. W. Galton. He was elected to Parliament in 1929.

cash in upon its most productive human asset. 'All Tickets Sold Out,' we are told in mid-1907, 'for Bernard Shaw's lecture at Queen's Hall'—a foretaste of the money-making series of the future. But, aside from all the miscellaneous lecturing and other educational efforts, the great weight of Fabian discussion (and controversy), during the latter part of this period, was concerned with two main issues, both arising directly from the social conditions of the time; these were Abolition of the Poor Law and the Control of Industry. Of these, the first enlisted the full united energy of the Fabians and may be described as the last throw of 'permeation', old-style; the second, generating no less energy, divided the Society from top to bottom, and but for the war was likely to have split it altogether. The emotional drive behind both, however, was fundamentally the same in origin—indignation at the exploitation of human personality in a class society.

Disillusion with Liberalism

By the beginning of 1909, the bright hopes of radical change recalled by Ensor were fading fast—and not only in the eyes of Mrs Pankhurst and her Suffragettes.[1] Some reforms, it is true, had come about: in the first flush of Liberal alarm at the Labour Party successes Trade Unions had been relieved of the consequences of Taff Vale; Trade Boards for the defence of those most scandalously sweated were about to be set up; a measure for the feeding from public funds of necessitous schoolchildren had been passed; and a pension of five shillings a week granted to persons of seventy years and more who were not 'of bad character'. But none of this did anything much to bridge the gulf between the 'two nations'; the appeals of Hardie, the 'Member for the Unemployed', that something should be done to relieve the suffering of those whom fluctuations in trade, through no fault of their own, had deprived of their livelihood, were without avail; and any fractional improvement, when trade improved, in the standard of living of the working classes was to a large extent offset in effect by the increase in 'conspicuous waste' and vulgar, costly ostentation which followed the South African War, when the restrictive hand of the old Queen was removed from high society. Today, the reminiscences of those who grew up in the glittering if slightly tarnished sunset of Edwardian society make pleasing romantic or nostalgic reading for those who know little

[1] See Christabel Pankhurst, *Unshackled* (1959).

or nothing of the poverty which formed its foundation; then, the contrast between the splendours of the coming-out ball of the future Countess of Warwick and the lives of those below the 'poverty line' in York [1] roused Blatchford to his fiercest denunciations in the *Clarion*, and converted Lady Warwick herself, the friend of Edward VII, who in all innocence asked Blatchford what she had done to deserve his abuse, to a Socialism from which through a long life she never departed.

Insecurity—the fear of unemployment—came only second to actual low wages as a determinant of working-class standards. Unemployment was considered an inescapable necessity of industrial society—a philanthropist of the stature of Beatrice Webb's cousin Charles Booth thought that the alternation of work and no work was as healthily bracing for the population as the alternations in temperature of summer and winter; and unemployment, once a man's savings or his Union benefit had been exhausted, meant, not falling behind in hire-purchase payments, but the Poor Law. It is true that the passage of time and the growth of humanitarian sentiment (and common sense) had softened in some measure and in some places the pristine rigidity of the Poor Law. Not all masters of workhouses enforced strictly the principle of 'less eligibility'—meaning that the recipient of 'indoor relief' must be forced to live in conditions worse than those of the worst-paid labourer outside; [2] not all Boards of Guardians insisted on removal to the workhouse as a condition of any relief at all being given, or refused admission to anyone who was not absolutely 'destitute', i.e. had not sold or pawned all available household possessions. Some Boards, some Relieving Officers, made efforts to provide tolerable medical care for the sick and the old, and some sort of education for the children. But all this was by way of grace; any Board *could* enforce the 'principles of 1834' to the full, and any Board *might*, if its personnel were changed or if it yielded to scolding from inspectors of the Poor Law Division of the Local Government Board.

The whole system was in confusion; but, whatever the policy and practice in different areas, Poor Law relief in general was a disgrace to the recipient—a stigma made plain by the refusal

[1] Seebohm Rowntree, *Poverty: A study of town life* (1901).

[2] But see the account of workhouse conditions in George Lansbury's *My Life*, or in his biography by his son-in-law Raymond Postgate.

of the civic right of voting to any person 'in receipt of relief', whatever the circumstances which had caused him to seek it. He became, in effect, not a 'person' at all but an encumbrance on society tolerated only because one day he might again be of some use to it. And this deprivation of personality, though made clearest in the Poor Law, in fact ran, so the Socialists began to say, right through the economic system as a whole. The worker in industry existed not as a person, but as a bit of labour-power maintained by his employer so long as a profit could be made out of him; when things went wrong and profit was no longer made, he was thrown aside with no more compunction than a piece of obsolete machinery. He was a 'wage-slave', worse off than a chattel-slave, because his employer did not even have to keep him alive when his services were not required; he was 'free' to keep himself—or to starve[1]—in any way he chose. Protests against this attitude, against treating men and women as cattle or tools—anything but people—had of course been made continuously since the days of the Chartists and earlier. But as the new century went on its way, as the effects of public education and of lip-service, at least, to democratic political principles began to be felt, the protests grew in number and in volume. Why should employers, such as the railway companies, refuse to meet in discussion the representatives of the railwaymen's own organisations? Why should working men, now in process of being granted a vote in politics, be denied any voice in the running of the industry which controlled their lives and that of their families? Were they not far more deeply concerned with its efficiency than absentee landlords, uninterested debenture-holders, or capitalists thinking only of increasing fortunes already large enough? So, with the aid of Syndicalist theorists from France and Industrial Unionist followers of Daniel de Leon from America and Australia, the idea of 'workers' control of industry' came to Britain;[2] but 'right to control' was closely bound up with 'right to live' free from the shadow of destitution. 'Status', a word of which the Guild Socialists were very fond, in some measure covers them both.

[1] Starvation was, in fact, a real alternative: it was not until many years later that the Government publication called *Return of Deaths from Starvation in the Metropolis* was discontinued from lack of casualties.

[2] For an English statement of the case against the employer, in fiction form, see Robert Tressall's *The Ragged-Trousered Philanthropists*.

The Poor Law Commission and the Poor Law Campaign

The Poor Law agitation came first in time, because the anomalies mentioned above had become so large—and so inconvenient to the public servants administering it—that there was a general feeling that something must be done. The Fabian Society, as well as other bodies, had long been attacking the Poor Law, and its first Tract on the subject—which called, among other things, for the removal of all care of the sick from the Poor Law and its transfer to other public authorities—had been published as far back as 1891, so that it was not surprising that when the Balfour Government, with almost its last breath, decided to appoint a Royal Commission, the Prime Minister should have included in its membership the eminent Fabian lady who was also his personal friend, Mrs Sidney Webb. It seems, however, that Mrs Webb's Fabian convictions were not very well known in civil service circles; otherwise Mr J. S. (later Sir James) Davy, the chief Poor Law officer of the Local Government Board, would scarcely have committed the magnificent and most fortunate *gaffe* of seeking a private meeting in which he confided to her his intentions that the Commission should advocate a tidy and speedy return to the 'principles of 1834'. 'Today,' wrote Beatrice gleefully, 'I put Mr Lansbury [a fellow-Commissioner] on his guard.' [1]

There is no need here to re-tell the story of the Royal Commission on the Poor Laws, of how Beatrice moved into the attack from the start, and deploying a battery of secretaries and special investigators,[2] endeavoured to bully the very varied collection of personalities on the Commission to recommend the total abolition of the Poor Law, or of how she failed, getting only two signatures besides her own and Lansbury's to her *Minority Report*; the story is told in all its vivid and often amusing detail, by the chief actor, in the pages of *Our Partnership*.[3] At the beginning of 1909 emerged the *Minority Report*, one of the greatest State papers of the century, which not merely damned the Poor Law root and branch, with supporting evidence, but laid down in detail the only possible conditions for its supersession, viz. a proper evaluation of all the various causes of destitution—old

[1] *Diary*, December 2nd, 1905.

[2] Partly paid for by sympathisers. The Fabian Executive in July 1907 decided to invite 'the richer members of the Society' to contribute to the cost.

[3] *Our Partnership*, Chapter VII.

age, accident, sickness, feeble-mindedness, unemployment—and the establishment of specific provision by the State to deal with each of them. All that is implied in the later phrase 'Social Security', including some things not yet put into effect, is to be found in essence in the *Minority Report* of fifty years ago.

The *Minority Report*, however, was the product of a small minority; after little more than a year of wrangling, it would appear from *Our Partnership*, Beatrice had decided that the majority were hopeless material from her point of view, and that she would do better to ignore their discussions and get on with the production of her own report. She was convinced that there was in the country a strong opposition to the Poor Law, which could be used to force the hands of the political leaders; but it would have to be mobilised, and the obvious centre at which to start was the Fabian Society, with its long tradition of interest in local government and the Poor Law. The campaign was to open immediately, and Beatrice, in her *Diary*, indicated that more than a single campaign was in her mind. 'I mean,' she wrote,[1] 'during the next ten months, to turn my attention to the Fabian Society, and the London School of Economics, and to cultivate the young people who are members of either organisation. There is coming over the country a great wave of reaction against Liberalism and Labour.'

The campaign began, actually, in January 1909, when an appeal was launched for voluntary assistance in the distribution of the special cheap Fabian print of the *Minority Report*, which Sidney's ingenuity and gift for remembering odd facts had succeeded in getting published in spite of the Treasury attempt to cling on to the copyright; by March it was reported to be 'going off like wildfire'. But the decision to make the Fabian Society itself the vehicle of the propaganda was quickly changed, as Beatrice came to the view that a body more neutral in appearance was needed to gain the support of influential non-Socialists in the task of 'permeating' the whole nation—since 'permeating' the Royal Commission had proved impossible. In June, *Fabian News* carried to the members the prospectus of the newly formed National Committee for the Break-up of the Poor Law, which soon changed its name to National Committee for the Prevention of Destitution; it had offices in Norfolk Street, Strand, and it invited adherence (no subscription necessary) from all who

[1] *Diary*, April 4th, 1909. *Our Partnership*, p. 427.

were in sympathy with, and prepared to work for the proposals of the *Minority Report*.

The campaign, like the reprint, went off like wildfire. Running a large office organisation was a new venture for Beatrice, in her fifty-first year, but she took to it like a duck to water.[1] Within a very short space of time the N.C.P.D. had enrolled over sixteen thousand members—many of whom, of course, paid their way; it was gathering subventions from all quarters and all parties; it was running a weekly paper, the *Crusade*, edited by Clifford Sharp, the future editor of the *New Statesman*, pouring out propaganda leaflets and sponsoring large enthusiastic meetings all over the country. Beatrice, aided by her band of secretaries,[2] neglected no avenue of approach. Persons of influence and importance were bidden to luncheon at 41 Grosvenor Road and there subjected to the combined attack which became so well known, when Beatrice and Sidney, as it were, batted the object of their attentions across the room from one to the other; in places such as gatherings of bankers, which might seem unsuitable for a woman, an invitation was secured for Sidney; 'experts' were found to explain the feasibility of the medical and financial proposals of the Report, and speakers suitable for Trade Union branches and professional societies; the young university Socialists were pressed into the kind of service typified by Rupert Brooke delivering leaflets to villages on his bicycle. As the campaign gathered force—during the years of Lloyd George's Budget and the struggle with the House of Lords—it became increasingly clear that there was a real popular demand from all classes, which the N.C.P.D. was canalising, for the ending of the destitution which drove men to the Poor Law. The report of the Majority, notwithstanding the grave approval given to it by much of the Press on publication, was drowned in the Minority clamour and never heard of again.[3]

[1] See *Diary* for May 27th, 1910, for a very candid and interesting analysis of both the organisation and her own feelings.

[2] Beatrice once admitted that their main extravagance was secretaries! Since the publication of Christabel Pankhurst's *Unshackled*, it is an interesting exercise to compare the methods of the Webbs with those of the Pankhursts, who were operating at the same time. Mrs Webb had more in common with Mrs Pankhurst than she would have cared to admit; of course she had less blind and furious prejudice to encounter.

[3] One eminent ex-Fabian, however, held different views. 'What a mass of stuff it all is,' wrote Wells to Beatrice in February 1909, acknowledging a copy

But the popular demand was for the relief of destitution and not for the positive proposals of the *Report*. However many were prepared to welcome them in principle, or at least not to oppose, the very moderate dose of collectivisation which they contained was too much for Edwardian England as a whole to swallow. This became plain in 1911, when Lloyd George, and his advisers, hastily borrowing an expedient from Bismarck's Germany, introduced the National Insurance Bill, under which, in return for weekly contributions from employers and employed, the State, adding a contribution of its own, undertook to provide sickness benefit and medical attention for insured persons (not for their families) and out-of-work benefit for those in a few trades most liable to heavy fluctuations.

The Fabian Society and the I.L.P. were furious, particularly at the 'contributory' character of the Bill; it had been their contention all along that 'distress', whatever its cause, ought to be recognised as a public liability and its cost met out of public funds. But the non-Socialist supporters of the N.C.P.D. were naturally pleased to learn that a method had been found of ending a great deal of misery without introducing a State Medical Service[1] or any such socialistic horror; equally important, the Trade Unions, whose members were well used to paying regular contributions, both to their Unions and to club doctors,[2] and who were also attracted by the prospect of becoming 'approved societies' for the administration of State insurance to their members, decided not to oppose; the Parliamentary Labour Party obediently followed suit; and though Hilaire Belloc denounced the whole scheme as a device for turning Britain into a Servile State,[3] he was generally regarded as a

of the *Minority Report*. 'You don't by any means make the quality of your difference from the Majority Report plain, nor your case in the slightest degree convincing. Perhaps I have been led to expect too much, but at any rate I am left wondering just what it is you think you are up to. All literature and all science is digestion and I've been wondering at times lately whether your later views as to dietary couldn't with advantage be applied to intellectual things.' From a letter in the Webb Collection.

[1] See Tract 160, *A National Medical Service* (1911), by Dr F. Lawson Dodd, treasurer of the Fabian Society from 1911 to 1936.

[2] And regarded contributions, therefore, as giving them a 'right' to service which they would not have felt to services provided free but necessarily 'at the discretion' of officials. The point, though overlooked by the N.C.P.D. propagandists, was of considerable importance.

[3] Belloc, *The Servile State* (1912).

crank. The Fabian Society passed angry resolutions—overruling Pease, who counselled them to agree with the Trade Unions and the Labour Party—and set up a committee to run another campaign in opposition to the Bill. The campaign was energetically pursued; nor did the N.C.P.D. go out of existence or cease to agitate against the Poor Law when the Bill had become an Act; but, as Beatrice observed, 'all the steam had gone out' of the nation-wide movement, and John Burns[1] metaphorically rubbed his hands at the thought that Lloyd George had 'dished the Webbs'. The great campaign had succeeded in waking the country up to the miseries of the Poor Law and in forcing the Government to take action; it had not succeeded in slipping over a semi-Socialist programme while no one was looking. 'Permeation', secret or open, of the two older parties, may be said to have died from that date; Beatrice, like Mr Davy at the beginning of the Commission, had disclosed her hand, and there are signs, in the *Diaries* and elsewhere, that she was realising it.

Whatever faults the Webbs may have had, crying over spilt milk was not one of them. When the Insurance Bill had become an Act they stopped fighting against it, and encouraged young Fabians to take jobs in the administration, as managers of the new Labour Exchanges and in other capacities.[2] At the urgent request of Clifford Sharp, they kept the N.C.P.D., and the *Crusade*, in being. But they encouraged both to interest themselves more in general social policy and enquiry (in August 1912, for example, the *Crusade* printed an article on 'Syndicalism'), with a view to the next stage in the struggle for Socialism—when they had decided what that should be. They themselves, however, in 1911, had left the problems to look after themselves while they went on a world tour, visiting India and the Far East, and concluding *inter alia* that the Japanese were a very pleasant cleanly people and that the morals of the Chinese were

[1] Then President of the Local Government Board. If the Webbs had had the forethought to make an ally of him at an earlier stage instead of offending him by their superior attitude, it is just conceivable that the result in 1911 might have been different.

[2] See memoirs of W. J. Braithwaite in *Lloyd George's Ambulance Waggon*. Two of these were Frederick ('Ben') Keeling, one of the most energetic of the Cambridge Fabians, who was killed in the war, and Arthur Colegate, who died a strong Tory and member of the House of Lords. 'The Webbs' young men' did not invariably remain Socialists.

deplorable. Neither the problems nor the Fabian Society, however, remained quiescent while they were away.

The Fabian Reform Committee

It was mentioned in the preceding chapter that the new membership of the Fabian Society showed itself anxious to have a say in its government and was unwilling to leave it all to the Old Guard. This, though naturally anathema to Pease, was not received without sympathy by the old leaders, some of whom were themselves contemplating retirement. Shaw in particular, though his victory over Wells had been so easy, did not attach excessive importance to it, and as early as the end of 1906 was begging Beatrice 'not to underrate' the effect Wells's writing 'produces on the imagination of the movement', and suggesting that 'we must spend the next few years in educating these chaps in Committee work and public life; then throw the whole thing into their hands as a federation of Fabian Socialist Societies, formally wind up the old Fabian and make our bow, as we shall both by that time be too wise, too various [*sic*] and too old to play with them any longer'.[1] Nothing more was heard of this suggestion at the time; but towards the end of the Poor Law agitation the subject of the Old Guard came up again, and Shaw, in a very amusing and Shavian letter, unfortunately too long for quotation, proposed that all Old Guard members should retire, and that a Fabian Senate should be formed out of members of the Executive with a number of years' service who should have the right to attend all Executive meetings, 'wearing togas if necessary', but should 'renounce all powers except that of persuasion (and intrigue)'.[2]

Shaw submitted his idea 'as a provision against senile decay of the Society' to the Executive, which on Webb's notion agreed to propose to the Annual Meeting the creation of a class of 'Consultative Executive Members', to be appointed for three years at a time by the elected members from those who had served for ten years or more; they were to have no vote, but any two of them were to have the right to circulate a memorandum on any subject to the whole membership. When Webb put his motion to the Annual Meeting it was hotly attacked as undemocratic;

[1] Letter in Webb Collection, November 25th, 1906.

[2] *Ibid.*, March 5th, 1911. And see Executive Minutes, April 7th and 21st, 1911.

and though a small majority was in favour, he withdrew it on the ground that it was undesirable to change the constitution by a narrow vote.[1] The net effect was that Shaw and Bland (who was already in poor health and died in April 1914) left the Executive, as did Ensor (first elected in 1907). The Webbs remained, and the rest of the Executive was much as before.

This outcome did little to allay the discontent—it is doubtful whether Webb's proposal or indeed any other procedural change would have had much more effect; and the wrangles, particularly about the attitude to be adopted towards the Labour Party, continued. In the autumn of 1911, there appeared a Fabian Reform Committee, whose principal members were Clifford Allen, Dr Marion Phillips, later chief woman officer of the Labour Party, St John Ervine, and H. H. Schloesser (now Lord Slesser), which issued an angry manifesto attacking generally the policy and practice of the Society, and complaining that its democratic control was a farce, since neither policy nor practice was ever adequately discussed. The committee declared that its views were shared by MacDonald (which may have been true enough, though he was not then a member of the Society), and by Philip Snowden, who later said that he had been misunderstood. Apart from their wish to tie the Society more closely to the Labour Party, a suggestion unlikely to have been accepted by the membership at that time, there seems nothing very drastic in the suggestions of the committee; but their language may have been intemperate, and the Executive Committee, which seems to have forgotten, with the departure of Shaw, Bland, and Webb, something of its former patient common sense in dealing with insurgents,[2] lost its collective temper, ordered Schloesser to 'explain and justify' his conduct, and issued a strong, angry statement in *Fabian News*. It agreed, however, to

[1] *News*, July 1911. It had been suggested that Shaw should become the Society's permanent Chairman; but he refused to countenance such a departure from the traditions of twenty-seven years. (Letter in Fabian files, October 10th, 1911.)

[2] 'It is the most difficult and uncertain body to work on imaginable,' wrote Sharp, who had appointed himself *rapporteur* to the Webbs in their absence. 'It runs about from week to week—a minute's speech is often enough to change the views of the majority on any point—and another minute's speech to turn them back again.' (Letter in Webb Collection, March 29th, 1912.) Beatrice, on her return, commented that the E.C. seemed to have let the Reform Committee get on their nerves (*Diary*, October 11th, 1912).

the appointment of a joint committee, which produced nothing more staggering than a demand for a 'new bright office *with a common-room* for the Society'—this desirable end was achieved two years later when the Society moved into new offices in Tothill Street, Westminster. However, by the end of the year the committee was satisfied enough to dissolve itself, partly because Allen was now involved with the official Labour *Daily Citizen*, whose directors did not want him mixed up in internal squabbles. But a much more formidable attack was preparing.

Pease, in his history, commenting upon Beatrice Webb's late entry into the inner counsels of the Fabian Society, says that she brought a fresh mind to bear upon its problems; and the mind was not merely fresh but forceful, and certainly very fertile in ideas. The period after 1911, when Shaw and Bland had left the Executive, and the former, instead of employing his remarkable talents as a conciliator and framer of policy[1] used them outside as the Society's most profitable but increasingly irresponsible counsellor and commentator, is the period when 'Fabianism' connoted to the public the Webbs (as presented by Wells) and not much else, their faithful followers, like Emil Davies of the L.C.C. and Leo (later Sir Leo) Chiozza Money,[2] attracting comparatively much less attention; and what Beatrice was thinking and planning at that time, therefore, became of day-to-day importance.[3] While still on world tour, with the printers' ink scarcely dry on the leaflets attacking the Insurance Bill, her mind had already begun to work on a new scheme for the education of the British public towards Socialism, this time through a new series of special enquiries, in which, under the beneficent guidance of herself and Sidney—so it was assumed—the younger

[1] See *Sixteen Self-Sketches*, Chapter XI.

[2] Authors, respectively, of *The Collectivist State in the Making* (1913) and *The Triumph of Nationalisation* (revised edition, 1920). The latter book, in particular, shows State Collectivism beginning to become more important, in Fabian propaganda, than municipal Socialism. Davies, the creator of the important Supplies Department of the L.C.C., was a municipaliser, but mainly so far as his own Authority was concerned. Money's first and best-known book was *Riches and Poverty* (1905); he gave up support of Labour following the first Labour Government, according to Webb (*Political Quarterly*, January 1961), because he failed to get a place therein.

[3] For the next twenty years, whenever Executive elections were held—on several occasions there was no contest—one or both Webbs headed the poll. 'What appals me is the fear that we may never be able to get quit of leadership again.' (Beatrice Webb's *Diary*, August 19th, 1910.)

members of the Fabian Society, particularly the university members, were to employ their unquestioned abilities on expert investigations, of the kind which the Executive had itself conducted in times gone by, into current questions of importance. These she considered to be, first, political organisation, national and international—on international matters the Society, as Shaw never tired of telling it, was very ill-informed—and secondly on the practical running of socialised industry. The first she proposed to tackle in co-operation with the I.L.P. and the Joint Committee, and the second by calling together all those who had views on the subject. She further suggested that the Fabian Summer School which, started in 1907 as a semi-private venture, had after four years been taken over by the Society officially, might usefully devote a part of its regular six- or eight-week session to intensive educational discussion of these problems, over which discussion she was prepared to preside.

It sounded, on the face of it, a simple and feasible project; but when it came to putting it into effect, the result was not at all what she intended. The I.L.P. and the politicians co-operated willingly, though not to much practical effect. But when it came to the organisation of industry, she found herself confronted, a year after the great transport strikes which paralysed docks and railways and brought the city of Liverpool to a complete standstill, and when the national mining dispute of 1912 had barely terminated, with battalions of Guild Socialists all arrayed and rarin' to go.

The Guild Socialist rebellion and the Research Department

The fact of the strike wave is relevant. For the essential of the movement known as Guild Socialism,[1] associated in its early years with A. R. Orage of the *New Age* weekly and S. G. Hobson, and later with G. D. H. Cole, that stormy petrel of the Fabian Society, who resigned from its Executive Committee no less than four times and died its President, was that it attempted, *via* the Trade Unions and particularly *via* their work-based institutions, workshop committees and shop stewards, pit committees and checkweighmen, and their like, to 'marry' the 'workers' control' theories of the Syndicalists and Industrial Unionists referred to earlier, with what its leaders considered worth while preserving

[1] See Hobson, *National Guilds*; Cole, *Self-Government in Industry*, *Guild Socialism Restated*; and many other books.

of the orthodox collectivist demand for the public ownership of 'the means of production, distribution and exchange'—this main approach being also influenced, to a greater or less degree according to the sympathies of the individual propagandist, by a yearning after the status-society of the Middle Ages, as recreated above all by William Morris,[1] by the 'pluralist' political philosphers such as J. N. Figgis, and by the vision of an individualist, peasant-proprietor, 'Distributivist' type of society preached principally by Hilaire Belloc and G. K. Chesterton.[2] Simplified, the idea was that while the public authority, national or local, was to be the *owner* of the productive machine, the organisation of all production should be in the hands of Guilds of Producers run on democratic lines.[3] As the public ownership side of this programme had already been fully stated in many Fabian Tracts and other Socialist publications, it was natural that the Guild Socialists should lay most stress on the side that was new, viz. industrial self-government; but to the leading Collectivists, Webb and Pease in particular, the very notion of management of industry by the workers engaged in it was at that date intolerable, savouring of the many Victorian enterprises in 'Cooperative Production' which, according to them, had uniformly either failed disastrously or turned into little closed corporations of self-employed not differing in any essential way from capitalism. (It is not true, however, that Fabian proposals for nationalisation, even at that date, completely ignored the working-class organisation; the miners were consulted on the content of Tract 171, *The Nationalisation of Mines and Minerals* (1913), before it was published; but this was an individual case.)

There was thus a clear difference of theoretical approach between the Webbs and their followers and the Guild Socialists,

[1] *News from Nowhere, Signs of Change,* and *The Dream of John Ball* expressed the vividest dreams of the majority of Guildsmen.

[2] Chesterton was never a Guild Socialist in the strict sense; his dislike of the State was too strong. But the anti-capitalist and pro-working-class attitude displayed in his early poems and his *Daily News* and *Daily Herald* articles made him a strong and moving ally.

[3] This happened in part, soon after the war, when under Hobson's inspiration the building Trade Unions formed a National Building Guild which built houses for local authorities under the Addison Housing Act. When the slump came, however, and Government housing subsidies were abruptly cut out, the programme of State-aided housing came temporarily to an end; and the Guild collapsed.

as there had not been in the case of the earlier disputes within the Society; the Guild Socialists wanted to make large and definite alterations, which could be expressed in written terms, in the form of society for which the Socialists and Labour movements should be working. Both sides, as is usual, tended to overstate their case. The Webbs had a fundamental faith in the civil servant and the trained administrator; they were natural bureaucrats in the best sense of the word, and admitted it—Beatrice said they were 'B's, benevolent, bourgeois and bureaucratic', contrasting themselves with the 'A's', who were 'aristocratic, anarchist and arrogant'—and they were, perhaps more than they realised, distrustful of the common man's ability to take important decisions unless he were wisely guided by his superiors and presented only with simple and definite choices—at election time, for example. 'A discreetly regulated freedom' was a frequent phrase of Sidney's which peculiarly exasperated the opposition;[1] and while one can accept many of its implications, it is easy to understand how infuriating was the assumption that Fabians like the Webbs were to do the regulating. The Guild Socialists, on the other hand, displayed an equally naïve belief in the virtues and abilities of Trade Unionists—at least, of such of them as were not 'hide-bound reactionary officials'—and of factory-elected representatives which they would probably have had cause to revise if their movement had lasted longer than it did; but they were on strong ground in pointing out the likelihood of the unimaginative official turning into a jack-in-office.

The difference of theoretical approach does not, however, strike one as absolutely fundamental; it might have seemed that there was right on both sides, and that a full discussion, with a little give-and-take, might have produced a reconciliation. But the difference was more than theoretical; it was a difference of temperament, of emotion, and even of style. The Guild Socialists and their allies fell in love with Trade Unionism and Trade Unionists much as the Webbs, twenty years later, fell in love with Soviet Communism; they regarded the Unions, not as institutions important for study by the reformer or social philoso-

[1] As also did another, 'the Average Sensual Man', opponents pointing out, with much truth, that Sidney had not the remotest idea of what 'average sensuality' was like. Shaw, of course, had no opinion at all of the common man—an aberration which later landed him in support of Mussolini.

pher, but as the living forces which could bring about a better world, not by persuasion and propaganda campaigns, though these had their uses, but by the exercise of their industrial power. Every strike, therefore, especially if it were a strike for status or recognition, was to be welcomed with cheers, and every blow struck against capitalism and its profits applauded, no matter who got hurt in the process. Furthermore, the Guild Socialists were most of them young, energetic, intellectually very able and articulate, with a strong dash of anarchism in their composition, making them impatient of regulation of any kind, and arrogant both in their convictions and in their methods of expressing them. They enjoyed being rude controversialists; they would butcher anybody to make a Guild Socialist holiday, and Beatrice's *Diaries* display considerable resentment at their shocking behaviour at 'her' Summer School. 'Freely laughing at ourselves', which Shaw had recorded as a merit of Fabians, did not, she felt, include undergraduate horseplay. They, for their part, regarded the Webbs and any who supported them as pestilent old obscurantists, and lampooned and abused them privately and publicly on every occasion.

There was therefore an emotional antagonism between the two parties (increased by the general tension of the years preceding the war and the political hamstringing of the Labour Party after the 1910 elections) which made reconciliation impossible. Nevertheless, the clash should not be exaggerated. The abuse, though violent, had none of the vicious spite which the Communist Party later brought into the Labour movement.[1] The antagonists played fair and did not deliberately cheat or trick one another; nor, whatever they may have felt and said at times, did either really desire the other's destruction—in fact they often collaborated amicably and without reservation on matters which did not touch the inflamed spots.

The Fabian Society had been aware for some time of the existence of Guild Socialism—though the National Guilds

[1] Jingles like 'O that Beatrice and Sidney Would get in their kidney A loathsome disease—Also Pease' suggest schoolchildren putting their tongues out rather than serious class-enemies. The Guildsmen did not call the Collectivists 'hyenas', 'lackeys', or any other choice epithets. See also my chapter on 'Labour Research' in *The Webbs and Their Work*, and the relevant parts of my *Growing Up Into Revolution*, for the atmosphere of the controversy as it appeared to a young Guild Socialist recruit.

League, the organisation formed to propagate it, did not come into existence until 1915, after the attempt to capture the Society had failed. The first intimation was the publication, in 1906, of *The Restoration of the Gild System*, by Arthur J. Penty, the architect-disciple of Morris and himself a Fabian at the time. Then, in 1907, A. R. Orage and Holbrook Jackson bought up the *New Age*. Orage also was a Fabian, and *Fabian News* of May, announcing that it was distributing his circular to all members, guaranteed that the paper would be run 'on Fabian lines'—a paragraph for which Pease must subsequently have kicked himself when Orage proceeded to turn the *New Age* into a brilliantly polemical journal of the left of all kinds, getting writers of the standing of Arnold Bennett to contribute weekly articles for nothing,[1] and, on the economic side, violently attacking Fabian Collectivism. Hobson's articles on National Guilds, afterwards collected into a book (and reviewed with meticulous contempt by Webb[2]), appeared serially in it, and 'everybody who was anybody' in the left-wing world read both it and Lansbury's *Daily Herald* with Will Dyson's cartoons as a matter of course. One of its contributors and strongest supporters was G. D. H. Cole, who had joined the Oxford Fabian Society in 1908, just after coming up to Balliol, and whose *Oxford Reformer* (a monthly) had received a kindly notice in the *News* of December 1909. He had been very energetic in the Poor Law campaign, and was ready to be equally energetic in the matter of Control of Industry.

In the summer of 1912, on Beatrice's suggestion, the Executive appointed two Committees of Enquiry. The first was to consider Rural Problems; its chairman was H. D. Harben, son of the chairman of the Prudential, and in August 1913 its findings were published as a book. The second, on the Control of Industry, was to be a much more imposing affair; it was to have a large membership, including 'consultants' who were not members of the Society; it was to examine all possible forms of industrial organisation, and papers 'propounding definite questions' were to be sent out to local Fabian Societies for discussion—the article on Syndicalism already mentioned was so distributed, but does not appear to have been followed up. By December the committee had already 85 full members and 66 'consultants', and was moving towards a distinct organisation of its own. William

[1] Under the pen-name 'Jacob Tonson'.

[2] *Fabian News*, July 1914.

Mellor, Cole's Oxford comrade and collaborator, later to be editor of the *Daily Herald* and afterwards of the *Tribune* weekly, was appointed full-time secretary, succeeding Julius West;[1] in the New Year it found lodging in the Norfolk Street offices of the N.C.P.D., levied a subscription on its members, and called itself the Fabian Research Committee. Cole, who had become a Fellow of Magdalen College, joined it in May; Beatrice was its chairman.

In October appeared a long printed Report of the Committee (written, on internal evidence, by Sidney) setting out a detailed scheme of work and announcing that it had set up four sub-committees, on Associations of Consumers, Associations of Producers, Public Services, and Associations of Wage-Earners; it intended to study also Industrial Assurance, asked for formal recognition as a group—which was granted—and set out to raise subscriptions and donations. Several of these sub-committees, it may here be mentioned, conducted extensive research in a calm and non-contentious manner and published their findings as Supplements to the *New Statesman* (see below). But with the fourth the fat was almost immediately in the fire; not only was the subject contentious, but it was already tangled with the political future of the Society. For in April Gillespie had moved, with Cole seconding, that the Society should disaffiliate immediately from the Labour Party on the ground that 'it had ceased to be capable of formulating a policy. We should endeavour to influence all parties [an odd revival of "permeation"] and our business was research.' The last words were a new argument in an old controversy; notwithstanding the support of Harold Laski, whose name appears for the first time in Fabian records, the resolution was lost by a two-to-one majority. Cole was not, however, at this stage, dismayed; in an article in the *Daily Herald* of December 12th he appealed to critics not to stand aside, but to join the Society as a useful fact-finding organisation. 'If only rebel thinkers would come in and fight, instead of scoffing from outside, we would soon alter the Fabian attitude . . . it is at least no more hopeless than the attitude of the T.U.C.' To a quite considerable extent they did come in, but not sufficiently to enable the rebels to carry at a members' meeting in March 1914, which was considering possible developments

[1] H. J. Gillespie, another Oxford Socialist and at one time editor of a journal called *The Smart Set*, became Honorary Secretary in March.

of the 'unifying' proposals of the International Socialist Bureau (see below, p. 169), a resolution declaring that the Society's function was 'primarily to conduct research'. The logical conclusion from that would have been to disaffiliate from the Labour Party. Shaw, whose attitudes, after he had left the Executive, became less and less predictable, supported the resolution, but an amendment by Webb to make research '*one* of the primary functions' was carried by a single vote. In the following month Cole was elected to the Executive, and carried on his battle from the platform. He might well have expected a victory in the third round.

At the delegate conference in August, just on the outbreak of war, he had a field-day, and does not seem, to say the least of it, to have gone out of his way to win over the opposition. He was, in fact, concerning himself more with the research organisation, with its young Guild Socialist recruits, and may have thought that the older Fabians did not really matter. At all events he intervened in a discussion on Parliamentary candidatures with a proposal to amend the Labour Party constitution so as to enable candidates standing under its auspices to describe themselves as 'Labour and Socialist'; this, he said, would result in the disruption of the Party, which would be excellent. 'Next business' was carried; but undismayed he then moved an amendment to an Oxford motion to revise the Basis, which Pease from the chair ruled out of order. Cole then moved that 'the chairman leave the chair'; being defeated on a small vote, most of the delegates sitting silent, he went on to move the rejection, on 'control of industry' grounds, of a motion of Webb's dealing with Trade Boards; the motion was carried.

The atmosphere of August 1914 may have affected the tone and temper of these discussions, though the disagreement between pro- and anti-war politicians did not develop for some time—and when they did, scarcely affected the Fabian Society, both parties agreeing that it was not a suitable forum for that debate. But the delegate conference, as already mentioned, was not the governing body of the Society, and the Guild Socialists prepared to do battle in the spring. By this time the Oxford contingent had been joined by a good number of the Cambridge Socialists, including Allen, W. N. Ewer, later foreign correspondent of the *Daily Herald*, A. L. Bacharach the chemist, and by others from other universities, among whom may be specially mentioned R. Page Arnot,[1] long to be secretary of the Fabian (later Labour) Research Department. It was not the case that all young Fabians were Guild Socialists; some were vehemently opposed. But I have very little doubt that at that time and for some years to come the majority of young intellectual Socialists were Guildsmen, or that Guild Socialism, which, as S. G. Hobson observed, was not by any means alien to Fabianism in spirit, gave a tremendous sense of purpose and excitement to its devotees.[2]

By the beginning of 1915 the Fabian Society, having outgrown its quarters at Clement's Inn, found a new home at 25 Tothill Street, Westminster, a very short distance from the Houses of Parliament, in a house to which was attached a lettable hall for meetings. This house was large enough to provide, as well as offices for the Society proper and the Fabian Women's Group, a common-room, opened in the new year, a Fabian Bookshop which under Howell's charge commenced operations in the following August, and accommodation for the N.C.P.D. and the Research Department. The latter, acquiring very rapidly a team of enthusiastic young volunteers (Guild Socialists naturally, for the most part), began to publicise itself as a general enquiry bureau[3] of the left, and to collect for study a reference library of books, journals, and press-cuttings dealing with current Trade Union and Labour questions. It soon was effectively occupying the room belonging to the N.C.P.D. as well as its own, and made full and frequent use of the common-room, a nest of rebels thus establishing themselves actively (and noisily!) just over Pease's head in his own office. The fact that, as time went on, and the Military Service Acts came into operation, some of the research workers, paid and voluntary, refused service on grounds of conscience and upon occasion took to the roof of the building to avoid visiting military police, only added to the fun.

[1] Later one of the founders of the Communist Party of Great Britain; author of the official *History of the Miners' Federation*.

[2] 'Theory, linked with logic, youth, good-fellowship, is apt to lead to genial heresy-hunting . . . gaily starting a revolution armed with split hairs,' wrote Hobson in *Pilgrim to the Left*, reminiscing on the battles of formulae which soon developed in the National Guilds League.

[3] An instruction to the Fabian Executive that it established through the Research Department a bureau of enquiry had been carried *nem. con.* at the excited August meeting.

Meanwhile, however, a furious battle was raging in the Committee on Associations of Wage-Earners. Webb's draft report was torn to pieces by Cole and Mellor, who proceeded to write an alternative—which turned into several books before it was finished—and early in 1915 the rebels opened their new campaign. A new long manifesto, entitled 'The Right Moment', signed by twenty members of the Society,[1] was published in the *News* of February, by leave of the Executive and at the signatories' expense, the title, of course, deriving from the Fabian motto. Now was the moment, it suggested, to abolish altogether the Basis or any other statement of faith, to confine the functions of the Society entirely to research—members, presumably, conducting their propaganda through other vehicles—but to deny membership to those who associated themselves publicly with any organisation opposed to the Labour movement, i.e. with the Liberal or Tory parties. Rejoinder and reply followed, and in June a series of resolutions embodying the proposals of the manifesto was put to the members' meeting; after long and heated debate they were one and all rejected. Cole then resigned, from both the Executive and the Society. The only Executive member to follow his example was Mrs Emily Townshend, who sent in her resignation 'on account of sympathy with the policy but not the manners of the Guild Socialists';[2] no resignations of ordinary members were recorded, though certainly many young Socialists who might have joined the Society contented themselves with enrolling in the Fabian Research Department.[3] There was no split; but the dissidents had in effect given up the battle, and the delegate conference in August was a shadow of itself—the war itself having by that time removed the active leadership of all the university societies and most of those in the

[1] Including, besides those already mentioned in this connection, Ivor Brown, afterwards editor of the *Observer*, T. W. Chaundy of Oxford, J. S. Middleton, Assistant Secretary of the Labour Party, Herbert Morrison and Ellen Wilkinson.

[2] Minutes, June 25th, 1915. Beatrice Webb, commenting in her *Diary* on May 15th, on the young people who 'do violent and dishonourable acts just for the sake of doing them' considered winding up the Fabian Society and retiring into research, but decided that that 'would be a mean proceeding'.

[3] Frank Horrabin, the Guild Socialist cartoonist and cartographer, endeavoured to join the Society in the spring, but Pease held up his application until after the vital meeting. There may have been others similarly placed.

provinces. The 'second blooming' of the Fabian Society was abruptly brought to an end; it had to its credit no achievement so concrete and unmistakable as the Education Acts, since the ending of the Poor Law was a generation and more away, and despite the rush of new ideas, the organisation itself would probably have proved unstable. No one can tell what would have happened but for the war. Before, however, we turn to the story of Fabianism after 1914 there is one important Fabian 'offshoot' (or Webbian child) to be mentioned.

The 'New Statesman'

It was during her world tour that Beatrice convinced herself of the need to establish a weekly journal of fact and discussion which should play its part in converting the British public, particularly the intellectual public, to Socialism. Nothing that was presently on the market served the purpose; the existing 'serious' weeklies were anti-Socialist and insufficiently concerned with fact; Keir Hardie's *Labour Leader* was the property of the I.L.P.; Blatchford's *Clarion* was also *sui generis*, and the *New Age* patently pursuing false gods. She did not, however, wish to revive the proposal of the special committee that the Fabian Society should itself run such a journal, even if it could have raised the necessary funds; she felt that any journal which called itself Fabian would be labelled sectarian and start its life in hobbles. 'Permeating' as ever, she wanted a paper which would influence the public mind, insinuating Socialist ideas and publishing the results of the enquiries which she was then proposing to initiate without continuously reminding its readers of their provenance. At first she contemplated making use of the already existing *Crusade*; but Sharp's reaction was unfavourable;[1] and on reflection she decided that the *Crusade* was already too much associated with a specific policy for subscribers to be forthcoming in sufficient numbers, and that an entirely new venture was preferable. Shaw, brought into a consultation a little later, was discouraging; he declared that they (the Webbs and himself) were too old and too truculent, and would quarrel with subscribers and contributors. If Beatrice insisted on going ahead, he would pay up his share as an old friend—but he would have nothing else to do with it. 'Nobody doubts', he concluded in a long letter to Beatrice,[2]

[1] Letter from Sharp in Webb Collection, March 11th, 1912.
[2] July 10th, 1912. (Letter in Webb Collection.)

'that you and Sidney can found a paper far more easily than you founded the London School of Economics. But of what use is the London School to us? us specifically?'

No answer was given to the last question, and Beatrice went ahead with an ingenious scheme which bears all the Webb hall-marks. A modest nest-egg of capital was secured—£5,000, contributed by Shaw, Harben, Edward Whitley of Oxford, and Ernest Simon (the late Lord Simon of Wythenshawe); and *Fabian News* carried an announcement that the new journal, though independent and to be run by an independent company, would have Shaw, the Webbs, and other Fabians as regular contributors—and that any Fabian taking out an annual subscription before a certain date would get it at a considerable reduction. This bait worked. A thousand subscribers at most were hoped for; but over 2,000 were secured—a pretty good send-off for a weekly in those days. Clifford Sharp was appointed editor, with full powers; and the first number, which appeared on May 12th, 1913, announced that the paper was not an organ of the Labour Party, but a journal of Fabian Socialism—this indicating no party bias, since the world movement towards collectivism was above and beyond party.[1]

Though Shaw made difficulties from the start, refusing to sign his articles, and clashing in personality with the editor to such an extent that his contributions practically ceased,[2] it will be seen that the *New Statesman* did not fulfil his gloomy presages, being far more 'Fabian' than ever was the School of Economics. Its rival in the weekly field was the Liberal *Nation*, edited by Massingham (which it eventually absorbed, though not until 1930); to compete with the *Nation* in journalism it enrolled such personalities as C. M. Lloyd, afterwards head of the Ratan Tata department of Social Science at the L.S.E., who was for many years assistant editor, J. C. (later Sir John) Squire, who was the first editor of the literary side and signed his articles 'Solomon Eagle', Desmond MacCarthy ('Affable Hawk'), the

[1] See further in chapter by S. K. Ratcliffe in *The Webbs and Their Work*, and the 21st anniversary issue of the *New Statesman*, 1934.

[2] With the notable exception of the brilliant and provocative Supplement called *Commonsense about the War*, which was published late in 1914. Sharp, however, refused to allow the author to follow it up with a second blast. In 1917 Shaw declared that the paper was now 'an organ of suburban Tory Democracy'. (Letter to Pease in Fabian files.)

essayist Robert Lynd ('Y.Y.'), C. W. Saleeby, who wrote scientific articles under the pen-name of 'Lens', and (after 1918) G. D. H. Cole, who from then to his death in 1959 wrote articles, leaders, notes and reviews on economic and industrial subjects, contributing to practically every issue of the paper, and becoming eventually Chairman of the Company.

The most distinctive, however, and most 'Fabian' feature of the *New Statesman* was the Special Supplements, whose appearance dates from the paper's very earliest days. Of these, which, produced in similar format, were often more bulky than the journal itself, the regular one was the monthly *Blue Book Supplement*, edited first by F. W. Keeling, and after he had joined the army, by S. K. Ratcliffe; it consisted of full summarising reviews of important official documents and a classified list of all those that had appeared during the month. At a moment when the intellectual left-wing public was only just beginning to appreciate the importance of really studying Government publications, however unappetising their format—and their style—might sometimes be, the *Blue Book Supplement* showed that the paper was seriously written for serious students, and, in the opinion of Sharp,[1] was indirectly well worth the time and money spent on its preparation and publication, for it won 'a certain solid authority and prestige in public circles which was never lost'. Of more permanent interest were the many Supplements which arose directly out of the work of the Research Committee: to mention only a few, *State and Municipal Enterprise* (1915) summarised all the achievements of collectivism to date; *The Co-operative Movement* and *Co-operative Production and Profit-Sharing* (1914) did the same for two methods of organisation of industry; Leonard Woolf's *Suggestions for the Prevention of War* (1915), later issued in book form, provided one of the first blue-prints for the League of Nations; and Beatrice Webb's *English Teachers and Their Professional Organisation* (1916) remained for very many years the only study of its subject, and is still indispensable for the student.

All the *New Statesman* Supplements were written by Fabians; the editor and the chief regular contributors were members of the Society, as were the bulk of the initial subscribers; its professed intention to be 'an organ of Fabian research' was therefore, at the first, almost completely fulfilled. It did not so continue;

[1] *New Statesman*, 21st anniversary issue.

war difficulties, particularly the shortage of paper, killed the characteristic Supplements, which were only faintly revived, in after years, by the production of an occasional *New Statesman* political pamphlet—several written by G. D. H. Cole; it took many years to get safely on its financial feet, and the struggle with competitors, such as the *Nation* and the *Week-End Review*, both of which it finally swallowed, caused it to become much less distinctively Fabian and more like other 'serious' weeklies. Nor was Sharp, with his strong dislike of what he called 'the emotional concerns' of early and contemporary Radical journalism, and his tough and sometimes dictatorial manner, always *persona grata* with the Radicals. Today, it cannot, and probably would not wish to be, described as Fabian, though it is not without sympathy for Fabianism. But for many years that was undoubtedly its character and made its reputation.

PART FOUR

The Ways Divide

1914–1938

CHAPTER XIV

War and Post-War

THE outbreak of war in 1914 found Fabianism as confused and bewildered as any other movement in the country, indeed as 90 per cent of the country's inhabitants. So long a time had passed, so many wars and threats of war have intervened, that it seems worth while stressing again the profound shock which the newspapers of the first days of August dealt to a people of whom only the barest handful—reinforced later by a few who claimed hindsight—had the remotest idea that anything of the kind was conceivable, much less possible, who had been brought up in a world in which there were no passports, except for those who wished to venture into 'uncivilised' countries such as Tsarist Russia or the Ottoman Empire, no immigration regulations to speak of, no vaccination certificates or fingerprints, no exchange control, 'foreign parts' places where 'indidents' took place from time to time, made headlines, and in due course disappeared; and where the armaments of other countries were little more than scare stories, themes for serials in the *Daily Mail*, stage melodramas, or election cries like 'We Want Eight [Dreadnoughts] and We Won't Wait!' [1] There was nothing remotely resembling the feverish propaganda of the 'thirties—books like *What Would Be the Character of a New War*, films like *The Shape of Things to Come*—to warn the doomed generation what it might expect; rather, visions of perpetual peace (which some of them, reared on stories of pioneering war and the White

[1] For example, novels of German invasion by the prolific William Le Queux, a popular spy play called *An Englishman's Home*, and Blatchford's *Clarion* articles on the German peril, which so little suited the mood of his public that the sales of the *Clarion* fell heavily. A long-ago novel by Mary Agnes Hamilton, *Dead Yesterday*, gives a still-vivid picture of the chaotic feeling of the time. So, later, did Wells's *Mr Britling Sees it Through* (1916).

Man's Burden, appreciated all too little)[1] and increasing prosperity were served out to them; Dr G. P. Gooch, in a volume of the Home University Library published in 1911, wrote of war between nations being shortly as dead as prehistoric monsters, and Sir Norman Angell's *The Great Illusion* (1910), interpreted in a way not intended by its author, was taken to prove conclusively that since major wars did not pay the victor, major wars would never occur. So it happened that a sizeable section of England's eligible-for-army youth, enjoying tramping holidays in Europe, was caught in the storm and spent the war years in the camps at Ruhleben. It should not be forgotten, either, that however much people disliked the idea of 'Prussianism', Uhlans in spiked *Pickelhaube* and jack-boots, and the Kaiser's bombast, there had been nothing in the pre-war years comparable with *Mein Kampf*, the streams of refugees, or Munich. The invasion of Belgium did indeed swing the bulk (but not the whole) of the nation behind Kitchener's appeal, but up till that moment the organised Labour movement and a good part of the popular Press had been opposed to any British participation, and two Cabinet Ministers, John Morley and John Burns, resigned rather than support it. Beatrice Webb noted that within a few days they had been approached by two practically identical deputations, one inviting them to join a demonstration of protest against the war, the other suggesting agitation supporting it;[2] this pictures very clearly the state of the more-or-less 'informed' public mind. This chapter has no need to re-tell the course of the war; but if the story of Fabianism is to be followed, its main effects on the working class and on the left-wing movement generally need to be noticed.

The Impact of War; Orthodoxy and Rebellion

The first immediate effect was a closing of the ranks on the home front. 'Unity', so long vainly sought, became something of a reality on August 6th, when the War Emergency, Workers'

[1] 'No more with England's chivalry at dawn to ride;
No more defeat, faith, victory—O no more
A cause on earth for which we might have died!'

Sir Henry Newbolt, author of *Drake's Drum*. See also the war sonnets of Rupert Brooke, the Cambridge Fabian, who in 1915 died of septicaemia in the Aegean.

[2] She recalled this in a symposium entitled *What I Believe*, published much later.

National Committee, met for the first time. This awkwardly titled body united the Trades Union Congress, the Labour Party, the General Federation of Trade Unions, the Co-operative Union and the Co-operative Wholesale Society, the Women's Labour League and the Women's Co-operative Guild, the London Trades Council, the Socialist Societies, the Miners, Railwaymen, and Transport Workers, and—an unprecedented event—the National Union of Teachers in an alliance which, first formed to protect the working classes against the results of immediate dislocation—unemployment, food shortages, price rackets, and the like—soon found itself, as the war went on and the longer-term problems began to show themselves, standing on guard to preserve the rights and living standards of those who remained at home, in the occupations and the cities and towns to which those in the forces would return, against the 'natural' results of inflation and the vigorous attacks by many of the better-off—notably landlords on crowded Clydeside and engineering employers delighting in the opportunity to engage cheap female labour on repetition work.[1] This new-found solidarity of labour was never broken and not substantially affected, as might perhaps have been expected, by the differences of opinion about the war which existed almost from the first. The pacifists of the I.L.P. (who included, after some hedging, MacDonald), the Marxist class-warriors of the Socialist Labour Party and the left wing of the British Socialist Party—the militants, under Hyndman, having split off to resume the old S.D.F. name—were abused and attacked from time to time, but never boycotted or thrown out of their organisations; a policy which served MacDonald well when the war and the post-war shouting were over.

Secondly, as the war continued and drained manpower, this united movement became a much more serious factor in society by reason of its sheer indispensability, because without a reasonably satisfied working force the war could not be fought, let alone won. The first success was the strike of munition workers on the Clyde in February 1915; the realities of the situation were brought home to the public in the summer of 1915 when Lloyd

[1] 'What the war has clearly shown', said a leader in one of the prominent engineering journals, 'is not that women are paid too little, but that men have been *paid too much*.' One Trade Board had recently fixed *2d. per hour* as a minimum in certain sweated women's trades, which indicates considerable scope for saving on the wages bill by dilution.

George discovered that the penalty clauses of the Munitions of War Act could not be enforced against 200,000 striking Welsh colliers whose product would be lost to the factories if they were put in prison, and hastily evolved a wage settlement. Direct representatives of the working force—shop stewards and the like—had to be recognised and negotiated with as plenipotentiaries by people, such as directors of railway companies, to whom even constitutionally built Trade Unions had been anathema only a few years previously. And their official Trade Unions had to be taken into consultation. As Government control was slowly extended over vital parts of the economy, organised labour had to be given representation on such organisations as the Cotton and Wool Control Boards, and even in the War Cabinet itself. An altogether new status and importance were thus given to the bodies which a reviewer of the Webbs' *Industrial Democracy* (1897) had once considered so unimportant and so uninteresting as to marvel that anyone should think it worth while writing a book about them; and their importance, for all that it was *at the time* largely a result of an exceptional situation and was sadly reduced when the war was over and the 'hard-faced men' again took brief command, had considerable effect, while it lasted, on all Socialist thought—an effect which outlasted the war.

Thirdly, before controls were imposed, and even, to a considerable extent, afterwards, the war provided infinite opportunities for greed—which were generally not neglected. (The action of the ironmaster Stanley Baldwin in donating secretly his excess gains to the Inland Revenue is still regarded as an awesome exception to the common practice.) Such gains were not, of course, confined to capitalists and company promoters; the high rates of pay and piecework earned by miners and engineers were publicised plentifully in newspapers which featured agonised reports of wives in the coalfields getting grand pianos and fur coats and refusing to send their daughters out to be maidservants to their betters—who suffered horribly until from 1921 onwards the long-drawn-out depression in mining and agriculture came to bring them temporary relief. Though wages, as a whole, rose considerably more slowly than prices—and came down with a run after 1920—the first known period of really 'full employment' brought prosperity, even with anxiety, to a great number of families; and really large working-class incomes appeared in sufficient amount to make 'the economy of high wages' seem something more than the notion of a crank American. But the growth in 'profiteering'—a word coined by the *New Age* to denote excessive profit-making—was far more spectacular, as were the scandals of trafficking in public property disclosed by Government reports such as that on the Army and Navy Canteens Board. Anyone could draw the contrast between the huge casualty lists, the rates of pension paid for the dead and the mutilated, and the records of company dividends on ordinary shares and bonus issues made; the result was first, a considerable sharpening of class-consciousness, a conviction that if 'we' could get a slightly increased taking while 'they' were getting a vast deal more, there ought to come a time when 'our' share, the share of organised labour, would be much bigger than 'theirs'; secondly, a feeling that the Socialists had all along been right in their arguments, that there did exist in society a mass of surplus productive capacity and 'conspicuous waste' which, communally owned and directed in the common interest, could provide a happy living for all. If the present owners and controllers showed no enthusiasm for the necessary readjustment, the organised workers, flexing their muscles and inspired, after March 1917, by the Revolution which had thrown down an ancient tyranny and destroyed the master-class in Russia, were willing to show them.

Finally, and far outside the economic field, the circumstances of the war itself, of its clumsy, stumbling outbreak and of its equally stumbling but after 1915 far more deadly continuance, convinced the more thoughtful members of the movement, in all classes, that *il fallait en finir*, and that means to prevent its recurrence must—and could—be found. Whatever hand had triggered off the explosion, the Tsar's, the Kaiser's, even a wicked combination of the 'Merchants of Death', as later propaganda picturesquely labelled Vickers, Du Pont, and the rest of their kin, nobody could possibly have intended the long-drawn, wholesale slaughter on the eastern and western fronts; if those results could have been foreseen, the powers and the people would certainly have found ways other than war of resolving their problems, of redressing grievances, and setting free the oppressed. So ran the argument for all but dogmatic Marxists and Anarchists; and the ignominious collapse of the pre-war International and all its vague plans for popular resistance to war only went to show that better machinery must be devised, better foundations laid, and such cynical share-outs as were contained in the Secret Treaties which the Bolsheviks so shockingly disclosed to the world, prevented in advance. Almost from the outbreak of war, the theorists were considering not only how to end it, but how to ensure that it really was the war to end war; the wild welcome accorded to Woodrow Wilson showed that by 1918 the mass of people agreed with them—so far.

These influences came to bear on a Fabianism which, as the previous chapter has shown, was already in a state of confused conflict which looked like leading to a split. There was in fact no split, in the sense of physical division of the Society; scarcely anyone followed Cole into exile, and even he, whatever the state of his emotions, showed no desire to cease from any intercourse with, for example, the Webbs;[1] war conditions, moreover, auto-

[1] A vivid illustration of the varying Cole–Webb attitude is to be found in some correspondence of 1917 with Beatrice Webb, preserved in the Webb Collection. Beatrice had suggested a federal form of government for the Research Department, with the Fabian Society, the Labour Party, and the Unions sharing control. Cole replied in a furious letter:

'. . . if I find myself secretary of a "group of the Fabian Society" it is from the basest financial motive and without any feeling of obligation to or friendship for the Fabian Society which to be candid I detest. I am no less averse than I am to the Fabian connection to the proposal to hand over the Research Department to the Labour Movement. . . . Nor do I regard the federal suggestion as practicable. I want to split the Research Department right off from the Fabian Society, as soon as it is strong enough to stand the strain. I do not for a moment accept the view that the sanction of the Fabian Executive is required, and I would certainly be no party to asking for their sanction. . . .

'I believe this is a rude letter; but I cannot write temperately of Fabians. . . . I don't want to force an issue at the moment, though every time I am confused with the Fabians I feel like the Pope being mistaken for Mr Stiggins.'

Beatrice's reply has not survived; but that it must have been soothing appears from Cole's next letter, dated eight days later than the first, which ends,

'I infinitely prefer our present purely nominal Fabianism to actual dependence on the P[arliamentary] C[ommittee] or the Joint Board [of the T.U.C. and the Labour Party].

Yours very sincerely,

G. D. H. Cole'

Those interested will find similar differences in Beatrice's estimate of her correspondent scattered through the text of her *Diaries* in the Webb Collection. In 1916–17 she was hoping still to found a new 'Labour Research Society', with Cole's collaboration; in May 1924 she committed herself to the view that he was 'finished'; by November 1928 she had revised this opinion completely.

matically brought to an end the majority of internal discussion meetings, national and provincial, in which the struggle between ideologies had been most loudly conducted. There was, however, a large difference in emphasis and temper between the members of the two pre-war camps which led them into different spheres of activity; the historian of wartime and post-war Fabianism has therefore to follow not only the documented story of the Society itself but also two only partly connected but highly important developments. The first of these, associated in the main with Sidney Webb and Arthur Henderson, may be summarised as the formation of a new Labour Party very different from the old semi-pressure group; the other was the work of the 1914 Rebels, through the Labour (Fabian) Research Department and the National Guilds League, in supplying information and ammunition, and endeavouring to formulate philosophy for the burgeoning industrial movement. The permanent results of the former are a matter of record; of the latter, once the post-war boom was over, little but 'influences' remained—though these should not be too lightly written off. Both, however, were essentially of the Fabian tradition, and reacted upon one another and upon the Society itself; there was a good deal of common membership, however complicated by the 'love-hate' attitude of the Rebels to the orthodox as exemplified in the footnote to p. 166; and when, many years later, reunion was formally completed by the reorganisation of the Fabian Society into a body whose President was Beatrice Webb and its Chairman G. D. H. Cole, this no more than underlined the fact that the growth of 'Fabian Socialism' had continued without any real break.

Webb, Henderson, and the Labour Party

To begin with the Labour Party. After returning from their world tour, and having digested the failure of the Poor Law campaign, the Webbs, at any rate, had made up their minds that permeation of the older parties was dead, and that the Labour Party—'a poor thing, but our own' [1]—was the only possible vehicle for Socialism in the country. Counting her chickens rather hastily, Beatrice had concluded at the end of 1912 that the alliance of the Fabian Society and the I.L.P. referred to in the last chapter was well on the way to 'controlling the policy' of the Labour and Socialist movement,[1] and was correspondingly

[1] *Diary*, October 11th and Christmas, 1912, and July 5th, 1913.

indignant when the Labour M.P.s declined to play or to bring in the Parliamentary Bills drafted for them by the Socialists. For this reason, perhaps, her *Diary* scarcely notices the conference of August 6th, 1914, at which the War Emergency Committee was born; yet this was perhaps the most important single event in the 'permeation' of the Labour Party. Sidney held no official position on that body, whose secretary was J. S. Middleton, Assistant Secretary and after 1935 Secretary of the Labour Party, and its Chairman, until he joined the Government, Arthur Henderson, who had become a Fabian in 1912; but from the first moment his ability to draft and to organise assured him a leading role. Within a week he had prepared, and the Fabian Society had issued on behalf of the committee, a thirty-two page pamphlet, *The War and the Workers* (Tract 176), intended for use throughout the country by local organisations such as Trades Councils, Trade Union branches, and branches of Socialist Societies, drawing attention to the kind of problems which would have to be faced immediately, and urging that local committees, constituted on the same lines as the National Committee, should be set up to co-ordinate local opinion and to press upon municipal and other authorities the need for action to prevent dislocation and distress.

> In all fields of social necessity . . . the National Committee was constantly engaged in promoting special measures, legislative and administrative, and urging them by deputations to Ministers, through the Parliamentary Labour Party, by steady press propaganda, by regional conferences, demonstrations and platform campaigns, and the regular circulation of the informative minutes of the Committee's weekly meetings to a wide network of national and local organisations and individuals.[1]

In its early days the Committee produced plans, not adopted until much later in the war, for the fixing of prices and the rationing of staple necessities, which were originated by Webb;[2] it campaigned with varying success for improved separation allowances for the families of servicemen, for provision for Belgian refugees, old age pensioners, relatives of prisoners of war, and

[1] J. S. Middleton, 'Webb and the Labour Party', Chapter XI of *The Webbs and Their Work*.

[2] 'All they ask', wrote Beatrice rather crossly, 'is that Sidney's name shall not appear.' *Diary*, September 9th, 1915. The tone of the whole passage suggests some dissatisfaction with this anonymity.

for adequate disablement pensions. Webb's greatest triumph, however, was to arrange a conference of the National Committee with representatives of building societies, ratepayers' organisations, and representatives of small property owners, which agreed upon a basis (drafted by him) restricting the level of rents and mortgage interest—thus laying the foundation of the whole subsequent structure of Rent Restriction.

As the war continued and its constituent bodies stepped up campaigns of their own, the Committee's importance declined; but Webb's position was not impaired. At the end of 1915 he became the Fabian Society's official representative on the Party Executive, Sanders having taken a commission.[1] By this time Henderson was in the Cabinet, but he had not given up the secretaryship of the Party, and the relationship between him and Webb became very close. It may even be hazarded that Henderson at that time took something of Shaw's place in Webb's life. Shaw, since becoming a successful dramatist with large earning power and retiring from the Fabian Executive—in 1916 he also severed connection, rather loudly, with the *New Statesman*[2]—had divorced himself to a large extent from the day-to-day political grind; he was also disposed to slightly impish support of the Fabian Rebels, with whom Sidney had no sympathy whatsoever. He was therefore no longer Sidney's 'partner'; and the void may have needed some filling. Be that as it may, the connection between Webb and Henderson grew rapidly from 1915 onwards, and in 1917–18 bore large and significant fruit. It would appear that they were both agreed on the need for a stronger Labour Party, and that the Labour Party could not become stronger unless it possessed both an organisation and a policy; both of these were secured by the time the war ended. Chronologically, the first move of importance came in the international field, and was connected by a tenuous trail with the abortive 'unity' discussions before the war.

In March 1914 the International Socialist Bureau had made a last endeavour to knock the heads of the three English Societies together by calling a conference at Newcastle. Beatrice Webb, who at that time was disposed to think well of the intellects of

[1] The I.L.P. had asked the Fabian Executive to suggest Fred Jowett in place of Keir Hardie; this was the Fabians' *quid pro quo*.

[2] See letters from Shaw and Sharp reprinted in *Beatrice Webb's Diaries, 1912–24*, p. 75.

some of the foreign Socialists such as Jaurès, Emile Vandervelde, and Camille Huysmans, was pleased to note that, influenced by the benign wisdom of the Fabian representatives (with Sidney in the chair), the intransigent others agreed to try co-operation, and that she herself was chosen chairman of the standing joint committee of the three executives. The intention was to form a single Society divided roughly into sections, of which one would be mainly educational; it was this suggestion which gave Cole the opportunity to try to confine the Fabian Society to 'research'. The attempt, as already related, failed; and under the stress of war the standing joint committee (whose stability was in any event very doubtful) broke up immediately. Huysmans, however, the secretary of the Bureau, who as a Belgian became a permanent exile, never ceased to try and make some sort of plan for the future, however often rebuffed by the 'fight-to-a-finish' brigade which existed in Socialist as well as other ranks, and kept close touch with Mrs Webb particularly. The Fabians, for their part, proceeding on more theoretical lines, had employed Leonard Woolf, in co-operation with a Research Committee, to work upon *Suggestions for the Prevention of War*, which were published in 1915 as a *New Statesman* Supplement.[1]

In 1917, after the first Russian Revolution and the Stockholm fiasco, these two lines of effort came together. The Labour Party Executive and the Parliamentary Committee of the T.U.C. held a series of discussions, as a result of which a document prepared by Huysmans, Henderson, Webb, and MacDonald in collaboration was laid before a special conference in December. This document, published as *Labour's War Aims*, included all the demands which became the subsequent stock-in-trade of Liberal-Socialist thought: universal democracy and the abandonment of imperialism and secret diplomacy; limitation of armaments and the abolition of profits therefrom; collective security, a supranational authority, an international court, and international legislation on social matters; plans for the settlement of 'burning' questions such as Alsace-Lorraine, Palestine, and the future of the subject nationalities of the Ottoman and Austrian empires; economic controls and an international commission for 'war damage and reparations'. It antedated the Fourteen Points, and before ever the Labour Party had completed its reorganisa-

[1] Later reissued in book form under the title *International Government*—one of the earliest blueprints for the League of Nations.

tion proclaimed it to the world, as well as to its fellows in the International, as a body with a policy of its own for world affairs.

Meantime, internal reorganisation of the Party was getting well under way; and the factor which did most to speed it up was the Stockholm incident, when not merely was Henderson's advice to allow facilities for representatives of British Labour to go to neutral Sweden and confer, along with other Allied Socialists, with the Russian revolutionaries, rejected by the Government out of hand, but Henderson himself, though a member of the inner War Cabinet, was not admitted to its deliberations, but brutally informed of the answer.[1] Will Dyson's angry *Herald* cartoon, 'On the Mat', only put into line drawing what the whole of the movement felt; and Henderson, who while never a stickler for his own personal dignity could be a lion in defence of his Party, regarded his treatment as a calculated insult to Labour, an indication that he himself was nothing more than a hostage 'for the duration'; and resolved that his opponents should find that they had something much tougher to deal with than they had suspected. Accordingly, with the help of Webb and others on the Executive, he drafted the new constitution for the Labour Party. This constitution, which, with certain modifications, has remained in force until the present day, established the Party as a federation of affiliated bodies, Trade Unions, Socialist Societies, the Royal Arsenal Co-operative Society, and local Labour Parties, all these having their representation on the National Executive. The local Labour Parties were empowered to accept affiliation from local branches of Trade Unions, etc., and also to enrol as members individual persons who had hitherto had no way of joining the Labour Party direct, and could only come in through one of the Socialist Societies.[2] The new constitution was a very 'Fabian' compromise between the Trade Unions which provided the sinews of war—the wherewithal, in fact, to run any organisation at all—and the Socialists, shortly

[1] See Mary Agnes Hamilton, *Arthur Henderson,* G. D. H. Cole, *History of the Labour Party,* and a host of other sources.

[2] Eventually, as the local parties developed and strengthened their membership and the I.L.P. became highly critical of the actions and policies of successive Labour Governments, this change spelt its doom as a political force, but in the immediate post-war years the strong interest in peace, coupled with the genius of Clifford Allen for raising money from his Quaker and pacifist friends, postponed this dénouement.

to be reinforced by a number of disaffected Liberals, who would have liked to control Party policy; and its passage was not completely smooth. At the Nottingham Conference of the Party in January 1918, it was all but rejected by suspicious Union delegates—made more suspicious, possibly, by the loud noises about 'workers' control' proceeding around the Labour Research Department's stall at the back of the hall—and was only saved when Henderson made a powerful appeal and promised to remit it to the constituent bodies for detailed discussion. It may have been a realisation of this background which prompted Henderson early to discard a suggestion for a 'national branch' of the Party, consisting of individuals who would join at Head Office directly and not *via* any Society or local Party. This may have been Webb's idea originally—Cole certainly agreed with it; and it would obviously have suited the London-based Fabian Society down to the ground, but the Fabians were not to gain influence so easily.

The Trade Unions were not, however, unamenable. At the resumed Party Conference in February the new constitution went through with scarcely a murmur; and in June the first Conference under the new constitution proceeded to adopt a full-dress programme—the first the Party had ever possessed—which was as nearly as possible the purest milk of the Fabian word. This was *Labour and the New Social Order*.

This event was, of course, no accident. Arising out of the work of the War Emergency Committee, Webb, with other Fabians, had been considering at intervals what lessons the war and the experiences of wartime finance and wartime controls might have taught the Socialist movement. The most noticeable result of this was a series of studies entitled *How to Pay for the War*—prepared nominally by a committee of the Fabian Research Department, but actually by Webb—and published as a whole and in separate parts in 1916. The separate parts advocated the nationalisation of mines and minerals, of railways and canals, the setting up of a State Insurance Department, the reorganisation and rationalisation of the Post Office and a 'revolution' in Income Tax.[1]

This book in itself provided a start for a programme, but *Labour and the New Social Order*, which the Labour Executive

[1] With the exception of the third, all these proposals were in course of time put into effect.

brought to Conference as the report of a special committee of its membership, went a great deal further. Too long for extensive quotation here, it bears in every line (even to the capital letters!) the unmistakable Webb trademark.

> What this war is consuming [it begins] is not merely the security, the homes, the livelihood and the lives of millions of innocent families, and an enormous proportion of all the accumulated wealth of the world, but also the very basis of the peculiar social order in which it has arisen. The individualist system of capitalist production has received a death-blow. With it must go the political system and ideas in which it naturally found expression. We of the Labour Party . . . must ensure that what is presently to be built up is a new social order, based not on fighting but on fraternity—not on the competitive struggle for the means of bare life, but on a deliberately-planned co-operation in production and distribution for the benefit of all who participate by hand or brain—not on the utmost possible inequality of riches, but on a systematic approach towards a healthy equality of material circumstances for every person born into the world—not on an enforced dominion over subject nations, subject races, subject colonies, subject classes, or a subject sex, but in industry, as well as in government,[1] on that equal freedom, that general consciousness of consent, and that widest participation in power which is characteristic of Democracy.
>
> What we now promulgate as our policy, whether for opposition or for office, is not merely this or that specific reform, but a deliberately thought out, systematic, and comprehensive plan for that immediate social rebuilding which any Ministry, whether or not it decided to grapple with the problem, will be driven to undertake. The Four Pillars of the House that we propose to erect, resting upon the common foundation of the Democratic control of society in all its activities, may be termed, respectively:—
>
> (*a*) The Universal Enforcement of the National Minimum;
> (*b*) The Democratic Control of Industry;
> (*c*) The Revolution in National Finance; and
> (*d*) The Surplus Wealth for the Common Good.

Subsequent paragraphs set out these four principles in greater detail. The first was to include all the proposals for wages, hours, health, safety, housing, education, public works, and the prevention of unemployment which the Fabian Society had from time to time advocated; the second adult suffrage, the abolition of the House of Lords, common ownership of land, the nationalisation

[1] A crumb for the Guild Socialists?

of mines, railways and canals, electric power, steamship companies, the municipalisation of coal distribution, the 'elimination of private profit' from industrial assurance, the liquor trade, etc.; the third a steep increase in taxation and death duties 'with the nearest possible approximation to equality of sacrifice', and including a capital levy; the fourth (which largely repeated the arguments in *Labour's War Aims*) envisaged Democratic Co-operation and a common plan, scientifically evolved, for solving the problems of mankind.

With this resounding and comprehensive declaration on its campaign plans—so comprehensive, indeed, that successive policies and programmes have done little more than modify it according to circumstances[1]—the reorganised Party marched into battle in the Hang-the-Kaiser election—and of course lost heavily, particularly on the intellectual side, though certainly no more heavily than might have been expected, in that atmosphere, of a party so recently grown to stature. Henderson was ousted; Webb, after putting up a good fight, was beaten for the University of London, much to his wife's relief;[2] and the fate of his immediate attempt to supply the newly elected M.P.s with suitable information and statistics is amusingly recorded in Beatrice Webb's *Diary* for January 14th, 1919.[3] Within a very short while, however, he was fully occupied as Miners' Federation representative on the famous and dramatic Sankey Coal

[1] 'Although the Purpose of the Labour Party', the pamphlet ended, 'must, by the law of its being, remain for all time unchanged, its Policy and its Programme will, we hope, undergo a perpetual development, as knowledge grows, and as new phases of the social problem present themselves, in a continually finer adjustment of our measures to our ends.'

So Webb, envisaging a more orderly sequence of events than in fact occurred. Henderson, however, at one time wanted a much faster pace. Beatrice's *Diary* of September 24th, 1919, describes him as asking Sidney to draft a complete scheme for socialising the whole of industry—'Why should the miners and the railwaymen have the privilege of being socialised?—the engineers and other operatives resented this partiality; it would be far better electioneering [*sic*] to have a complete scheme for all industry and get it accepted by the L.P. Conference.' The Webbs poured very cold water on this idea.

[2] Of the 49 other Fabians who stood only four were elected, one (Athelstan Rendall) as a Coalition Liberal.

[3] 'Two clerks—and three typists—and *at least* one messenger'—was what William Adamson, the miner who became Leader of His Majesty's Opposition, thought essential. But Henderson was already doing more than this for the Party Executive. See pp. 171 and 182.

Commission, where with two other Fabians, Chiozza Money and R. H. Tawney,[1] he publicly tore the pretensions and performance of the mineowners into such small fragments that no intelligent person could doubt, thereafter, that nationalisation of the mines was bound to come; the immediate result of this was his heading of the 1919 poll for the Labour Party Executive, and four years later his presidential address to the Party Conference of June 1923, in which he reaffirmed the Fabian faith in a phrase which was picked up by the revolutionists of the day and used again and again as an epitome of all that was abominable in non-Communist Socialism.

Let me insist [he said, winding up a review of the history and prospects of the Party which had just doubled its representation in Parliament] on what our opponents habitually ignore, and, indeed, what they seem intellectually incapable of understanding, namely *the inevitable gradualness* of our scheme of change. The very fact that Socialists have both principles and a programme appears to confuse nearly all their critics. If we state our principles, we are told 'That is not practicable.' When we recite our programme the objection is 'That is not Socialism.' But why, because we are idealists, should we be supposed to be idiots? For the Labour Party, it must be plain, Socialism is rooted in Democracy; which necessarily compels us to recognise that every step towards our goal is dependent on gaining the assent and support of at least a numerical majority of the whole people. Thus, even if we aimed at revolutionising everything at once, we should necessarily be compelled to make each particular change only at the time, and to the extent, and in the manner which ten or fifteen million electors, in all sorts of conditions, of all sorts of temperaments, from Land's End to the Orkneys, could be brought to consent to it. How anyone can fear that the British electorate, whatever mistakes it can make or may condone, can ever go too far or too fast is incomprehensible to me. That, indeed, is the supremely valuable safeguard of any effective democracy.

But the Labour Party, when in due course it comes to be entrusted with power, will naturally not want to do everything at once. . . . Once we face the necessity of putting our principles first into bills, to be fought through Committee clause by clause; and then into appropriate machinery for carrying them into execution from one end of the kingdom to the other—and that is what the Labour Party has done

[1] Professor Tawney's great work in historical study and adult education has tended to overshadow his service to Labour politics—the more so because of his modesty. But there are few, in fact, who have contributed more to the Fabian and democratic Labour tradition.

with its Socialism—*the inevitability of gradualness* cannot fail to be appreciated.

This presidency of the Conference, held, be it remembered, in the year immediately before the Labour Party became the Government, combined with his remarkable triumph at the election of the previous year in 'our constituency' of Seaham, seems in retrospect to mark the high-water mark of the leading Fabian in the counsels of the Labour Party; within two years he had lost his seat on the Executive, and neither in Parliament nor subsequently in office could he be regarded as a conspicuous success. But the presidential address,[1] however much it annoyed the 'direct-actionists' on the left, who until 1926 were still strong in the industrial wing of the movement, was a clear-cut statement of Fabian principles of action; it is difficult today for anyone with any knowledge of the history of British Trade Unionism, to say nothing of the British people as a whole, to find anything to cavil at in a conclusion so apparently obvious. The former Rebels, though, were not yet ready to accept it.

Guild Socialism and the Labour Research Department

The story of the Rebel movement is rather more complicated to follow, partly because, as already explained, its legacy to Fabianism lay rather in emphasis than in achievement, and partly because documentation is lacking. There is no history of Guild Socialism—Carter Goodrich's *The Frontier of Control* (1920), a study by an American observer, gives some of it to the date at which it was written; the rest has to be sought in publications of the National Guilds League and (scrappily) in memoirs of those who lived through it. Nor is there any history of the Labour Research Department except a pamphlet by R. Page Arnot, published by the L.R.D. in 1926; the Department's own *Monthly Circular* (see below) was an austerely factual journal very unlike *Fabian News*, eschewing any gossip helpful to historians. Chapter V of my own *Growing Up into Revolution* (1949) gives the fullest picture I know of the nature and atmosphere of 'The Movement' which ran it; there is little else available.

The documents in the 'Right Moment' controversy—two from the Right Moment group and two from the Executive, Cole and Allen dissenting, were printed in full in *Fabian News* of April and May 1915. The dust lies on them now, yet not so

[1] Reprinted in full as Tract 207.

thickly as to obscure the fact that the Executive had, on paper, the best of the argument, and that it was not surprising that they carried the day. The amendment forbidding any Fabian to belong to either of the two major parties was at that stage of the Labour Party's development quite premature—also rather puzzling to the uninitiated, in view of the language which its promoters were in the habit of using about the leading Labour M.P.s—and would have disfranchised most of the Society's membership as effectively as would Blatchford's Fourth Clause. The other principal amendment, which declared the object of the Society to be to carry out research into 'contemporary Socialist and Trade Union problems' and to undertake propaganda based upon it, involved both a considerable narrowing of the scope of the Society's work—as the Executive pointed out, most of its educational effort, lectures, book-boxes and summer schools, as well as nearly all that the Women's Group and other groups were doing, would have been ruled out—and a somewhat insulting devaluation of most of the past activities and publications of the Society. It was rather absurd, on the face of it, to demand that the Webbs, for example, with the *History of Trade Unionism*, *Industrial Democracy*, and a great corpus of local government study behind them, should in 1915 be called upon to recognise the importance of research.

This, of course, was not the intention. The object of the exercise—which its organisers can scarcely have hoped would succeed—was to capture the Society for the 'research into contemporary Socialist and Trade Union problems' already initiated by the Fabian Research Department, which they controlled, and for propaganda arising therefrom, which would be Guild Socialist propaganda. Beatrice Webb, in several passages of her *Diary*, shows that she saw this quite clearly, but was not at all convinced that the Rebels, if they won, would achieve anything. 'No one', she had written on April 8th, 1913, 'in the Fabian Society is capable of running the Research Department but ourselves.' And again, in April 1914, 'Each Rebel in turn—J. R. MacDonald, H. G. Wells, S. G. Hobson, Schloesser & Co.—have attacked the old gang without being able to do the work. I am wondering whether this new lot of rebellious spirits—Cole, Gillespie and Mellor—will prove any more capable.'

These doubts were without foundation. Not only Cole, whose almost single-handed output of books and pamphlets rivalled that of the Webbs before the end of his life, but a dozen other of his collaborators in the Research Department were fully capable of running the kind of research laid down in their amendment, and of running it without any guidance or instruction from the Webbs. As Arnot frankly put it, when the latter were engaged in bringing their *History of Trade Unionism* up to date—and had, with their unusual common sense, invited criticisms from their harshest critics—'Why not leave it for your successors to finish—you have ploughed the furrow up to a certain date—leave it to us to complete it.'[1] For the propaganda side, since the Fabian machine was denied them, they founded in 1915 the National Guilds League;[2] for research they retreated on positions 'prepared in advance' in the Research Department. Shaw, who was showing sympathy with the Rebel outlook—though not with the Rebel resolutions—was already a figurehead Chairman of the Department, and Cole its Vice-Chairman; its membership, though in 1914 not more than a couple of hundreds, were faithful and eager helpers, some having served an apprenticeship in the Poor Law campaign. The human material was ready to hand.

The essential difference in outlook between the Rebels and the Old Guard has been described in the last chapter; in the field of research, it was displayed in the enormous amount of attention devoted to details of Trade Unionism and Trade Union problems—to the practical exclusion of almost all other current questions. The Guild Socialists had pinned all their hopes for the British worker to his industrial organisations—their break with the Old Guard had come over the question of Control of Industry through Associations of Wage Earners; and Trade Unionism, and the local groupings of industrial workers, were their prime object of study, not to say their mystique.[3] The

[1] *Diary*, December 25th, 1919.

[2] Much to the annoyance of S. G. Hobson, who prophesied that it would become just another Fabian Society with a slightly different slant. In its early years association with the Clyde engineers (see Privićević, *The Shop Stewards Movement*), who provided its first secretary, John Paton, removed some of the likeness; but a study of its literature will show that Hobson was not very wide of the mark.

[3] An illustration of the enthusiasm may be found in the *Gazetteer* of Trade Union branches. Early in 1916 the Statutory Committee on War Pensions (of which Beatrice Webb was a member) proposed that local Pensions Committees, to which branches of Trade Unions might be invited to appoint

modern reader may comprehend the difference in attitude if he re-reads the Webbs' *Industrial Democracy* along with G. D. H. Cole's first book, *The World of Labour* (1913). Lenin translated the former for his followers; he would have scorned the latter as 'infantile left-wing deviationism', if not worse.

The Fabian Research Department, therefore, set out in the first instance to learn about Trade Unions in full detail, as living organisms. A large library of press cuttings, journals, and every sort of publication bearing on their activities was started; new recruits, who came in fairly rapidly, to the voluntary staff, were expected to get by heart the names, initials, and pet names of all the leading Unions and their general secretaries; a series of studies in Trade Unionism in various industries, of which *Trade Unionism on the Railways*, by Cole and Arnot, was the first, was set on foot. Later, in July 1917, a *Monthly Circular* of information, statistics, etc., likely to be of interest and value to Trade Unions, Trades Councils, and similar bodies, was initiated. Starting as a document of which two hundred copies were run off on the office duplicator, this last-named was so well received by those for whom it was intended that it very soon attained a circulation of several thousand printed copies, without advertising and all sold within the Labour movement. As far as industry, Government reports, or actions affecting industrial workers and working-class organisations was concerned, the Research Department's *Monthly Circular* did what *Fabian News* in its earliest issue had promised, but never performed, namely to provide day-to-day facts as ammunition for Socialists in their day-to-day struggle; it was a kind of left-wing *Ministry of Labour Gazette*.[1] At the same time the Department followed the time-honoured Fabian practice of

members, should be set up. Neither the Government nor the Trades Union Congress having at the time any available record of branches or their secretaries, Mrs Webb suggested that the F.R.D. might help; and for many months the Research Department volunteers (of whom the present writer was one) worked night after night at the superficially somewhat depressing task of copying out and indexing long lists of names and addresses furnished by Union head offices. The finished product was eventually published by the Ministry of Labour.

[1] As time went on it added to its contents facts about 'the other side', such as profits, bonus shares, and combinations of capital, of which there was a fine harvest to be gathered; still later, it introduced sections on Parliament and Local Government, and an International Section edited by that cuckoo in the Socialist nest, Rajani Palme Dutt—now editor of the Communist *Labour Monthly*.

producing pamphlets, small and large, on subjects of Socialist importance. These were not called 'Tracts', for that name was the Fabian Society's copyright; they were called Memorandum Series, Syllabus Series (for students), Studies in Capital and Labour, and (happy improvisation) Labour White Papers;[1] but to all intents and purposes they were Tracts just as much as *Facts for Socialists*. As such, they were gobbled up by the affiliated organisations.

For the study of Trade Unionism soon became a two-way traffic. The clearest sign of this was the appointment, in 1915, of G. D. H. Cole, while a Fellow of Magdalen College, to an unpaid position as research adviser to the Amalgamated Society of Engineers, in which capacity he handled a good deal of complicated Union business in the matter of wages, prices, and 'dilution' discussion under the Treasury Agreements and the Munitions of War Acts,[2] and was deep in the counsels of the A.S.E. Along with this went a steady mixing of Mellor, Arnot, and their colleagues with Trade Union officers, particularly branch and workshop officers, and the gradual self-establishment of the Research Department (which roped in as voluntary assistants much of the university Fabian membership that was not in the army) as an Enquiry Bureau to which perplexed individuals and organisations could address themselves, confident that if an answer to their problems were not immediately forthcoming, one would be earnestly sought and if humanly possible found. A *Labour Year Book*, collecting and summarising information of all kinds likely to be useful to the Labour movement in wartime, was projected as early as December 1914, under the auspices of the Fabian Society, the Research Department, and the Labour Party, and appeared only a year later.[3] In the summer of 1916, again with

[1] A full list of L.R.D. publications, down to the end of 1925, is given in an appendix to R. Page Arnot's pamphlet, *History of the Labour Research Department*.

[2] See G. D. H. Cole, *Trade Unionism and Munitions* (Carnegie Endowment, 1923).

[3] 'I have tried to inspire new work without controlling the direction of it,' wrote Beatrice Webb (*Diary*, February 14th, 1915). It seems that she had learned that the Webbs were not indispensable; the same entry indicates that she was taking up the serious study of the organisation of the professions as a counterblast to the Research Department's 'obsession' with manual workers. Her work on this subject was issued as a *New Statesman* Supplement; it was Arnot and Cole, however, who were mainly responsible for the formation in 1920 of the first Federation of Professional Workers.

the support of the Fabian leaders, membership of the Department was opened to admit anyone belonging to a Trade Union, Co-operative or Socialist society, whether or not he professed 'Fabianism' or adhered to the Fabian Basis;[1] and with the approval and encouragement of Mrs Webb, and partly with the purpose of gaining the effective support of the Parliamentary Committee of the Trades Union Congress, a 'Trade Union Survey Committee' was established with prominent Trade Unionists in its membership, for the ostensible purpose of overseeing the Trade Union work of the Department. As, however, the Trade Union officials had plenty of work on their hands in wartime, they were not likely to do much 'overseeing' of the work of the eager teams of enthusiastic irregulars,[2] a few paid (or, in the Fabian tradition, underpaid), but for the most part not paid at all but working in their spare time for the love of it—the majority were under thirty, or even under twenty-five, and without personal ties or responsibilities. The Research Department was obviously fulfilling a felt want, and so long as its employees did not tread on the toes of friendly Unions—which they would have died rather than do—let them get on with it. The most important effect, therefore, of the new committee and the new rules, apart from the partial independence of the Fabian Society, was the affiliation to the Department of an increasing number of Trade Union and Labour associations, national bodies paying ten pounds a year and local societies and branches ten shillings,[3] and the enrolment of a good few individuals belonging to them. The Research Department made no to-do about beliefs or qualifications; it was no more than a logical development, even if it hurt Mrs Webb's feelings, when in the middle of 1918, with the full assent of its Chairman Bernard Shaw, it sloughed the Fabian name altogether and called itself simply the Labour Research

[1] This involved the ending of the Department's status as a group of the Society, with representation on the Executive.

[2] An exception should be made of W. H. Hutchinson (Chairman after 1920), and F. S. (later Sir Fred) Button, of the A.S.E., whose interest was keen and continued. But personal friendship with Cole and Mellor accounted for much of this.

[3] No one appears to have found anything ironical in the fact that the largest crop of these local affiliations was secured by means of a circular which offered, additionally, copies of the 1920 revision of the Webbs' *History of Trade Unionism* at a derisory cost; it is another indication that the feud was not fundamental.

Department. In the new year, having outgrown its quarters at Tothill Street, it moved bag and baggage into the Labour Party's new headquarters at Eccleston Square, where it remained for some time; but the scope and temper of its activities were unaffected.

Cole's appointment as research officer to a large union was something quite new in the Labour movement, which had hitherto not merely been unwilling to pay for brains, but had not seen any necessity for specialised skill of that kind.[1] A man's native wits should be sufficient for him to handle negotiations with employers; and if he had ambitions as a politician, say, there were books he could read. But one of the effects of war was to make ordinary life as well as the future more complicated for the simple-minded. Arthur Henderson saw at an early stage the need for fresh and competent thinking, and before ever *Labour and the New Social Order* had come into existence he was discussing with Cole and other intellectuals in or just outside the Fabian Society the formation of a number of voluntary Labour Party advisory committees to work out aspects of Labour policy against the time when it should form a Government; and when in 1919 the Party made up its mind to appoint a secretary for research Cole was the first to hold the post.[2] During the same period he was closely associated with the discussions which resulted in the constitution of the General Council of the T.U.C.

Even closer to day-to-day problems was the hiring of the Labour Research Department by Trade Unions engaged in wage negotiations or disputes to prepare their cases for them, a job which frequently involved a good deal of specialised *ad hoc* research. Details of several of these cases may be found in the pamphlet by Page Arnot already mentioned; the occasion which attracted by far the most public attention was the national railway strike of 1919, when the National Union of Railwaymen, faced with a threat of heavy cuts in railwaymen's wages, invited the L.R.D. to handle the publicity for them, and a lightning press and propaganda campaign organised by Arnot, in which Shaw and Webb as well as the staff of the Department and many others took part, not merely swung public opinion round within

[1] See many instances in Raymond Postgate's *The Builders' History* (1923).

[2] He had been Honorary Secretary of the L.R.D. since 1916, Gillespie having gone into the army, and his successor, G. P. Blizard, serving only for a short while.

a week from almost universal hostility to part-support, but helped to secure a final settlement much better than the original offer. The L.R.D., in fact, during the war and immediate post-war years, was actually fulfilling the Webbs' aspiration of twenty years before of becoming 'clerks to Labour'; and though this side of its work was bound to be gradually superseded as Unions learned to organise their own research departments and fight their own statistical battles before Industrial Courts and Commissions of Enquiry,[1] the reputation so achieved served to keep it alive and working long after it had ceased to be in any other way Fabian.

The workers in the L.R.D., as has been said, were Guildsmen to a man. This book cannot tell the story either of Guild Socialism or the National Guilds League;[2] but, besides the fact that so many Fabians were enrolled, it is necessary for the student of Fabian thought to have some understanding of the way in which the doctrine grew and the causes of its decline.

The semi-syndicalist movement among miners, railwaymen, and dock workers received a great strengthening, early in the war, in what was called roughly 'the engineering industry'. From the angle of Trade Unionism, this was scarcely an industry at all, but a welter of competing craft unions (of which the A.S.E. was only the biggest fish in the pool) more concerned with fighting one another over 'demarcation disputes' than in showing a common front against anyone.[3] The rapid growth of 'engineering' during the war, however, and the inevitable consent of the skilled men to the use of 'dilutees'—semi- and unskilled workers and women—to perform operations hitherto reserved for the skilled, which was effected under the Treasury Agreements and the Munitions of War Acts, rendered essential a coming together of workers of every kind in order to see that the agreements were observed, to maintain wages and conditions of

[1] The outstanding public example being, of course, Ernest Bevin, 'the Dockers' K.C.'. (See Alan Bullock, *Ernest Bevin*, Vol. I, pp. 116 ff.) Bevin never quite forgave the L.R.D. for a tactless (and quite incorrect) suggestion made in the *Labour Leader* that he had had the Department's assistance.

[2] See Carter Goodrich, *op. cit.*, and for the shop stewards and their connection with Guild Socialism see a recent study by Branko Privićević, with preface by G. D. H. Cole, *The Shop Stewards' Movement and Workers Control, 1910–1922* (1959). See also Cole, *Workshop Organisation* (Carnegie Endowment, 1928).

[3] See J. Jeffreys, *The Story of the Engineers* (1945).

employment during the war, and to ensure that there was no barrier to 'the restoration of pre-war practices' when the war should be over. Hence—as the recognised Trade Union machinery was hamstrung partly by the disputes already referred to and partly by the fact that strikes were nominally illegal—the shop steward, hitherto not much more than a dues-collecting agent, became almost overnight a power in the industry. The Shop Steward Movement made its first public impact on the always troubled Clyde, where its leaders were almost all trained in the Socialist Labour Party, a violent 'Industrial Unionist', anti-Parliamentarian organisation inspired by the teachings of Daniel de Leon; but it appeared simultaneously in many other centres such as Sheffield and the Tyne, and by 1917 was already a national movement working out a constitution for itself. The Guild Socialists seized on this locally based organisation as a contributor to their theories of industrial democracy; and to the proposals for National Guilds mentioned earlier was added a demand for 'Collective Contract and Encroaching Control', under which, whether or not an industry or plant were publicly owned, the workers therein, organised in a single body, would bargain as a whole for a collective price for any job they were asked to do, would divide the proceeds according to principles fixed by themselves, would appoint their own foremen and rate-fixers, and generally speaking would wrest bit by bit the functions of management out of the hands of the employers.

This doctrine, which seemed to offer practical fulfilment, in more fields than engineering, for the aspirations towards 'status in industry' and the end of 'wage-slavery' which had inspired so much of the pre-war unrest, caught on very rapidly. Of course, those who considered the matter coolly would have observed that the possibility of 'encroaching control', as much as that of National Guilds, depended (unless there were no resistance, which seemed unlikely) on effective control by the workers' organisations of the supply of labour, i.e. on a situation of full employment. But by 1915–16 there was, as near as no matter, full employment, and shop committees, union branches, I.L.P. branches, etc., all over the country began welcoming Guild Socialist speakers, buying Guild Socialist pamphlets, and passing resolutions on industrial democracy and workers' control. All of this was given a tremendous fillip by events in Russia during 1917, particularly the October Revolution, coming at a time when war-weariness was well developed, and there was a feeling abroad that the workers might make peace—and a new world—in their own way. Several Unions incorporated 'Control of Industry' in their rule-books, as in the days of Owen they had incorporated 'communities'.

Nevertheless, it was the Russian Revolution itself which soon spelt the end of Guild Socialism as an organised movement. Immediately, the Russian factory workers did in fact take over control of the factories, and the resultant chaos was so disastrous that the Bolsheviks quickly put a stop to it and introduced centralised discipline—this fact being underlined when, in 1920, Lenin refused to allow the British Shop Stewards' Committee's application for membership of the Communist International on the grounds that political parties alone were eligible. 'Workers' control', as has subsequently become much clearer than it was then, had no place in a Communist society. That apart, the Revolution itself soon created deep division in the ranks. The majority of Guild Socialists welcomed it as a fulfilment of syndicalist and 'direct action' hopes and were delighted when in 1920 the united Labour and Trade Union movement played at least a considerable part in stopping by threatened strike action Lloyd George's attempt to destroy the Revolution by force; but a few, who hated the reports of physical violence and enforced atheism emanating from Russia, repudiated the Revolution[1] and took refuge in the 'Social Credit' proposals of one Major Douglas; and among the pro-Bolsheviks a further division developed between those who joined the Communist Party of Great Britain on its formation, and those, including Cole and his wife, who while sympathising strongly with revolutions in general remained suspicious of an organisation controlled in the last resort—and after 1923 much more closely—by authority from outside.

To add to this, in 1920–1, the paper post-war boom broke; full employment, and for many any sort of employment, vanished overnight. When the Government subsidy for public housing was withdrawn, the Building Guilds—which had done some very good work—collapsed; after 'Black Friday' (April 15th, 1921) no more was heard of National Guilds for miners, railwaymen,

[1] In this they were supported by several leaders of the I.L.P. and by Mrs Webb, who in *Fabian News* of June 1921 published a fierce denunciation of the Revolution and all its works in the form of a review of a book by M. Philips Price, later M.P. for Forest of Dean.

or transport workers; in the following year the engineering employers roughly pointed the moral by successfully locking out the members of the Amalgamated Engineering Union (the enlarged A.S.E.) for 'interfering with the functions of management'. In the same year the National Guilds League came to an end, and though workers' control propaganda continued for some time to be listened to, particularly in the Workers' Educational Association,[1] in which Cole was a very active tutor, as a practical movement it was dead. It had been killed by a combination of slump and what we have since been taught to call 'democratic centralism'; but later industrial experience, particularly in the nationalised industries since 1945, has shown that many of the questions it propounded remain still unanswered. The Guild Socialists in the L.R.D. continued to work for some time at 'practical' research, i.e. at producing pamphlets and endeavouring to help the unions in their struggles against wage-cuts, along with such Fabians as Bernard Shaw and Barbara Drake[2]—Beatrice Webb's niece, alderman of the L.C.C. and an authority on women's wages and women's organisations—until the determination of the Communists to get control became too strong for them. In December 1921 Arcos, the trading organisation of the U.S.S.R., offered the Department a large annual subsidy, and Shaw and Mrs Drake resigned sooner than accept it. In 1924 Cole, the Honorary Secretary, was needled into resignation; Margaret Cole, a paid servant, followed him in 1925. But for a brief 'all hands to the pump' get-together during the nine days of the General Strike, the L.R.D. from then on had no real connection with Fabianism, though the tradition of research and useful information persisted to an extent sufficient to preserve it from destruction in the most vehement anti-Communist campaigns of Transport House.

[1] The W.E.A., being 'non-party political', was never Fabian; but the influence of such Fabians as R. H. Tawney, the late Lord Lindsay of Birker, J. J. Mallon, long the Warden of Toynbee Hall, and many others, has always been very pervasive. A short-lived journal called *New Standards*, edited by G. D. H. and Margaret Cole, endeavoured for a while to 'marry' the twin causes of workers' education and workers' control; but the response was inadequate.

[2] The ebullient sniping at 'Sidneywebbicalism' (*Punch*) had died down by the end of the war, as mud-slinging in Communist language became a regular feature in discussion.

The Fabian Society to 1920

It remains to link up these two streams in the development of Fabian Socialism with that of the Society itself during the war and immediately post-war years. Much of this, it will be clear, has already been told by implication; and it would be impossible and idle to try to separate out what was done by Fabian Socialists *qua* Fabians, or *qua* advisers of the Labour Party, or *qua* members of the L.R.D. In the field of publication, for example, the tangle is inextricable. All the early products of the L.R.D. appeared under the imprint of the Fabian Society and of George Allen and Unwin, who acted as co-publishers; so did *International Government* and *How to Pay for the War.* At the beginning of 1917 Shaw wrote to the Executive that now was the moment for the Society to issue a republican manifesto, for which he offered the text, and an alarmed meeting proposed as an alternative a committee to discuss 'Empire Reconstruction', to which Shaw agreed; this committee eventually, in 1920, produced a book by H. Duncan Hall, entitled *The British Commonwealth of Nations*, which was very unlike a republican manifesto.[1] A brilliant documented study of imperialism by Leonard Woolf, *Empire and Commerce in Africa*, was begun under the auspices of the Society and 'handed over' to the L.R.D. in 1919; but Tawney's *Sickness of an Acquisitive Society*, perhaps the most powerful of all post-war appeals for Socialism, was published by the Society itself early in 1921. In membership the cross-fertilisation was no less. Most of the older members of the L.R.D., in London at any rate, were also members of the Society; and it may be conjectured that more of the younger ones would have joined but for the fact that until 1919 they were able to make fairly constant use (to the accompaniment of some Fabian grumblings[2]) of the Fabian common-room for chatter and the Fabian Hall for meetings. Fabians, such as were not away at the war or definitely on war work, were taking part in discussions of many kinds, more especially after the setting-up in February 1917, under the chairmanship of Edwin Montagu, of the Reconstruction Committee which became the Ministry of Reconstruction.

[1] Minutes, January 13th, 1917, and *Fabian News*, March 1917.

[2] One of the Research Department's voluntary helpers, Pease indignantly reported, had caused a Fabian letter containing a postal order to be lost by putting it down casually on a window-sill. (Minutes, July 28th, 1916. A sidelight on both Pease and the volunteers.)

Beatrice Webb was a member of that Committee, whose many sub-committees soon became honeycombed with Fabians or what might be termed Fabian fellow-travellers; she herself sitting on the Haldane Committee on the Machinery of Government and the Maclean Committee on the Poor Law, which she quickly converted to produce a version of her own *Minority Report* of nine years back. Education, oddly enough, in view of the Fabians' past, seems not to have concerned them; the Fisher Act came into being without Sidney's aid. The other Reconstruction Reports reek of Fabianism; but little space need be spent on them here, for after the war and its aftermath they all went down the drain as surely as did the Building Guilds and the other Guild Socialist projects.[1] At the time, however, they took up a great deal of time and energy.

The Fabian Society was partly, at any rate, occupied in keeping alive and in keeping open its offices and its newly furnished common-room as a rendezvous for Socialists on leave. Like many other societies in 1914, it wondered for a while whether it would survive financially, many members (apart from the lost university Societies) being unable to keep up subscriptions, and many outside functions having lapsed; in the middle of 1915 Sidney Webb produced an alarmist report on finance and 'deficit'. But nothing very serious happened. The Fabian Lectures, which had begun in 1913 to make a substantial profit, now entered upon their long life as cash-earners (mainly, of course, owing to Shaw); and as people recovered from the immediate shock, hirings of the Fabian Hall began to bring in a modest return. Pease's authoritative *History of the Fabian Society* came out in 1916. But the production of Tracts stopped almost completely; only eleven were issued between the outbreak of war and the Armistice, of which one was a prior commitment, one Webb's pamphlet on *The War and the Workers*, and a third (185) a brief appeal by Beatrice to end the Poor Law; this, however, was on the whole a gain rather than a loss to the immediate finances—in the middle of 1915 it was suggested and agreed that the form of Fabian publications should be 'less repellent'. Sales, however, at the Bookshop increased as the war went on. The Summer School continued to be held, and to flourish, particularly when

[1] See R. S. W. Pollard, *Reconstruction Then and Now* (Fabian Research Series 98, 1945), for the whole melancholy story—re-told then as a warning for the future.

holidays overseas were impossible. Contributions of some size were forthcoming from members and sympathisers, some of whom, such as the Quaker Joseph Rowntree, had earlier helped to finance the Poor Law campaign, both for general work and for special enquiries such as produced *International Government*; and a more melancholy subsidy was received from the estates of some young Fabians killed in action. Possibly, however, the major relief to the finances came indirectly, through the commission taken by Stephen Sanders at the end of 1915, since Pease emerged from his retirement to oversee the work at a cost to the Society of only £5 a month for expenses; as most of the enquiries were by then handed over to the Research Department to answer, his task was not a heavy one.

Differences of opinion about the war itself troubled the Society no more than they did the Research Department. Early on, at the members' meeting of April 1915, a pacifist motion had been defeated, William Mellor (himself a conscientious objector) urging that the Fabian Society was not the right arena in which to fight that battle. The opinions of individuals ranged from the fire-eating Ensor, who wished to see Germany cut into fragments, to Clifford Allen, whose provocative pamphlet, *Is Germany Right?*, was almost, but not quite, banned from the Fabian Bookshop; but they pursued their 'war aims' in their appropriate organisations, the bulk of the Society, as far as can be ascertained, being content to accept the war as a fact and to work for Socialism during and after it. There were a few attempts on the Executive during the war to initiate enquiries, into 'democratisation of the army', for example; but these came to nothing, largely because the available personnel was already fully occupied in the activities described earlier in this chapter.

When peace came, however, the Executive expected it as a matter of course to bring a full revival. Webb drafted new Rules and a new Basis, and in April 1919 the Executive published them both in the *News* with the following call to action:

> There are indications that we are on the eve of a great expansion of Socialist thought and activity, in which the Society can play a useful and distinctive part. The Executive Committee feels that the Society should now put its constitution in order, reorganise its machinery, call upon the members for renewed effort, and develop all the branches of its work, with a view to exercising through an enlarged membership and increased financial resources, all the influence in

these formative years to which its work and its thirty-five years' record entitle it.

The 'indications' included the revulsion from the mood of the khaki general election shown in the local elections of the spring, when several London boroughs went over to Labour, and on the L.C.C. the number of Labour members rose from one to fifteen. Three of the fifteen were Fabians[1]—in addition to those Fabians elected as Progressives—and Emil Davies, most faithful of 'second-generation' Fabians, who succeeded Lawson Dodd as Treasurer in 1936, was chosen as the single Labour alderman.

In May the new Basis was passed, the members' meeting rejecting what Pease calls a 'harmless proposal' to insert words advocating 'a steadily increasing participation of the organised workers in the management both central and local of industries transferred to the community';[2] it was confirmed in December. In July *Fabian News* printed a lengthy 'Scheme of Activities', which included new Tracts, a large growth in membership, a series of Hutchinson Lectures, a Tutorial Class at Westminster on 'The Aims, Policy and History of the Labour Party', etc.

These were brave words; unfortunately, the results did not bear them out. New entrants were only a trickle;[3] and there was no noticeable increase in the provincial organisations, though three university Societies appeared in Cambridge, Glasgow, and the Royal Holloway College. The lectures were duly given, and the tutorial class held; but of Tracts there were only ten issued in three years, of which six were on Local Government, and one a reprint of a lecture by G. D. H. Cole on Guild Socialism. The failure to make a 'revival' deeply disappointed the Executive; but in retrospect the reasons are clear enough. First, and up till 1921 most important, was the fact that the Rebels—the L.R.D. and the Guild Socialists—were still in the field and still recruiting strongly among young Socialists; the Communist Party was not yet born. Secondly, and through the deliberate action of the

[1] Harry Snell, Susan Lawrence, and L. Haden Guest. One of the Labour candidates defeated was Major C. R. Attlee.

[2] Pease, *History*, p. 259. The most important change made in the Basis, apart from some tidying up of phraseology, was the definite commitment of the Society to association with the Labour Party—indicating that 'permeation' was finally dead—and to the International Socialist movement. (Text in Appendix I.)

[3] Membership for the years 1919–20, 1920–1, and 1921–2 (March figures) were: 1,658, 1,707, 1,760.

Fabian leaders, the newly formed local Labour Parties, with their membership open to individuals, were making calls upon the time and energy of those who might otherwise have revived local Fabian Societies in the provinces;[1] even in London the Westminster Labour Party, founded at the end of 1917, with E. J. Howell, the Smart Boy, now grown to the status of Bookshop Manager, as secretary, was enrolling and using a large number of Fabians and potential Fabians. The Westminster Labour Party was Webb's idea, replacing Henderson's rejected suggestion for a 'national' branch of individual Party members; he does not appear to have foreseen that most Fabians would scarcely have time to work actively in the Society as well. A third factor was certainly the loss of the war generation, but this was common to all organisations; much more serious was the personality of the new General Secretary. Pease handed back the office to Sanders when the latter came out of the army, but Sanders did not stay. In the summer of 1920 he took a post in the newly formed International Labour Office; the Executive chose to succeed him F. W. Galton, a Fabian of over fifty who had been one of the Webbs' secretaries when they were working on the history of Trade Unionism twenty-five years earlier.

He is . . . exactly like his old self [wrote Mrs Webb]:[2] strong [she meant physically strong] and full of cheerful energy: he drops his h's as vigorously and defiantly as of old: he dismisses ideas and sentiments with the same goodnatured tolerance to weaker brethren, and he is still a friend and admirer of the Webbs except that he regards them as very distinctly 'Old Folk' who may be a little past their work. He has plans for the Fabian Society and declares that it still has life left in it [*sic*]: but his mind runs on somewhat commercial lines. He scans the new movements and wonders whether they have anything in them. 'I have seen four-and-twenty leaders of revolt' is his attitude towards Cole and Co. . . . He is disgusted with the old political parties, and does not much believe in the Labour Party.

The choice was indeed an unfortunate one, and it is difficult to understand why the Webbs (who, it will be remembered, had headed the Executive polls since 1912) ever came to recommend

[1] They might not, in any event, have received much encouragement from the centre. Pease's *History* states forthrightly that provincial Fabian Societies, other than university Societies, had proved a waste of time and money and had made no contribution to Fabian thought.

[2] *Diary*, June 8th, 1920.

it. Frank Galton was certainly cheerful and amiable, and shrewd as well as cynical; but that fairly sums up his qualities. He had little education; the reminiscences which he wrote remain unpublished because they were so badly written; he could not meet any intellectual on his own ground. His physical strength was due largely to the fact that he had never overtaxed it; Fabians who were young in the 'twenties remember to this day how punctually on the stroke of five he closed the office and departed. Pease may have been gruff and, in his later years, conservative and suspicious of all who were not Sidney Webb; but he was a thinking Socialist who contributed to the Society's output and wrote vigorous English, as both his reviews in the *News* and his Fabian *History* attest. Galton was none of these things; he had not an idea in his head, and in his hands both the *News* and the Annual Report (which were his sole literary contribution to the Society) came to be made up, month by month and year by year, of paragraphs with identical headings whose text was often word for word the same. This lazy repetition gives the impression that the work of the Society was far less and far duller in the 'twenties than in fact it was; its author, a man whose amiability was matched by his obstinacy and who had no views whatever on Socialist policy, was a depressing secretary for a Society hoping to stage a revival among the generation returning from the war.

CHAPTER XV

The Nineteen-Twenties

THE ending of the war was followed, as has many times been told,[1] by a chaotic paper inflation, in which the hopes of Labour, only slightly dashed by the 1918 election, were as inflated as the selling price of cotton mills. Demobilisation riots, the miners' demand for nationalisation which led to the setting up of the Sankey Commission, a national railway strike and even a police strike, the nation-wide protest, given expression by organised labour, which forced the ending of military attack on the Soviet Union—all belong to those two years. After the boom had broken, the story of the Labour movement during the 'twenties is one of industrial defeat and (comparative) political success. In the case of Fabian Socialism, the Fabian Society itself, like other Socialist societies, was mainly concerned with the political fortunes of the Labour Party. The previous chapter mentioned the efforts by Fabians to assist in the creation of local Labour Parties under the new constitution; there are naturally not detailed records of this, but the results of national elections and by-elections, for which the Society raised special funds, as it did for the triennial elections to the L.C.C., are proudly detailed in the *News*. Ten Fabians—eleven, counting Henderson, who got in later at a by-election—were elected to Parliament in November 1922, and formed part of the Party which chose MacDonald as Leader. How the Fabian M.P.s voted is not recorded, but Beatrice Webb's comment was 'if he is not the best man for the post, he is at any rate the worst and most dangerous man out of it',[2] from which it may be concluded that Sidney at any rate supported his election, though MacDonald havered for some time before deciding to invite him to sit on the

[1] Very vividly, for modern readers, in Charles Mowat, *Great Britain Between the Wars* (1955).

[2] *Diaries*, November 23rd, 1922.

Front Bench.[1] Twelve months later the Free Trade versus Tariffs election naturally caused the *News* much greater excitement. Twenty-two Fabians were elected (with Henderson, again, to be added at a later date); of these five—Henderson, Webb, Olivier, Noel-Buxton, and C. B. Thomson[2]—were in the Cabinet; Attlee, Percy Alden, Arthur Greenwood, William Graham, and James Stewart were given minor posts, and several more Fabians became Parliamentary private secretaries. It was a pleasant pendant to the election that on March 14th, 1924, the Society celebrated its fortieth birthday with a dinner, attended by some 230 members and presided over by R. H. Tawney, at which 'the Right Hon. Sidney Webb, M.P., was received with musical honours'.[3] The nature of the music is regrettably not recorded; but the Society may well have felt that a Labour Government, even a minority Labour Government, was a fitting crown to forty years of Fabian effort. So at any rate it seemed to Pease, whose *History* was revised that year, with a lyrical chapter bringing it up to date. Even the Red Letter election at the end of the year removed only five of the twenty-five Fabians from Parliament.

The Fabian Society in the Twenties

It does not appear that the Society as a whole concerned itself much with Labour or Socialist policy in the mid-twenties. Presumably it felt that *Labour and the New Social Order* was enough to be going on with—as indeed did the Labour Party itself until, jabbed by the I.L.P. on its left and faced on the right by the Liberal research and propaganda financed by Lloyd George and published in the *Liberal Yellow Book* and *Orange Book* and elsewhere—giving the Liberals two by-election victories early in 1928—the Party leaders reluctantly admitted that some revamping was called for.[4] Unemployment, remaining at the dreary dead-level of between a million and a half and a million and a

[1] See Webb's contemporary private memoranda on the 1924 Government, first published in the *Political Quarterly* of January 1961.

[2] Secretary for Air in both Labour Governments; perished in the crash of R101.

[3] *News*, April 1924. The Autumn lecture series of 1922 had been entitled, prophetically, *Can Labour Govern?* Unkind people professed to read significance into the title for 1923, which was *Is Civilisation Decaying?*

[4] The result was *Labour and the Nation*—not a very impressive statement of policy notwithstanding Tawney's able writing-up of it, though it was generally assumed to have done the trick as far as the 1929 election was concerned.

quarter out of work year by year, seemed to evoke no Fabian response more practical than the declaratory resolution sent to the International Bureau during the war, that 'the recurrence of any extensive or lasting unemployment in any country is now as much a disgrace to its Government as the occurrence of cholera'—and should be prevented by public works; the sole reference, in the Executive Minutes, is the response to an appeal from the Longsight Unemployed Committee, 'that they be sent some spare pamphlets',[1] which might, in itself, be regarded as callous. It was not until December 1927 that the Executive announced the setting up of a committee in order to draw up a new programme for the Labour Party, whose conclusions would be published in pamphlet form. Four pamphlets (Tracts 227–230)[2] were in fact published in 1929–30; but by then there was a Labour Government in office, and no more was heard of the 'programme'.

There was, in fact, very little sign of discussion of principle at national level. The Annual Conference had ceased to exist early in the war and was never revived, even when a few local Societies had woken up; the annual members' meeting continued, but only on two occasions were any motions brought before it, and one of these, a request to the Labour Party to come to an agreement with the Liberals for mutual withdrawal of Parliamentary candidates in three-cornered fights, was opposed by Laski on behalf of the Executive and collected two votes only. The *News* carried no word of the struggle over Communist affiliation, which was taking up so much time and energy at Labour Party Conferences; in the Executive Minutes the only reference to Communism is a decision (November 19th, 1925) to allow the admission of a member in Birmingham 'if he is not a Communist' —which presumably indicates that the Executive had accepted the ban on Communists imposed in that year by the Labour Party Conference, though in accordance with tradition there was no inquisition into the acts or allegiances of existing members. In the exciting days of the 1926 General Strike the Society played as safe as it had done during the South African

[1] Minutes, July 27th, 1923.

[2] *Labour's Foreign Policy*, by H. M. Swanwick; *National Finance*, by F. W. (now Lord) Pethick Lawrence; *Agriculture and the Labour Party*, by G. T. Garratt; *Imperial Trusteeship*, by Lord Olivier. It may be noticed that the Society had now at length ventured into 'foreign affairs'.

War,[1] though without so much publicity. On May 12th the Executive, invited by letter to state its attitude, decided to reply in effect 'we haven't one'; this reply was not to be printed in the *News* nor submitted to the membership. It would like, the Executive observed, to see the strike settled on fair terms, and a different Government in power; and it passed a resolution expressing sympathy with the Miners' Federation and condemning the Government for 'forcing the strike'. In mid-June, when all was over but the hopeless struggle of the miners, Laski moved an 'urgent' motion at the Annual Meeting condemning without reservation the Government's proposals for settlement, and offering 'warmest sympathy and support' to the M.F.G.B., and *Fabian News* collected subscriptions for the Miners' Relief Fund. At the beginning of 1927 a sub-committee was set up to consider publishing something on the General Strike; nothing came of this, though at the Annual Meeting the Society passed a resolution violently attacking the vindictive Trade Disputes and Trade Unions Bill, and published a pamphlet by W. A. Robson denouncing it in detail.[2]

The only other noteworthy expression of political feeling was a violent outburst of complaint at the end of 1927, when Shaw, having spent eight weeks of his summer holiday at Stresa 'in continuous and flattering interviews with Fascist officials of charming personality and considerable attainments',[3] embarked on a Press controversy with Adler, the secretary of the International, and Gaetano Salvemini, in which he lauded Mussolini and Strong-Man Government.

'We must get the Socialist movement', he declared in a letter to Adler, 'out of its old democratic grooves,' and three days later,

[1] So also, during the war, it had refused to send delegates to the Leeds Soldiers' and Workers' Conference of 1917, and only after a good deal of argument had agreed to appoint representatives to go to Stockholm on Henderson's recommendation.

[2] Tract 222. The Act was repealed *en bloc* by the Labour Government in 1946. The attitude of the Executive over the strike itself, though never put to the membership, would probably have been endorsed. A good few Fabians, including the Webbs, thought the strike lunacy; others, while deploring, would not have condemned; while others again, such as Susan Lawrence, found themselves emotionally committed to the last throw of militant Trade Unionism. See, however, p. 209.

[3] Webb *Diaries*, October 21st, 1927.

We, as Socialists, have nothing to do with liberty. Our message, like Mussolini's, is one of discipline, of service, of ruthless refusal to acknowledge any natural right of competence. . . . *Liberty belongs not to the day's work which it is the business of a Socialist government to organise, but to the day's leisure, as to which there is plenty of room for Liberal activity* [my italics].[1]

He followed this up, in his Fabian Autumn Lecture, by declaring that democracy had proved *incompatible* with Socialism, which could only be brought into existence by a dictator determined to thrust himself forward without scruple. That this was not just a passing bout of impatience was shown by his subsequent praise of Stalin, and, more shockingly, in the last Fabian Lecture he ever gave, when, referring to Hitler, he said that

his efforts had been obscured in this country by the natural indignation and horror at the persecution of the Jews. But he was no mere Titus Oates, and *his violence and brutality were the regrettable but natural retorts to the continual kicking, the exploitation and robbery to which his people had been subjected since 1919.*[2]

By the end of 1933 Socialists had ceased to pay much attention to Shaw's political antics; but in 1927 they were furious, and this public Shavian approval of the Fascists may have helped to inspire contemptuous reviews, by Laski and S. K. Ratcliffe, of *The Intelligent Woman's Guide to Socialism and Capitalism*, which, according to Mrs Webb, put Shaw in 'the devil of a temper' and caused him to come to a Fabian gathering and denounce the Society as 'a collection of dull dogs who could not write English and did not know what they were talking about'.[3] It was quite a little storm, though Shaw's resentment did not lead him to resign or to punish the Society; it was in the middle of 1928, when 25 Tothill Street was condemned to demolition, that he agreed to lend it a substantial sum towards the purchase of its present home in Dartmouth Street, only two or three hundred yards away.[4]

[1] Letters dated 11th and 14th October, 1927; copies in Fabian Society's files. Further letters and leaders in *Manchester Guardian* of October 13th, 19th and 23rd.

[2] *Fabian News*, February 1934. My italics.

[3] *Diaries*, February 20th, 1928. For summary of Shaw's lecture see *News*, January 1928.

[4] He forgave the loan in 1944.

The direct influence of Fabians on the Labour Party is distinctly less noticeable than during the war period. This was partly due to the new constitution and partly owing to the gradual retirement of Webb, who was defeated for the Executive in 1925. Passfield Corner was bought as a 'retreat' in 1923, and it had been generally assumed that the Webbs were going out of politics; this was certainly the view of Beatrice, for whom the first Labour Government (which no one had expected to see for many years) came as an unwelcome break.[1] There was no leading personality to take his place; Harold Laski, first elected to the Fabian Executive in 1921, had yet to rise to prominence. Apart from Laski the best-known members of the Executive who served throughout the decade were Susan Lawrence,[2] the woman M.P. who became a junior Minister in 1929, Harry (afterwards Lord) Snell, the Rationalist who led Labour on the L.C.C. before Herbert Morrison brought it to power, Emil Davies, Barbara Drake, and R. H. Tawney, whose unquestioned eminence was in education rather than politics. The governing committee of the Parliamentary Party always included a number of Fabians; but the Leader had long since ceased from membership and, though as 'gradualist' as anyone, regarded Fabian doctrine and Fabian practice with continued suspicion.

Apart from Sidney's presidential address of 1923, the most distinctively Webbian contribution to the Party in the 'twenties was Mrs Webb's Half-Circle Club. Many years previously, in a letter to the newly-weds,[3] Shaw had casually flung out the suggestion, 'Will Madame Potter-Webb undertake a salon for the social cultivation of the Socialist Party in Parliament?' In 1892 there were only three of these, scarcely adequate material for a *salon*, and when the Labour Representation Committee came

[1] It is noticeable how *Diary* references to the Fabian Society decline in number after 1924.

[2] Susan Lawrence came of a well-to-do family, and sat on the L.C.C. as a Moderate until indignation at the shabby treatment of cleaners in the London schools caused her to change sides. She was also an unpaid organiser for Mary Macarthur's National Federation of Women Workers, a tough, vehement, and emotional fighter—much too emotional for Mrs Webb's taste—and later an excellent *raconteur* of Socialist and Trade Union history. She shared 41 Grosvenor Road with the Webbs from 1925 until they left London altogether, when she took over the house. See the obituary article by Clara Rackham in *Fabian Quarterly*, Spring, 1948.

[3] August 12th, 1892, Webb Collection.

into being the Webbs were engaged with 'permeation'; but the seed had been planted, and germinated with the post-war Labour Party.

The idea [Beatrice wrote][1] arose in my mind in a long talk with Mrs Frank Hodges[2] steaming up the Lake of Geneva at the International Socialist Conference last August. After some shyness she let herself go about the loneliness of her life in London. In Wales she and her husband had their own set, their relatives and childhood friends, they had a complete life together. But since she came to London she lived in complete isolation. She knew no one in her immediate neighbourhood. Frank was always away and was making his own friends. . . . When he came home he was too dead tired to talk about his work or about public affairs. 'I can talk politics as well as anyone else, and the wives of the Labour Party and Trade Union officials feel just the same as I do. Some of them are becoming hostile to the whole Labour movement in consequence.'

This cry enlisted Beatrice's fears as well as her sympathies. She had more than once, in private conversation, dwelt on the danger that the wives of the Labour men might turn out so 'unpresentable' in the circles of their social superiors that they would be left behind in their kitchens as their husbands rose. Even if the phrasing could have been more tactful, the risk, both to politics and to family life, was a real one. So 'I got hold of Mrs Henderson and Mrs Thomas, who happened to be at Geneva, and opened up communication with Mrs Clynes when I got back to London and induced them to issue a private letter asking other Labour women to meet at my house. Hence the Half-Circle Club.' The name was given because it was intended for the principal benefit of one sex only, though of course its object would not have been achieved if men had not been invited to some of the gatherings.

The project did not proceed without difficulty, some of which sheds a light on the attitude of some Labour men towards their womenkind. 'Little dinners' of Labour M.P.s at 41 Grosvenor Road, which had started in 1919, were all very well, but when it came to the women . . . Henderson, notwithstanding that his

[1] *Diary*, July 16th, 1921.

[2] Wife of the Secretary of the Miners' Federation, who lost much of his influence there as a result of the part he played in 'Black Friday'; he became M.P. for Lichfield, and Civil Lord of the Admiralty in the first Labour Government, but soon afterwards went into industry.

own wife was helping to set it up, was dubious, and Egerton Wake, the Labour Party's national organiser, commented bluntly, 'Not all your genius for organising, Mrs Webb, will make the wives of Labour men come out of their homes and hob-nob with the women organisers and the *well-to-do women*' (my italics). There were not wanting, also, voices among the more class-conscious of the Labour wives who resented the hint of patronage and criticism of their manners and bearing (which the promoter would have been wiser to keep to herself); and others thought they detected a flavour of intrigue and 'New Machiavellism'[1] about the project. The latter criticism was entirely without foundation; there is no trace of any desire on Beatrice's part to intrigue with anybody or to influence Labour policy through the wives, her main purpose being to provide some sorely needed social centre for a Party newly come to importance which had nothing of the sort—the hospitality sometimes extended by a few middle-class adherents who had houses large enough for entertainment being clearly inadequate. As such it served very well until in 1924 a Parliamentary Labour Club (itself owing a good deal to Mrs Webb's initiative) more or less superseded it; and nearly forty years later there were those who remembered its *soirées* of coffee, sandwiches, and discussion with affection and gratitude.[2] Mrs Webb herself was naïvely delighted with her protégées.

Mrs Clynes [she wrote][3] turns out to be a woman of strong character and good intelligence. She dresses immaculately [which was more than the diarist did], looks a Duchess! She reads G.B.S. with appreciation and delights in good music. . . . Altogether the 150 women of the Half-Circle Club would compare well, alike in character and intelligence and even in personal charm, with the 150 principal ladies of the Coalition or Free Liberals. There is not the smallest reason

[1] 'You must be very happy,' Ellen Terry had written a generation ago to Bernard Shaw, 'with Mrs Webb to "arrange" you. Do you think she'd arrange *me* if I asked her?' Beatrice's tendency to push people around, always with the best intentions but sometimes with inadequate appraisal of their potentialities, was always liable to set up resistances.

[2] e.g. Mr W. Surrey Dane, in a letter to the present writer.

[3] *Diaries, loc. cit.* Mrs Clynes had, in fact, been known for some time as a personality in the Labour movement, considerably more so than her husband, whom Beatrice described (when he was Leader of the House) as 'a snowdrop shivering in an icy wind'. She would have been quite capable of running any club all by herself.

why they should not become real leaders of society under a Labour Government.

The Fabian Society supported the Half-Circle Club and loaned its common-room for functions as required. It also, while resigned to the non-fulfilment of the large hopes mentioned in the preceding chapter, occupied itself with a number of less grandiose activities. Early in 1922 the Education Group, which had died during the war, was revived by Barbara Drake and Helen Keynes; in the same year the Society succeeded in appointing all the Trustees to the Sara Hall Fund.[1] Promptly the Executive decided to use the Fund for research and discussion of the problems of the Co-operative Movement. Six pamphlets[2] were published in 1922–3, one by Leonard Woolf, two by Webb, one by Lilian Harris, one by Lilian Dawson, the secretary of the Fabian Women's Group, and one by a leading Co-operative politician, Alfred Barnes, who entered Parliament in 1922. Conferences of co-operators and other interested persons were arranged, and the response was said to have been a numerous attendance with keen discussion, though the higher organisations of co-operators remained unmoved, maintaining the attitude of bovine complacency with which that vast movement had received all criticism and all suggestion, including the Webbs' large treatise on co-operation and co-operators published two years earlier.

Much more fruitful and hopeful was the Local Government Bureau, which came into existence a twelvemonth later, also with the aid of a special trust, in this case the Henry Atkinson Fund deriving from a legacy to the Society. The successes in the municipal elections of 1919 had, after a temporary set-back, been followed by a steady series of Labour gains, with the result that there were now sitting, or campaigning for seats, on local Councils, a good many Socialists and Trade Unionists who had little or no experience or knowledge of local government, and

[1] This was an estate left by an old lady who died in 1900 and who was a great admirer of Robert Owen, to be expended for the furtherance of objects which would have interested Owen. Fortunately Owen's interests were wide, but for twenty years the application of the Fund to Fabian interests was frustrated, as Pease reported to the Executive, by an obstinate solicitor. When he died, the Fabians took over an annual income of £300–£400, which was for some years used to finance a lecturer on co-operation at Ruskin College.

[2] Tracts 201–206.

very little idea of what a Borough Council or other body could do, how it should set about doing it, or how the Borough or other Councillor could tackle the various problems brought to him by his constituents. In order to fill that gap, and also to 'permeate' sympathetic officers with the ideas of the Fabian Municipal Programme, the Society, in October 1923, in co-operation with the Labour Party, established a Local Government Information Bureau, with W. A. Robson as its part-time secretary, and started a penny journal, the *Local Government News*, which appeared ten times in the year. (The Labour Party was given the option of taking the Bureau over completely at the end of two years; but did not exercise it.)

For some years both the Bureau and the *News* were very successful; the latter was enlarged before a year had passed and reached a circulation of 2,000 copies. It printed regularly summaries of legislation, of Ministerial decisions and Circulars, of court cases, of local government statistics, and of questions in Parliament; it answered queries and reviewed important books; it gave news of local government in other countries, particularly the United States; and it published a great number of informed and critical articles, both on the day-to-day problems of municipal life, such as the conduct of elections, the organisation of staff, the superannuation of officers, and the behaviour of the District Auditor—a special *bête noire* of Robson's—as well as on all aspects of 'municipal enterprise', from concerts and libraries to cemeteries, swimming baths, and the design of petrol stations. Shaw gave a highly individual contribution on Public Libraries, in which he declared that libraries ought to be nearly empty, for if they were full of people it showed that they were supplying low-class periodicals and other such 'mere' reading matter; and Robson, under the title of 'Local Government in Poetry', reproduced parts of Crabbe's *The Borough* for the benefit of his readers. Indignant attacks were printed on the surcharges made on the Poplar Borough Council for fixing wage-rates at levels disapproved by the District Auditor and on cuts in public education proposed by Lord Eustace Percy after the return to the Gold Standard; the *News* was, in fact, a Fabian guide and policy-promoter on municipal affairs.

Unfortunately, the financial support accorded to the Bureau did not measure up to its usefulness. The *News* did not cover its costs; and though when the original subsidy was exhausted help was forthcoming from E. D. Simon and Noel-Buxton (later Lord Noel-Buxton), one of the most eminent of the Liberals who had come over to Labour during the war, difficulties continued. Early in 1928 a Municipal Information Bureau was set up, which for five shillings per annum offered to supply the *News*, a copy of all new Fabian pamphlets on local government, and to answer questions. 'Over 100' subscribed; but at five shillings a time this did not go far to meet the gap. In January 1930 the format was changed and the size reduced; twelve months later the size was again reduced and the price doubled, and in December 1931 the sponsoring bodies succumbed to fear induced by the 'crisis', and in a disgusted article[1] Robson announced its demise.

There were four Tracts on local government for subscribers, Nos. 214, 218, 225, and 231, the last being Webb's exposition of the 1929 Local Government Act which by abolishing the *ad hoc* Guardians of the Poor implemented a small part of the *Minority Report*. Just previously there had appeared a long and vigorous programme for the improvement of State education.[2] The output of publications in the mid-twenties was in fact considerable; in addition to those already mentioned there were four biographical Tracts, *William Lovett* by Barbara Hammond, co-author of the *Town Labourer*, *William Cobbett* by Cole, *Tom Paine* by Kingsley Martin, and *Jeremy Bentham* by Victor Cohen. Laski contributed no fewer than five; there were two political ones, on compulsory voting and proportional representation, and several others, including reprints of Webb's presidential address,[3] of Dr Charles Childe's similar address to the B.M.A. Conference,[3] and of a highly Shavian lecture on the League of Nations;[3] longer contributions were published, as earlier, in the form of booklets, of which Laski's study of Marx was the most important. Pease's revised *History* has already been mentioned.

This adds up to a not unimpressive total, though it does not, of course, compare with the remarkable spate of the years just before the war; and the sales, of both the new and the older publications, appear to have been satisfactory. Lectures, particularly the Autumn Lectures,[4] collected large audiences; book-boxes

[1] See p. 215. [2] Tract 198, by Barbara Drake.

[3] Tract 207, *The Labour Party on the Threshold*; Tract 208, *Environment and Health*; Tract 226, *The League of Nations*.

[4] The Autumn Lectures, given at the King's Hall, Covent Garden, and after 1924 at the Kingsway Hall, with Shaw regularly winding up, had begun

and travelling speakers were sent into the provinces, and questions answered. But there is no doubt that the Society's impact on the outside world was declining; the membership figures alone tell their own tale. As early as September 1923 the Executive was admitting publicly that the membership was not increasing commensurately with the work done, and trying to account for this distressing fact; it remained practically stationary, throughout the period, at round about 1,800 all told, including the membership of the (comparatively few) provincial Societies. There were short-lived spurts following the general elections of 1924 and 1929; but the gains then made were offset by 'purges' reluctantly undertaken of those whose addresses had been lost or who persistently omitted to pay subscriptions. Of the thousands who bought tickets for—and attended—the Autumn Lectures very few stayed to join the Society; they had paid for their entertainment and departed. The Summer School, between 1922 and 1926 at all events, had to compete with the attractions of the I.L.P. Summer School, during the period when the organising genius of Clifford Allen, first as treasurer and then as chairman, was working that body up to an imposing size, making a strong appeal, particularly at the Schools held in Lady Warwick's Easton Lodge, to left-wing intellectuals of the middle class; the Fabian School complained that neither the General Secretary nor the Executive took any interest in it. The 'permeating' type of Fabian, on the other hand, was tending to find his propagandist satisfaction in the League of Nations Union, which until the beginning of the 'thirties was supported by an idealistic enthusiasm hardly to be credited by those who have been reared in the cynical hard-bargaining atmosphere of the 'United Nations'.[1]

Stagnant membership, combined with expensive activity, spelt financial crisis and debt. In 1924, when the accumulated deficit had reached £800, and a special appeal was issued to members, the Executive was informed that the annual salary bill was

to pay in 1913; there were also post-Christmas series—in the early 'thirties one of these was given by Oswald Mosley, and William Joyce, afterwards executed for treason, debated with A. L. Rowse—and courses arranged by groups such as the Women's Group, but these were not expected to make money.

[1] See, for example, Sir Alfred Zimmern's book, *The League of Nations and the Rule of Man*. Few now remember how near the League of Nations seemed to be to success, in 1929.

£1,337, of which the General Secretary got £600 and five others shared the rest between them,[1] while the income from subscriptions was only £1,005; notwithstanding the revenue from lectures, books, trust funds, and some investments, this seems an unfortunately large disparity.

Some part of the decline was due, I have suggested, to the unimaginative routine-following mind of Galton himself; it was certainly not lack of zeal and loyalty on the part of the existing membership. Publications and lectures have already been mentioned; the deficit was cleared—and cleared again four years later—by special gifts from the better-off. In January 1922 the Fabian Nursery which, like the old Education Group, had faded away during the war, was re-formed, with a flourish of trumpets, an annual subscription of a shilling, Ernest Davies, son of Emil Davies, and later M.P., as its first secretary, and W. A. Robson and Anne Corner (sister of Sir John Squire) on its committee.

> Young Fabians awake! [its manifesto said]. An opportunity awaits you. No matter where your talent lies the Fabian Nursery will appreciate it. If you have a new constitution, a new credit scheme, or what you will, we will let you lay it before us. . . . Do you act? We will give you training. Do you write? We want a revue; or perhaps, if you lend us your talent young Fabian Essays may one day appear.[2]

A little later it was announcing that having taken two months to dispose of Guild Socialism and the Douglas Credit Scheme and to settle the affairs of Egypt, it would now 'tackle Webbism and solve the problems of India', and was asking fellow-Fabians to 'tell your children and the children of your friends about its existence, and thus help to bring up the adolescents of Great Britain in the way of truth'.[3]

Gallant words, even if an upper age-limit of thirty-five does not exactly suggest 'adolescence'; and the Nursery, enrolling somewhere between 150 and 200 members, did bring a brightness into the Fabian records. It sang songs; it gave a revue, and a musical show called *Tothill Nights*; it ran week-end and Easter Schools on the Continent; it twice repainted the Fabian Hall with its own hands; it arranged 'rambles' and other expeditions;[4]

[1] Minutes, April 11th, 1924.

[2] *News*, January and March 1922. [3] *Ibid.*

[4] Once to meet at Beaconsfield and travel on a Mystery Train—maximum fare two shillings. Those were the days!

it camped (appropriately) on a meadow belonging to a don at Oxford. It worked hard, withal; it set up study groups and arranged debates; at the end of 1927 it was instructing its members to read the reports of the Colwyn Committee on National Debt and Taxation—a moderately stiff assignment; it tried to write a collective Tract, but was turned down by the Executive. It had a good many ups and downs, its membership at one time falling as low as twenty-five; but it managed to survive until the second world war.

In 1925 it ran into a tea-cup storm. For some reason, which appears to have been connected with a 'research programme', its secretary quarrelled with the committee, and resigned; when this was reported to the members they reinstated the secretary, whereupon the committee, led by Robson, resigned *en bloc*, and decided to form a New Fabian Group; the Executive, apprised of these happenings, took the news calmly, and agreed to 'recognise' both parties for representation on it; both presented regular reports for inclusion in *Fabian News*. The New Fabian Group, reaching at its peak a membership of seventy-odd, took itself very seriously—though it did occasionally deign to 'ramble'; it formed six study groups, and proposed to run a journal, *The Cunctator*, of which only one issue seems ever to have appeared; it collected some young members of distinction from universities—Colin Clark read a paper to it in 1928; it had a Research Organiser and a Pamphlet Committee. Not a very great deal came out of all this, however, except a few publications. A Tract by Lionel Elvin, now Director of the London University Institute of Education, was rejected by the Executive; Tracts on *Jeremy Bentham* and on *Seditious Offences*[1] were published, and the third effort by a Group member, Robson's *Socialism and the Standardised Life* (Tract 219), with its attack on the standardisation produced by the class system, anticipates much of what was said thirty years later in *The Organisation Man* and similar criticisms of American life, and well bears re-reading today. But the Group's own confession of faith, *A Socialist Philosophy for Fabians*, was a very thin and halting production; Laski, called upon to write a preface, could say no better for it than that 'Mr Fraser and his colleagues have, it is clear, an inspiration and an outlook far more complicated than the [Fabian] essayists. . . . Most of its readers will, I think, agree that it is a beginning of real

[1] Tract 220, by E. J. C. Neep (1926).

promise.'[1] At the time when this faint praise appeared the Group was dying; in the following month it was dissolved 'for lack of support'.

'Fabianism' in Oxford

'Rebel' Fabianism had come to an end as a movement by 1925. Guild Socialism had long been a lost cause, despite the last-minute support of the I.L.P., whose 1922 Conference carried a resolution in favour of workers' control in industry. This was due to the influence of Clifford Allen, himself a Guildsman, whose four-year leadership of the I.L.P. began that year. Allen's leadership was vigorous, if a trifle tortuous; he devised a plan whereby the I.L.P. should fight Parliamentary seats on a series of *ad hoc* programmes, tailored to suit the interests of each constituency, while an inner ring of leaders of revolutionary faith was to be prepared, when sufficient seats were won, to take control and unflinchingly establish a Socialist State.[2] This curious version of Leninism was not at all well adapted to a body like the I.L.P., and nothing came of it; nevertheless, Allen's enthusiasm, and his unique gifts as a money-raiser, lifted the number of I.L.P. branches within a year or two from 600 to over 1,000, turned its organ, the *New Leader*, under the editorship of H. N. Brailsford and the management of Dick Plummer (now Sir Leslie Plummer, M.P.), into a brilliant propagandist journal, and made considerable Socialist converts from the middle classes.

The older I.L.P. leaders did not appreciate the workers' control resolution. 'At least it won't make any difference to *our* propaganda,' growled Philip Snowden. Nor did it, to any noticeable extent. The policy of *Socialism in Our Time* and *The Living Wage*, produced in 1925–6, which was the I.L.P.'s contribution to the politics of the 'twenties, though drafted by the able quartet consisting of J. A. Hobson, Brailsford, Arthur

[1] Tract 234, December 1930, edited by R. Fraser—now Sir Robert Fraser of Independent Television.

[2] M. A. Hamilton, *Remembering My Good Friends*. See also Fenner Brockway, *Inside the Left*. Allen's leadership ended in 1925, when the I.L.P. decided to quarrel with MacDonald and turned him out of the editorship of the *Socialist Review*. Allen had by that time decided that MacDonald was indispensable, and thereafter followed him to the end of his career; the leadership of the I.L.P. was taken over by James Maxton, who led it rapidly into the wilderness.

Creech Jones, and Frank Wise, the ex-civil servant on the staff of the Russian Centrosoyus, of whom the first two had been ardent Guildsmen, contained little that was distinctively Guild Socialist—or Fabian for the matter of that. The Labour Research Department had passed lock, stock, and barrel under Communist control. Cole himself, it seemed, had turned aside from politics; he had removed himself from London to the retreat of Oxford University, and was producing detective novels and a Life of Cobbett. Beatrice Webb, in 1924, confided to her *Diary* that Cole was finished.

This proved to be a misjudgment, though disappointment with the London political scene certainly played a part in the move to Oxford. But what Mrs Webb failed to appreciate was that before leaving London Cole had spent four years in service to the adult education movement, with which he had been continuously connected since before the war. In 1921 he became the first full-time Tutorial Class Tutor in the University of London and created the professional Tutors' Association (of which Margaret Cole was later London secretary). He thus joined the great company of leaders of working-class education which included Albert Mansbridge, the founder of the Workers' Educational Association, A. D. Lindsay, Tawney, J. J. Mallon, Arthur Greenwood, Lord Privy Seal in the 1945 Government, and many others;[1] and while he in no way used his classes for propagandist ends, his views were of course well known, and his influence was spread and consolidated in the many conferences of Trade Union branches and other working-class bodies addressed by him under W.E.A. auspices; conversely, his own development, and his effect on Fabian thought after he had rejoined the Society, owed much to what he had learned from those discussions.

He did not give up working-class education when he returned to Oxford; but he added to it, and to his 'straight' teaching as Reader in Economics, a field of activity, small at first, among the undergraduate population. Almost immediately upon his arrival there he and the writer began to invite undergraduates of radical and Socialist leanings to their house in Holywell for weekly dis-

[1] The W.E.A. is of course 'non-party political'. But the social status and experience of its students and its membership have always meant that the vast majority were on the radical side—and not only in matters educational. A very large number of the M.P.s of 1945 looked back to the W.E.A. class as their 'university education'.

THE LABOUR CABINET, 1924

Left to right, seated: W. Adamson, Lord Parmoor, Philip Snowden, Lord Haldane, J. R. MacDonald, J. R. Clynes, J. H. Thomas, Arthur Henderson. Standing: Sir Charles Trevelyan, Stephen Walsh, Lord Thomson, Lord Chelmsford, Lord Olivier, Noel Buxton, Josiah Wedgwood, Vernon Hartshorn, Tom Shaw. Behind: Sidney Webb, John Wheatley, Fred Jowett.

William Heinemann Ltd and the Ashmolean

Sidney Webb on his birthday by Max Beerbohm from *A Survey* (1921)

cussions on Monday evenings. There was nothing, in the beginning, particularly novel about this. Tawney and Lindsay, to take two names only, had long concerned themselves to discuss social and philosophical problems with their pupils and others; it was the 'left-wing' aspect of the concern with politics which has always been the tradition of Oxford, above all other universities. It was commonly believed, between the wars, that the destinies of England were settled in the common-room of All Souls; conversely, when the Oxford Union declared that it would not fight for King and Country there was a nation-wide furore. (The Cambridge Union—*pace* the good Socialists who have come out of Cambridge—can vote what it pleases, and no one takes much notice.) The 'Cole Group', as it came to be called many years afterwards, was, however, more important than would have been guessed at the moment of its foundation, for several reasons. First, because it was so long-lasting; it provided the initial personnel for the movement described in the next chapter, without which it is doubtful whether there would have been any revival of the Fabian Society in the 'forties; and as it endured, renewed year by year by fresh generations of undergraduates, until its founder's retirement, it resulted in a continuity of Socialist discussion in Oxford which was not to be found in any other university. Secondly, because its beginning coincided very nearly with the arrival at maturity of the first really post-war (and very remarkable) generation of young men and women; thirdly, because it had barely come into being when its members were brought sharply up against reality by the outbreak in 1926 of the General Strike.

The drama of the General Strike, coming right in the middle of the post-war world, the world of the Bright Young Things and *The Boy Friend*, was certain to wake up, on one side or the other, the young members of the university. For the majority, of course, it was a rousing and unexpected call to Save the Country, in pleasant and picnic fashion, from the perils of Bolshevism, Anarchism, and Trade Unionism (regarded as much the same thing). But the workers who marched out with such astonishing unanimity on the morning of May 4th were moved not only by the economic fear of the general attack on wages already in progress, but by a conviction that the miners had been twice betrayed, first by Lloyd George and Bonar Law in their refusal to honour the pledge to carry out the Sankey Report 'in the spirit and in the letter' and again by their own Union comrades on 'Black Friday': this feeling of shame was intensified by the Government's decision to treat the 'purely industrial struggle' (J. H. Thomas, the railwaymen's leader) as a threat to society which must be fought to a finish, and particularly by the belligerent attitudes struck by Churchill, the creator of the strike-breaking Organisation for the Maintenance of Supplies and editor of the fire-eating *British Gazette*. As Hugh Dalton, himself no ultra-revolutionary, wrote, 'In this struggle, so sharply joined, between "the masters" and "the men" it was impossible for any generous spirit to be emotionally on the side of "the masters".'[1] The 'Cole Group', and a good few outside it, were among those who were emotionally so moved.

To be moved, however, was clearly not enough. In face of the urgent appeals being made by the O.M.S. to undergraduates and others to come forward in the national emergency and volunteer to drive cars, trains, buses, unload cargoes at the docks, etc., it was clear that if something more positive than emotional sympathy were not demanded of the 'generous-minded' they too would soon be away on this exciting mission. Accordingly, there was formed in Holywell a 'University Strike Committee', co-operating with its counterpart in the city; and throughout the nine days of the strike this committee worked full time, drawing in many who were not members of the original group. It wrote, duplicated, and distributed leaflets; it sent speakers out through the city and into the surrounding villages; it arranged to ferry from London copies of the T.U.C.'s *British Worker*, and to keep liaison between the Oxford strikers and the T.U.C. headquarters in Eccleston Square. It was a baptism in the rough waters of politics and organisation for the Oxford Socialists, and its effects long outlasted the strike itself.

[1] *Call Back Yesterday* (1953), p. 164. See also my *Growing Up into Revolution*, Chapter 8. There is a good account of the General Strike, with full bibliography, in Mowat's *Great Britain Between the Wars*. Julian Symons's more recent *The General Strike* contains more detail, but is inadequate on the historical background. There were several contemporary accounts; but the most vivid presentation of the feelings of the time is to be found in G. D. H. Cole's unpublished 'Operetta', *The Striker Stricken*, which presented the miners, the leaders of the T.U.C., and the Government in satire and song. (Copy in the Cole Collection in the library of Nuffield College.) For the effects of the defeat on Trade Unionism, the best recent account is in Alan Bullock's *Life and Times of Ernest Bevin*.

For when the strike, with its demonstration of amazing working-class solidarity, and inept and confused working-class leadership, had ended in the complete defeat which, given the attitude taken by the Government and upheld by the lawyers, was pretty soon recognised to have been inevitable, a serious rethinking of Socialist policy, Fabian or non-Fabian, was bound to follow. The 'myths' of Georges Sorel, the Syndicalists, the Industrial Unionists, and 'Direct-Actionists' in general, died once and for all. No 'purely industrial struggle' in future had any hope of achieving fundamental change, even had the Trade Unions, with their funds depleted and their membership falling, the penalties of the 1927 Trade Disputes and Trade Unions Act hanging over them, been willing to try another fall. No more was heard of sympathetic strikes or strikes with a political flavour; the strikes of the years after 1927 *were* 'purely industrial disputes', with the Communists fishing as they could in troubled waters. In some of the foreign-policy debates of the next decade, it is true, there were heard pre-war echoes of 'a strike against war', but these were nostalgic murmurs merely; thenceforward it was political and Parliamentary action or none.

It was in this atmosphere that the young organisers of the University Strike Committee continued their discussions, and it is of importance, for later history, that they included a number of unusually able young men. Intellectual ability, in Oxford, seems to run in generations; one, just prior to 1914, had produced Cole, Mellor, Ivor Brown, and the other Guild Socialists of whom so many fell in the war, and another, twenty years earlier, the brilliant group of which Hilaire Belloc and J. L. Hammond were members, immortalised in Belloc's poem on 'Balliol Men'; this, the third, was of no less distinction. The best-known of them today is Hugh Gaitskell, one-time Chancellor of the Exchequer, and now Leader of the Labour Party, who was a pupil of Cole's;[1] they included Colin Clark, most adventurous of professional economists, later to be adviser to the Government of Queensland and head of the Department of Agricultural Economics at Oxford, John Parker, M.P., whom we shall meet again, John Dugdale, M.P., afterwards secretary to Lord Attlee and Minister of State for the Colonies (who when 'coming up' to

[1] He did not, however, join the Group until the General Strike had shown him where his sympathies lay. See his chapter in Briggs and Saville, *Essays in Labour History* (1959).

Oxford had met Cole in the train and peremptorily demanded to be taken on as his pupil), Evan Durbin, also in office in the 1945 Government, whose book on *The Politics of Democratic Socialism* continued to influence young men for years after his untimely death, Lord Listowel, Governor-General of Ghana at the time of writing, Michael Stewart, M.P., the Labour Party's authority on education, and other Labour politicians of the future, as well as others who became civil servants or university professors (sometimes both) and poets of the calibre of John Betjeman and Wystan Auden. All these future shapers of policy, stimulated rather than shattered by the experience of 1926, were engaged during the years immediately following in deep and ranging though informal discussions, of the kind of problems which might confront a Socialist Government at some time in the future, and the way in which they might be solved; in this discussion of non-revolutionary procedures they had the full collaboration of the man who had originally called them together.

For the events of 1926 had considerably affected the thought of Cole himself, following as they did upon the heels of his breach with the Communists of the Labour Research Department. He had long ceased from open opposition to the Webbs—who, for their part, had distinctly modified their earlier unqualified hostility to workshop representation of any kind; and he and his wife had stayed several times at Passfield Corner. In 1928, after lecturing at the Fabian Summer School, he rejoined the Society; in the following year he delivered an Autumn Lecture, with Beatrice Webb in the chair, in which he explained that he now hoped to meet the aspirations of the workers in industry by schemes 'practical rather than idealistic';[1] and almost simultaneously he published a long book, *The Next Ten Years in British Social and Economic Policy*, in which he set out a series of reforms which might well have been put into effect, without any industrial action, by a determined Labour Government possessed of an adequate majority and blessed with a favourable economic situation. In the preface to this book he expressed the opinion that 'Pre-war Socialism could afford to seek after perfection, because it was not in a hurry; post-war Socialism needs practical results', and thanked the Webbs for 'suggestions made for improvement' while the work was in progress; and in 1930, at their and Henderson's instigation, he actually took on a Parlia-

[1] *Fabian News*, December 1929.

mentary candidature, although ill-health—the onset of the disease which afflicted him for the rest of his life—forced him to give it up in the following year. Several of the Oxford Group, notably Clark and Parker, joined the Fabian Society, and by 1929 there might have seemed no reason why the two streams should not come together again. But for several reasons, of which, ironically enough, the second Labour Government was one, this development was delayed for another decade.

CHAPTER XVI

The Nineteen-Thirties

The Decade of Frustration

FOR the general historian the 'thirties, that dolorous decade, begin with the Great Slump, with the fall of the second Labour Government and the Weimar Republic, the triumph of reaction and Fascism in one country after another[1]—with war at the end of the road. The student of British Socialism, however, sees the story starting a few years earlier, even before Labour took office.

Right up to election day, in the summer of 1929, few if any had expected to see another Labour Government in the near future. Baldwin himself, as his biographer G. M. Young has related, was astonished and disappointed when his election cry of Safety First and the posters inviting the voters to trust the Man with the Pipe in his mouth failed of their effect; for the 1924 Government had ended in a fall so ignominious as to suggest to the well-informed that Churchill was right and Labour really Unfit to Govern. The industrial movement was down and out, the political movement helpless to stop the passage of the Trade Disputes Act; if there were any serious rival to the Tories it was thought to be the Liberals, armed with the Lloyd George propaganda and with what was made available of Lloyd George's million-pound election fund. Few realised the resentment that was building up against the post-strike behaviour of the Government and its failure to do anything about the long-continued unemployment; but on election day Labour proved in effect to have stolen Lloyd George's slogan, 'We Can Conquer Unemployment', and was returned with a Parliamentary following which made office inevitable.

[1] Not in the U.S.A., where it was the Republicans who were swept away in the storm—a fact used by apologists for the British Cabinet, who maintain that, had the Tories been in power in 1931, they would have crashed as surely as did Labour.

But in fact the slogan had been stolen, not thought out by Labour. Practically nothing had been done in the intervening years, in official Labour circles, to think out policy afresh or to grapple with the problems which would have certainly presented themselves, however the economic future had turned out. It seems to have been more or less assumed that the first Labour Government had done pretty well in spite of its handicaps—as was not far from the truth[1]—and that all that was necessary was to proceed on the same lines with a clear majority, whenever that should come about. The Labour Party had a Research Secretary, but no Research Department worth the name, and the Advisory Committees set up in the first flush of reorganisation by Webb and Henderson which, eager amateurs though some of them were,[2] were at least better than nothing, had been allowed to fall into decay. W. A. Robson, in the article in the *Local Government News* already referred to, angrily recounted the fate of one of them.

Extended provision [he wrote] in regard to education, housing, public health services—these are three of the main planks in Labour policy. Yet the Parliamentary Labour Party and Transport House have never been fundamentally interested in the municipal instruments by which these services are administered. . . .

The Local Government Advisory Committee, of which I am a member, has not met for some years. . . . The last occasion on which it did meet was for the purpose of rushing through a recommendation [on 'Travelling time' for local Councillors] which somebody wanted the Executive to have . . . as if the House of Commons was prorogued for seven years and then summoned in order to consider the price of admission to Kew Gardens. . . .

. . . [it] never met once even during the passage of the 1929 Local Government Act. . . . It is not in the true interests of the Labour Movement [he ended] to smother the criticism of the past two and a half years which every intelligent supporter of the Party feels to be unavoidable.

This general intellectual inertia was not, of course, altogether deliberate, though there is plenty of evidence that MacDonald's

[1] See a friendly and careful appraisal in Professor Lyman's book, *The First Labour Government*, and the memorandum by Webb mentioned on p. 194.

[2] One of them, the Rural Advisory Committee, began by taking the advice of its three agricultural members and sending in a memorandum asking for protection for agriculture, which naturally, in 1920, scandalised Henderson into all but disbanding the lot of them. Its secretary was the present author.

preference for eloquent and cloudy sentiments as against hard and sometimes inconvenient facts was growing rapidly. But the shortness of the interval between 1924 and 1929 meant that not only had there been no reappraisement of programme and policy, there had been no reappraisement of leadership either. The second Labour Government was more firmly based than the first; it did not need to call upon experts from outside, such as Lord Chelmsford, to man offices of State. But it was headed essentially by the same people, Bourbons who saw no need for any different line to be pursued;[1] and the junior Ministers and the flock of new members who wanted to see something new soon found themselves struggling in a bog. Well before the tide of unemployment, for which they had so cheerfully promised a cure, overwhelmed them, doubling in volume in two years, Mary Agnes Hamilton, member for the depressed town of Blackburn, was noting that from beginning to end unemployment 'dominated our lives' at Westminster,[2] and the I.L.P.'s 'forward' policy had little or no effect. A hundred and ninety-seven of the Members of Parliament were members of the I.L.P.; but when the latter's executive committee, under Maxton's leadership, attempted to make them into a disciplined force acting as a Party within a Party, pledged to the policy of the I.L.P., it rapidly became clear where the allegiance of the great majority of them lay, and the few who accepted the discipline were manœuvred, first into quarrelling with the mass of the Labour Party, and finally, soon after the crash, into disaffiliation. The education projects of the Government were killed by sectarian opposition; and though there were some mildly useful measures put through with Liberal aid during the first year or so, the record, apart from the fine and strenuous effort put in by Arthur Henderson at the Foreign Office,[3] makes uninspiring and (until the very end) uninteresting reading.

[1] There is no indication that Webb was any exception—not that MacDonald consulted him. But, as I have already indicated, the Webbs were really on their way out of politics by the end of the 'twenties. For them, Sidney's second term of office was an interlude, and not a happy one, even if the disasters in Palestine were scarcely his fault. 'People will say,' he said to his wife, with unusual pessimism, 'that your husband has not been a success as a Minister.' He was correct.

[2] *Remembering My Good Friends*, p. 184.

[3] Which had the unfortunate incidental result that the organisation of the Labour Party, of which he retained the secretaryship, was almost completely neglected. When he returned to it he was an exhausted and a dying man.

After the deluge and the ensuing confusion of explanation—not altogether unlike the confusion of 1959, since, after the first shock had passed, few really believed that the defection of three leaders with a few followers, however venomously expressed by Philip Snowden, was an adequate explanation of the overwhelming vote—there followed the dismal story of unemployment without precedent, Walter Greenwood's *Love on the Dole*, hunger-marchers, and Ellen Wilkinson's *Jarrow*, *The Town that was Murdered*; and as the state of trade gradually and almost imperceptibly improved a little, so did the international sky darken, the Japanese in China, the Fascists in Austria, the Nazis in the Saar and the Rhineland, Right and Left clashing *en pleine vue* in the Spanish Civil War—these being only a few of the highlights which pointed, as anyone could afterwards observe, to Munich, Prague, and Danzig. The political story of Labour and Socialism during those years is of pathetically hopeful but unsuccessful little combinations, Popular Fronts, United Fronts, Five-Point Groups, People's Charter Groups, National Petition Groups, and the like, all now forgotten, all trying in their various ways to create some common resistance to the march of Fascism, and all breaking themselves, apparently upon the refusal of the leaders of the established parties (excepting of course the Communists) to have anything to do with them, and in reality on the deep reluctance of the British people to realise that the world war was not, as for at least a dozen years after its ending most of them had believed, the last, but only a prelude to another and to civil wars all over the world. Only the L.C.C. election of 1934, when Herbert Morrison led the London Labour Party to a victory so lasting as later to deceive some optimists into the belief that the national Labour victory of 1945 might be as permanent, showed any solid gain for radicalism; what that admirable journalist and war correspondent Henry Nevinson called 'the Stage-Army of the Good' was in a very poor way.

Concurrently, however, there was growing, mainly as a result of the patent scandals of depression, of 'over-production', ploughing-in of crops and burning of coffee, coupled with revelations about the standard of living, not only of the unemployed but of their fellows in work, a rousing of the social conscience as it had been roused in the long-ago days of the 'eighties and again in the early years of the century. Books like the Pilgrim Trust's *Men Without Work*, Robert Sinclair's *Metropolitan Man*, Sir John Boyd

Orr's *Food, Health and Income*, and publications of the impeccably respectable British Medical Association,[1] proved beyond criticism that there were still, nearly a hundred years after Disraeli, Two Nations in Britain, of which the smaller still flourished, albeit with rather less sumptuous glitter, on the poverty of the larger, and that the 'generous spirits' mentioned by Dalton had Robert Blatchford's work to do all over again. As some of those who were young then recalled twenty years later with something like nostalgia, in the 'thirties, particularly after the outbreak of the Spanish War, and the growth of the Left Book Club (founded in 1936) to an astonishingly large membership, 'in the 'thirties you at least knew where you were; Left was Left and Right was Right, and Right was *wrong*'. But little happened until war dissolved the frozen pattern.

The Fabian Society in Stagnation

The story of the Fabian Society proper, during these years, can be very briefly told, for it is one of inertia amounting almost to complete stagnation. All the factors listed in the last chapter, including the activities, or rather absence of any activity, on the part of the General Secretary, were still operating; but the records give no indication of any new idea or new leadership to counteract them. In July 1929 the *News* rejoiced greatly, and not without reason, at the election results—forty-seven out of ninety-nine Fabian candidates[2] successful, eight Fabians in the Cabinet, eleven in office as under-secretaries; a small rush of new entrants to the Society appeared in the next few months, and in April 1930 there is a satisfied reference to the growth of Socialism in Oxford contained in a notice of a pamphlet called *Red Oxford*, by C. T. Saunders and Maurice Ashley (members both of the Fabian Society and the 'Cole Group'). Thereafter there is no reference at all to the Labour Government or its doings until November 1931, when it was reported that of the eighty-six

[1] Most of these were summarised in *The Condition of Britain*, by G. D. H. and M. I. Cole (1937). They did not show that the condition of the working class as a whole had fallen, for owing to the break in world prices it had in fact risen over twenty years; what they did show was the disgraceful standards which were still tolerated.

[2] Meaning, of course, 'members of the Society who were candidates'. The former Fabian Parliamentary Fund had ceased to make any but very small contributions to election expenses.

members who stood under Labour auspices four only—Attlee, Lansbury, Stafford Cripps, and Tom Williams—had been elected, as well as six (including Sir William Jowitt, soon to change sides) who fought under MacDonald's banner. The 4–6 did not represent the balance of feeling in the Society, as is shown by the Executive vote of 'unabated confidence' in Henderson, and the publication of Webb's *Political Quarterly* article on the fall of the Government as a Tract[1] and of a booklet by Harold Laski on *The Political Crisis.* The Society might have taken a little pleasure—though if it did it did not express it—from the fact that of the four survivors two became Leader and Deputy Leader of the attenuated Party; but even the London victory of 1934, though it brought sixteen out of the twenty-six Fabian candidates home, gave the Society six out of eight new aldermen and the Chairman of the Council (Snell), did not move the *News* to the faintest semblance of a cheer. Membership dropped, though owing to the tender behaviour of the Society towards defaulters,[2] not so much on paper as it did in reality; provincial Societies faded away, though the Societies in Scotland, partly owing to the energetic efforts of Baillie Raffan of Aberdeen, maintained a sturdier life and held annual conferences of their own. Funds fell, lecture receipts declined; stock was sold, and salaries reduced; the housekeeper resigned and was not replaced; the second floor at Dartmouth Street was let, and payments on Shaw's mortgage fell into arrears;[3] recurrent appeals for special donations appeared in the *News*. The Jubilee celebrations of June 1934—a sandwich reception held in the Suffolk Rooms—had little to celebrate but longevity.

The Society was indeed suffering sadly from the extent to which it had committed itself under Webb's guidance to the fortunes of the Labour Party. It had issued, in 1929–30, no pamphlets the like of the one published in 1906,[4] saying what

[1] Minutes, October 29th, 1931. Tract 237, *What Happened in 1931.*

[2] Pease, in a letter to John Parker after the reorganisation of 1938, explained that a 'purge' was undertaken only every three or four years, and even then distinguished non-payers were allowed to remain; he added that when Mrs Pankhurst swept out in wrath over the South African War, her distinguished subscription had been for years in abeyance. (Letter of November 23rd, 1941, in Fabian Society files.)

[3] E.C. Minutes, January 25th and May 23rd; January 24th, 1934; March 3rd, 1935; September 26th and October 29th, 1936.

[4] See p. 115.

Socialists ought to do in Parliament; when the blow fell, therefore, it had nothing to say, and its position was all the more melancholy because Webb, the last of the old leaders and the chief architect of the post-war alliance with the Labour Party, in effect abandoned the Party and the Society simultaneously, in favour of the U.S.S.R.[1] It was in 1932 that the Webbs went to Russia, and 'fell in love', as Beatrice said, with the Soviet system; for three years thereafter they were engaged in the preparation of their massive *Soviet Communism*, and tended to judge all political characters—and all their visitors to Passfield Corner! —by the amount of interest they showed in Soviet affairs. Granted the tremendous general curiosity which existed in the fortunes of the 'Socialist Sixth of the World', it could scarcely have been to the interests of a Socialist Society in England to discuss nothing else at all.

Nor did the discarded Webb mantle fall upon any other leaders in the Society. The most considerable personality on the Fabian Executive of those years was Harold Laski, who three times headed the poll, and whose writings made a fair-sized contribution to the Fabian output. But, as one who served with him in many capacities and fully appreciated his gifts pointed out to the present writer, Laski had always too many irons in the fire and was constitutionally incapable of giving the close and prolonged attention to detail which Fabian Socialism, as Shaw had said in 1892, demanded, if it were to be made a real force; he would come to a meeting, make a brilliant and convincing speech to the effect that such-and-such and so-and-so must be done, cause a sub-committee to be set up—and then be too busy to attend any of its meetings. One example may serve for many. At the end of 1930 Shaw, in a letter to the Executive, suggested once again that the time had come for a new *Fabian Essays*; this was eagerly supported, and a group, including Laski, set up to consider it, which held one or two meetings, but after that was never heard of again; a similar fate befell a group on Land Reform, set up at about the same time.[2] Just before the Jubilee, Laski moved for a special committee to consider 'the future

[1] He remained on the Fabian Executive until 1935, completing his half-century; but of interest there is little evidence. For details of the Webbs' conversion to the U.S.S.R. see my introduction to *Beatrice Webb's Diaries, 1924–32*.

[2] E.C. Minutes, January 20th and February 26th, 1931.

organisation and activities of the Society'. This committee did report;[1] it said that 'the Fabian Society does not undertake publication of pamphlets upon specific issues of policy, since this function is already performed in the research stage by N.F.R.B. [see below] and in the definition stage by the Labour Party'. The sub-committee went on to suggest that the function of the Society was rather to 'restate principles', with a possibility of eventual publication, and that it would report again later—which it never did. Confession of futility could hardly go much further; and it is not surprising that in 1936 Laski left the Executive to become a director of the rapidly growing Left Book Club and a representative of the Divisional Labour Parties on the National Labour Executive.

Apart from Laski, and Tawney, who left in 1933, those who served continuously on the Executive during the 'thirties included Susan Lawrence, Pease, Sanders, Davies, Mrs Drake, Eric Fletcher, later M.P., and John Ramage—not a very forceful combination, and one which seemed, moreover, at one time to have lost control of the Society. In 1935 and 1936 small Annual Meetings carried motions against the advice of the Executive, on the second occasion demanding that the Labour Party should promote a pact with the U.S.S.R. and admit the Communist Party to affiliation; neither of these, however, created any stir outside the Society, and by the following year the Executive had recovered sufficiently to defeat motions to invite Harry Pollitt to deliver one of the Autumn Lectures and to oppose the expulsion of the Socialist League from the Labour Party.[2] The faint stirrings of 'United-Front'-ism had, it seemed, been crushed; and in 1936 a new group was formed by D. M. Fraser, which called itself 'the 1936 Group'; it did little more, however, than interest itself in methods of propaganda, which the results of the Saar plebiscite and the activities of Mosley's Fascists had recently made interesting, and call a couple of conferences of representatives of black-coated workers, of which nothing came. In the years between 1934 and 1938 the Society issued only twelve Tracts, of which four were reprints of lectures or articles elsewhere and one Emil Davies's history of the L.C.C. in its jubilee

[1] Minutes, February 21st and June 21st, 1934.

[2] *Fabian News*, June 1935, June 1936, and June 1937. 'It was hoped', the Executive Minutes recorded in June 1937, 'that members of the E.C. will attend the A.G.M.' Apparently some of them did.

year,[1] and nothing else but one or two volumes of reprints of Autumn Lectures. Students at the Summer School sent in an angry request that 'complaints against petty restrictions should not be autocratically dismissed by the Manageress as youthful idiosyncrasies'.[2] Towards the close of the inter-war period the Society was, in fact, all but moribund. That it did not perish entirely, as others had done before it, notwithstanding the patience with which the British public continues to cherish elderly organisations, was accounted for by three main facts; it had a famous name, which in people's minds still retained significance; it had a number of devoted adherents of long standing and some financial resources, who, partly for the same reason, again and again contributed substantial sums to stave off bankruptcy; most important, it was an integral part of the Labour Party, and so provided an entry thereto for people, particularly middle-class professionals, who did not want to enrol in a Divisional Labour Party either because they feared the local publicity, or because the business agendas of local parties bored them to extinction. How long this twilight existence could have continued is matter for conjecture; a vigorous blood-transfusion was on the way.

New Beginnings

This chapter has already drawn attention to the uneasiness felt, even before it had taken office, about the second Labour Government and its policies, an uneasiness felt, not only by Beatrice Webb, who was already flirting with the Soviet Embassy, but by the Cole Group in Oxford and by a good few Socialists up and down the country. In the summer of 1930 Margaret Cole and H. L. Beales, later Reader at the London School of Economics and at that time one of Cole's most effective allies in the Tutors' Association and the W.E.A., talking over lunch, felt that there was a real need to bring back, somehow, into the Labour movement a sense of Socialist purpose and a programme of Socialist action. They took their idea to Cole, who took some convincing, but eventually agreed on the desirability of at any rate starting

[1] Tract 246, the last before the reorganisation, appropriately had as its title, *Our Ageing Population*.

[2] Minutes, October 14th, 1937. The Executive affirmed that the Director of the School should be responsible for any necessary discipline—upon which the Manageress resigned her post.

discussions to find out whether there were others who felt the same, and if so what they were willing to do about it. The three were joined by C. M. Lloyd and a newcomer to Socialism, the barrister G. R. Mitchison (now M.P. for Kettering); and the immediate result was the first of a series of week-end conferences held at Lady Warwick's Easton Lodge in Essex—next door to H. G. Wells's Easton Glebe. The hospitality was provided gladly by Blatchford's aristocratic convert, who had never forgotten the lessons he taught her, and had given lavishly to many Socialist causes; it was enjoyed by a number of persons disillusioned by 'Labour politics', who came by personal invitation to exchange ideas and possibilities. From these conferences emerged, first, the short-lived Society for Socialist Inquiry and Propaganda (S.S.I.P., pronounced ZIP).

Some earnest enquirers, delving in the meagre records of S.S.I.P., have been moved to ask what it was *for*—what it conceived its purpose to be. This is not altogether an easy question to answer. At the outset, the Socialists who assembled at Easton Lodge had no fixed intention of forming any organisation at all—it was not until the third of the week-ends that one emerged—and certainly not one which would seek in any way to rival or oppose the Labour Party; what they wanted to do was in some way to counter-balance the lack of purpose and the sheer ignorance of facts which they felt, in the winter of 1930, were making the MacDonald Government to all intents and purposes useless. Many of them had stood for Parliament in 1929—some successfully—on individual programmes more positively Socialist than *Labour and the Nation*; and they were hopeful that the Labour Government could be made into the Socialist Government which they believed they had helped to put into office. They were amateurs, in the strictest sense of the term, and the nickname which Francis Meynell coined for them, the 'Loyal Grousers', expressed pretty accurately the role which they envisaged for themselves.

These amateurs, however, came from all over the field of active Labour, and Cole's efforts in working-class education and in the university, added to his earlier Guild Socialist and Trade Union connections, began to bear effective fruit. The chief recruits were the young Oxford Socialists, who came in practically *en bloc*; but from the *Daily Herald* (not yet taken over by Odhams Press) came George Lansbury, his son-in-law Raymond

Postgate, Labour historian and later editor of *Tribune* and of the remarkable monthly *Fact*, and Francis Meynell; from the Parliamentary Labour Party C. R. Attlee and Stafford Cripps; from the quondam Guild Socialists William Mellor, Ellen Wilkinson, M.P., W. H. Thompson, the Labour solicitor, defender of dozens of conscientious objectors, shop stewards, and others in trouble with the authorities, and the cartoonist Frank Horrabin, then M.P.; from the I.L.P. Plummer and Brailsford; from the W.E.A. Tawney, E. S. Cartwright and H. P. Smith of Oxford and many other tutors and organisers; from the Co-operative Movement W. R. Blair, director of the C.W.S. and a tower of strength until his sudden death; from the Trade Unions Ernest Bevin, fresh from the Mond–Turner discussions, and Arthur (later Sir Arthur) Pugh of the Iron and Steel Confederation, that most conservative of Unions. This is only a selection of names; except for the dyed-in-the-wool Communists, scarcely a section of Labour was unrepresented, all recruitment, in the early days, being done by personal canvass and meeting hardly any refusals.

The gatherings of the amateurs in the curious ramshackle premises of Easton Lodge,[1] once patronised by Edward VII, with its wide and ill-kept park and gardens and its chatelaine with her Edwardian curls and her Lily Langtry smile, were informal to a degree. There was nothing that was stiff, arranged, or dull about them. Peacocks strutted up and down the terrace outside the windows, screeching 'Pigou! Pigou!' to speakers propounding unorthodox economic theories; on one occasion an intrusive cuckoo interrupted Lansbury so persistently that he broke off to admit 'Yes, brother, I *know* I am.' Accommodation was of very varied character, causing one university lecturer to enquire of another whether he would mind exchanging beds, 'as I feel sure mine is damp'; meals might be large and luxurious, or almost non-existent; minuting, and the circulation of papers, was casual. Nevertheless, work and discussion were eager, and the enthusiasm generated, the feeling of being together again for a Socialist purpose, was so strong and vivid that by the new year the new society had come into being almost of itself. Ernest Bevin was its chairman; Cole, Pugh, Blair, and D. N. Pritt, K.C. (a new convert) vice-chairmen; Mitchison treasurer; Beales and Margaret Cole joint secretaries; with Lloyd, Post-

[1] It was pulled down in 1948.

London Express News and Features Services

Short Cut
by Low

Ruth Gollancz, Dr Stella Churchill, Margaret Cole, Victor Gollancz

FABIAN SUMMER SCHOOL
DARTINGTON HALL, 1941

Hubert Humphreys addressing
typical School audience

gate, Horrabin, and Colin Clark completing the committee. It had a few voluntary assistants, a nominal subscription of five shillings, with donations from some of its wealthier members, and an organisation that was skeletal. But obviously there were a good few Labourites, up and down the country, who were anxious for an opportunity to 'grouse loyally'; in its short life of a year and a half S.S.I.P. founded fourteen branches and several study groups, gave lectures, held conferences, and published more than a dozen pamphlets as well as a cyclostyled bulletin, and by all the evidence provided a sorely needed heartlift to Socialists who had been near to leaving the Labour movement in despair at its sterility.

The New Fabian Research Bureau

It was not the only new foundation of the winter of 1930–1. Cole's organisationally inventive mind was already contemplating, besides 'information and propaganda', the possibility of a programme of solid Socialist research, following up the suggestions he had thrown out in *The Next Ten Years*, and filling the yawning gap in the work of the Labour Party. His original idea, which he propounded to the Easton Lodge conferences, was that the members should follow his own example, join the Fabian Society, on whose Executive he was then sitting, and proceed to make fruitful use of the Fabian offices and funds. Some of those to whom he appealed were, as we have seen, already Fabians; but this new variety of 'permeation' did not appeal greatly to others who had in the not-so-distant past shaken the Fabian dust from their shoes and were dubious about the possibility of removing the old-stagers from control of the Society. Cole therefore changed his tactics, and, early in 1931, having secured the support of the Webbs, he approached Arthur Henderson and some others with a proposal for the foundation of a new body, to be called the New Fabian Research Bureau, which should follow the Fabian tradition of Socialist research—to such an extent had former animosities been forgotten!—but should not embark on direct propaganda or take part in political or electoral activities. Henderson reacted favourably, and the idea was put across at a dinner in the House of Commons on March 2nd, which (Henderson being ill in bed) his assistant, J. S. Middleton, with the Webbs, Hugh Dalton, and Philip Noel-Baker, benignantly attended, as well as the Coles and the officers of S.S.I.P. already mentioned. 'It was a very pleasant family party,' wrote Beatrice;[1] 'and may lead to something.' Galton, who was also present, reported the proceedings to his own Executive, which on April 30th solemnly sanctioned the use of the Fabian name. By then the Bureau was already in being. Attlee was its chairman, Lloyd vice-chairman, Mitchison again treasurer; Cole was honorary secretary with Hugh Gaitskell[2] to assist him; its committee included, as well as Beales, Clark, and Cole, W. A. Robson of the School of Economics, a Fabian of long standing, Philip Noel-Baker, Mary Agnes Hamilton, M.P., Professor Hyman Levy, Harold Clay of the Transport Workers and the W.E.A., and Madeleine Symons, a former comrade of L.R.D. days;[3] it acquired an office in Abingdon Street, opposite the House of Lords, which it shared with S.S.I.P., and soon issued a printed appeal for funds, in which it stated that it had no intention of overlapping the work of the T.U.C. and Labour Party headquarters by offering to provide information on day-to-day affairs, nor did it promise immediate results.

> It is setting out [the manifesto concluded] on a programme of research meant to be spread over a considerable period of time, and is setting out to do its work patiently and with all the skilled help it can command, conscious that what the Labour Movement needs above all is the constant expansion and adaptation of policy in the light of changing conditions, on a basis of accurate research and collation of available experience.

These were ambitious words, and the Bureau started with high

[1] *Diary*, March 8th, 1931.

[2] Gaitskell played a very considerable part in the early days of N.F.R.B., and was assistant honorary secretary until 1933–4, when he left England on a Rockefeller Fellowship to Austria—in which capacity he distinguished himself in succouring the Social-Democrats arrested during the Dollfuss *coup* of February 1934. On his return to England he resumed active participation and continued until the amalgamation was complete. He and Evan Durbin were joint assistant honorary secretaries in 1937–8, and he was a member of the Executive of the amalgamated Society until 1940; then, however, he was drawn into the wartime civil service and subsequently into Parliament and high office, and though he maintained close relationship he did not again, save for a brief period of membership of the Executive between 1951 and 1953, have direct responsibility in the Society.

[3] Once an assistant to Mary Macarthur in the National Federation of Women Workers, she later became until her death in 1958 the distinguished magistrate Madeleine Robinson.

intellectual ambitions, though small funds—the income necessary to make a start was provided largely by Cripps, Pritt, and Mitchison. Cole began by drafting for what was called its Economic Section a vast programme of work, occupying thirteen large printed pages, and covering all and more of the contents of *The Next Ten Years*. Gaitskell was put in charge of this programme, assisted by a committee of economists and social theorists of enthusiasm and experience. (By the following March it had developed no fewer than eleven sub-committees, all of which were reported to be in working order.) Two other sections, the International Section and the Political Section, run by Leonard Woolf and W. A. Robson respectively, were gradually established with similar supporting committees, and set about preparing similar though slightly less portentous programmes of work. Legal matters, questions of civil and political liberties, were to be handled by co-operation of the Bureau with the association of Labour lawyers which called itself the Haldane Society. The honorary secretary, meantime, occupied himself with writing the Bureau's first published pamphlet, *The Essentials of Socialisation*, which appeared a very short while after its foundation.

This work was all in hand, several conferences had been held, and some though not all of the proposed organisation completed, even before the Labour Government fell; its complexity goes far to explain why the members of the two newly formed organisations, staggered as they were, like everyone else, by the size of the electoral defeat, were not shattered by it. They had realised, more than a twelvemonth back, that something was going gravely wrong; and were already busily trying to discover what it was. The winter of 1931–2 saw them holding a variety of meetings and conferences; and in April, again at Easton Lodge and again by private invitation, a week-end was arranged at which members of the late Government attended to discuss with others what were the causes of the disaster and what ought to be done to retrieve it. Simultaneously, and following the example of the Webbs, the N.F.R.B. decided to send an investigating team to Russia, 'the land where there was no unemployment'. The Webbs sailed for Leningrad in May, to be received 'as a kind of minor royalty'; the Bureau team, for which the present writer was organiser and editor, followed in July.

The Bureau researchers were not received like royalty; but

it can safely be said that they had what used to be called 'the whale of a time'. The team was a mixed one: from what could be reckoned official Labour circles came Hugh Dalton, who wrote on Soviet planning, and F. W. (now Lord) Pethick-Lawrence, who specialised on finance; from the N.F.R.B. Executive Mitchison, who wrote on the conditions of the Soviet worker and on foreign trade, Beales on politics, D. N. Pritt on the legal system, and Margaret Cole (Cole's health prevented him from going) on the position of women and children. 'Outside experts' were Graeme Haldane, the electrical engineer and cousin of Professor J. B. S. Haldane, John Morgan the farmer,[1] Geoffrey Ridley the architect, and Raymond Postgate on radio, press, and publishing. The novelist Naomi Mitchison contributed a highly individual chapter on 'Archaeology and the Intellectual Worker', and the late Rudolph Messel (cousin of Oliver Messel) wrote on films. None of the party spoke more than a smattering of Russian, though Postgate conducted a study-class consisting of himself, Mitchison, and the author in a lifeboat of the *Alexei Rykoff*, the ship which transported them through the Baltic, in elementary Russian based on *Hugo*. They were, therefore, to a considerable extent, in the hands of the guides and interpreters, except in so far as they used their own eyes and ears; they spent, in all, some four to six weeks in the Union, mostly in Leningrad, Moscow, and the Ukraine, though some went as far as Saratov on the Volga and Magnitogorsk in the Urals.

The resultant report, *Twelve Studies in Soviet Russia*, which appeared in 1933, after its several authors had given lectures to London audiences on their own subjects, was one of the earliest appraisals to appear of the Soviet Union after the first Five-Year Plan had been running for some time, when the Trotskyite opposition had been driven out and the collectivisation of agriculture had been called to a halt[2] and then resumed with more concentrated vigour. As at that date and time, it was perhaps as good an effort as could have been made. Its authors believed it to be objective and impartial; of course it was nothing of the kind, though not all of its chapters were so uncritical as the lyrical encomium which Pritt composed about Soviet People's Justice (of all things!), and John Morgan wrote with unhappy honesty of the conditions on the farms in the south—the chief

[1] Labour M.P. for Doncaster; died in 1940.
[2] By Stalin's *Dizziness from Success*.

victims of collectivisation—which as a farmer he knew quite well could not be attributed to bad weather. The investigators could see for themselves the enthusiasm of planners and guides, and of foreign settlers like the American correspondent Walter Duranty; they discounted the evidence of the few who wished to complain to them, and they accepted as part of the price to be paid for Socialist planning the shortages both of food and of the day-to-day amenities of western civilisation to be seen on all sides—unaware, of course, of the extent to which this was caused by deliberate Government policy. Apart from the pure pleasure of travelling in a new country and seeing in the flesh the faces which Eisenstein had made familiar to them on celluloid, the investigators, like the Webbs, rejoiced to see what they wanted to see—the 'spirit of the Revolution', the sense of collective purpose and planning so notably lacking in Europe and America in 1932; and like the Webbs again[1] did not see, or minimised, what they did not want to see. They were in good company; the cold war, and the revelations of the Twentieth Congress, have made it difficult for this generation to understand the unique and compelling force of the Soviet appeal in the dark years of depression. Only a minority in the Labour movement, at that date, was so sharply alive to the oppressiveness involved in 'democratic centralism' as to forget the rest.

The desire to explore the Soviet Union, in 1932, was not peculiar to the N.F.R.B.; all manner of visitors were flocking across the opened frontier, being guided about the cities by Voks, visiting prisons, crèches, Parks of Culture and Rest, and shopping with foreign exchange at Torgsin establishments. The Easter post-mortem on the election was much more the Bureau's own unaided idea; it was welcomed by Henderson, who, writing to Cole from the Disarmament Conference at Geneva, told him,

> it is clear . . . that we would greatly benefit by working out for ourselves a more clearly defined programme of action which we should seek to apply. I think we cannot do too much constructive thinking on those lines, and the more that you and your group can get done in that direction, the better for the Party,

[1] It is often forgotten, however, by anti-Stalinists who bitterly criticise the Webbs for *Soviet Communism*, how much criticism of what they called 'the disease of orthodoxy' was in fact contained in the first edition of their book. Where they erred materially was in believing that the elements they disliked would shortly, in Marxist parlance, 'wither away'.

and asked to be sent any written memoranda for his consideration.[1]

It will be observed that the Secretary of the Party raised no objection to an unofficial group discussing matters of Party policy; and discussions went ahead rapidly. By the beginning of June this group, consisting, according to the records, of Attlee, Bevin, Cripps, Hugh Dalton, Lansbury, Laski, Mellor, Pugh, Emanuel Shinwell, and the Coles, had produced a 'draft programme of action', which was duly forwarded to Henderson and to George Lathan, brother of the present Lord Latham and then chairman of the Policy Committee of the Party; it was also circulated to a large number of persons holding office in the political or industrial sections of the movement, a good number of whom signified their adhesion with or without some reservations. The intention of the promoters was that it should influence the Party Executive in its preparation for the Annual Conference to be held at Leicester in October, and so it undoubtedly did. But before the Conference met, developments had occurred which caused the N.F.R.B. to define its role a good deal more sharply.

The observant reader will have noticed a considerable coincidence of names between the original governing bodies of S.S.I.P. and the New Fabian Research Bureau. The coincidence, in fact, went much further; for of the handful of slightly over a hundred who joined N.F.R.B. (just about equalling the membership of the Fabian Society at the date of *Fabian Essays*) very nearly all were also members of S.S.I.P.; and several were beginning to enquire what was the purpose of having two separate organisations. E. A. Radice, the ex-Oxford Socialist who in 1931–3 was the paid secretary to both, more than once suggested that they should be amalgamated. Cole, however, would have none of it, having the functions of the two already separated in his mind; S.S.I.P. was to be the 'talking' body, with a wide, or moderately wide, membership and a branch organisation, doing propaganda and dealing with day-to-day propositions on Socialist lines, while the Bureau confined itself to hard thought and study and looked for a restricted membership among those

[1] April 27th, 1932. Letter in Cole Collection. After the issue of the 'draft programme' some of the signatories, mysteriously calling themselves the 'Friday Group', continued to meet and discuss private papers in Lansbury's room at the House of Commons.

who might not want to be mixed up with politics and political propaganda—though enrolments were not to be made, except as Associates without voting rights, of persons who adhered openly to any political party other than Labour.

In practice, whatever Cole's intentions, up to the summer of 1932 the outsider would have found it difficult to see much difference between the two organisations. Even the published pamphlets looked very much alike, both having white and scarlet covers;[1] and it seemed a matter of chance which of them organised any particular meeting or conference. But in midsummer the situation changed abruptly owing to the action of the I.L.P.

The tension between the I.L.P. and the Labour Party during the lifetime of the MacDonald Government has already been mentioned. Under Maxton's leadership it now came to a head, and the I.L.P., by a majority, disaffiliated, much to Lansbury's indignation. But the minority, which was considerable, had no wish to be cast out into a political wilderness; and its leaders, particularly Frank Wise and Brailsford, conceived the idea of amalgamating with S.S.I.P. in a new Socialist organisation, which should seek affiliation to the Labour Party. The Labour Party chiefs were understood not to be opposed to the idea, and Horrabin, a former I.L.P. member of Parliament who was also on the S.S.I.P. Executive, acted as go-between. Cole was vehemently opposed, being convinced that any such body would inevitably be deflected from 'inquiry and propaganda' into purely political and Parliamentary activity, of which he now found himself as suspicious as ever he had been in 1913–14. But he had not clearly thought out what should be the organisational future of S.S.I.P., which was beginning to outgrow the very loose structure which had served it well at the start; with all his energy, he was not in good health and could not possibly have run it himself in addition to all his other commitments, and a good number of his colleagues (including Cripps and Pritt, who provided a large part of the funds of S.S.I.P.) did not share his aversion to Parliament, felt much more akin than he did to the I.L.P. dissidents, and thought that amalgamation would eliminate unnecessary and unfruitful competition. (Wise had already spoken to at least one of the Easton Lodge conferences.)

[1] The N.F.R.B. made a change with its sixth issue, by which time the Socialist League had preempted the scarlet and white.

Cole yielded, protesting, to a majority on his own Executive, and negotiations began; but in the course of them the I.L.P. contingent took a step which had far-reaching consequences.

Bevin, as chairman of S.S.I.P., had been informed of the negotiations and had not, apparently, disagreed, though he took no part in them. But when the question of officers came up, the I.L.P. negotiators were determined that Wise, and not he, should be the chairman of the new body, to be called the Socialist League, and, being the stronger party, they prevailed. Bevin made no public comment, but he was extremely angry. He refused to have anything to do with the new body; and the whole incident helped to create in his mind that deep belief, already suggested by his experiences with Mosley and MacDonald, that 'intellectuals' were people who stabbed honest loyal Trade Unionists in the back. The results of this were plain enough in his attitude in the troubled Party conferences of the later 'thirties—towards Lansbury, for example, and Stafford Cripps.[1]

The members of S.S.I.P. were by no means unanimous in support of the amalgamation; at the final meeting a good-sized majority, whose chief spokesman was Evan Durbin, voted against it, and many of them refused to join the Socialist League, preferring to retain connection with N.F.R.B. only. Cole, as part of the agreement, took his seat on the Executive of the new body and was present at its formal inauguration meeting during the Leicester Conference of the Labour Party in October, at which the League scored an immediate success by carrying in a snap vote an amendment to an official resolution, demanding the nationalisation of joint stock banks. Very soon, however, he found the atmosphere of the League too uncongenial. He resigned in the spring of 1933; and it may be said at once that in so far as preoccupation with politics was concerned the League proceeded to fulfil all his prognostications. In addition to formulating programmes which it tried to induce Party Conferences to accept, it embroiled itself very soon, in association with the disaffiliated I.L.P. and the Communist Party, in attempts to run a Unity Campaign against Fascism and war. The official Labour Party reacted violently; at the beginning of 1937 the League was

[1] See further in Bullock, *Life and Times of Ernest Bevin.* It should be observed, however, that there was not at any time any suggestion of 'intrigue'. Whatever the advantages or disadvantages of Wise's candidature, it was openly pursued, and the stronger party won.

expelled from membership, and later in the year, in order to prevent the expulsion of its members individually, it dissolved itself. Some of its members, however, continued to carry on propaganda for unity, and four of them, Cripps, Aneurin Bevan, George Strauss, and Sir Charles Trevelyan, were expelled by the Party Conference of 1939. What the episode showed was, first, that those who tried co-operation with the Communist Party needed to take a very long spoon; and second, and more important, that there was now no place within the Labour Party for any organisation running a private programme of its own.[1]

S.S.I.P. thus came to an end, after a life too short to enable anyone to judge what would have happened to it had it survived; and the Cole brand of Fabianism thenceforward pursued its course through the New Fabian Research Bureau. It should be emphasised, however, that though there had been a strong disagreement on tactics and there was a clear difference of temperament involved, there was no quarrel, open or secret. Many members of the Bureau were members of the Socialist League as well, for some time at all events—some, as we have seen, were members also of the Fabian Society—and many engaged themselves, more or less deeply, in one or more of the political movements mentioned at the beginning of this chapter. After 1936, moreover, and the beginning of the Spanish Civil War, many threw in their lot with various pro-Republican movements[2] and especially with the Left Book Club, founded by Laski, Victor Gollancz, and John Strachey, which, though taking no direct part in politics, played such an enormous part in forming opinion, particularly among the young.[3] Gollancz himself, who was a member of most of the listed organisations, became *the* publisher of the Left; in 1932 he had issued Cole's first (since 1913) political best-seller, *The Intelligent Man's Guide Through World Chaos*, and went on to publish popular books by the same

[1] This paragraph is not, of course, a history of the Socialist League; that is part of the history of the Labour Party and is to be found fairly fully recounted, from different points of view, in books like G. D. H. Cole, *History of the Labour Party since 1914*, Fenner Brockway's *Inside the Left*, or J. T. Murphy's *New Horizons*; the facts given here are those which bear on the story of N.F.R.B.

[2] One member, Lewis Clive, author of an N.F.R.B. book called *The People's Army*, was killed fighting in Spain.

[3] See, for a vivid description of those to whom it appealed, Jessica Mitford's *Hons & Rebels* (1960).

author which followed in a steady stream; he was also co-publisher of pamphlets and books for the N.F.R.B.—and afterwards for the Fabian Society. The handful who made up the roll of N.F.R.B. kept their research independent, but led their political lives in many other organisations.

After the end of S.S.I.P., the Bureau began to grow, though slowly at first. Radice resigned in July 1933; he was succeeded in September by John Parker, the young Oxford Socialist who two years later distinguished himself by being the first candidate to win for Labour a really populous Parliamentary division in the south of England—Romford in Essex, out of which his present constituency of Dagenham was subsequently carved.[1] His nomination was due very largely to the work he had done in tutoring a W.E.A. class in Barking, which was then included in the Romford division—another instance of the connection between working-class education and Fabian Socialism. Parker, whose term of office was to cover the long period before the next Labour Government, set himself to expand the Bureau and to attract new membership, a goal which had not interested his predecessor. The initial roll of 133 soon doubled, and this membership, though small, was a real not a paper membership, since N.F.R.B. could not afford to retain on its books those who did not pay their subscriptions—it was, of course, like the Fabian Society itself, partly dependent on a few who gave substantially more than the minimum of 10*s*. 6*d*. a year. After Radice left, it moved out of the Abingdon Street offices into rooms in Bloomsbury, and soon found itself having to take on staff. John Cripps, son of Stafford, and the present editor of *The Countryman*, served for a year as unpaid assistant secretary, and there was from time to time a fair amount of voluntary assistance given in the office, though the changed conditions of life and work over twenty years never permitted the existence of such a constant band of volunteers as had worked and sung in the upper rooms of Tothill Street in the early days of the Fabian Research Department and the National Guilds League. As the Bureau did not set out to be either a propagandist body, a purveyor of travelling lecturers, or a general enquiry office, it had no need of such constant assistance on its own premises. Its main business was

[1] He was also, for a very few days, the 'baby' of the House of Commons—until the last returns brought in Malcolm Macmillan as member for the Western Isles.

research, most of which could be done by its distinguished collaborators in their own homes or offices.

The output of N.F.R.B. did not quite fulfil the comprehensive plans laid down for it at the outset; no programme of research carried out by voluntary workers[1] in their spare time can ever be tidily fulfilled. But the volume of work produced by its exiguous membership was so large that to recount it in detail would be tedious; a general summary is all that can be attempted here—but the comparison with the range of subjects studied by Fabians before the wars is interesting.

Forty-two solid 'Research Pamphlets' were published between 1932 and 1938. Two of these were contributed by the Haldane Society; one was a N.F.R.B. revision of *Facts for Socialists*; another—one of the earliest—a document on *Workers' Control* bearing the names of G. D. H. Cole and William Mellor, but incorporating the conclusions of a committee of sympathetic Trade Union officers. Four dealt with the reform of local government and three with education; one with standards of nutrition, one with the forty-hour week, and one (by Cole) with the problem of a living wage; one followed the life-story of children's milk 'from Cow to Consumer'. Public finance and taxation policy claimed four, mostly by Colin Clark and Evan Durbin—the new Bureau was rich in professional economists, though it could not persuade Keynes to join except as an Associate; an anonymous financier contributed a study of *The City To-Day*, for the better instruction of those who had been alarmed by the role played by finance in 1931, and Cole edited a book of *Studies in Capital and Investment*. Philips Price, long M.P. for Forest of Dean, produced a pamphlet on *Marketing Boards and Imports*. The greatest difference in emphasis, however, was, as might have been expected, in the prominence given to external affairs; there was one pamphlet on the Colonies and another on India, and the International Section sponsored no fewer than ten, culminating in a book edited by Leonard Woolf, *Hitler's Route to Bagdad*, which saw the light a few days after the outbreak of war.

The Haldane Committee contributed a pamphlet on *A Ministry of Justice*; and the Political Section—to which a sub-section dealing with local government was shortly added—a

[1] The Fabian Society had paid a modest fee for some Tracts not written by members of its Executive; N.F.R.B. paid nothing at all, except in cases of proven need—a policy which has continued, broadly speaking, until this day.

pamphlet by Robson on *The Relations between Central and Local Government*, and an important book by Ivor (now Sir Ivor) Jennings on *Parliamentary Reform* (1934). The proposals made in this book were accepted by the Labour Party and the greater part of them put into effect in 1945; had that not been done, the legislation of the session 1945–50 could scarcely have been got through.

On nationalisation (or socialisation) there were five pamphlets, one of which was a translation by Cole of the *Plan du Travail* of the Belgian Socialist Henri de Man, which excited a good deal of attention, particularly among the ex-Guild Socialists; two short books set out proposals for the socialisation of iron and steel and of electricity supply (both appeared anonymously, since their authors were experts who were unable, owing to the nature of their employment, to allow their names to be publicly used); and a very long document on the socialisation of the gas industry remained unpublished—partly by reason of its length—in the office files. Apart from the *Plan du Travail*, however, these gave little or no attention to the old question of 'workers' control'; and the same is true of the Bureau's first serious book, *Public Enterprise*, edited by W. A. Robson, which appeared in the spring of 1937. This book was the first full-length study of what did happen, in contrast to what ought or might be expected to happen, to industries and services brought under public or semi-public control. It contained nine chapters dealing with such organisations as the Post Office, the B.B.C., the London Passenger Transport Board, the Coal Reorganisation Committee, etc.—including one on the Co-operative Movement, whose potentialities were thereafter promptly forgotten, and its researches undoubtedly played some part in the formulation of Labour policy with regard to nationalisation. It is interesting, therefore, to observe that though it was not uncritical its general tenor was to accept the idea of the independent corporation as exemplified in the B.B.C. and the L.P.T.B. sponsored by Herbert Morrison (himself a Fabian of long standing); it did not anticipate the attacks made in the 'fifties.

The unpublished memorandum on gas mentioned above was only one of several, and its existence merits a word of explanation. The founders of the Bureau had envisaged that it would become a kind of specialised library of reference for those who wished to study the scientific application of Socialist principles to different aspects of society—in the 'thirties the sources available were unbelievably few. For reasons of finance it could not hope, even with the aid of friendly publishers, to put on the market all the work and the conclusions of its many committees. Some of these, also, were unpublishable for other reasons—because they were too long, for example, or—since ability to do research is not always accompanied by a parallel ability to write English—because the result was unreadable, or, in one or two cases, particularly where the socialisation of monopolies was concerned, because the arguments might have involved the authors and the publishers with the law. English law of libel permits any amount of criticism—or abuse—of colliery-owners, say, in general terms; but direct attention to the behaviour of a specific capitalist combination in chemicals or milk-distribution and you may well be hauled before the Courts. And however well founded the indictment and however useful the resultant publicity, small organisations, as some have found out to their cost, cannot afford the costs of a libel action, successful or unsuccessful. The Bureau, however, was anxious that this mass of work should remain available to anyone who wished to consult it; accordingly, the first volume of the *Quarterly*—see below—contained, issue by issue, lists of studies and 'finished memoranda' which were in the office and might be read or borrowed. Some of these were also discussed at week-end conferences, of which some dozen were held between 1934 and 1936—one, a conference on International Socialist Planning, whose genesis was largely the *Plan du Travail* already mentioned, took place at Geneva.

The date 1934 is given because early in that year the *N.F.R.B. Quarterly* was started; and from then on the documentation of the doings of the Bureau, which is very jejune for earlier years, becomes more ample. The *Quarterly*, an ambitious project, resembled much more the *Bulletin* of the early Labour Research Department than it did *Fabian News* at any stage in its career, though its 'slant' was naturally much less directed towards Trade Union and industrial matters than was the case with the former. It had twenty large quarto pages; it regularly contained a statistical section written by Cole (whose monumental statistical compilation on *British Trade and Industry* had appeared in 1931), surveys, some by Parker, of the political and international scene, a diary of current events, articles on particular problems, a couple of pages of brief notes on useful publications, and a few paragraphs on Bureau activities. The last-named took the place, for the Bureau, of the 'What Members are Doing' section of *Fabian News*; unfortunately for the historian in search of 'the human side', it was extremely austere, containing nothing but dry announcements of publications and 'forthcoming events'. It did not even deign to mention the election to Parliament of its General Secretary—or of course of anyone else; the impression of unrelieved study conveyed by it can only be supplemented and humanised by personal recollection, e.g. of conferences held in the Royal Star Hotel, Maidstone (a frequent rendezvous), where younger members enlivened their laborious days by adjourning to the travelling fun-fair and swinging on flying-boats or a large whirling apparatus called a Chairoplane.

Up to the end of 1935, however, the Bureau remained a small group—with less than four hundred members—concerned almost entirely with research; from then onwards a gradual change and widening may be observed. For this there were several reasons. In the first place, the general election of that year, while disappointing to the many who had hoped to see something more like the L.C.C. triumph of 1934,[1] had at least improved the political atmosphere, and, more important, brought into Parliament a good few of the intellectuals who had been swept away in the earlier flood as well as one or two of the younger generation. Secondly, the machinery at Labour Party headquarters was pulling itself together and really realising that solid work on the essentials of the Labour programme was needed. There was much scope, in the sub-committees set up by the Policy Committee of the Party (whose first efforts appeared in the document *For Socialism and Peace*, presented to the 1934 Conference), for 'permeation' by Fabian Socialists; at the same time, the advantages of having, within the Labour movement, a body of non-committed and non-committing persons who could publish, for study and criticism by the movement at large, 'kite-flying' suggestions which if they proved unacceptable would not be albatrosses hanging round the necks of Labour Parliamentary candidates,[2] became gradually more apparent. A proposal put

[1] Of the twenty Fabians elected the majority were also members of N.F.R.B.

[2] The risk was a real one, even if not quite as great as some of the more timid imagined. As far back as 1920, the present writer, then in the service of the L.R.D., produced a *Labour White Paper* which in a very simple table

out by a group which had no official standing, no vote at Conference, and no pledged M.P.s could easily be repudiated, whereas anything bearing the imprint of Transport House was liable, so it was said, to be widely thought of as part of the official policy of the Labour Party. The third factor was the darkening international situation, which was slowly forcing the Labour Party to define its attitude, to repudiate, at its 1935 Conference, both the pacifism of Lansbury and the Socialist League's policy of 'arm against the dictatorships, but no arms for a Tory Government',[1] and was simultaneously forcing the most quietist, the most 'research-minded' of Labour supporters to become personally involved in politics, in such issues as sanctions against Italian aggression and later the war in Spain; and the fourth, a domestic reason, was a change in the personnel of the Bureau itself.

After his election to Parliament, John Parker had to give up full-time service, though he remained as part-time General Secretary. A full-time assistant was already a necessity; and on the retirement of the gentle and modest Cripps, a paid post was created and filled by an energetic young man from Oxford, W. A. Nield, who within a very few months raised the Bureau membership—and the number of affiliated Labour organisations—by 50 per cent. Nield left after a brief while to take service with the Labour Party, and was succeeded by H. D. Hughes, another Oxford Socialist,[2] who continued a vigorous 'expansionist' policy. (Posts in the N.F.R.B., and after 1938 in the Fabian Society, became a recognised training-ground for aspirants to service in the Labour and cognate movements, or to Parliamentary candidatures.)

These influences quickly made themselves felt. The membership rose to 800 in a couple of years; in the autumn of 1936 the *Quarterly Journal* (partly for financial reasons) changed its format, appearing as an octavo, orange-covered magazine of

drew attention to the amount paid out of national funds for the armed forces and the interest on the war debt compared with that spent on all social services—and some indignant persons wrote to Arthur Henderson demanding whether this meant that the Labour Party intended to repudiate the National Debt.

[1] The year before, the League had put down no fewer than 75 amendments to *For Socialism and Peace*—a remarkable example of how not to do things.

[2] Afterwards M.P. for West Wolverhampton and now Principal of Ruskin College.

between forty and fifty pages, dropped its statistical and other heavy surveys and printed, instead, articles on topical political subjects such as 'How to Win a Labour Majority', and symposia on such non-research questions as 'The Future of the Labour Party', 'Labour Propaganda', 'Class Favouritism in the Armed Forces'. A formal series of public lectures in London, comparable with the Fabian Autumn Lectures, was initiated in the winter of 1937, and the conferences, of which the number was increasing, began to be concerned more and more with immediate affairs. This did not mean, however, that the amount of research in hand or projected was in any way diminished; in the autumn of 1936, borrowing the currently fashionable phrase, the Bureau announced that the greater part of its original Five-Year Plan had been fulfilled, and that it was now formulating a second one; in the following year an assistant was engaged full-time to make a study of retail distribution. This project eventually proved to be too ambitious both for the research assistant and for the Bureau itself and had to be left unfinished; but in 1938 Lord Pakenham provided the funds for three young workers to be employed for a year at least on somewhat more manageable assignments. The three selected were Polly Hill, niece of Maynard Keynes, Christopher Mayhew, the future M.P. and television personality, and Charles Smith, M.P. for Colchester from 1945 to 1950 and now General Secretary of the Post Office Engineering Union; and the results of their work, on *Unemployment Services*, *Planned Investment*, and *Food Policy* respectively, were all in due course published, notwithstanding the outbreak of war.

In 1937, finally, the Bureau had sent a team of enquirers to study conditions in Sweden, where the apparent success of the Social-Democratic Party in dealing with the depression had excited interest all over the world—see, for example, the best-seller *Sweden: the Middle Way*, by the American correspondent Marquis Childs. This expedition was much more 'scientifically' organised than its Russian predecessor; it stayed for periods of up to six weeks in the country, and had contacts prepared for it with all the experts it wished to see, and all preparations made—including fishing tackle for Graeme Haldane, who was sent on a mission to the far north! Ministers, including Per Alvin Hansen, the Premier, put themselves at its disposal. Besides the two Coles and Parker, Gaitskell, Hughes, and Mitchison from the Bureau's central organisation, the team of writers included H. R. G. Greaves and David Glass of the London School of Economics, James MacColl, now M.P., the barrister Geoffrey Wilson, Raymond Postgate, Molly Bolton, long personal secretary to the Webbs and now on the London County Council, Dunstan Skilbeck, head of Wye Agricultural College, R. W. B. Clarke, the future civil servant, Mayhew, and Charles Smith. It is hardly surprising that the study provided by this team, edited by Smith and Margaret Cole, appearing early in 1938, afforded much material for discussion and propaganda among those who fervently desired to see the return of economic catastrophe prevented without recourse to the methods of either Hitler or Stalin.

The most pertinent comment upon all this record was made, in 1936, in a private letter to Sidney Webb by Emil Davies, who had just taken over the treasurership of the Fabian Society, to the effect that he was 'applying to Parker for membership of the N.F.R.B.' as an insurance. By that time, the existence of two organisations with names very similar, of which one had the historical prestige (and the association with the Labour Party), while the other did nearly all the work, had become both anomalous and confusing. Membership overlapped—and some were asking why they should pay two subscriptions, while 'Fabian-minded' recruits were in some doubt which they should join. The Fabian Society, it will be remembered,[1] had recorded in 1934 its resignation of long-term research into the hands of the Bureau, which now appeared to be taking over its educational propaganda as well. In 1936, when the Bureau was faced with the necessity of moving office, it had been suggested that it might help out the Society by renting the top floors at Dartmouth Street, which would have made confusion worse confounded; but this proposal was abandoned, largely because it became apparent that Galton's somnolent régime and the bustle of the Bureau were oil and water and would not mingle at all happily in the same premises. But Galton was ready to retire by 1939, as was Howell, the Bookshop Manager; and Davies, by a herculean begging campaign, had succeeded both in clearing, for the time being, the deficit in the funds of the Fabian Society—though this would certainly have reappeared in another year or two—and in securing a fund which helped to pay modest pensions

[1] See p. 221.

to the two officials. The road was therefore clear for amalgamation; negotiations began in the summer of 1938; N.F.R.B. lecturers took over a week of the Fabian Summer School, where one of their number observed, not without amusement, a number of once-familiar faces which she had not seen since, nearly twenty years before, the School had devoted a week to discussion of Guild Socialism; and after protracted discussion a 'contract of marriage' was arranged.[1] The terms were accepted by both sides in November and December, and were to be fully effective by the following summer. Under the older name the two streams of Fabian Socialism came together at last.

[1] According to Parker's recollection, agreement was facilitated by 'Munich', as Galton and some other Fabians were convinced that war was coming and would destroy the Fabian Society altogether, so that it might as well amalgamate at once.

PART FIVE

Amalgamation and Revival

1938–1960

CHAPTER XVII

A Marriage Arranged

Amalgamation and the new constitution

THE amalgamation of N.F.R.B. and the Fabian Society into a single body was the logical—one might even say the obvious—conclusion to their history in the 'thirties; and by the end of 1938 the scheme had been accepted by meetings of both bodies without dissent. The final draft of the scheme had, however, been preceded by discussions and negotiations lasting over some months; and the constitution which resulted—fairly satisfactory, one must assume, since it has remained in force for over twenty years with only minor amendment—registered some changes and concessions made on either side.

The first 'point of discussion' was the name to be borne by the amalgamated society; and it was decided that this should be 'Fabian Society' *sans phrase*. The reasons for this decision, which was reached by all except Cole without serious hesitation, are clear. One was tradition; however elderly and comatose the Fabian Society of 1938 might be, the word Fabian still meant a good deal to older members of the Labour movement and to many outside it, and if the word were to be retained, the older name was both simpler and more euphonic. It was also suggested, by the Fabian Society's negotiators, that the members of the Society, particularly those more advanced in years, would not understand or take kindly to a new appellation, and might abandon membership or alter their wills, which it was hoped contained legacies to the Society;[1] it was assumed that the young

[1] It may be said at once that these hopes were in the main disappointed; the reconstructed Society received practically nothing from unsuspected bequests. It is true that since the death of Sidney Webb in 1947, the Passfield Trust, which incorporated the Webb estate, has provided annually a substantial contribution to the Fabian Society; but as the Webbs were strongly in favour of the fusion the amalgamated body would presumably have received their money, whatever it had chosen to call itself.

adherents of N.F.R.B., if they had any money to leave, would not have any comparable loyalty to overcome. Of greater practical importance was the question of affiliation to the Labour Party; the Fabian Society, as a founding body, was in a special relationship, and might be expected to remain so, even with an altered constitution,[1] and Fabians to continue to be recognised as members of the Labour movement and eligible for adoption as Labour candidates; it was not at all certain that a new body, with a new name, would be acceptable on the old terms. It was on this point that Cole found himself hesitating; he had of course long ceased to object to being described as a Fabian, but he continued to dislike the idea of the supremacy of Parliament and to distrust the political machine, and would have preferred to keep clear of any definite political commitment. It was quite evident, however, that he was in a very small minority, and that if the point were pressed negotiations would break down altogether; he accordingly gave way with no more than a protest, and the Labour Party accepted that the Fabian Society's life had been prolonged.

The name being settled, what of the objects and purpose of the reorganised Society? What, in fact, was to be done about the Fabian Basis? The new entrants could not stomach signing what they felt to be an obsolete and unintelligible document, unchanged since 1919, and the negotiating Fabians were not particularly concerned to defend it in detail. When it came to re-drafting, however, it appeared that everyone concerned had his or her own pet ideas—as indeed might have been expected—and discussion was becoming completely bogged down when Cole came to the rescue by suggesting that the Basis should simply be scrapped and replaced by a single Rule. The text of this Rule as finally adopted, after some discussion centring partly round the phrase 'methods of political democracy', was as follows:

> The Society consists of Socialists. It therefore aims at the establishment of a society in which equality of opportunity will be assured, and the economic power and privileges of individuals and classes abolished through the collective ownership and democratic control of the economic resources of the community. It seeks to secure these ends by the methods of political democracy.
>
> The Society, believing in equal citizenship in the fullest sense, is

[1] But see p. 278.

open to persons irrespective of sex, race or creed, who commit themselves to its aim and purposes and undertake to promote its work.

The Society shall be affiliated to the Labour Party. Its activities shall be the furtherance of socialism and the education of the public on socialist lines by the holding of meetings, lectures, discussion groups, conferences and summer schools, the promotion of research into political, economic and social problems, national and international, the publication of books, pamphlets and periodicals, and by any other appropriate method.

So the Fabian Basis vanished for ever, much to everyone's relief; and in order that the Society might not be tempted to be perpetually juggling with its own objects—a peculiarly unfruitful form of discussion—a further Rule (Rule 8) prescribed that the first six Rules of the constitution, of which the text cited above became No. 2, should be unalterable save by a special procedure designed to prevent snap votes. No amendment to Rule 2 was in fact made or proposed until 1959.

Of the other 'Fundamental Rules',[1] as they came to be called, much the most important is Rule 3, which is unique among societies of this nature. It runs as follows (my italics):

The Society as a whole shall have no collective policy beyond what is implied in Rule 2; its research shall be free and objective in its methods.

No resolution of a political character, expressing an opinion or calling for action, other than in relation to the running of the Society itself, shall be put forward in the name of the Society. Delegates to conferences of the Labour Party, or to any other conference, shall be appointed by the Executive Committee without any mandatory instructions.

This Rule, commonly known as 'the self-denying ordinance', was reinforced by part of a later Rule (13) enjoining that 'all publications sponsored by the Society shall bear a clear indication that they do not commit the Society, but only those responsible for preparing them'. This is not a 'fundamental rule', and could be repealed by a bare majority, if anyone thought it worth while to attempt it.

The 'self-denying ordinance' is of the greatest importance to anyone wishing to understand the history and influence of the Fabian Society in its third blooming. It was a new idea to the

[1] See Appendix I. The Rules were formally adopted at the first Annual General Meeting of the Amalgamated Society, held in June 1939.

Fabian Society, though the N.F.R.B., as a purely research organisation with no political ties, had never felt any desire to pass resolutions; and Beatrice Webb, in a long welcoming message published in *Fabian News* of February 1939, was at pains to defend it in some detail as the really logical conclusion to what she felt—or said she felt—ought to have been the proper development of the Society. As far back as 1912, she said, her intention and Sidney's had been greatly to increase the research work of the Society, an intention which had been frustrated by the war and the rise of the Labour Party. The considerable 'frustration' caused by the Guild Socialists was politely (?) ignored, and the Labour Research Department not mentioned; nor was the disillusion with Labour politics and the Labour Party produced in her thinking by the record and the fall of the second Labour Government (a disillusion so great that at one time she had publicly expressed doubts about the sacred 'inevitability of gradualism'). But it was certainly at the back of her mind; and the 'Message' concludes that

> as research entails attracting individuals interested in discovery, we shall inevitably have a conflict about immediate policy between those who are to the right and those who are to the left in the Labour movement, or those who are neither the one nor the other. . . . The plain truth is that research and active propaganda of immediate proposals are uncongenial companions: the one insists on an open mind, the other prefers a closed one. If Fabians want to influence the immediate policy of the parliamentary Labour Party, they can fall back on their local Labour Party or their trade union.

The 'self-denying ordinance' was in part a concession to Cole in return for the retention of the name Fabian Society, and of the Labour Party affiliation; it was, however, obvious common sense, given the existence of the Labour Party and the political history of the previous few years, and it brought some immediate advantages which Beatrice's 'Message' did not specifically mention. The amalgamated Society had deliberately and publicly barred itself from formulating or promoting policies of its own in opposition to or at variance with the official policy of the Labour Party; it was not going to fall into the traps which the defunct Socialist League had dug for itself. And the rule was not simply a declaratory or paper rule; it was enforced. Early in 1940, the Labour Party expelled D. N. Pritt for the pro-Soviet attitude he took up over the Finnish war; though he had given generously to N.F.R.B. in its early life and had been closely associated with it ever since, the Fabian Executive would not entertain a suggestion that it should protest. Shortly afterwards the Executive refused to allow the reorganised Women's Group to send in a resolution for the National Conference of Labour Women, despite the Group's plea that the Conference was advisory and not mandatory; and when in September 1942 the dangerous situation between the British Government and the Indian National Congress so moved the Executive itself that it sent to the Press and the Party an 'emergency statement' on India, it got rapped very hard over the knuckles and had to promise never to do it again.[1]

The new rule also made explicit the conviction, which we have noticed expressed at the time of the South African War, that the correct way for a small society to pull its political weight is not by passing resolutions, however sonorous, and endeavouring to thrust them down the throats of larger organisations, but by making its individual members trustworthy and so getting their opinions invited and listened to. Finally—a more humdrum but none the less valuable result—it rid the Society, once and for all, of attempts by Communists or any other organised group of opinion to capture its machinery and use it for its own purposes. This had been a danger, for a brief while, and could easily have been so again; but there was no advantage in trying to pack an annual or any other meeting which was expressly forbidden to pass policy resolutions or mandate representatives. After the constitution was finally passed in June 1939, Fabian Society meetings could not be a happy hunting-ground for political sectaries, and much unprofitable discussion was thereby eliminated.

Apart from establishing a fixed rate of subscription—minimum, in 1939, 10*s*. 6*d*. per annum—instead of the 'moral obligation' to contribute a reasonable percentage of one's income, which in the recent years had scarcely proved a satisfactory way of keeping the Society alive, the only other matters of importance in the new constitution concerned the election of the Executive Committee and the question of honorary officers. On both these points there was discussion, for the practice of the amalgamating societies had been different as regards officers. The Fabian Society had only one honorary officer, the Treasurer—Pease had

[1] Minutes, April 29th, 1940, and September 28th and October 26th, 1942.

been Honorary Secretary for a while, just after Sanders' appointment, and had so continued during Galton's term of service—and no chairman at all, the chair at Executive meetings being taken by members of the Committee in rotation, while at members' meetings, including the Annual Meeting, a chairman was elected from the floor. The paid General Secretary was also an elected member of the Executive with voting rights. N.F.R.B., on the other hand, followed the more common practice of having a paid Secretary who was not a member of the Executive, a more or less permanent Chairman (G. D. H. Cole), and a whole row of honorary officers—at the time of the amalgamation these were: *President*, Lord Addison, who had succeeded Attlee in 1934; *Vice-President*, Harold Clay of the Transport and General Workers; *Vice-Chairman*, G. R. Mitchison; *Treasurer*, George Wansbrough; *Honorary Secretary*, Margaret Cole; *Assistant Honorary Secretaries*, H. T. N. Gaitskell and E. F. M. Durbin. The Bureau valued its officers, and wanted to retain them; and on balance it succeeded, a contention by Davies that the Fabians would not stand for two Coles both holding office having been negatived by a vote of the combined Executives which controlled the amalgamation until the new constitution had been ratified.[1] Davies the Fabian became Treasurer with universal acclaim and Wansbrough (temporarily) assistant; Cole was Chairman; the vice-chairmanship was dropped; and the Honorary Secretary was Margaret Cole, with Durbin as assistant—later he was given the title of Research Secretary. The General Secretary (Parker) and the Assistant Secretary (Hughes) remained voteless, as did all paid officers subsequently appointed. The Chairman of the Society took the chair at Annual Meetings without question.[2] As to the Presidency, Addison wished to retire, and there was a general feeling that a President, as a permanent ornament, was not required. But Cole had the happy idea of inviting Beatrice Webb, as a mark of special honour and in order to 'seal' the alliance, to become President. She agreed, attended the inaugural meeting in 1939 and delivered her welcoming address. In 1941 she resigned; some time after her death a similar honour was conferred on Stafford Cripps, who remained President until

[1] Minutes, January 16th, 1939.

[2] Cole was Chairman until 1946, and again from 1948 to 1950, Harold Laski filling the chair during the interim. After 1953 the chair was taken by a different member of the E.C. every year.

his death in 1952; and, after another brief interval, on Cole, who was President from 1952 to 1959. Addison was made an honorary life member of the Society—a distinction granted to very few.

It might be thought that the N.F.R.B. representatives had got all they wanted. But they were still very much concerned to secure in the supreme counsels of the Society the services of those whose value for the conduct and direction of research—now recognised to be the Society's most important object—they believed to have been amply proved, but whose names and merits they feared might not be well enough known to the Fabians to secure their victory in a contested election. Accordingly, they carried in the new constitution a rule providing for the *election* by postal ballot of fifteen members (in addition to the Treasurer) and the *co-option*, by the elected members, of not more than nine others. It may be said at once that, with the exception of the case of Ivor Montagu,[1] the 'co-option rule' was responsible for more disputes within the Society than all the rest of its activities put together. There was a determinedly purist element in the membership which abominated the idea of any Fabian attaining Executive rank by any other than the strait path of democratic election, and insisted that co-option led to backstairs influence and the admission to the Executive of unwanted persons for reasons of friendship or compassion. Ian Mikardo, M.P. for Reading and Treasurer of the Society from 1947 to 1950, was the protagonist in the recurrent campaign to rescind the rule; there was something, perhaps, in the suggestion that the elected members, being kindly souls, might be inclined to bring back an old comrade rejected at the polls, but the democratic argument, applied to a Society less than 30 per cent of whose membership ever voted—and more than once elected members whose records showed that they had attended no Executive meetings at all—was largely nonsense; nevertheless, this crumpled roseleaf caused heated discussion at meeting after meeting until it was settled, for some years at least, by a reduction of the number who could be co-opted to seven out of twenty-four (excluding the Treasurer) and a 'gentleman's understanding' that members should not be co-opted unless good reason could be shown, e.g. chairmanship of an important committee of the Society, or distinguished service to research which was not yet widely known—

[1] See below, p. 277.

and that 'co-optees' should be expected to run in due course the gauntlet of election. In practice, the great majority of Executive members proved to have entered in the first instance by the co-option route, though a few of the 'co-optees', naturally, never got elected at all.

Webb and Cole

By the summer of 1939, amalgamation was complete, the Executive elections had been held, producing seven from the N.F.R.B., five from the Fabian Society, and two who had been members of both, standing orders approved, the necessary committees set up,[1] and the N.F.R.B. staff and records had moved into Dartmouth Street. From this time onwards, notwithstanding Mrs Webb's acceptance of the Presidency, the name chiefly associated with the Society and its work was not Webb, but Cole. Until 1951, when Cole resigned—Margaret Cole remaining as Honorary Secretary until 1953—the elections to the Executive were headed by the Coles; if to this be added the earlier years when both similarly headed the N.F.R.B. polls, the record is pretty well comparable with that of the Webbs mentioned on p. 145.[2] This therefore seems a convenient opportunity for some comparison of the work of the two men whose careers as leaders of 'Fabianism' followed one another almost end to end.[3] Cole's influence may be said to have begun as soon as N.F.R.B. was well on its feet—about 1933—when Webb's was already almost at an end, for though the latter remained on the Fabian Executive until 1935, his political interest, as well as that of Beatrice, had already in effect left England for the U.S.S.R. After their Russian tour, and even after the publication of *Soviet Communism* in 1935, the hearts of the Webbs were in Russia and Russia alone. Beatrice's *Diaries*, up to 1938, contain very little

[1] In the first instance, the principal ones were Finance and General Purposes, Research, Publications, Tracts and Propaganda, Social Activities, and Summer School; these were altered and added to from time to time. The Women's Group was reorganised by Margaret Cole and Mrs M. D. Spikes, later succeeded as secretary by Agnes Murray, now an inspector for the Home Office; the Nursery continued to function for a while, but fairly soon faded away under war conditions.

[2] As President from 1952 onwards, Cole took no part or responsibility for day-to-day work, but his influence did not cease to be felt.

[3] For Cole's view of Webb at its kindliest, see his obituary article in *Fabian Quarterly* of Winter, 1947.

about either Hitler or the Nazis, and her private reference to the first conference of the amalgamated Fabian Society called it a 'thin and shabby affair' (*Diaries*, June 18th, 1939). She had really little concern to influence the British Labour movement.

Some may wonder about the influence of *Soviet Communism* itself on Labour thought; my own impression is that that enormous political guide-book, for all its sheer size and weight and the fame of its authors, had, in fact, remarkably little. The many whose enthusiasm had been kindled in the years of the world depression and the first Five-Year Plan had no need for the Webbs to tell them of the satisfactions of Socialist planning, the 'dedicated order' of the Communist Party, full employment, and extensive social services; and by the time the book appeared some of the facts about the collectivisation of the kulaks, the famine, and the purges which began after the assassination of Kirov were beginning to seep through and to cause deep disquiet. Though the Webbs did criticise what they called 'the disease of orthodoxy'—having no notion, of course, of the frightful growth of that disease which was in the future—nevertheless their acceptance of the easy doctrine that all such disagreeables would 'wither away' before long as the Soviet State became firmly established, their admiration of the Communist Party as an instrument of government, and their refusal to be moved to indignation by accounts of cruelty and oppression did give, to minds beginning to be critical, the impression that their attitude was not unlike that of Shaw to Mussolini, that, having 'fallen in love' (as they themselves said) with an economic and political framework which they recognised as Socialist, they had become advocates rather than researchers, and were ignoring the human values of liberty and democracy which were at least as strong a part of the Socialist tradition in Europe.[1] It was interesting to observe that the Webbs were so impressed; but it convinced scarcely anyone who was not already convinced; and as it did not take them the length of admiring the Communist Party of Great Britain, it prevented them contributing anything—even if Sidney had not been partially disabled by a stroke—to British political thought in the later 'thirties.

Comparing Webb and Cole, one finds certain common traits leaping instantly to the eye. Both were indefatigable and very

[1] See, for an acute analysis, Leonard Woolf's chapter on 'The Political Thought of the Webbs' in *The Webbs and Their Work*.

rapid workers; both had a remarkable gift for quickly assessing reports, documents, statistics, etc., and distilling the gist of them in communicable form. Pease had once written 'in the absence of evidence to the contrary it may be assumed [of any anonymous Labour document] that Webb wrote it'. Cole, when his attention was drawn to this statement, commented that he could see nothing extraordinary about *that*; and it is true, therefore, that a good deal of the writing of both men is concealed in drafts and memoranda—often very lengthy memoranda—drawn up for committees and commissions of all kinds. Both, further, were extremely competent in negotiation, in administration, and in the conduct of business from the chair; both believed in democratic practice, though in the last resort, when a committee went crazy, as committees do, or became impossibly contentious, Webb's reaction was to bully it, Cole's to walk out in pain and wrath.

Cole, however, was only gradually recognised as a leader of 'Fabianism'—the speeches at the Albert Hall rally of 1946[1] did not even mention him—nor did he ever create a 'school' of Fabianism as Webb and his collaborators did in the early days of the Society; there was never a 'Coleism' recognisable in literature and caricature as 'Webbism' was, for example, in the days of the Poor Law Campaign and *The New Machiavelli*—Cole would have disliked it very much if there had been. Part of the reason for this was, undoubtedly, the change in the social and political atmosphere which the years had brought. The founders of the Fabian Society were a handful of pioneers facing a world which hardly knew enough of Socialism to formulate a reasoned hostility to it; they could with comparative ease arrive at a common view both of Socialist theory and the means for its application which, even though it was never allowed to turn into dogma, could be recognised as something to which in general all Fabian Socialists would subscribe. By the 'thirties this was no longer possible: there were many more Socialists and potential Socialists about, for one thing; for another, there was the Labour Party already organised and in the field; and there was also, particularly since the Russian Revolution, very much more genuine doubt of what ought to be the correct 'steps towards Socialism'. 'Fabianism' still remained clearly recognisable, both as a system of ideas and, even more important, as a method of approach and

[1] See p. 254. This was partly accidental.

working; but, as the abolition of the Fabian Basis indicates, it had become less and less 'formulable'.

But, even if it had been 'formulable', Cole was certainly not the man to formulate it or to force it upon anyone else. Not only was he temperamentally unable to dragoon anyone, he was also far less 'of a piece', politically and intellectually, than his predecessor. Webb was fond of saying that 'he had no inside', physical or psychological, meaning that he could digest anything which Beatrice or anyone else provided for him to eat, and that, once his mind was made up on any issue, he felt no qualms or uneasiness but pursued his objective until facts or reasoning induced him to change it. Cole, on the other hand, had a great deal of 'inside'; he was not a healthy man—the diabetes of which he died had been diagnosed when N.F.R.B. was barely founded—and there were points in his career at which illness quite clearly influenced his actions. Much more important, he was never so benignly sure of himself and his convictions as was Webb; his Socialist faith was very vivid, and he knew what he meant by it, but it included such personal idiosyncrasies as atheism and republicanism, which Webb would have regarded as irrelevant and which Cole himself knew were not shared by people to whom (whatever he might say in moments of wrath) he could not deny the name of Socialists. Webb was not without emotion in his Socialism (particularly where his own city of London was concerned);[1] but Cole was much more moved by emotion, and was therefore more liable to be disturbed when persons or movements to which he had given allegiance acted in a non-Socialist manner, whether by accepting a title or by liquidating their opponents. The case of the U.S.S.R. may be taken as an example. Webb received the news of the October Revolution and the establishment of the Bolshevik State with unqualified repudiation; by 1931, before he had even set foot on Russian soil, he had convinced himself that the U.S.S.R. was the Fabian State in being, and his visit only confirmed his happy faith in it, from which he never wavered, even when Beatrice was really shaken by the treason trials and the Nazi-Soviet Pact.[2] Cole, in contrast, welcomed the Revolution wholeheartedly, defended the Russians

[1] See *The London Programme* and others of his writing on the L.C.C. And see also the book, *The Decay of Capitalist Civilisation.*

[2] *Diaries,* August 28th, 1936; and particularly July 23rd and August 23rd, 1939.

both publicly and in private for a great many years, and only at long last, and with much personal distress, brought himself to the point of outright public condemnation of Stalinism.[1]

Temperamentally, then, they were unlike, and their collaboration, as earlier chapters of this book have shown, ran regularly into difficulties: with Beatrice, in spite of occasional clashes in which both parties thoroughly lost their tempers, Cole had a good deal more sympathy. In their interests, also, they diverged a good deal. Cole was essentially an intellectual in the aristocratic-cultural tradition, a product of Balliol and of the Honours School of *Literae Humaniores*; Webb had never been to a university, and though he could not be accused of lack of concern for higher education, his 'favourite child' was the London School of Economics which, whatever its merits, bore little resemblance to the Oxford of Edwardian days. Webb started his career in the civil service—an organisation which Cole tended to regard with repulsion as both centralised and hierarchical—and the people whom he liked most to talk with and to influence were, on the whole, administrators of various kinds—public servants of one sort or another, or business men engaged in the running of large organisations; he certainly did not actively enjoy, as Beatrice did, the gossip of high-placed persons around political dinner-tables. Cole, though he could get on with administrators and business men if need be, found much more congenial audiences among teachers and students, both in the universities and the working-class movement; it is not an accident that, whereas the first expansion of Fabianism among university students resulted in violent quarrels with the leadership, the second provided the Society with its most fertile and persistent source of recruitment. Finally, Cole was a man of culture far outside politics, a connoisseur of English literature, Greek verse, Bohemian glass, and wine; Webb was a contented philistine as

[1] 'Mr G. D. H. Cole', a friend had written in the days of the L.R.D.,
'Is a bit of a puzzle,
With a Bolshevik soul,
In a Fabian muzzle.'

This epigram would be more correct if 'anarchist' were substituted for 'Bolshevik'. It was the individualist-anarchist element in Cole (of which Webb had no trace) which made him condemn 'democratic centralism'; it also prevented him from becoming anything remotely resembling a dictator. For Stalin, see the final judgment in his *History of Socialist Thought*, Vol. V.

regards all those realms of taste;[1] and while both were scientific ignoramuses, Webb's ignorance—as, for example, of whether sweet-peas did or did not produce the peas eaten at table—was that of a man who had just had no time to study science but was perfectly prepared to allow it a suitable place in the universe, whereas Cole from time to time exhibited a positive hostility to both science and scientists, on the ground that they made arrogant pretensions, attempted to reduce qualitative values to quantitative terms, and deliberately fostered a mechanisation which was ultimately destructive of the good life.

The above paragraphs are not intended, of course, to be a full description of either Cole or Webb, but merely to indicate the particular characteristics of both which marked their contribution to the character of the Society at the dates of their ascendancy, and had certain clear effects on its history—the comparative lightness, not to say rowdiness, of some of the Fabian schools and conferences of the post-amalgamation years owes something to Cole's appreciation of satire and his gift for verse parody. But there remains to be added one very important thing which they possessed in common: complete political disinterest. Neither of them had any 'career' interest in Socialism; both pursued it for its own sake alone. It is true that neither, during their Fabian years, had any 'struggle for existence' or needed to curtail their Socialist activities in order to earn a living in uncongenial ways or to direct their political activities into money-making channels solely.[2] Many others, of course, have given service and writing freely to the Fabian as to other Socialist societies, but very few to anything like the same extent or with such tenacity over so long a continuous period; and few have been so conscious of the need for steady attention and effort in detail if a Socialist grouping was to go on working and not fly into fragments. However much their contributions differed, and whatever value posterity will assign to either of them, it is difficult to over-estimate the

[1] The famous story of his enjoying a performance of *Parsifal* because during the interval he had met Herbert (now Lord) Samuel, and had had a 'very interesting discussion on the incidence of sickness during pregnancy' is only the best of many anecdotes.

[2] Beatrice had an income inherited from her father; Cole, in his early years, had an Oxford fellowship, and eventually inherited money from his own father; and, it may be added, the wives of both contributed to their literary earnings, though Beatrice's contribution was much the larger. Sidney's brief tenure of Cabinet office does not affect the picture.

importance, to the Fabian Society, of the fact that its two principal leaders stood to gain no material advantage at any time from their efforts on its behalf.

Revival and the 'phoney war'. Wartime organisation

It was accidental that the union of N.F.R.B. and the Fabian Society was completed only just before the outbreak of war—as we have seen, this might well have come about some years earlier. But the coincidence of date was felt to have some symbolic significance, to indicate that a newly made Society was entering stripped for action into a world in which action would be peremptorily needed. 'Stripped', indeed, is almost literally correct. For, some months before the war, the N.F.R.B. members of the joint Executive had suggested that the membership lists should be rationalised, and 'paper' removed, by the expedient of striking off from circularisation all those whose subscriptions were now more than three months in arrears. This was agreed—with somewhat startling results. For whereas the Bureau had entered amalgamation with a nominal roll of about 800 and the Society with one of about 1,600, the new 'purge' reduced the numbers of former Fabians by nearly 50 per cent—one so purged, for example, being on record as having last paid half a crown ten years previously—even though a kindly decision allowed all over eighty years of age to have arrears forgiven. At the Summer School of the previous year one week had been organised by the N.F.R.B., represented by Hughes and Margaret Cole, and a member of more than twenty years' standing wrote appreciatively in *Fabian News*, 'when debate waxed fast and furious there was a happy reminiscent murmuring all round "how like the good old days" '—it is to be hoped that not too many of the happy murmurers found themselves coldly thrown out in the spring for non-payment. Those who remained appeared to enjoy the shake-up which they experienced;[1] but the net result was that at New Year, 1940, counting all new accessions, there were only 1,715 members—hardly more than the nominal roll of the Society alone six months earlier—and 10 per cent more 'in arrears'; these 1,715 included 24 'subscribing bodies' and 6 Local Fabian Societies, of which one was in South Australia, and one, in Manchester, had absorbed the local

[1] 'A mixture of old and young Fabians can be achieved with complete success,' wrote the reporter in the *News* of September 1939.

N.F.R.B. It is not surprising that *Fabian News* of November contained a fervent appeal for more Local Fabian Societies.

There is no need here to describe the 'war situation' of 1939 as fully as that of 1914; it is within the memories of far more people, and also came upon a country far less emotionally unprepared—this is not to minimise the undoubted fact that a stage in society did end then, though with less finality, less abruptness, than on the earlier occasion. What may, however, be emphasised, as it is often forgotten, was that no one, at the beginning of September, anticipated a phoney war lasting for nine months. When the London sirens blared out on Sunday, September 3rd, so little time after Neville Chamberlain had announced that Britain was at war with Germany, the immediate thought of many was that Hitler had been slightly quicker off the mark than was anticipated, but that anyway the devastation foreshadowed in *The Shape of Things to Come* and already seen in the unprovoked German bombing of Guernica would be upon us in a very few hours or minutes. Even when this failed to happen, and the most noticeable immediate results of war turned out to be the black-out, petrol rationing, the short-lived closure of cinemas, etc., and the evacuation of the working-class mothers and children of the cities[1]—and let no one minimise the effect of these at the time—there remained the conviction among people like Fabian Socialists, first, that their work must go on, and secondly, that the War for Democracy—not, this time, the War to End War—must this time be made to fulfil its ostensible purpose.

The Fabian Executive was called together for an emergency meeting on September 4th, the day after the declaration of war; its immediate decision was to carry on, as far as possible, removing the archives and a duplicate membership list to safer keeping at the Coles' house in Hendon and that of Hughes's father in Derbyshire. Some work of reorganisation had already been done; Parker and Hughes had gone during Whitsun on a lightning tour to the comparatively live Scottish Societies, in order to get their support for the new régime, and a questionnaire had been sent to all members of both former organisations, inviting them to state their qualifications and what they could

[1] Perhaps there should be added to this the Ministry of Information and William Joyce on the radio ('Jairmany Calling'). The effects of the electoral truce, which did not become apparent for a while, are discussed on a later page.

do to help the Society. *Fabian News* of August had taken on a different aspect, with a change of type face, the abandonment of the antique Gothic headlines, a series of new announcements, a general air of bustle, and an appeal for up-to-date news for 'Personal Notes'.[1] But obviously much more needed to be done. To the next meeting, held a week later, the Honorary Secretary and the General Secretary presented a joint memorandum on policy, sources, and possibilities; this in effect began the régime under which John Parker and Margaret Cole (the former, of course, spending much more regular time in the office) were in effect responsible for the day-to-day running under the direction of the Executive, Margaret Cole taking over the 'full responsibility' when the General Secretary, as at the beginning of 1945, was out of the country, and Hughes, until he was called up to the Army, acting as the third member of the triumvirate. Mayhew, one of the research workers paid for out of the Pakenham donation, was called up immediately, and other young Fabians were in the armed forces; but there was, of course, no such general exodus as in 1914.

On September 18th the third wartime meeting of the Executive took decisions arising out of the memorandum. The office was not to be evacuated, but to remain in Dartmouth Street—the staff would have rioted against any other decision. The Autumn Lectures (like the Windmill Theatre) were 'never to close', though they were to be held on Saturday afternoons instead of the hallowed Thursday evenings; the Executive and the Finance Committee were to be combined and to meet at lunch-time in the blacked-out National Trade Union Club in Great Newport Street, where also lunch-time meetings addressed by interesting personages were to be held—the first was Ellen Wilkinson, the future Labour Minister of Education. The contents of the Fabian book-boxes, which an earlier meeting had decided had served their time and were obsolete, were to be dis-

[1] Unfortunately for the historian, 'Personal Notes' were apparently crowded out, and never appeared again; the section, which later became so large, of Local Societies' news past and present is no substitute. The fact that *Fabian News*, like other journals, suffered severely from the paper shortage, and that the minutes of Executive and other committees were confined to strict statements of fact, makes 'gossip' about the revived Society hard to come by, except through personal recollection. (*Fabian Quarterly*, continuing the N.F.R.B. journal of the same name, contained many interesting articles and discussions, but of internal news very little.)

posed of in a jumble book sale, which the *News*, with doubtful candour, advertised under the heading 'Black-Out Time is Reading Time'. Two conferences were to be held, one called *War for What?* and the other *War on the Home Front*; and Cole was to write a Tract (No. 247) on the second subject, and a leader for the *News*. The following extracts from the latter give the gist of what the Fabian Society believed to be its role in war-time.

First, there is the question of what may be called broadly War Aims. What Great Britain is fighting *for* is fully as important as what we are fighting *against*. We, as Socialists, have to set to work now to think out the nature of the peace settlement at which we are to aim, so as to avert the calamity of a second Versailles and a second abortive League of Nations. We have to think out plans for a democratic peace . . . to work out new economic policies for commerce and finance . . . to devise a solution of the problems of colonialism and imperialism, and to lay plans for a democratic League of Peoples. . . .

Secondly, and even more immediately, we have to keep a watch on what is being done in our own country during the war—from the double standpoint of securing that war-time 'controls' shall be efficiently and impartially conducted in the general interest, and that our democratic liberties shall not be unnecessarily invaded . . . no profiteering and no entrenchment of vested interests under cover of government control . . . no regimentation of Labour by employers or bureaucrats. . . .

Moreover, as war-time control necessarily embodies a large element of 'Socialism', in the sense of public control over industry, commerce and finance, it is our business as Socialists to see to it that this 'Socialism' shall be real Socialism, and not a bastard form of State Capitalism under which the monopolists can get ready to exploit us more efficiently than ever. . . .

Thirdly, there is the task of keeping the people well informed about their rights as well as their duties . . . this will mean keeping a constant watch on the orders and regulations issued under emergency laws, and on the methods of administration. It will mean issuing practically useful leaflets and pamphlets, and giving advice where it is wanted.

These three essential tasks are already plain before us. But we do not propose to attempt them alone. The Fabian Society is already taking steps to consult with other bodies that are likely to be active on similar lines. It has already offered help to the Labour Party, whose Research Department has been badly depleted by the removal of its principal workers. We are also in touch with the *New Statesman and Nation* . . . with the Union of Democratic Control and with several other bodies.[1]

The article went on to invite Fabians to act as watch-dogs in certain named fields, to pay their subscriptions promptly and in full, and to volunteer in small numbers for help in the office—one of those who responded to the last appeal was the late Zita Crossman, wife of R. H. S. Crossman, afterwards a member of the Fabian Executive and joint editor of the *New Fabian Essays* when at length they appeared.

The two conferences were held in October and November, and collected a full audience; the practice, initiated by N.F.R.B., of preparing duplicated reports for distribution to any attender who would pay the out-of-pocket costs was continued and reports, both of conferences and of lectures, thereafter ceased to appear in the *News*.[2] Meantime the work suggested in Cole's article began to get under way. Fabians were advised of the powers and duties of local authorities with regard to evacuation, wartime education, and war legislation generally, and what Labour locally should be doing about it; one of these sets of instructions was printed and published as *Fabian Information Bulletin No. 1*—there never seems to have been a No. 2; and subscriptions were sought and obtained to pay for the production of a news-letter, *Fabians at the Front*, which was sent out regularly for some time to Fabians who had been called up. In the early autumn, Margaret Cole and the new Research Secretary, Richard Padley, began work on the first large wartime study, *Evacuation Survey*. This was a large piece of work, in which a great many people collaborated; it included a section on Government action, the various Government circulars and their results, contributions on the effects of evacuation in various centres, and essays on some of the problems presented. It was published, as a good-sized book, in the summer of 1940; it was, of course, an amateur performance, in no way comparable with the official accounts, such as that by Professor Titmuss, issued years later, but as the evidence given to the Government's Shakespeare Committee of Enquiry never saw the light, it remained for some

[1] *Fabian News*, September–October 1939. Published mid-September.

[2] The Society had begun, two or three years previously, to publish the text of the Autumn Lectures in book form, and this was continued for some time; the 1939 series was brought out by Macmillan under the title *Where Stands Democracy?*

time the only story, other than scarifying reports and wild correspondence in the newspapers, of what had really happened when the slums of the cities were decanted upon an unsuspecting countryside and a cruel light thus thrown upon the conditions still tolerated in Britain. At the same time, out of funds provided by the Ethical Union, two research workers, Peggy Jay[1] and Marjorie Pollard, embarked on an enquiry into the effects of war on a single small town—Aylesbury—which also was published in the following autumn—later on, after the blitz had done its worst, came a similar study by Doreen Idle, *War Over West Ham* (1942).

The first fruit of the discussion on war aims was the second wartime Tract, H. N. Brailsford's *Democracy in India*, published in November;[2] the same month saw the establishment of an International Discussion Group, whose secretary was Paul Lamartine Yates, which through the whole of the winter and spring met weekly at the National Trade Union Club.[3] Towards the end of the year a more ambitious venture was tried, when Margaret Cole and Rita Hinden, later secretary of the Fabian Colonial Bureau and then a voluntary member of the staff, called together a group of European Socialists in exile with the purpose of making plans for an after-war map of Europe; it may be said at once that this attempt was unsuccessful, as the various representatives of European Socialists quarrelled so violently that the room at Dartmouth Street in which they met became known as the 'Anschluss', in recollection of Hitler's forcible union of Germany and Austria. Only Wenzl Jaksch, the leader of the Sudeten Germans (who subsequently married Joan Clarke, Research Secretary of the Fabian Society from 1940 to 1943, and returned to honour in post-war Germany where he still presses the claim

[1] Wife of Douglas Jay, M.P., and at the time of writing member of the London County Council.

[2] The titles of the first three war issues in the Research Series taken over from N.F.R.B.—*Planned Investment*, by Christopher Mayhew, *Scottish Local Government*, by W. H. Marwick, and *The Reform of the Rating System*, by J. Sullivan—may seem to lack immediacy; they were, of course, the result of work initiated long before the crisis.

[3] Unlike the official Labour Party, the Fabian Society looked for no 'orthodoxies' among the Socialists to whom it issued invitations. 'Enemy' and 'Allied' were alike treated as Socialists, which naturally resulted in meetings and conferences being far better attended than those in which discriminations were made.

of the Sudeten exiles to return to Czechoslovakia), seemed to have any conception of or desire to reach an agreement. Finally, in the spring of 1940, on the initiative of Konni Zilliacus, now M.P. for Gorton, a conference was called to promote co-operation, for the duration of the war, between French and English Socialists. An Anglo-French Committee was set up, of which the most prominent members were, in addition to Zilliacus and the two Coles, Leonard Woolf, Henri Hauck, the French Labour Counsellor in London, W. E. (now Sir William) Williams, editor of *The Highway*, and William Pickles of the B.B.C., son of a veteran 'Clarion Vanner', the well-known translator, interpreter, and broadcaster in the Foreign Service.[1] This committee, collecting funds and employing a part-time secretary, Marguerite Desnières, started a journal, *France and Britain*, whose first number, which was in preparation before the fall of France, came out as a Supplement to the *New Statesman* of June 29th, 1940.[2]

A good many other ploys were undertaken to maintain social and political life in London when so many normal gatherings had been abandoned in an alarm which turned out to be unnecessary. The Fabian Bookshop, which in the last years of the old Society had become a somnolent retreat where Fabian Tracts could be obtained, and other publications if members insisted, abruptly woke up, started stocking books and touting for orders; at a counter set up on the pavement outside, possible recruits could be seen in their lunch-hour sampling Penguins and Pelicans—then a comparatively new venture—as well as Fabian, Labour, and other products. If lured into the interior, they might find pinned up notices of Fabian lunches and Fabian dances. The lunches have already been mentioned; in the first years of the war they provided a succession of well-known speakers, including Cabinet Ministers and the ambassadors of China and the U.S.A. (Quo Tai Chi and John Winant)—the most successful was that addressed by Maynard Keynes, which was packed to the doors. The dances, also, were more important than they might sound. They had started just before the war, with an Amalgamation Dance, with floor-show given by the Unity Theatre, at the Burlington Galleries; another dance was announced for Christmas, and this was followed by many more, at which the younger members of the Society regularly made

[1] In May he and his wife had produced Research Pamphlet 48, *Is France still a Democracy?*

[2] See further, p. 288.

social contact with one another, and particularly, after the summer of 1940, with the foreign Socialists in exile; the revived Social Activities Committee arranged other functions.

For the first Fabian Christmas Frank Horrabin produced the first Fabian Christmas card, bearing the design which now appears on the cover of Fabian publications, of a tortoise with front paw uplifted, proclaiming 'When I Strike I Strike Hard'. This card was issued for two seasons only, the members pointing out, reasonably enough, that whatever its artistic merits they did not really want their mantelpieces covered with tortoises presented to them by their friends; but the Society fell in love with Horrabin's design and thereafter used it as a permanent colophon, notwithstanding the protests of a few who repudiated the association of the progress of Socialism with that of a tortoise, whose picture, they added, suggested to them nothing so much as an infuriated old age pensioner.

All in all, the amalgamated Society, during these first months of its life, well deserved the encomium contained in a letter from Pease to the General Secretary, printed in the February *News*:

I want to congratulate you and your colleagues on the new life you have put into the Society. I once wrote that I suspected that Socialist and political societies (not parties) could not long survive their founders. This is substantially true of all the other Socialist societies in England, but not of the F.S. The founders are all politically dead, but the F.S. looks good for a good many years to come, after we, the founders, are all cremated.

The *News* of December announced that 'the Fabian Society is now settling down to its programme of wartime research', gave details, and called for volunteers, members, and contributions; in March it invited suggestions for new work. Margaret Cole prepared for the Executive a detailed 'costing list' for various types of venture, and in April the reorganised Women's Group told the membership that it was beginning to organise research on its own and sending out a questionnaire and arranging discussion groups on 'The Family and the State'; in the first six months of 1940 two research pamphlets, in addition to the one on France, appeared, as well as four Tracts, one by Sir John Boyd-Orr on *Nutrition in Wartime*. The book on *Britain's Food Supplies*, the result of the year's work by Charles Smith, came out in June; the Ministry of Food expressed a desire to interview the author, but by then he was out of reach, a private in battledress.

All this work, moreover, was done on a membership which was still very small; the Annual Report for 1939–40 gives a figure of only 1,859, including eleven Local Societies, by the end of March, though 120 more enrolled during the next quarter. The 'third blooming' did not really begin until the war had started in earnest.

After 1940

In the late summer of 1940 the Fabian Society, like many others, was feeling in considerably better spirits than the war news would seem to have warranted. The first reason was certainly the fall of Chamberlain, and the change in Government, which meant, among other things, that there were now four Fabians—Attlee, Dalton, Greenwood, and Morrison—holding high office; four more were junior Ministers and, in the course of time, fifteen Parliamentary private secretaries. Stafford Cripps was Ambassador in Moscow; and there were also, of course, many other members of the Society (including Gaitskell and Durbin) rising fast in the wartime civil service. One of the immediate results of the change was that Cole joined Sir William Beveridge in the task laid on him by Bevin, the new Minister of Labour, of making a rush Survey of Manpower for the whole kingdom. Cole, becoming a temporary unpaid civil servant for the period of the Survey, enlisted the help of the various contacts he had made, through the W.E.A. and other sources, in different towns; for London the Fabian Society undertook the job, and throughout July a team of twenty-three, organised by Hughes and Margaret Cole, rushed about the city making enquiries and drawing up reports, having armed themselves, somewhat to their own surprise, with permits, hurriedly made out in the office and signed Ernest Bevin, which authorised them to enter all manner of officially closed territory, such as the docks. (Some patriotic Trade Union officials were slightly suspicious of these home-made documents and sought confirmation from the Ministry of Labour—an incident which confirmed the researchers in a sense of their own immediate importance.) The London report was finally finished on a fine Saturday afternoon before Bank Holiday, just in time to enable the organisers to scramble into a Great Western train for an over-subscribed Summer School whose average age, the *News* delightedly recorded, had come 'hurtling downwards'—there being no Continental holidays for students (or others) then and for years thereafter—and which was eagerly discussing problems of a new world after the war.

A while earlier, Beatrice Webb's presidential address to the Annual General Meeting, which she delivered in person, had displayed much more enthusiasm than a year previously; its text (printed in full in *Fabian News* of July) went into appreciative detail about the research work done and doing, praised the Society for its 'persistence in its own policy combined with tolerance towards the views of other individuals and other organisations', and ended with the hearty conclusion 'Long Live the Fabian Society'; the Executive had decided that the Autumn Lectures, to be delivered under the title 'Programme for Victory', could again be held in the evening. More important, in the course of the Summer School one of the longest-lived developments of the new Society was conceived. Rita Hinden, wearying of the futile discussions on War Aims described earlier, had the idea of separating from the problems of post-war Europe the problems of dealing with the British dependent Empire and of establishing a special section or department of the Society in order to get into touch with the leaders of the colonial peoples, to ask and answer questions, and to work out policies for the redevelopment and ultimate 'freeing of the Colonies'. The suggestion being favourably received, she turned to seek the help of others with similar interests, notably Arthur Creech Jones, afterwards Secretary of State for the Colonies, and Frank Horrabin—and so, later in the year, was born the Fabian Colonial Bureau, of which there will be more to be said later.

The Summer School was hardly over when air-raids forced the Lectures to return to daylight performance; but, apart from that, the beginning of the blitz produced no curtailment of activity. The offices suffered no more than a chip or two; the staff, after a brief trial of public shelters, refused to have anything more to do with them, the office boy coming to work on his bicycle through shattered streets and being packed off home by Enid Jeeves, the head of the office, if possible before the sirens sounded.[1] Callers and enquirers continued

[1] 'Jeeves', most efficient of organisers, had been office secretary to N.F.R.B. almost since its foundation, the book-keeper, Agnes Gibson, being taken over from the Fabian Society. The boy, Ronald Gantlett, had been bookshop boy to the Fabian Society; he was killed, unhappily, in Belgium in the last months of the war.

to come in, and there was a considerable increase in correspondence.

For one of the immediate results of the changed situation was an increase in membership outside London. The first reason for this was obvious enough—evacuation of offices and departments and difficulties of travel. The evacuation, or some of it, had of course happened before the blitz, but the arrival of the latter meant that the evacuees had to stay put, could not come running up to London for week-ends, and began to feel as lost and lonely as observers on searchlight sites. 'Cries of despair reach us from all over the country,' the *News* wrote picturesquely in November, 'from Bristol, Blackpool, Liverpool. . . . Can the Society do nothing to end General Boredom?' This plea reads ironically, in the light of what was soon to happen to Bristol and Liverpool, which could scarcely be described as 'boring'. The cries were, however, taken seriously, and in January Margaret Cole, in a New Year message in the *News*, wrote a strong appeal to exiled Fabians to enrol for service, which apparently produced some effect, for in the next issue an article headed 'Fabian Frontiersmen' said that the response had been 'remarkable' and printed a series of suggestions on what individuals so marooned could do to keep the flag flying.

Boiled down, what these recommendations in effect amounted to was an instruction to revive as far as possible local interest in politics. For, ever since the outbreak of war, what had been normal political activity had been almost completely abandoned. Local Councils, for example, had almost completely blacked themselves out at the beginning of the war, without waiting for any orders from Whitehall; some even ceased to meet at all, leaving business to be done by the officials supervised by an emergency committee of three or four, and many more dispensed altogether with the normal committees and sub-committees.[1] The action of the Government in creating Regional Commissioners with plenary powers, and the enormous rate subsidy, with corresponding central control, involved in Civil Defence and Air Raid Precautions, no doubt accounted for much of this, as did the absence of many councillors in the services or on war work of various kinds; but for Socialists and the Labour Party the largest single factor was undoubtedly the electoral truce. With

[1] See an interesting if pessimistic article by John Sullivan in *Fabian Quarterly* No. 28, 'Local Government in Decline'.

no possibility of fighting elections, the local Labour Parties, even where their active personnel was not deeply involved in the war, had lost their main reason for holding meetings, and opportunities for political discussion were therefore down to a minimum. At first, this was hardly noticed; but soon after the stormy business about evacuation died down, active political minds began to feel the gap, and, as early as March 1940, the Fabian Society had staged a discussion between George Ridley, M.P., and Michael Stewart, on the desirability of ending the truce—Ridley, as befitted a member of the Labour Party's National Executive, being strongly opposed to its termination. The beginning of the blitz, and the resultant partial resumption of evacuation, in some measure slowed down the argument; but there were a good many towns where neither was very important, and Local Fabian Societies, where they existed, began to realise that one of their important wartime roles would be to fill the void, to make themselves the focus for political and social discussion within their areas. Fabians exiled to the provinces were urged, in the article mentioned above, to try and get together with other Fabians or like-minded persons and form a Local Society or at least a discussion group, in the towns to which they had been drafted; *Fabian News* of February 1941 contains a list of a dozen names of members offering themselves to act as convenors and by March there were fifteen Local Fabian Societies; but the great development came in the following winter, when the blitz was over.

The ending of the blitz was not, however, by any means the chief reason. Already, the mere existence of the National Government with Labour Ministers in power and authority, and the far-reaching measures of State control of economic life accepted by Parliament within a few hours of its formation, had given a new and immediate meaning to the I.L.P.'s old slogan of 'Socialism in Our Time', and Socialist organisations were growing and new ones springing up. At the beginning of June the Fabian Executive agreed to take part in the formation of a Socialist Advisory Committee which was to include representatives of the Left Book Club, with its comparatively huge membership, a small, recently founded body called the Socialist Clarity Group which had done some very thoughtful work—one of its reports, called *Labour's Next Step*, had been published as a Fabian Tract—and possibly others. To the Annual General Meeting, held on

June 23rd, the retiring President sent a written message urging the Society to initiate, by these and other means, a great forward leap into Socialism, with special reference to the achievements of the Soviet Union; only the day before, press and radio had announced the German march into Russia.

The excitement and enthusiasm produced by that event have been largely forgotten today, overlaid by recollections of Stalinism, Beria, and cold war; but it is attested by the upward leap in war production, and the eager rush into pro-Soviet activity, quite apart from the overnight *volte-face* in the attitude of the Communist Party. Those Socialists who had been made most unhappy by the signing of the Nazi-Soviet pact, the annexation of the Baltic States, and the war on Finland were now ready to see excuses for the Russian action—or to forget all about it—in the joy of feeling 'together again', Russian Communists and British Socialists fighting the common enemy; the complete cold-shouldering of Cripps, the British Ambassador in Moscow, was overlooked or thought to be of no importance. The Fabian Society was moved no less deeply than any other body. Early in July the Executive voted to set up an *ad hoc* committee on 'International Work with special reference to Anglo-Soviet Co-operation'. From that, immediately, came only a short propagandist pamphlet called *How the Russians Live* and a more serious study of *The Soviet Home Front.*[1] In August, however, Victor Gollancz, bubbling with enthusiasm, came down to lecture to a Summer School even more crowded than that of the previous year, and delivered, on the general theme that as we were now allies of the great Socialist State it was our opportunity and our immediate duty to work for Socialism in Britain, an address so impassioned that it brought his audience to its feet cheering and demanding to be told what to do next. Before the School had dispersed, discussions had been held, and decisions tentatively made, that now was the time for a great forward effort in Socialist propaganda; and back in London the Executive Committee set

[1] Research Series 67, by Noah Barou, the remarkable Russian banker and co-operator, who held doctorates from the Universities of Moscow, London, and Berlin, and was one of the most vigorous of Fabians as well as a pillar of the World Jewish Congress. His pamphlet was a best-seller for months. A volume of essays entitled *Our Soviet Ally*, written by Margaret Cole and three Russian contributors, Barou, A. Steinberg, and I. Narodny (a pseudonym), was also projected, but did not appear until 1943.

about forming a Socialist Propaganda Committee which should carry the message through the land. An enormous list of names was put forward, covering all branches of the movement; Cole was to see Middleton, the Labour Party Secretary, to make sure of Party approval; branches were to be founded and regional committees set up; propaganda pamphlets 'up to twelve' were projected; Dorothy Fox, long to be secretary of the Local Societies' Section of the Fabian Society, was appointed in December to be part-time assistant for Socialist propaganda; shortly afterwards a project appeared to expand *Fabian News* into a regular journal of Socialist propaganda, to be edited by Raymond Postgate.[1]

This somewhat grandiose scheme, like some others, turned out to be too large to be carried out in full. A committee of thirty-six 'persons of importance' was indeed set up, including, according to the Annual Report for 1941–2, six M.P.s, the editors of *Reynolds' News* and the *New Statesman*, all three directors of the Left Book Club (Gollancz, Laski, and John Strachey), the Publicity Officer and the Chief Woman Officer of the Labour Party, as well as such 'coming names' as Barbara Betts (Barbara Castle, M.P.), Ritchie Calder, Roy Jenkins, and William Pickles; and a number of short propaganda pamphlets were issued, one of which, *A Letter to a Woman Munition Worker*, by Susan Lawrence,[2] was bought up in large quantities by the general workers' Unions. But the committee itself was too full of important people with important commitments ever to function effectively; the Paper Control refused to issue paper for the projected journal, and funds were not forthcoming to finance the widespread organisation which had been contemplated. What did happen, however, was that Hughes, who acted as secretary and organiser to the committee until he was called up in May, found, as he toured the country making speeches on its behalf, a growing inclination to form Local Fabian Societies. By March there were forty of these (fifty-seven a year later); and in addition a number of local Labour Parties had been stimulated to set up Socialist Propaganda Committees, some of which in due course became Fabian

[1] Minutes, September 22nd and December 18th, 1941; and February 16th, 1942. *Fabian News*, December 1941.

[2] No. 4 in the Fabian *Letter Series*; others were addressed to members of different occupations (including the Army!) inviting them to become Socialists; they had some success.

Societies on their own. At the 1942 A.G.M., Cole, from the chair, devoted most of his address to advertising the new developments, and the Local Societies took the first steps towards becoming a permanent section in the constitution of the Fabian Society. The Colonial Bureau, already mentioned, had been established in October 1940, with a committee of its own[1] of which Creech Jones was chairman, a membership roll of its own, and a journal, *Empire*, which it had taken over from a previously existing organisation. In March 1941 an International Bureau had been proposed, and took shape in December, with Philip Noel-Baker, M.P., as chairman, Doreen Warriner, the expert on the Middle East, as honorary, and Mildred Bamford as paid secretary. Both these Bureaux presented ecstatic reports of their conferences, their research, and their publications to the 1942 A.G.M., and it may be said that by that summer the structure of the modern Fabian Society was fairly well established, at any rate in outline. The organisation of the main bulk of the work, which came gradually to be called Home Research, was rather more fluid than that of the rest, and will be discussed in the following chapter.

[1] Membership of the original committee included Julian Huxley, Margery Perham, Professor Arthur Lewis, Professor W. M. Macmillan, Leonard Woolf, and Frank Horrabin. Many other distinguished names were afterwards added.

CHAPTER XVIII

The Third Blooming

THE years after 1941 saw the real 'third blooming' of the Society, during which its increase in size and output astonished itself. By March 1942 it was already claiming that its membership was higher than at any previous peak. The Annual Report for 1946–7 suggested that the total had nearly trebled in five years, and now reached well over 8,000—with 800 more who subscribed to the Colonial or the International Bureau alone; this included some 160 'subscribing bodies', i.e. Labour, Trade Union and Co-operative organisations, public libraries, etc. There were over 120 recognised Local Fabian Societies in Britain and a handful known to exist overseas; this compared with the total of six in all in 1939. The headquarters had developed into quite a large organisation. The staff, of whom there were about eight at the beginning of the war, now numbered thirty-one, twenty-five being on full time; there was a Staff Association, and a system of 'joint consultation' over salaries and conditions for those other than heads of departments, which worked reasonably well, although the conditions of war and post-war meant a fairly rapid rate of change in personnel. The salary bill had grown a great deal, as the ancient tradition of all-round parsimony was gradually left behind—though for directing staff the Society could never afford high salaries, and the reasons which attracted applicants, other than the work itself, were still those mentioned on pp. 222 and 239.[1] Along with all these worked 'office' volunteers, doing much to help in the day-to-day routine and being rewarded by the gratitude of the paid staff and a paragraph of praise in successive Annual Reports.

[1] Of those who served as assistant or research secretaries after Hughes left, one, Joan Clarke, as already related, married a leading German Socialist, one went into industry, and one into the civil service, one opened his own bookshop, and one, Donald Chapman, after a period as General Secretary, became M.P. for Northfield.

To house all these the Society had filled the whole of 11 Dartmouth Street, evicting previous tenants, and had expanded into two nearby buildings; even so, the 'level of occupancy' was such that there was sometimes scarcely a vacant chair. The opening and closing paragraphs of every Annual Report up to 1947 express amazed satisfaction at the rate at which the Society was expanding, not merely its membership but its work in all fields and its influence outside and inside the Labour Party. The *Fabian Quarterly* of Spring, 1944, commemorating the official Diamond Jubilee, was a paean of self-praise, only slightly salted by some leg-pulling in an article by Bernard Shaw.

The self-praise, considering the facts and figures, was not surprising, and the officers and the Executive were too pleased and too busy to ask themselves what was the reason; if asked, they would probably have replied that the cause was sheer merit, that people needs must love the Fabian when they saw it. While the claim was not without justification, there were other reasons not immediately apparent; there was a tide of public opinion beginning to flow. Since there were practically no by-elections and very few meetings of political parties, since newspapers were minute and filled with war news, since the actual membership of the Fabian or any similar society, however much increased, was still tiny in relation to the population, it was not surprising that the swelling of this tide was unperceived—though the heavy Parliamentary vote of February 18th, 1943, against the Government's refusal to promise 'Beveridge' might have given some warning—until the 1945 election gave so astonishing a demonstration. Looking backward, though, this is not hard to understand.

Effects of war on Socialist thought

In 1939, the importance of the 'common people' and of their organisations had to be recognised far more quickly than in 1914, in a war which had to be total but was not to be won by the reckless expenditure of cannon-fodder.[1] This much had been made plain even at the beginning, when Arthur Greenwood was invited by an excited Tory patriot to 'speak for England', and plainer still when Churchill called upon Labour leaders to occupy key posts in his Cabinet; but there was much more to it

[1] Except, of course, in Russia. Politicians and people in Britain were extraordinarily slow to realise the sheer size of the Soviet war casualty list, and of its effects on later Soviet policy.

than that. In the first place, the 'shame of the 'thirties' was being purged. Not merely, nor for this argument principally, the shame of Munich and the betrayal of the Spanish Republic, but the shame of the Two Nations, of unemployment and the treatment of the unemployed, of the cuts in social services and the shocking standards of food, health and housing, against which, as already described, Socialists and non-Socialists had alike campaigned unsuccessfully during the dreary years. People could see with their own eyes that in a war which was making greater and greater demands on material resources, it was possible, for example, to provide quickly help, food, milk for those who needed it, to raise remarkably the standard of health and nutrition of British children, and to impose, with the minimum of resistance and the minimum of evasion, a system of fair shares without favour upon the whole population. This had been done, moreover, by what was in effect partial nationalisation, centralised control administered by non-profit-making servants of the community, a good few of whom were—and many more might have been—members of the Fabian Society.[1] Britain was operating a society of Planned Production for Communal Ends, and operating it with far less confusion, friction and inequality than was to be seen in the war production of the capitalist United States—also less than in Germany, though that was not known at the time; the bankers, those villains of 1931, were toeing the line with scarcely a squeak. And this régime was not only agreed to be more just than the pre-war scramble, it was also more efficient; it was standing up to attack and bringing gradually victory out of disaster. There seemed no reason why a system, tried and triumphant in war, should not be carried over with equal success into peace, when material resources, enhanced by wartime scientific discovery, would again be available, no reason why mass-unemployment, human squalor and misery, gross inequality between man and man, should ever come again. The 1944 Education Act, symptom of the times, though it was criticised by Fabians as inadequate, was passed in the year of the Society's Diamond Jubilee; the Beveridge Report, which

[1] The fact that a good few of the boards and controllers were in fact the same individuals as had run the industries in peace-time, though matter for loud comment, did not really affect the argument. Business men *could* be socialised, it was said; and stern control would prevent them 'getting away with it' after the war, as they had in 1919.

had been preceded by the Fabian study on Social Security,[1] and the enthusiasm which acclaimed it, is even more indicative.

This summary omits, no doubt, elements which though present at the time, did not become apparent until after the Labour Government had fallen; but it represents, I am sure, the mood of the active Fabians at the time,[2] and accounts for the supreme self-confidence exhibited in their public statements and the eagerness with which the Society—without, as will be seen, altogether counting the cost—took up almost any and every suggestion for new work. During the 'forties, in fact, its range became so wide that a strictly chronological account would be an intolerably dreary recital of detail; the following pages, therefore, will tell the important developments, first of the lesser sections, the Local Societies, the Colonial and International Bureaux, and finally with the core of it all—called Home Research.

The Society and the Labour Party. The Local Societies

One of the main differences between the old Society in its days of activity and the new lay in the fact that there was now a fully organised national Labour Party, with branches all over the country, presenting, now, the only possible alternative to a Conservative Government, and that this Party had both a national policy and a national discipline which it was interested in maintaining against attacks from outside, particularly from Communists. These developments had a noticeable effect upon the Fabian Society and its organisation, which this section will proceed to discuss.

The Fabian Society, as a political Society, was in a position which had no parallel in any other country in the world. It was older than the Labour Party, which it had helped to found, and had therefore never been subjected in detail to any rules which the Party might see fit to impose upon the Local Parties created by itself; its members, before the war, had not been individual members of the Labour Party, though they were recognised as being part of it by virtue of being Socialists and signatories to

[1] See p. 294.

[2] Not, altogether, of Cole himself, who in the winter of 1944–5 composed a very long draft or synopsis for a possible New Fabian Essays, at the opening of which he laid down the thesis that Socialism was on the decline all over the world. This view was not found acceptable by the suggested collaborators, and contributed to the dropping of the project.

the Fabian Basis. Originally, the I.L.P. and the S.D.F. had been in the same position, but by 1940 one was defunct[1] and the other disaffiliated; the Fabian Society was therefore unique. Early in the war what might have turned out a difficulty developed suddenly. The Fabian membership, made up of the former Fabians and adherents of N.F.R.B., included a few who still belonged to other political parties, who were therefore ineligible, by Conference decision, for membership of the Labour Party. When amalgamation was complete, John Parker, the General Secretary, taking what seemed to him to be logical action, informed them that they were no longer eligible for membership and suggested that they become Associates, i.e. non-voting members. Nothing happened immediately; but when ballot papers were issued for the 1940 Executive elections, Ivor Montagu, a Fabian of long standing who was also a member of the Communist Party and had recently engaged in a heated controversy with Will Arnold-Forster, a member of the International Discussion Group, on whether the war was or was not an imperialist venture which no Socialist could support, complained that he had not received one. Being informed that he was no longer a member, he wrote very angrily to the Chairman and to various other influential members saying that he had been arbitrarily deprived of his rights. His letter was brought before the Executive on June 10th, accompanied by strong protests from Bernard Shaw, Beatrice Webb and Leonard Woolf. Beatrice was the recently chosen President of the Society, and Shaw held the mortgage on the offices; it would have been embarrassing to quarrel with them publicly over one man, even had a majority of the Executive been willing to treat all Communists as implacable enemies. Accordingly, after a long debate at a special meeting, the Executive declared that

> in the opinion of the E.C., on the existing rules of the Society and the constitution of the Labour Party, the eight persons[2] who have been named as having been transferred to associateship have not ceased to be members of the Fabian Society by reason of the fact that they ceased to be eligible to be individual members of the Labour Party;

and forbade the Secretary to expel any members in future without consultation. At the same time, in order to make it clear that

[1] The S.D.F. came to an end in that year.

[2] Some Communists, some individually expelled from the Labour Party; the other seven had 'gone quietly'.

this leniency referred to the rights of past members and not to the future, it stated that 'the Executive Committee does not propose to accept for membership candidates who are not eligible for individual membership of the Labour Party'.

None of this was made public, or put before the membership in any shape or form; if it had been, in the days of Dunkirk, it is difficult to be sure what would have happened. There was a note of warning struck in a letter from George (later Lord) Shepherd, the Labour Party's National Agent, to whom the problem had been submitted, to the effect that it would not have arisen had the Society's rules been submitted to the N.E.C. of the Labour Party, *as they should have been.* The Fabian Executive ignored this, holding that the Society's own rules were no business of the N.E.C.; and Shepherd, it seems, was satisfied to leave the situation as it was for the time being, it being improbable that one swallow out of 1,800 could make much of a Communist summer in the Fabian Society. (Later, in 1946, Montagu, who had maintained his lonely membership, elected to assert a right to stand for office. This, being refused, led to a stand-up fight in which Montagu, a skilled and ingenious debater, at two Annual Meetings running played so successfully on the 'civil rights' principles of the membership as to prevent a valid decision being given against him; the Executive had finally to resort, somewhat ignominiously, to the expedient of taking a postal ballot to insert an explicit provision in the rules, which was carried by a very large margin. It was an embarrassing situation for successive Chairmen, and amusing for onlookers; it had little significance except in so far as it indicated that the vocal members of the Society were neither subservient to their Executive nor in awe of the Labour Party.)

More difficulty might have been experienced over Local Fabian Societies. These—to which Pease, it will be remembered, attached small importance—were originally all but independent of the parent Society, which gave them no money and received little. There were in existence 'By-Laws for Local Societies', which said little more than that their membership must accept the Fabian Basis. At the time of the amalgamation, with only half a dozen in existence, and those mainly in Scotland, it did not seem worth while bothering to re-draft the by-laws, and they were accordingly held over for later consideration. But after the Socialist Propaganda Committee got to work, and Local Societies began to grow in numbers and to make demands on the resources of the office for meetings, speakers, and enquiries, it became clear that some more formal relationship was desirable—particularly since the Basis had now ceased to exist. At the end of 1941 there was a joint meeting of the Executive with representatives of the Local Societies then in existence, and by the following September draft rules for them were in being.

There were two main points which the draft was intended to cover. First, the Local Societies should make some contribution to the cost of the Society itself; this meant an affiliation fee on the one hand (and a minimum local subscription to assure the wherewithal to pay an affiliation fee), and, on the other, some concession by way of rebate to those national members living in the area of a particular Local Society which they were willing to join. Secondly, if a Local Society was to have the use of the Fabian name, it must observe Fabian principles, i.e. it must subscribe to Rule 2 of the Fabian constitution, it must run its affairs in a democratic manner, it must exclude from voting membership anyone not eligible for membership of the Labour Party, and it must, emphatically, insert in its constitution Rule 3, the 'self-denying ordinance', and apply it strictly to any participation in local political affairs. These provisos were eminently necessary if Societies calling themselves Fabian were to spring up all over the place; for however tolerant the National Agent might be and however much Fabianism was accepted at the Labour Party headquarters in London, the ancient prejudice against Fabians as superior, smug, interfering intellectuals whose loyalty could not be relied upon,[1] was still very much alive in many provincial towns. Two incidents may be recorded as illustrations.

In the winter of 1942, at a week-end conference called partly to discuss the promotion of Local Fabian Societies, a Labour Party agent from Essex—he subsequently became an M.P.—who had arrived in a mood of deep suspicion, got up at the close of proceedings to deliver a recantation. He had intended, he said, to oppose the establishment of any Fabian Society in his own area; but having listened to the discussion and to Margaret Cole in particular, he had changed his mind; he now thought

[1] Cf. the story of Tract 70. As late as June 1941, 'John Stone', in a *Fabian News* article criticising the Tracts generally, wrote of the 'dreadful smugness' characteristic of Fabians.

'it would be a good thing for a Labour Party to have a snob section in it'. This candid compliment was accepted in the spirit offered. The other risk was exemplified in a letter once received by Dorothy Fox, proposing the foundation of a Fabian Society in the town of X. The letter, with very fortunate indiscretion, was signed 'Smith, late Chairman X Labour Party, Jones, late Treasurer ditto, Brown, late Secretary, ditto'—this innocent give-away saved the Fabian Society from being made a pawn in a private Party quarrel in X.

The obvious way to deal with these and other possible troubles was to give the Executive, and the Executive alone, the right to grant the use of the Fabian name to any Society, and to make this approval dependent upon the presentation of a constitution satisfactory on all essential points. But when proposals on those lines were submitted to a meeting of Local Societies in December 1942, they revolted—not against the suggestion itself, but against the 'undemocratic' nature of the means by which it was to be carried out. Their members, they pointed out, were not members of the Society itself; they had not voted for the Executive, but they were to be disciplined by a body over which they had no control whatever. The Local Societies, at that moment, had some very vigorous and vocal representatives; the opposition was led by Gwyneth Morgan, for many years secretary of the Cardiff Society and of the Welsh Regional Council, John Diamond, secretary of the large Central London Fabian Society (not to be confused with the John Diamond, M.P., who became Treasurer of the Society in 1950), and James Callaghan, now M.P., and refused to abate its demands until at a lengthy Conference with the Executive they had gained their principal points of difference, and had secured that members of Local Societies certified by their secretary might vote in Executive elections. (About 10 per cent, at a guess, availed themselves annually of this hard-won privilege.)[1]

After this brush, however, the Local Societies settled down, became more and more numerous and more and more estab-

[1] The Socialist Propaganda Committee after this developed into a full Standing Committee of the Executive, containing representatives from the Local Societies, the national Labour Party office, as well as others directly interested in education and propaganda. It has been chaired since 1944 by Arthur Skeffington, now M.P. for Hayes and Harlington, and the most prominent of the 'new Fabians' who were members of the old Society and had not joined N.F.R.B.

lished, though it was always to be impossible to rely on the permanence of an organisation which depended, inevitably, on the disinterested enthusiasm and available time of a few people to keep it alive and in working order. One or two removals from a district, a local squabble, the arrival of a baby to the secretary, can too often be sufficient to cause the rapid decline of an apparently flourishing Society, and names come and go, over the years, from the official directory. Nevertheless, the growing interest of the Executive, which at the beginning of 1947, for all that the financial situation was becoming unpropitious, set aside a modest 'Fund for Local Society Development', and even more the fostering maternal care expended by Dorothy Fox on Societies from their first birth pangs onwards gradually began to have their effect. As early as mid-1942 *Fabian News* printed a brief summary 'News from the Societies'—a feature harking back some thirty years—and this column gradually grew until it occupied a good half of the much slenderised wartime *News*. (Some energetic Societies also ran local journals of their own when paper supplies permitted.) Soon, the Local Societies Committee took to having an annual meeting of its own just preceding the A.G.M., as well as its own recruiting tea-party held as one of the sideshows in the Labour Party's Annual Conference. By 1946, under the guidance first of Margaret Cole and then of Mary Stewart, wife of Michael Stewart, M.P., it was planning research of its own on matters of local interest such as public libraries and museums, the use made by local Councils of their statutory powers, the working of some of the welfare services—some of these enquiries formed the basis of pamphlets or *Quarterly* articles. It also encouraged Societies to help Fabian writers on cognate subjects by answering questionnaires and sending in the results of local study. In the financial crisis of 1948, the Local Society movement was strongly enough established to make a considerable direct contribution to the urgent appeals made by the Revenue Campaign Council (see below), and it is worth noting that when the national membership of the Society came down with a run after the peak, the number of Local Societies and of their members fell much less in proportion.

The Fabian Colonial Bureau

Of the two other departments of the Society the Fabian Colonial Bureau (renamed the Fabian Commonwealth Bureau since 1958) was the more successful and the more self-contained; at one time, indeed, it was for a while almost a society-within-a-society, drawing a regular subsidy from the central funds, but keeping its own separate accounts and more or less conducting its own affairs.

From its foundation in 1940 the Colonial Bureau's work was rather different from that of the rest of the Society; it provided, in fact, a sort of microcosm of what the original founders would have liked to do for the whole of the British social scene, had there ever been funds enough or workers enough to make this practicable. The very first plans presented to the Executive make this clear. Its purpose was to be to formulate, in practical terms, that part of 'War Aims' which dealt with dependent Empires—British, for the most part—their liberation and transformation into self-governing states, as laid down time and again in the declarations and programmes of Socialist and Labour parties the world over. This purpose it proposed to achieve by the bringing together of Socialists of experience and knowledge for discussion and conference, by setting up committees of enquiry—three of these came into existence during the Bureau's first year of life—and by publishing books and pamphlets.

So far, this was just what the Society as a whole was doing. But the Bureau intended to carry matters further. It set out to compile a library of current journals and press-cuttings, and offered itself as a general enquiry office on colonial questions—two fields which the Society itself had deliberately decided not to enter, though it was of course forced from time to time to try to answer questions put to it by members and others. It began quickly to follow up its research and the information gathered by practical effort, notably by deputations to Ministers and departmental officials and by questions in Parliament. The latter soon involved it in close relations with a 'panel' of interested M.P.s, who were willing and anxious to put down prepared questions and to receive from the Bureau briefings for speeches to be made in debate—some of the questions and speeches were reported in *Empire*, which gradually built itself up an extra-European circulation; it also made contact with the leaders of nationalist movements in the colonies, a contact which naturally grew rapidly as colony after colony came nearer to self-government. In 1941 the formation of a Nigerian Fabian Society was announced; in 1948 the Secretary and R. W. Sorensen, M.P., a member of the Advisory Committee, were invited by the Nigerian Labour movement to tour Nigeria; and any important visitor or deputation to Britain from colonial territories was safe to be invited by the Bureau (sometimes in the House of Commons, sometimes in the town house of Lord Faringdon, a strong supporter from its inception and after 1951 its chairman) to formal or informal meetings with members of the Society. A 'midway' activity was the effort, partly with the assistance of Trade Unionists, Co-operators, and civil servants, working and retired, to anticipate in advance some of the social problems with which emergent nationalities would have to deal, to save them from some of the mistakes and disasters which had happened in England and elsewhere. *Labour and the Colonies* was one of the Bureau's first pamphlets; a much deeper study was that of the possibilities of co-operation, which was initiated in the first year with the aid of C. F. Strickland, the famous authority on village co-operation in India, and came out in 1945 as a book, *Co-operation in the Colonies*. *Local Government in the Colonies* followed it in 1950.

The Colonial Bureau was thus to some extent a *Dinge an sich*, seeking to combine within itself—though loudly and continuously complaining about the insufficiency of its resources—research, propaganda, information and political pressure.[1] It intended, in fact, to be the former S.S.I.P. and N.F.R.B. rolled into one, and to add to their functions that of a 'pressure group', lobbying and pestering M.P.s, Ministers and civil servants. No small ambition; and while the Bureau, naturally, never commanded resources enough to do all on these lines that it would have liked—what society of Radicals ever did?—it none the less did something, and sometimes some very effective things, on all of them. The large measure of success which it attained can be ascribed to a variety of causes.

The first, there is no doubt, was the quality of its personnel. Dr. Rita Hinden, who originated the idea of the Bureau and was its paid secretary for ten years and its honorary secretary for four more, was a remarkably able woman, South African born, who

[1] See, for a very clear summary of its purpose and working, Rita Hinden's article in the Diamond Jubilee issue of *Fabian Quarterly*. The 'political pressure' side of its work occasionally led to difficulties, when letters were sent to the Press under the Secretary's name which seemed to conflict with the principle of the 'self-denying ordinance'. This trouble was finally settled by giving the General Secretary of the Society a right of veto.

had gained her doctorate by work in the Jewish Agency on economic development in Palestine. She had, from the first, a very clear idea of what she wanted the Bureau to be and how she thought it ought to work, which in setting up a new organisation is at least half the battle. Moreover, her conviction and her clear-mindedness made it easy for her to persuade others to work for her Bureau and to help to pay for it. (Her successors, Marjorie Nicholson and Lady Selwyn Clarke, wife of the former Governor of the Seychelles, carried on the tradition which she had established.) The Bureau's first chairman was Arthur Creech Jones, of whom no more need be said here than that in 1945 he became, without question asked or doubt expressed, first Under-Secretary and then Secretary of State for the Colonies. He was succeeded by Frank Horrabin, whose interest in the ending of imperialism had been lifelong, and who did the Bureau the inestimable service of handing over to it a ready-made journal (*Empire*, renamed *Venture* in 1949); he was followed in turn by Lord Faringdon, the most 'colonial-minded' member of the House of Lords. The names and records of those 'experts' who from time to time assisted the Bureau with advice, writing, research and agitation would fill a small *Who's Who* pamphlet. Strickland's name has already been mentioned; to his might be added, as a selection, those of Leonard Woolf, Noel Brailsford, Lord Listowel (until 1960 Governor-General of Ghana), John Dugdale, M.P., sometime Minister of State for the Colonies, Sir Drummond Shiels, M.P., once Under-Secretary to Sidney Webb, James Griffiths, M.P., and the late David Adams, M.P., Sir Alan Pim, C. W. Greenidge of the Anti-Slavery Society, the anthropologists Margaret Read, Audrey Richards and Dr M. Fortes, Wilfrid Benson of the I.L.O., Neil Beaton of the Scottish Co-operative Wholesale Society, Andrew Dalgleish of the T.U.C.—and Dr Hastings Banda. In addition to all these, the Bureau was always able to count on the assistance of regular volunteers, some of these working almost full-time to help it in its day-to-day routine tasks. Retired colonial officials, who did not fancy spending the evening of their days walking about Cheltenham or playing golf, were a noticeable source of recruitment; a helper of a different kind was, curiously enough, the grandson of Henry Hutchinson of the Hutchinson Trust. One way and another, the Bureau had at its command a personnel of remarkably high quality.

The second source of strength was that it had mapped out its own field of operations as clearly as was possible under the circumstances. It was *British* imperialism, and the British colonies, with which it was chiefly concerned; other empires might sometimes be discussed in conferences, but except on one occasion, when it had a look at *America's Colonial Record*,[1] it did not seek to solve other countries' problems for them. It did not, except, again, for a single publication on Newfoundland before that distressed island linked itself with Canada,[2] involve itself in the affairs of the self-governing Dominions;[3] as regards South Africa, its interest was confined to the High Commission Territories. India was outside its purview and remitted to the Society itself, which organised an Indian Affairs Group from 1945 to 1947; and only once did it put a tentative toe into the troubled waters of Palestine, where the reputation of the first Fabian Colonial Secretary had foundered.[4] Its first published book, Rita Hinden's *Plan for Africa* (1942), struck the main keynote; African questions, not unnaturally, attracted more of its attentions than those of other parts of the world. By its third year of life, however, it had set up a committee on the West Indies; a year or two later it was producing plans for Malaya, and studying the awkward (and still unresolved) problems of the 'strategic colonies'—Malta, Cyprus, Gibraltar and Hong Kong; but it was never tempted to stray outside the colonial field.

The third fortunate factor was that this chosen field was one in which the broad principles of Socialist policy were agreed, and had been agreed for a very long time. Everybody was sure that imperialism must come to an end after the war and that the subject peoples must be freed. There was difference of opinion, naturally, over method and timing, but except in the case of Palestine (which raised issues that were not, properly speaking, the responsibility of the Colonial Office at all) there did not exist, in regard to colonial policy, the deep divisions which were to appear, for example, in the attitude of Labour to American loans, to military co-operation with the U.S.A., or to the U.S.S.R.

[1] Research Pamphlet 119, by John Collier.

[2] Research Pamphlet 86, by Lord Ammon.

[3] The Fabian Society, in July 1944, considered the possibility of setting up a group on the Dominions, but nothing came of it.

[4] *Palestine Controversy*, Research Pamphlet 101. For Sidney Webb and Palestine, see Chapter XIII in *The Webbs and Their Work*.

and the cold war. No doubt this was to some extent due to inertia, to the fact that delegates to Labour conferences left 'imperialism', as they did 'education', to experts to discuss while they went to have tea; the fact remains, and the Colonial Bureau's planners could therefore go ahead in the confidence that the Labour Party, and 'enlightened' opinion in general, were conditioned to receive the advice which it decided to tender, and it could resolve its own differences, such as they were, around its own office table and without recriminations or resignations. This may be part of the reason why, in 1945, when proposals for a new volume of Fabian Essays had again come to an impasse,[1] the Bureau was able to produce a book of *Fabian Colonial Essays*, edited by Rita Hinden, without any fur flying.

Between 1941 and 1949 the Colonial Bureau published eighteen pamphlets in the Research Series, as well as *Empire* (a monthly after 1946), and four more popular ones in a series called 'Colonial Controversy'. But it should not be assumed either from this record or from the factors listed above that its life was perfect sailing. There was, for one thing, occasional friction within the Fabian Society itself, whose officers sometimes complained that the workers in the Bureau mistook a highly efficient section of the Society for the Society itself, put its interests first of all, and were not sufficiently conscious of the heavy demands it was making on the central funds.[2]

Such disputes, though they troubled Executive meetings from time to time—especially when, as is recounted later, funds ran short and 'economy' had to be discussed—amounted to little more than the frictions which enthusiastic devotion to a cause is apt from time to time to generate. Much more serious was the outside criticism which the Bureau had to face, particularly after 1945, from those who wanted to go faster and farther to meet the demands of the leaders of the dependent peoples than the Bureau was prepared to recommend. There had always been 'whole-hoggers', such as some of the members of

[1] See p. 276. A volume of *New Fabian Colonial Essays*, edited by Creech Jones, was published in 1959.

[2] The Bureau did continually make efforts, and not without success, to raise funds for colonial work. But, aside from the inevitable arguments about 'earmarked' contributions, the sums so raised never came near to meeting the costs, even when account was taken of a proportion of the money brought in by 'all-in' subscribers to the Society's activities.

Fenner Brockway's League Against Imperialism, who wanted to do everything at once and regarded the Bureau as the home of 'inevitable gradualism'—or 'hopelessly reactionary', that convenient term of abuse; and after the Labour Government took office, when the Bureau tended to be regarded, rightly or wrongly, as responsible for all the actions of the Government, whether large or small, this form of criticism was naturally intensified.

> I resigned my membership of the Bureau [said an angry letter received at the close of 1947] after I had found that the Bureau merely seemed to be acting as a sort of Public Relations Officer for the Labour Government's Colonial Ministers, *whose policies are indistinguishable from those of the Conservatives* [my italics]. I cannot conscientiously support people who do not try to live up to principles they have maintained so long in opposition.[1]

This feeling, though at times very vocal and vigorous, was not sufficient to do great damage. However, the Bureau was very conscious of the change in its position from the days in which it could happily spread itself in calling attention to 'the state of miserable neglect' (Rita Hinden) in which the Colonies languished in the 'thirties, to the new dispensation in which it would have to accept at least part-responsibility for righting the abuses which remained. In its Annual Report for 1946–7, written well before the angry letter had been received, it said that it had thought very long about the attitude it ought to adopt to the new Government and had reached the conclusion that 'we would be true to the Fabian tradition if we maintained an attitude of independence and acted as a friendly critic and spur, rather than an uncritical supporter. This has not been an easy rôle, and we have at times received criticism from both sides.'

The criticism received from the Government side is not recorded; that it was less severe may be concluded from the fact that when the Colonial Development Council was formed in 1948 three members of the Bureau's Advisory Committee, together with the Secretary, were made members of it. The attitude of 'independent critic' was maintained where felt to be

[1] Quoted from *Fabian Quarterly*, Spring, 1948. The Secretary contributed a lengthy reply, in which she pointed out the necessity of distinguishing between policy at the centre and performance by local officers in the field, and in general defended the Bureau from the charge of being blindly uncritical.

necessary;[1] but it was not very often so felt. All in all, the Fabian Society could claim that in affairs colonial its influence had played no small part in formulating policy which was actually carried out.

The Fabian International Bureau

The International Bureau, founded only a few months after its brother, took under its wing the Anglo-French Committee whose beginnings have already been noted. This committee, because of obvious difficulties of personnel and communications appearing after the fall of France, hardly functioned at all as a committee, though it arranged a few meetings and lunches—one for André Philip, the Socialist deputy for Lyons, bringing news of the Resistance. Its chief preoccupation was running the journal *France and Britain*. The *New Statesman* declined to carry the publication for more than one issue; for a few months Sir William Williams, a member of the Committee, persuaded the W.E.A.'s *Highway* to issue it as a Supplement, but thereafter the Fabian Society had to conduct it single-handed. It continued to appear monthly until the midsummer of 1945, a modest octavo of 8–16 pages (according to supplies of paper), which yet managed to give its readers a very fair coverage from well-informed sources of French affairs and conditions in Occupied and Unoccupied France and in France beyond the seas. Looking through its back numbers, after reading the recent memoirs of De Gaulle, it is astonishing to find how much of the history of those years was explained in the pages of *France and Britain*, and how the paper, receiving De Gaulle at first with caution, then backed him strongly against the futile flirtations of the United States Government with the Pétainists and with nonentities like Giraud, returning, after the Liberation, to more strongly expressed doubts of the political intentions of the Liberator with his flaming sword and his mission to recreate France in his own image of her. The journal had a faithful following in Britain of friends of France who were anxious for news; it was something of a disappointment for the Society to discover, just before its demise, that a large number of copies of every issue, purchased by the Free French Government for circulation in France and overseas, had, by some misunderstanding all too common in those days, never left these shores at all, but had spent the war

[1] e.g., in regard to the handling of the case of Seretse Khama.

lying safely in a cellar. With the reopening of communications generally, so small a publication ceased to have much value, and it was discontinued: it was seven years before the Fabian Society again ran a journal of foreign affairs.

The history of the International Bureau was much less of a success story than that of its brother. For this—which indeed was all too easy to foresee—there were several reasons; but one of them was certainly not lack of quality in its workers. It is true that Mildred Bamford, who was its paid secretary from August 1941 to March 1946, was an organiser rather than a research worker of the status of Rita Hinden, but she was supervised by an honorary secretary, Doreen Warriner, who was an expert; its first chairman was Philip Noel-Baker, the Nobel Peace prizewinner and authority for uncounted years on international affairs, and on his resignation in 1943 Leonard Woolf held the chair for ten years; its first Advisory Committee included, in addition to the foregoing, such well-known names as those of Harold Laski, Noel Brailsford, R. W. G. Mackay (promoter of Federal Union and later M.P. for Reading), Kingsley Martin, Francis Williams and Barbara (now Lady) Wootton;[1] and it was able, particularly in the first few years, to call upon a great deal of outside goodwill. Its first conference, 'After the Nazis', held in December 1941, was very well received, by the exiles in particular, as was its first pamphlet, *Help Germany to Revolt*;[2] and in the autumn of 1942 it organised a most impressive week-end conference at Oxford, under the title 'When Hostilities Cease', at which the discussions, by English and foreign experts, were broadcast on the European, North American and Empire services, published shortly afterwards in book form, and contributed to the groundwork of UNRRA and other subsequent relief schemes.

This Conference was the Bureau's most spectacular achievement, though its use as a forum for Socialists in exile, and the similar use of its offspring, the International Youth Forum, set up early in 1944, was undeniable—at least until the war was over. What prevented it from being more successful was a weakness, not peculiar to itself, but of the Labour movement as a whole.

[1] Later comers included Lord Faringdon, for some time Vice-Chairman, Will Arnold-Forster, R. H. S. Crossman, M.P., Patrick Gordon-Walker, M.P., Jim Griffiths, M.P., Denis Healey, M.P., and Dorothy Woodman.

[2] Research Series 62, March 1942.

At its foundation, the International Bureau announced that it had three aims:

1. To promote research into international problems in order that there may be a wider knowledge of the facts and an understanding of the problems throughout the Labour movement.
2. To promote Socialist co-operation through personal contacts and discussions between British Socialists and Socialists from other countries.
3. To prepare the ground for an international Socialist policy in international affairs.

The first object, so far as funds allowed, it pursued steadily, even though the subjects on which pamphlets were published may seem rather erratically chosen;[1] there were pamphlets on the International Labour Office, on World Co-operation, on Labour in Latin America and in the U.S.A., on post-war Spain and post-war Jugoslavia, on world food supplies, on Reparations (by Cole), and a very interesting if highly visionary plan for a complete integration of transport in Europe by M. Zwalf, the research officer of the International Transport Workers' Federation.[2] Late in 1946 it despatched a party of six, led by James Callaghan, M.P., to study conditions in Czechoslovakia; their report, now an historical curiosity, was published shortly afterwards; later still—in 1950—a delegation went to Norway, to do for that country, on a much smaller scale, what the N.F.R.B. delegation had previously done for Sweden. The results of these and of other studies were of course made known to Bureau members and members of the public by the usual Fabian methods.

The second object was thoroughly pursued during the war, as has already been suggested; it would not be far from the truth to say that up till 1945 it occupied the major part of the Bureau's attention and accounted for the majority of those who paid subscriptions to it alone, and not as part of a general subscription. But with the ending of the war ended also the need for asylum and for rooms and platforms where exiled Socialists could discuss their hopes and plans. Except for the exiles who

[1] See, however, p. 297 f. for a note on the difficulties of 'pamphlet planning' in a voluntary society.

[2] Research Series 82, 87, 122, 133, 114, 94 and 109.

had no hope of return—and the Bureau was not disposed to turn itself into a home for perpetual *émigrés*—the Socialists-in-exile went back, and were promptly immersed, not to say overwhelmed, in the problems of their own re-created countries;[1] when some of them returned again as honoured visitors, it was, quite properly, the International Section of the Labour Party which received them if they were not guests of the Government, rather than the Fabian Bureau. This should, it seems, have been the moment to attempt seriously the third of the Bureau's objects—preparing the ground for an international Socialist policy; but it was exactly then that the difficulties appeared.

The International Bureau could not, like the Colonial Bureau, set to work on the assumption of a common idea among members of the Labour Party and radical opinion generally, on the essentials of policy in foreign affairs. For the Labour Party had not got a foreign policy at all. Before the war it was the least 'internationally minded' of all the constituents of the International.[2] During the inter-war years its policy could have been summed up as 'Disarmament and the League of Nations'; when that policy was kicked to pieces by Hitler the Party suffered long and agonising reappraisals in Party Conference after Party Conference until it ultimately decided that the Nazis must be fought with all force—a correct and even a heartening decision, but scarcely to be called a foreign policy. The other side of Labour 'foreign' policy was a deep if not quite universal conviction, reinforced after June 1941, that the first need for the future was an alliance between Great Britain and the Soviet Union.

The first essential for carrying out this policy [the unification of Europe] [said a Fabian Tract of 1942],[3] is to secure the fullest possible measure of agreement between Great Britain and the Soviet Union, the two great European powers upon which the defeat of the Nazis will leave the main burden of European reconstruction. Agreement with the United States is also important; for it is to be hoped that America will play a great part in the rebuilding of our shattered continent. . . . But agreement with the United States, important as it is, is secondary in relation to Europe to agreement with the Soviet

[1] This resulted, naturally, in some falling-off in the numbers of direct subscribers.

[2] See Cole, *History of Socialist Thought*, Vol. III, Chapters III and IV.

[3] Tract 256, *A Word on the Future for British Socialists*. Drawn up for the Labour Party Conference of that year, and put into the hands of all delegates.

Union, because America is far away and may again back out of European affairs when the menace of Nazism has been removed [this, it should be remembered, was written a very few months after Pearl Harbour]. The Soviet Union, on the other hand, is as bound to play the premier part in Eastern Europe, on the morrow of victory, as Great Britain is in the West. It will be a disaster for the whole world if Great Britain, the Soviet Union and the United States do not work closely together for world recovery; and the best hope of getting American help lies in European unity. If Great Britain and the Soviet Union pull opposite ways, no tolerable or durable settlement is even possible; there is no way of solving the German problem; and within a brief time after the peace the continent is likely to be again well on the road to war. [It went on to declare that] the only condition on which there can be real co-operation between the Soviet Union and Great Britain is that Great Britain shall become, in spirit, Socialist

—not Communist.

The sentiments of this passage—part of whose prophecy has been so sadly fulfilled—aroused no opposition in the Society or in the Labour movement; nor did its conclusion. As late as the Victory Conference at Blackpool in 1945 the delegates discussed post-war plans on the assumption that if Labour won the election Stalin would be delighted at the prospect of co-operating with Labour rather than with Churchill—having forgotten the advice of Stalin's predecessor to non-Russian Communist Parties that they should shake Social-Democrats by the hand in order to take them by the throat. But however desirable co-operation with the Soviet Union might be, it too could hardly be described as a complete foreign policy; and when it also began to fade into the distance there was little left but cause for dissension. The Labour Party's own 1945 document, *Let Us Face the Future*, devoted only a page or two to policy outside Britain, in which it committed itself merely to handsome-sounding phrases like 'we must consolidate in peace the great wartime association of the British Commonwealth with the U.S.A. and the U.S.S.R.'; but beyond calling for 'an International Organisation capable of keeping the peace for years to come' it did not suggest how that was to be done.

The Fabian Society had been a trifle more specific than that. In December 1944 a Tract (261) was rushed out, called *Dumbarton Oaks; a Fabian Commentary*, which traversed the first drafts for a United Nations Organisation and registered a fair amount of criticism. Just before Dumbarton Oaks the Bureau had produced a pamphlet by Leonard Woolf on *The International Post-War Settlement*,[1] covering the same ground, the preface to which stated that it was

> an attempt to show the general principles, or perhaps principle, upon which such a policy must be based and how, if that principle is translated into action, it immediately makes the solution of particular problems possible. The International Bureau hopes to be able to produce detailed studies of particular problems of the post-war settlement which may complete and fill in the policy outlined.

This hope, alas, was never fulfilled. As has been shown, there was a variety of pamphlets published, and the Bureau also issued a few memoranda, speakers' notes and reading guides, and early in 1946 held a conference on the Far East—not then an explosive subject. But of general policy nothing is heard until the report of the A.G.M. of 1947 discloses that 'the Bureau has been attempting to examine the whole question of Socialist Foreign Policy. Several papers putting forward conflicting views have been written by members of the Advisory Committee . . . the Chairman of the Bureau is endeavouring to edit all the papers.' This concise statement covers a period of wrangle which had been going on for months. When, in November 1947, the edited document[2] finally appeared it was clear that the 'conflicting opinions' were very far from resolved. The bulk of the text was written by Leonard Woolf, but there was an angry final section by W. N. Ewer, Foreign Editor of the *Daily Herald*, attacking Woolf as an 'appeaser' (of the Soviet Union) and comparing him to Lansbury, the extreme pacifist, or Chamberlain before Munich, and an explanatory preface by Laski, then Chairman of the Society, saying that he admired both contributors and did not agree entirely with either, but that the Executive thought that their combined effort should be published. This soothing approach to the 'Dilemma' did not prevent further criticisms from William Warbey, M.P., and Konni Zilliacus from appearing in subsequent issues of *Fabian Quarterly*.

So did the cold war come to hit the Fabian International Bureau and reduce it, not to extinction, but to comparative weakness. The dispute had really begun with the fierce though unrecorded opposition of Cole to the terms accepted for the post-war American Loan; the battle raged throughout the early

[1] Research Series 85.

[2] Research Series 121, *Foreign Policy: the Labour Party's Dilemma.*

months of 1946, and the general attitude of the Bureau (and of the Executive) towards co-operation with the United States, though it was never uncritically anti-Soviet, certainly contributed to his refusal to stand for the Executive in that year. Doreen Warriner, who largely shared his views, resigned the honorary secretaryship in 1947; the paid Secretary gave up her post, though not for political reasons—and though the Bureau staggered on with assistance, at first paid and afterwards voluntary, from Anne Whyte, who had succeeded in March 1947 in getting a group to agree on a Tract (262) on *The Future of Germany*, it was some time before it pulled itself together into moderate working order. Its troubles were little fault of its own; though 'information' on foreign affairs may be provided, as was done in several publications, research-leading-to-policy, which was the Fabian idea, cannot be effectively conducted when the body for whose benefit the research is designed neither controls the other factors in the picture nor has any idea what it would do with them if it did. It is not, however, entirely wrong to see the neglect of the outside world, with which Shaw had so often reproached the Fabian Society, coming home to roost.

Home Research

Notwithstanding the energy, enthusiasm and effective work of the sections of the Society described in the foregoing pages, its main work still lay, as it had always lain, on what its second wartime conference had called the Home Front—and research on the Home Front; and while the two Bureaux and the Socialist Propaganda Committee were getting under way, the home research side was steadily growing. Its most important product, in the first year or two of the war, was a large book of essays on *Social Security*, edited by W. A. Robson, with the assistance of Joan Clarke, who when Padley was called up took his place as Research Secretary to the Society. This book, though it did not appear in print until 1943, anticipated very much of what was in the Beveridge Report, and in the preceding year its contributors had given to Beveridge collective evidence, which itself was issued as a pamphlet in August 1942.[1] When the Beveridge

[1] Evidence was also given to the later Beveridge enquiry on full employment and was published as *The Prevention of General Unemployment* (Research Series 79). It was violently attacked in the *Quarterly* by two distinguished Fabian economists, Thomas Balogh and G. D. N. Worswick.

Report actually appeared, the Society discussed whether its Social Security sub-committee should undertake a campaign to popularise it, but eventually decided, as it had decided on earlier occasions, that it was a pity to waste scarce Fabian funds on doing jobs which other people could do better, and that it would prefer to lend its research secretary to an all-party Social Security League which would undertake the task—this eventually led to the resignation of Joan Clarke and her replacement by J. C. Gray. A month or two earlier, the Executive Committee had given permission for the setting up of an Industrial Advisory Panel, whose first secretary, receiving a nominal sum in expenses, was W. A. Fiske (at the time of writing the Chief Whip of the London County Council). This rather loosely organised body in course of time set on foot a good number of enquiries into various aspects of socialisation and the organisation of industry.

The 'step-aside' from propaganda in favour of the Beveridge Report is an illustration of the kind of problem which faced the Fabian Society month by month during the years of expansion—and indeed afterwards. The total output of Fabian publications for the ten years following the outbreak of war is set out on p. 305, and roughly analysed as to subject. The reader may justly observe that it would make more interesting reading if actual titles and authors were listed, and some appraisement given of the contents. So it certainly would; and if the space—a lot of space, be it noted—were available, this could have been done. But much of it would have been of interest only to exceptionally specialising specialists, since the great bulk of the output consisted of pamphlets, and pamphlets, whatever their immediate merits, can only be of marginal concern, twelve to twenty years after their date of publication, to anyone but a historian concerned with their particular subject-matter. Readers will have to accept the author's assurance that, as a result of the procedure described on a later page, no pamphlet or other publication was put out unless, in the words to be found on the covers of all, it 'embodied facts and opinions worthy of consideration within the Labour Movement'—and that a good few of them are in fact worth re-reading today. The main point of the table is that it shows a very high rate of productivity for a Society with so small a membership; and the additional fact of importance is that the total could have been much higher, had resources been available to meet the potential demand. 'Demand', here, is used in two senses. On the one hand, as the war progressed and the mood described earlier in this chapter grew, there came into being an increasingly large public which was avid for any sort of discussion of the possibilities of a brave new world, in books, pamphlets, periodicals, lectures—anywhere. A fraction of this public joined the Fabian Society; more bought and read anything it put out. The circulation of the *New Statesman* jumped to eighty or ninety thousand: the Left Book Club, with its outpouring of left-wing books in limp red covers—*Guilty Men* and *Tory M.P.* will probably be remembered today—outsold them all, particularly among the young.

Here was the selling demand. But here was also a demand that the Fabian Society, as a respectable Socialist body manned by expert and enquiring persons belonging to the Labour Party but not tied in detail by its declared policy, should undertake and publish enquiries into any and every problem on which an intelligent Socialist might wish to make up his mind. The number of these was legion, and it became almost a commonplace for the officers and Executive members of the Society to be asked why the Fabians had not published a pamphlet—set up a committee—on this or that. There were, also, not lacking those who, having in their desks or on their minds a pamphlet on, say, School Meals or Currency Reform, conceived of the Society as a suitable vehicle for bringing it before the public; and some of these creations, particularly when they had gone through the 'licking into shape' which was the lot of all Fabian work, turned out to be valuable additions to the *corpus*. A very few did not.

The Society, growing fast and feeling full of optimism, was, in general, ready to entertain as many of these propositions as possible, subject to inevitable limitations. The first of these, though by no means the most important, was the wartime supply of paper. The Society, in common with all other bodies, did suffer to some extent—though it was much helped, during the early days of the war, by a gift of a thousand pounds' worth of that precious commodity from a sympathiser, to be used for research pamphlets; *Fabian News* was reduced to a single sheet resembling a railway timetable, and the *Quarterly*'s size and make-up became erratic. But the Paper Control's attitude towards 'educational' publications was kindly; and the necessary paper was secured for the Fabian books and for a good number of other publications. As soon as the control was removed, the output went up with a rush.

The second limitation was that imposed by the Society's own standards. With a membership running into several thousands, it was no longer possible to submit drafts of Tracts or pamphlets for consideration by the membership or even by the Executive; that practice had indeed been abandoned years before. But every draft, commissioned or non-commissioned,[1] had to run the gamut of at least two readers appointed by the Executive, one of whom was, in theory, an 'expert' fully conversant with the subject, and the other was to satisfy himself or herself that the draft was 'Fabian' in its approach, and measured up to Fabian standards of presentation. (It may be admitted at once that not all of the second-strings were connoisseurs of style as well as of Fabianism; the standards set by Shaw and Hubert Bland would not have condoned some of the pedestrian work which appeared in print.) These readers took their task seriously; and successive General Secretaries or Research Secretaries were from time to time faced with the delicate task of conveying fundamental (and sometimes very forthright) criticisms to people who had spent a great deal of time and effort on writing between ten and fifteen thousand words—often to a syllabus agreed in advance—and asking them what they proposed to do about it. If there was real dispute or difficulty, the procedure might be repeated and other readers called in.[2] It was part of the earliest Fabian tradition, namely that everything that was put out by the Society should be, as far as humanly possible, accurate, tolerably sensible, and able to stand up to informed criticism; but it was a stiff standard for the writer, and it is not surprising that some projected pamphlets took a very long time to appear, and others fell by the wayside altogether. It is more surprising that very few indeed of the would-be authors resented the criticisms, and the re-writing expected of them, so much as to take themselves and their brain-children out of reach—some were in fact grateful for the trouble

[1] 'Commissioned' does not mean 'paid for'. Very few Fabian authors got a halfpenny for their work, except some of the contributors to books. 'Unsolicited' manuscripts, Pease had found, were rarely worth anything; later Fabian experience was rather less unhappy.

[2] 'Difficult' pamphlets—or pamphlets whose authors were particularly resistant—might be submitted to anything up to half a dozen readers.

taken and the improvements made; it is also noticeable that, even including the exceptional dispute about international policy, the occasions on which differences of opinion were so wide that they persisted into the final document could be counted on the fingers of one hand—pamphlets on the future of the House of Lords and of the B.B.C. are two instances that come to the mind.

The third limitation was of subject. As we have seen, the Society endeavoured, on the whole, not to attempt tasks for which it was not fitted, or which were beyond its strength. It had at the back of its mind, even though none of the present-day Executive may have read them, the restrictive phrases of Tract 70;[1] and though the restrictions might not be the same as in 1896—it was hardly possible, for example, for a Fabian economist of the 'forties to have 'no opinions upon the Currency'—they were still felt to be there, and some suggestions were turned down on that ground. One particular self-restriction arose directly from the relationship of the Society with the various branches of the Labour movement itself. It is illustrated by a proposal made by Laski to the Executive that a sub-committee should be set up to consider the present state of the Labour Party.[2] This proposal was never followed up; and the Society also trod very gingerly in its approach to the internal problems of either Trade Unionism or Co-operation. This attitude was strongly criticised from time to time, and may even be thought pusillanimous. It must be remembered, however, that the Society was not only affiliated to a Party very sensitive to criticism, it was also—increasingly, as time went on—appealing to Labour organisations for financial support,[3] and seeking to gain the confidence of Divisional Labour Parties. It is at least arguable that if the 'snob section' had started to poke its nose into the private affairs of Party and Unions it would have got that nose severely bitten and lost its standing within the Party; but it was certainly a limitation of scope, a price paid for acceptability. Later on, when the Labour Party's own research department had grown to a respectable size and efficiency, liaison machinery was introduced to avoid clashing and overlapping; and no sense of

[1] See p. 92. [2] Minutes, July 6th, 1942.

[3] In 1947–8, Transport House paid a subsidy to enable a research worker to do for it a study of commercial insurance; there were other grants to come later.

restriction prevented the Society from offering the Party a programme for its expected second term of office.[1]

Finally, there was the obvious limitation of the availability of authors. There might be literally no one—or no one sympathetic with Socialism—who was competent to tackle a subject which was crying out to be tackled; if there were, he might have no time, or at least no time to spare from his current work, for the 'by-product' of writing a Fabian pamphlet and re-writing it to meet the views of critics. The records of the Home Research Committee are littered with notes of projects which never came to birth or perished untimely, because the author had no time, lost heart, or in a war-time society continually on the move disappeared to China or Peru. The International Bureau decided at one time to publish a pamphlet on Oil—an obviously important subject; but after the chosen author, having accepted the assignment, had been chased from London to Washington, from Washington to Cairo and back again, the project was abandoned in despair.

These factors, taken together, made it difficult to formulate a plan of research, or to keep to it when planned—an ordinary member who did not follow what the Society was doing but relied on the pieces of printed matter which reached him month by month must have received an impression of something very like chaos. Even in the Minutes of the Executive and other committees the process is not always easy to follow. Sub-committees and *ad hoc* committees come and go; there is generally a record of their setting-up but not always of their doings or their demise—some, of course, never died officially but faded into limbo. The Executive made considerable efforts to co-ordinate. In the middle of 1943 it set up a Home Research Committee for that purpose, and eight months later ordered the Minutes of all committees to be sent to it for approval; a procedure of which it tired fairly soon. In the middle of 1944, after Dr Barou had developed in lively and strident tones the thesis that it was muddling and frittering away its resources and the A.G.M. had shown some measure of agreement with him, it appointed a Research Planning Committee (really the Home Research Committee under another name), and ordered it to produce a Plan, which it did by the end of the year.[2] This resulted, *inter alia*, in

[1] Research Series 124, *The Second Five Years*, by Ian Mikardo.

[2] Minutes, July 18th and 27th, and October 10th, 1944.

the appointment of assistant research workers for home, colonial and international affairs; but two and a half years later, it seemed, the job had to be done again. Nothing would really make it tidy, or prevent eager members from going their own way, singly or in groups, and producing what they wanted to produce—even if prevention had been really a good idea—and the Society resigned itself to what it could get. Which was a great deal.

Nevertheless, it is possible, by looking at the output as a whole and by studying the intermittent reports in the *Quarterly*, to get a general idea of what the Society was doing on the home front through the years in question. In the earlier part of the war it was very much occupied with problems arising directly out of it—evacuation, billeting, communal feeding, compensation for war injuries and the like. Soon, as we have seen, it turned to the social services, full employment and questions arising therefrom; it interested itself, naturally, in public education, in the discussions which preceded the 1944 Act[1] and in the provisions of the Act when passed; it proceeded tentatively into schemes for nationalising land and electricity supply, and it published two editions of *Facts for Socialists*. As the end of the war drew nearer and nearer it became increasingly concerned with the situation which would arise when it was over, and began to prepare studies, some of which appeared before the surrender and some soon afterwards, on the future of transport, coal and power, agriculture and the government control of industry and labour, as well as the omnibus warning mentioned earlier in this book, *Reconstruction Then and Now*; it started work, through groups, on the evidence it proposed to give to the Royal Commission on Population, the Royal Commission on Equal Pay, and others of the kind.

When the war in Europe was over, and the results of the election had been declared, astonishing all the leading politicians except Aneurin Bevan, the Fabian Society was loud in the general rejoicing. At the excited Blackpool Conference its honorary secretary had come to the rostrum to pledge wholehearted co-operation; the Local Societies had flung themselves into the battle, and its members were known to have contributed strongly

[1] See, for example, Research Series 76, *A New Charter for Education*, by Grace Leybourne, and 90, *The Education Act, 1944*, by Lady Simon of Wythenshawe.

to the discussions leading up to the production of *Let Us Face the Future*, written by a Fabian, Michael Young,[1] then the Party's research secretary, and generally agreed to be the most effective of all Labour manifestoes. In the new Parliament, it seemed to be reaping its reward; later in the year, Margaret Cole, in an ecstatic statistical study (pre-psephologist) of the election results joyfully listed the number of Fabians newly come to the seat of power—229 out of the 394 M.P.s elected as Labour, ten Cabinet Ministers, including the Premier, thirty-five Under-Secretaries and other officers of State, and eleven parliamentary private secretaries.[2] 'Why,' said John Parker's wife on being introduced to the new Parliamentary Party, 'it looks just like an enormous Fabian School!' The comment was not wide of the mark.

The Society was certain that it would find plenty to do under the new dispensation, even if it was not quite sure, immediately, what that was, except to try and ensure that the local elections to be held in the autumn produced as many Labour majorities as possible in county and borough, and to speed up its own research and publication programme; the second task it pursued with such enthusiasm that the Annual Report for 1945–6 had to list no fewer than *nineteen* research pamphlets published during the year, as well as four books—*Population and the People* (the reprint of the evidence given to the Royal Commission), *Co-operation in the Colonies*, *The Condition of the British People, 1911–1945*, by Mark Abrams, and a collection of essays, edited by F. W. Bateson, entitled *Towards a Socialist Agriculture*.

Fabian News of September observed, without too much tact, that 'we must continue with the work of educating our masters'. By the following June the Executive had done some reconsideration and suggested to the A.G.M. that the function of the Society in the forthcoming year ought to be:

first, to expound the principles and beliefs of Socialism in terms of the modern world; secondly, to look beyond the immediate Party programme to the subsequent tasks of a Socialist Administration and to

[1] Subsequently founder of Consumer Research and the journal *Which*.

[2] Research Series 102, *The General Election and After*. This bit of bragging had one unforeseen effect; a certain number of politically ambitious innocents, reading in it an indication that the road to Parliament lay through the Fabian Society, hastened to join its ranks. As it became apparent that there were not likely to be a number of winnable seats going begging, this 'band-wagon' membership as rapidly dropped away.

initiate full discussion on these well in advance; thirdly, to act as advisers and consultants as required during the execution of the current programme; and fourthly, to act as a recruiting and training ground for the thousands of people [*sic*], particularly in the provinces, needed to fill key positions in the administration and development of a Socialist Society.

This definition, though some would not think it very happily phrased, was accepted by the meeting; but meantime there had been a considerable change in the staff of the Society.

John Parker, having accepted the post of Under-Secretary to the Dominions Office, had to resign the part-time general secretaryship which he had held for ten years since his election to Parliament. As an immediate expedient, H. D. Hughes, now out of the Army and an M.P., was made Acting General Secretary on the basis of as much time as he could spare; he was already P.P.S. to Ellen Wilkinson, the Minister of Education, and by May he had to give up Fabian work altogether. Parker shared the honorary secretaryship with Margaret Cole, and the post of General Secretary was advertised. It was filled in April by Bosworth Monck, a Fabian of some five years' standing, who had been a production engineer and a wartime civil servant, and had toured China and the Soviet Union. He started to boost the Society with great vigour, his efforts culminating in November in a 'Jubilee Rally and Celebration Concert' in the Albert Hall, paid for by the *Daily Herald*, and graced by several Ministers and the London Symphony Orchestra conducted by Sir Thomas Beecham; but in February 1947 the Society was again advertising for a General Secretary.

To explain this unfortunate opening to a new era it is necessary to go back a little in the narrative. It would be pleasant to have been able to say that the Society's funds were as buoyant as its spirits and its programmes; unfortunately that was not the case. Though the membership roll had started to rise early in 1940, it did not produce anything like enough revenue to meet the rising costs in staff and printing alone, which the new masters of the Society were eagerly incurring. As early as October 1943 Emil Davies, whose depressing experience in trying to clear off debt in the old Society had made him apprehensive of a recurrence of crisis, delivered to the Finance and General Purposes Committee a warning that the end of the financial year would probably see a deficit of over £1,000. The committee did not show great concern. It made some minor economies, but preferred to rely on the securing of larger subventions from educational funds recognised as charities, which were available for the research work of the Society, as for that of many other bodies. As it was in fact research that was the principal cause of increased expenditure, this expedient solved the difficulty for a while. But the spenders had not learned caution; they continued a highly expansionist programme, taking on additional staff, hiring outside offices, etc., until at the beginning of 1946 the long-suffering Davies again announced that the funds of the Society were 'in the red', and that a bank overdraft was immediately necessary.

It was in this situation—aggravated by the fact that subscriptions had been allowed to fall heavily into arrears—that Monck took over; and for that situation he had the wrong temperament and the wrong ideas. He was an expansionist, who forty years earlier would have been an ardent supporter of Wells; he wanted to cure the deficit not by saving, but by spending—on circularising thousands of possible subscribers, on advertising, on making a splash, on writing the name FABIAN up in large letters—and this time there was no Shaw to laugh him out of court. His plans were no doubt well intentioned, but they came near to ruining the organisation. For the Fabian Society was not, either then or at any time since its birth, the kind of organisation capable of making a splash; it had no large sums to spend on advertising, and the money which Monck did persuade it to spend was mostly thrown away owing to injudicious use—the mass-circularisation, for example, was stopped half-way because it was producing no new members to speak of. Even the Jubilee Rally, though it cost the Society nothing (except in manpower) and provided a good evening of entertainment for several thousands, proved of no real value, because the emphasis was quite wrong. It featured the oldest leaders—as, indeed, it was bound to do under the circumstances—and recalled the ancient triumphs; it did not suggest, nor did any of the voluminous press reports, that the Society had any function in 1946. 'We're not merely tortoises,' a cynic in the audience remarked, 'we're prehistoric tortoises.' One new member, and one only, enrolled as a result.

Cole, had he been on the spot, might have helped to check the extravagances, but he had just resigned over the foreign policy dispute, and Harold Laski, who took his place as Chairman, had not leisure to give the attention needed (he was heavily involved with his own unfortunate legal action). Davies had already been worsted once and was getting old and deaf; he resigned in 1947 and died in the following year. The Honorary Secretaries, after a good deal of rather distressing argument, succeeded in getting a majority of the Executive to take notice of the discomforting facts; and the dispute was finally settled by Monck's resigning office but remaining on the Executive. The Executive then set itself in earnest to clear up the mess it had allowed to accumulate. It slowed down the publications programme, struck off a mass of defaulters, reduced staff, and made various other economies. The subscription, unchanged since the beginning of the war, was doubled at an emergency members' meeting in November, to come into effect in January; but the immediate financial result was doubtful, and a further alarmist report from the new Treasurer, Ian Mikardo, and his assistant L. A. Gossman, predicted another heavy deficit and suggested a further cut of £2,000 on an expenditure of £13,000: at this, however, the Executive balked, feeling that it might really be lethal, and decided, instead, to make a sustained effort to raise new revenue.[1] A Revenue Campaign Council was formed and set to work vigorously if unspectacularly, seeking subventions from Labour and Trade Union bodies and asking Local Societies to help get money in; and a much-chastened Annual Report told the 1948 A.G.M. that 'we must regretfully record that the last few years have been a period of over-optimistic spending in all directions, which has now turned out to be too much for the resources to sustain; and the Annual General Meeting must face the facts'.

The A.G.M. did so, blinking, and submitting to the death of *Fabian Quarterly*, an expensive product; but it refused to despair or to regard the Society as seriously sick, and it may be recorded now that the output of publications began to rise again, and that, though it took two years more to put the Society on an even financial keel, this was achieved by 1950.

Cole, who after Laski's resignation in September 1948 returned to the Executive and to the chair, showed no pessimism about the future; and though the membership continued to fall slowly, the regular flow of schools, lectures and conferences had not diminished, and in the midst of his wilder efforts Monck had

[1] W. A. Robson thought the cuts ought to have been made, and resigned his long membership of the Executive in protest.

found time to work with a group of high-up civil servants on the reform of the higher civil service, and to produce a long published report and a deputation to the Lord President of the Council. Some of the cuts made were true savings, in that they represented the elimination of waste due to hurry and inadvertence; others were inevitable as the fine flush of victory faded. But it would have been better, and consumed less time and argument in the first years of the Labour Government, if the facts had been realised sooner.

TABLE

Fabian Publications, 1939–1949

1. *Research Series*	[Octavo pamphlets of 24 to 56 pages]	*Total* 92
	War and Reconstruction	8
	Social Subjects	6
	Local Government	4
	Education	8
	Full Employment	4
	Nationalisation	8
	Trade and Investment	3
	Political Questions	3
	Colonial Problems	17
	International and Foreign	20
	Others	11
2. *Tracts*		40
	Note—Fabian Tracts after 1939 covered a variety of publications. Some might have been classified as Research pamphlets, except that they were shorter; some were semi-manifestoes, such as *A Word on the Future*, some reprints of Autumn Lectures, some syllabuses or bibliographies, and a few small cheap products intended for wide circulation.	
3. *Biographies*	*Keir Hardie*, *John Burns*, *Richard Carlile* (all by G. D. H. Cole)	3
4. *Letter Series*[1]		8
5. *Socialist Propaganda Series*[1]		4

[1] See p. 271.

6. *Booklets*	(priced at 1*s.* to 2*s.* 6*d.*)	8
7. *Books*	(priced at 6*s.* to 15*s.*) Eight of these were reprints of the Fabian Autumn Lectures.	25
8. *Periodicals*	*Fabian Quarterly*; *Fabian News* (monthly). *France and Britain* (irregular for first few issues, then monthly until 1945). *Empire* (bi-monthly until 1946, monthly thereafter).	

Note—During 1949 the *Quarterly* was discontinued, some of its material being incorporated in an enlarged *Fabian News*; this proved highly unpopular, and in the following year *Fabian Journal*, appearing three or four times a year, substituted for it.

By the mid-forties, the Fabian Society had reached the third peak in its history; and it seems worth while at this point to consider how far it had changed over the years, to what extent it differed, in organisation, scope or personnel, from the Fabian Society of 1892 or 1913.

In organisation, it was a much more closely knit body, as regards the connection between its headquarters and the provinces, than at either of the earlier periods. This did not mean any stern centralised control; the Local Fabian Societies were still independent organisations, not 'branches' to which orders could be given. But the single simple requirement of acceptance of the Fabian Basis as a condition for being allowed to use the name had been replaced by a prescribed constitution, a fixed affiliation fee, and formal recommendation by the Local Societies Committee. As a corollary, Local Societies received a good deal of assistance, direct and indirect, from the centre, and their members had been given by rule a definite voice in the administration. This in itself showed a large difference from the ephemeral collection of delegates who gathered in 1892, and from the advisory (or rather declaratory!) conferences of the years before the first world war. Provincial Fabianism, however loosely controlled, was now integrated with the main Society, and also, to an only slightly less degree, with the network of Divisional Labour Parties now established all over the country. An established Fabian Society was expected to make appropriate connections with its own Labour Party; conversely, the national Party accepted that any Local Society recognised by the Fabian Executive should be eligible for affiliation to a Divisional Labour Party without more ado. This gave the Fabians the right to a seat on the local executive and to representation (by members not mandated, of course) at delegate conferences, and so brought them into the heart of day-to-day discussion of local policy; it spread Fabian ideas, and sometimes Fabian councillors, around the constituencies. Issue after issue of the 'Directive', the periodic duplicated news-sheet which the Local Societies Committee sent out to its constituents, gave suggestions and examples of what Fabian Societies could do for Labour in their own home towns; and officers and Executive members went on regular speaking tours in order to drive home these recommendations as well as meeting provincial Fabians face to face.

The other most obvious change arises from the 1918 reorganisation of the Labour Party itself; the days in which Fabian candidates for Parliament stood as Liberals or Tories, and the advisability of killing the Labour Party was seriously canvassed, had long passed away. This did not mean that the Society was subjected to strict Transport House discipline; it is not generally known that in 1943, when a Labour Party Committee (which may have been moved by a recollection of the Montagu dispute mentioned on p. 227, or merely by a desire for administrative tidiness) proposed that the constitution of the Society should henceforth be submitted, like those of Divisional Labour Parties, for official sanction, there was an immediate outcry, supported so strongly by lifelong Fabians high up in the counsels of the Party and of the T.U.C. that the suggestion was *spurlos versenkt* and was never brought to Conference at all. The Society's constitution, on the (correct) assumption that it would behave tactfully, was never interfered with; but, as we have seen, the mere existence of the Party organisation and the growth of research departments both of the Labour Party and the T.U.C. did have the result of restricting to some extent the scope of Fabian enquiry. Some measure of restraint upon independent thought was the inevitable price to be paid for continued association and continued trust.

The visits of Executive members to Local Societies did not, however, produce a great deal more of direct contact with individual Fabians, particularly in the provinces. At summer schools, and at week-end schools and conferences, there was rather more; but only fractions (differing fractions) of the membership attended either, or even the large gatherings which were held during Labour Party annual conferences. The Annual General Meeting, the Society's supreme governing body, was attended by numbers varying from 150 to 250, the bulk of whom, naturally, came from London or the Home Counties—suggestions that the A.G.M. should be held outside London were made from time to time, but never implemented owing to lack of agreement on venue. The Fabian in the provinces, unless he was an active member of a Local Society, which for various reasons he often was not, seemed perfectly content to receive publications by post, to come occasionally to conferences and to support the Society with a subscription which (unless he had been persuaded to sign a banker's order) was generally a month or two in arrears. The low poll for elections to the Executive, rarely rising above 25 per cent, bears this out.

Not that the Fabians had become inactive. Besides those who actually wrote or spoke for the Society, there were many who toiled in less conspicuous ways. Questionnaires were regularly issued—to new entrants always—asking members to say what they were willing to do and what they were qualified to do—not always the same thing—as were adjurations to action of various kinds. But the latter were not quite so peremptory as those described in Chapter VII, partly because the membership had become too large to be controlled in this way, but more because it had become too busy and too distracted. For though the general picture of the nature and social class of the membership seems to have altered very little over seventy years, still being predominantly middle-class and professional, the tempo of their lives, and what one might call their technical equipment, had altered very considerably since before the wars. The Fabian of the last century, even leaving out those who had possessed, like the Webbs, an independent income, was a comparatively leisured person. If it is a libel to say that, like the Trafalgar Square fountains, he played from ten to four, he nevertheless had a good deal of time to spare from earning his living, and he did not have to spend a large part of that time straphanging from home to work or being carried by aeroplane from conference to conference in the remotest capitals of the world. He was able (except when lecturing on Socialism) to attend all Executive meetings for their full length, which must have been considerable, if Hobson's account of them is correct—and to meet and talk with Fabians outside of formal engagements; he could, and did, stroll in and out of the office and help the Secretary with answering enquiries, correcting proofs, or anything else that turned up. With the coming of the first world war his hours of work lengthened, and this tendency was greatly accentuated in the second, and even more when the Labour Government came in and made its own demands on the Fabian ranks. After a time—and partly for reasons of economy—meetings of the Executive came to be held in the precincts of the House of Commons; this was convenient for M.P.s, but one result was that the feeling of *continuous* association gradually lessened, as the M.P. members wandered in and out, voting in divisions, seeing constituents, or leaving to attend committees in the House. Some scarcely visited the offices, or saw the lesser staff, at all; this meant that they did not assist in day-to-day work, a fact which accounts in small part for the increase in numbers of staff and in the cost of running the Society. The Society was becoming slightly more professionalised, though far less so than many others.

The major part of the increase in cost, apart from general rise of prices, was, of course, the great increase in volume of work and in its complexity. The innate intellectual ability of Fabians was hardly likely to have changed; but the amount of knowledge which they were expected to have, and the quantity of other-provided information which they were required to absorb, to understand and make telling use of, had increased out of all measure. The kind of information published in the sixteenth edition of *Facts for Socialists* is a useful indication of the change. The demands of the pioneers for *facts*, and more facts, information and more information, had succeeded only too well; statistics, national and international, Government reports, and (later) reports of all the international agencies with all their initials poured in a flood over their heads. Research became continually more complicated, more expensive—and more specialised; and as it became more specialised, 'member-participation' in the research work of the Society, which had ceased to be much of a reality as soon as the numbers of members grew beyond a few hundred, became less and less possible. Research itself cannot be 'democratically' conducted by anything larger than a group small enough to meet face to face or at the least to correspond; and though there were from time to time debates initiated by members frustrated because their offers of assistance—deliberately solicited by questionnaire—had never been taken up, and supported by others who felt that the Society's pamphlets, however definitely they disclaimed collective responsibility, did in the eyes of the public commit the membership, which ought therefore to have some means of exercising some control over them,[1] and though experiments were tried of submitting *précis* or schemes of specialist research to meetings of members, these proved to have a very limited appeal and not really to repay the trouble and expense. The only method of widening collaboration which in the end proved practical—aside from discussions and suggestions at Annual General Meetings—was that described on an earlier page, of encouraging Local Societies to embark on enquiries whose scope was reasonably within their capacity and their resources. No satisfactory answer could—or ever can—be given to the lone member who ardently desired to do work on the nationalisation of joint-stock banks, for example, or prison reform, but had little specialised knowledge and was in contact with no group.

But specialised research, though accepted as being the most important part of the Society's work, was not the whole of it; nor indeed were publications, even if their sheer volume tends to suggest it. In other discussions, within local groups, at week-end gatherings and at Summer Schools,[2] Fabians talked on a variety of subjects which never reached the stage of publication, but

[1] 'Something should be done,' wrote a contributor to a slightly later discussion on the functions of the Society, '. . . For example, every quarter a report of the work of the Research Group on a major problem could be presented to the membership for discussion at an aggregate meeting or conference. If the report were generally approved, a campaign could be organised throughout the country to get publicity for the ideas it contained.' (John Diamond of Central London, writing in *Fabian Journal*, October 1950.) The short answer to this well-meant suggestion was, 'No, it could not—not without considerable cost and serious delay to the publication in question.' The Executive did, at the end of 1947, circulate to all members its new Research Programme, and the Minutes of June 23rd, 1948, record an instruction to Arthur Skeffington to call a meeting under the portentous title of 'Mobilisation of Fabians for Policy Preparation', from which nothing very much resulted. But the attempt had at least been made.

[2] The importance of the Summer Schools waned rapidly after the war; week-end schools, on the other hand, sometimes general, more often on particular topics, increased in interest and importance.

which showed a greater range of interest than the list of published pamphlets, etc., would indicate—particularly in 'the arts'. Fabians, at the third peak, were not as philistine as Shaw had said; there was a Fabian Dramatic Society, one of whose sponsors was Bernard Miles; in 1946 there was set up an Arts and Amenities Group, later taken over by the Central London Society, which, with its large and sometimes obstreperous membership, had in effect taken over the role of the former Fabian Nursery.[1] Much of this was staged at the Summer School at Dartington Hall in Devon, which had been thoroughly shaken and braced up by the newcomers and until a year or two after the war's end was a much-sought-after rendezvous for Fabians (and some non-Fabians) of all types, and incidentally a handsome revenue-producer for the Society. The proximity of the Arts Group at Dartington Hall itself was not without influence, and musical and dramatic Fabians got their chance to expand—in one year a performance of *The Striker Stricken*,[2] directed by its author's wife, gave young Socialists some instruction in past working-class history.

It has been noted that the 'class structure' of the Society had not changed much over the generations, and was still mainly bourgeois and professional, consisting of those whose incomes were high enough for them to be asked to pay an annual subscription which at the 'all-in' rate amounted to 60*s*. by 1947.[3] Working-class membership of Local Societies was a little larger than it had been in 1912; it was much less than in 1892, but, as we have seen, the 1892 membership was not really Fabian, but drifted away to the I.L.P. as soon as the latter was on its feet. There were also a good many more members of working-class *origin*; i.e. those who, *via* secondary school, Ruskin College or University Tutorial classes, or paid service in Labour organisations, had acquired middle-class incomes, although not all who had come up that way became Fabians. Two of the most prominent non-Fabians among Labour leaders were Ernest Bevin, for reasons which are obvious, and later Aneurin Bevan. It would be interesting to know more about the average age of

[1] In after years the Central London Society became the main organiser of non-regional functions in the metropolis, and shared the responsibility of organising the Autumn Lectures.

[2] See ante, p. 210.

[3] Raised to 80*s*. at the end of 1960.

members of the Society, in so far as 'averages', in a small organisation, mean anything. Undoubtedly the vocal element in the Society at the first peak was mostly in its 'thirties, and in 1912 appreciably younger. After the amalgamation there was a considerable access of youth which may partly have been balanced, statistically speaking, by the advancing years of a good many of the past-generation Fabians; but no age-census was ever taken, and as after 1914 there were no battles between the Old and the New, no reliable information is available.[1] There were no Angry Young Fabians; Old Faithfuls like Susan Lawrence, Miss Lucie Simpson and Hubert Humphreys were cherished and invited to entertain Summer Schools with their reminiscences.

There was, however, a recurrent streak of anarchism in the Society which, considering its respectability and the absence of any serious differences of opinion except on post-war foreign policy,[2] is rather surprising, and may perhaps have been indirectly due, in part, to the difficulties of achieving 'member-collaboration' alluded to earlier. Fabians were obstreperous creatures: the Executive Committee, as its Chairman confessed, was at times one of the most awkward and argumentative committees he had ever presided over; the Annual Meeting readily developed a passion for trying to alter the constitution, and showed a tendency to suspicion of its Executive;[3] and at the Summer School there seemed to be almost a code of honour for breaking rules, shouting and singing into the small hours, etc.—upheld not by exuberant adolescents but by adults, even fathers of families. This might have been held to derive from the behaviour of Cole, Mellor and the Guild Socialists which had so upset Beatrice Webb's idea of decorum; if so, it would indicate a remarkable longevity of tradition, but the Fabian Summer School was, for a fact, at least twice denied the use of premises because the owners disliked its behaviour—on one occasion the reason given was the distribution of duplicated song-sheets

[1] A partial questionnaire sent out to members in 1959 and summarised in *Fabian News* of February 1960 gave some information for a much later date; the most striking feature was the great preponderance of males.

[2] Resignations over questions of principle were very few indeed. But see next chapter.

[3] At the Annual General Meetings of 1950 and 1951 attempts were made, led on the first occasion by the irrepressible Montagu, to allow Local Societies to recruit outside the Labour Party membership; both attempts were defeated, but the minority was sizeable.

of Socialism which were considered to be obscene and blasphemous.[1] This sort of incident enlivened the Society and prevented it from being the set of solemn prigs which outsiders were apt to conjure up; the Fabians thoroughly enjoyed their political and sociological disputations. Of all this side of modern Fabianism little, unfortunately, remains recorded except in the memories of the participants; the sole paragraph in the attenuated *News* which recalls old times is an advertisement briefly inviting Fabians who would like 'a guaranteed income for life' to write to the advertiser;[2] practically all the songs and sketches of Summer Schools are lost beyond recall.

The personnel of the Executive changed, naturally, with the passage of years; of the twenty-four who signed the Annual Report of 1939–40 only Leonard Woolf and the two Coles (with John Parker) signed ten years later. The newcomers were mostly younger—ten in 1949–50 were members of the House of Commons;[3] but there was at no time any sudden change. They entered one or two at a time, generally, as has been said earlier, by co-option, having graduated by service on one or other of the Society's standing committees—the Home Research Committee of 1949, for example, contained seven members who were not on the Executive, and others had more 'outsiders'. Competition for Executive places was pretty keen. There were no more years of 'no contest', and the level of ability remained high, though the record of attendance was not, particularly after 1945, what it had been in Hobson's day. Meetings of the Fabian Executive were not quite, then, as exciting as he had found them; no one expected to lose or gain his immortal soul by serving on it; there were too many other places in which informed and intellectual discussion of social problems could be found. But the discussion was keen, and keenly pursued; real 'non-attenders' were very few, and disappeared after a year or two, not because they were voted down by the membership, but under pressure from the active. The most notable—and irreparable—difference between the old Society and the new was that the 'amanuensis and

[1] Much of the offending material was published later by the National Association of Labour Student Organisations, with no apparent damage to anyone. From 1941 the Society had made various efforts to produce a new *Songs for Socialists*, but without success.

[2] *News*, February 1942.

[3] Of non-Parliamentarians the best-known was Ritchie Calder.

mouthpiece' had gone. There was no more Shaw, rewriting his colleagues' imperfect drafts in incomparable English, drawing crowds to purchase full-course tickets for the Autumn Lectures in order to make sure of hearing him, and 'smoothing out frictions by an Irish sort of tact which in England seemed the most outrageous want of it';[1] there was only a mischievous voice in the Jubilee number of the *Quarterly* telling the jubilant members never to forgo their independence of thought and their belief in 'permeation'. 'The true Fabian', said Shaw, as he had said at Bradford in 1893, 'is not, and never can be, a Party man or woman. My Party, right or wrong, is not our slogan. All Fabians have their price, which is always the adoption of Fabian measures no matter by what Party.' Long, long ago Shaw had told the German Socialist, Eduard Bernstein, that he wanted the Fabians to be 'the Jesuits of Socialism';[2] sixty years later that most unjesuitical character thought so still.

[1] Shaw, *Sixteen Self-Sketches*, p. 68.

[2] Bernstein, *My Years of Exile* (English translation, 1920), p. 226.

Some Members of the Fabian Executive, 1946

Left to right, round table: E. F. M. Durbin, W. A. Robson, Michael Stewart, M.P., Christopher Mayhew, M.P., J. F. Horrabin, H. D. Hughes, Geoffrey Wilson, Ian Mikardo, M.P., Bosworth Monck (General Secretary), John Parker, M.P., Emil Davies, Michael Young.

Shaw and the Fabian Baby by Vicky, from *Fabian Quarterly Jubilee Number*, April 1944. Illustrates an article by Shaw called 'Fabian Failures and Successes', in which he wrote 'I have carried the infant children of [two generations of] Fabians to bed in my arms.'

CHAPTER XIX

The Latest Years

AT the time of writing nearly a dozen years have passed since the Fabian Annual Meeting was told so sharply that it was outrunning the constable and must take drastic measures if it wished to survive—twelve years during which a great deal has happened—and is still happening—to change the face of the world and to make speculations about the future of countries as a whole or of any particular institution more risky than ever before. Generalisations about the recent past of the Fabian Society, as of any other body, must therefore be very tentative and made in acute consciousness that the time for real appraisement is not yet; all that can be done is briefly to observe available facts and tendencies.

Of the Society, it may be said that the extreme fears of 1948 were not realised. There was a sharp decline in membership, which was not arrested until the mid-fifties;[1] but this did not produce any such immediate and obvious shrinkage as had taken place in 1894 or 1915. The tortoise did not disappear into its shell; the work went on. But the first few years were undoubtedly a difficult time, and Andrew Filson, who succeeded Monck as General Secretary from April 1947 to September 1949, when Donald Chapman, the Research Secretary (later M.P.), took his place, had an exceptionally depressing term of office. Not only had he to carry out the economies ordered by the Annual Meeting—always a hard task in a body whose efficiency depends so much on the enthusiasm of its staff and of those immediately associated with the day-to-day work; he had to do this on a membership roll which was falling fast. This was not due

[1] Figures cannot be given with any certainty, because as already mentioned the optimism and bad book-keeping of the boom years had inflated the picture on paper; it may, however, be guessed that the final level of national membership was not much above half of what it had risen to in, say, 1946.

only to the 'tidying-up' of the register, or to the inevitable failures to renew when the increased subscription came to be demanded, or even to the dropping-out of the 'band-wagon' recruits who had joined in 1945 and 1946, paying the lowest rate of subscription;[1] there was a good deal more to it than that.

For one thing, the rapid recruitment of the young fell away. Many had joined either in order to get admission to the Summer School, or as a result of the speakers they heard there and the discussions in which they joined. But when foreign travel, even on a shoe-string, again became possible the attractions of Dartington Hall became less unique; more important, when Labour was in office, leading Fabians, having become members of the Government or senior civil servants, were not able, even had they been willing, to come to the Summer School or anywhere else and discuss freely what Labour could or should do, and Fabians in school and conference, therefore, could no longer have the feeling that they were directly participating in the making of policy. This narrowed the field of recruitment; furthermore, as time went on, and the difficulties of the Labour Government began to loom more largely than its achievements, the enthusiasm of those who were already enrolled began to wane. Instead of planning and developing the world envisaged in *Let Us Face the Future*, Fabians and potential Fabians, after 1948, were more and more having to defend what nobody could pretend to enjoy—continued rationing, dependence on American loans, difficulties in the nationalised industries, the teething troubles of the Health Service, impatience among colonial peoples, etc. Some members—a few of very long standing—went the length of resigning their membership, giving one or more of these as the reason, or simply that they felt the Labour Party, and with it the Fabian Society, had 'ceased to be Socialist'; others silently lapsed; more serious was the number, including many at or just leaving the universities, who were influenced by

[1] Entitling the member to receive *Fabian News* only—sometimes with a pamphlet or two thrown in—in addition to normal voting rights. The highest rate—60*s*. after the rise—promised all pamphlets except a few of very specialised appeal which could be had 'on demand'. This class of membership was by far the most stable. Presumably it was also, on the whole, better off; but its stability suggests that it valued what it received. (Students could join at half-rate on any level.)

anti-government propaganda and laments over the plight of the middle classes, and so failed to come in.

Some of this was, of course, to be expected as a result of the general political situation; the fortunes of the Fabian Society, as we have observed more than once, have tended to 'follow th'illiction returns', i.e. the fortunes of the Labour Party, and it is really more surprising that the decline was not more catastrophic,[1] and that the Local Societies, though they lost ground, maintained their numbers and their strength to a much greater extent than might have been expected. The decline in membership resulted, of course, in a considerable decline in revenue; the outside offices had to be given up and part of 11 Dartmouth Street again rented out, and the staff was cut by degrees to about half the peak level—though, it should be said at once, these cuts, partly owing to better deployment of resources and partly to the dogged devotion of those who remained, did not reduce the volume of work anything like proportionately. The production of research and publication staggered, and was conducted for a while in a rather melancholy atmosphere of 'what we can afford'; but it went on. By 1950, when John Diamond, M.P., became the Society's fifth Treasurer,[2] the immediate financial crisis was over, and for ten years to come there were no more serious difficulties; this fortune was partly due to Diamond's level-headed financial ability, but even more to contributions received by the Society from outside its direct membership.

Beatrice Webb had died in the spring of 1943, and the Fabian Society had initiated a Webb Memorial Fund which, in charge of trustees drawn from all sections of the Labour movement, in the course of a few years purchased and equipped for schools and conferences a house near Abinger in Surrey, named Beatrice Webb House, which contains, in addition to rooms named after the Webbs, Shaw, Cripps and Cole, the stained-glass window of Edwardian Fabianism already described. Apart from the use it made of the House as a meeting-place, the Webb Fund in itself

[1] It should also be mentioned that the bitter personal disputes which from time to time attacked the Party do not seem to have prevented the Society from getting on with its work. 'The Bevanite quarrel' made no appearance in Executive discussions except in so far as it may have tended to make members sharper-toned with one another when disagreements arose.

[2] Small organisations do not change their treasurers so readily as they do their committee members. But to have had five Treasurers only, during seventy-seven years, must, one feels, be something approaching a record.

brought no gain to the Society; but when Sidney died in the winter of 1947 it was found that his will left nearly the whole of their estate, amounting to about £30,000, to be administered by five trustees, who were to expend it within twenty years in fostering social and economic research, mainly through the Fabian Society and the London School of Economics—specifically mentioned on this occasion! The publication of the will caused some embarrassment to the Revenue Campaign Council mentioned in the last chapter, which had only recently got off the mark and found its appeals occasionally meeting with raised eyebrows on the faces of those who had read the newspapers and failed to realise either the existence of death duties or the law's delays; within a year or so, however, formalities were completed, and the Society was able to receive, on presentation of a research programme to the trustees, something of the order of a thousand pounds a year. This important addition to the sums already available from educational charities mentioned in earlier chapters was enhanced by an annual subvention given by the Labour Party towards the work of the Colonial Bureau, and, as time went on, by a growing amount received in donations from Labour organisations (the first in 1949), including a number of the larger Trade Unions. Practically none of these were in any sense payment for services directly rendered—one important exception was a special grant from the Amalgamated Engineering Union which enabled Hugh Clegg, of Nuffield College, to prepare a report on industrial democracy and nationalisation—and did not involve the Society in becoming to the smallest degree a regular enquiry bureau or provider of services on a piecework basis. They were given without condition simply for the support of the Society itself, and their existence shows a real appreciation of its value in general terms, since the sums given had commonly to be renewed, year by year, by specific vote of the organisation concerned, or of its executive committee, which had to choose from many claimants on its financial resources.

These grants enabled Donald Chapman, who graduated from Research Secretary to General Secretary after Filson's resignation, and his new assistant, W. T. Rodgers, again to build up a research programme; and early in 1952 the latter, taking charge of the Society's weakest link, the International Bureau, succeeded in getting it to start a quarterly journal of its own, *Fabian Inter-*

national Review, edited by Kenneth Younger, then M.P.[1] Two years earlier, G. D. H. Cole, who had resumed the chairmanship in the autumn of 1948, wrote for the first number of the new *Fabian Journal*, which replaced the defunct *Quarterly*, a long 'Open Letter' which, while its optimism may have run a little ahead of the facts, certainly contained no suggestion that the Society was in decline, or even in a state of doubt.

'Why Are We Fabians?' he began; and went on to declare that

> it will not do to say that we belong because we are Socialists, or even because we are democratic Socialists; for these labels can be attached to a great many people who are not Fabians and probably would not be even if they appreciated our work. The Fabian Society . . . attracts, first and foremost, those for whom democratic Socialism is not a creed already worked out in full and simply there to be accepted or rejected, but rather a developing and highly adaptable corpus of social doctrine that needs to be continually thought out afresh as situations change and as notions that have been worked out only theoretically come to be applied in practice—and sometimes wrongly applied. We have, no doubt, our dogmas, like other people; but we do our best to prevent them from becoming our masters by questioning them constantly and refusing to write more than the barest minimum of them into our constitution or insist on any more than this bare minimum as a test of eligibility for membership. We are *freethinkers* to a man—and a woman—in the sense that we believe in freedom to think without blinkers. We duly revere our founders; but we by no means take what they say as gospel, or the last word. Nor do we delude ourselves that what we are saying and thinking to-day is the last word—or all of it right.

After a couple of pages explaining the conditions in which Fabian research had to be carried on, and describing some half-dozen projects, most of which came to eventual fruition in one form or another, the article went on to say

> I said we must work out the new answers 'bit by bit'; but 'bit by bit' is not of itself enough. Some of us have been feeling for some time that the Fabian Society cannot do its work properly without making an attempt to perform for the present generation the service which *Fabian Essays* performed more than two generations ago. So a small group of us has been meeting, with the Executive's endorsement, to discover how far we can agree on a restatement of the basis of our

[1] The *Review* had unfortunately to be discontinued, eventually, partly because of the difficulty of keeping pace, in a journal appearing at such rare intervals, with the swift changes in the international scene.

democratic Socialist faith in its relation to the problems of the next ten or twenty or thirty years. . . . Our purpose, however, must not be misunderstood. We are trying, not to produce a new Fabian 'orthodoxy', but only to formulate a line of approach without wishing to tie down anyone to accepting more of our conclusions than he wishes.

In the year following this confident appeal the Labour Government fell; but the Society showed little sign of being daunted—paradoxically, it seemed if anything a trifle invigorated by a half-conviction that it might not be a bad thing to end the intolerable strain of the year of bare majority and to start thinking afresh. Almost immediately it initiated discussions, in which Fabian ex-Ministers willingly participated, on 'What Went Wrong', i.e. in what ways had the Labour Government's practice and achievements, in various fields, failed to come up to the expectations of the participants or fulfil the promises made to the electors of 1945. The results of these discussions, several of which dealt with highly confidential information, were naturally not made public—some were not even written down in any shape or form, but they had their bearing on the Transport House enquiries into future Labour policy, in which Fabians took part along with other Socialists. In the spring of the following year the Society put out in the *New Statesman* an appeal headed 'The Job is Never Done', which brought in an appreciable bunch of new members, though not as yet sufficient to arrest the fall-off completely; eleven research pamphlets, five Tracts (or thirteen, including reprints of lectures) and two 'Colonial Controversies' were published in 1950 and 1951. The Society's main energy, however, was concentrated on *New Fabian Essays*.

This was the project referred to in the second quoted paragraph of Cole's article in *Fabian Journal*. Already, while Laski was Chairman, he had promulgated a fresh attempt to rewrite the *Essays*, which failed, the project, as on previous occasions, being eventually adjourned *sine die*. In the summer of 1949, however, Cole collected a group, not specifically for the purpose of writing new *Essays*, though that was certainly in everybody's mind, but for seeing how much of common Fabian thought would emerge from continuous discussion. The group met first for a long week-end in Lord Faringdon's Buscot House; discussions continued there, and in Oxford and London, for more than a year and a half. Twenty-one members of the Society participated from time to time—the list of names is given in full at the beginning of the book published in 1952; the mass of memoranda produced for these week-ends and preserved in several large boxes in the Fabian office would easily give the lie to anyone disposed to think that Fabian thinking had ceased to exist, or to range widely, as the Labour Government drew to its end. The subjects treated covered nearly the whole field of economic, political and social life; there was material presented there, and in part discussed,[1] which would have provided the basis for far more than a single volume, however enormous; and *New Fabian Essays* of 1952 was no more than a very select selection. Two other volumes were in fact projected; one was to be called *Fabian Economic Essays*, but disagreement among the authors combined with swift changes in the world outside destroyed it as a book before it was finished—though one chapter, Hugh Gaitskell's *Socialism and Nationalisation*, was published as Tract 300; the second, which was to be essays in sociology, was very much vaguer in conception, and never really got started at all.[2]

When the *Essays* finally appeared, the name of the originator of the discussion was absent from the title-page. During 1950, as he explained in a brief letter which appeared in *Fabian News* of March 1951, Cole had come to feel 'so unhappy about the trend in Labour foreign policy' (in particular its attitude towards both America and the Soviet Union) that he did not find himself able to continue in close discussion with those who supported it; he left the 'Buscot Group' in the autumn of 1950, and did not stand for the Executive a year later. The letter explained that he had no cause of quarrel with the Society itself over anything it had done or proposed to do; the estrangement was a part of the rift about foreign policy described in the previous chapter. He did not resign from the Society; and his continued interest in it (as well as its regard for him) was shown by the fact that in the summer following the letter in *Fabian News* he agreed to direct a Summer School at Broadstairs—although owing to illness he actually played only a small part therein—and, more important, that after Stafford Cripps's death he was immediately offered and

[1] Memory brings up an animated exchange on 'potting the baby' as a sociological factor.

[2] A book of *Fabian International Essays*, edited by Tom McKitterick, however, came out in 1957; the two sets of *Fabian Colonial Essays* have already been mentioned.

accepted the Presidency of the Society. In accepting he stipulated that, like his two predecessors, he should be regarded as 'above the battle', playing no part in its governance. Health would in any event have dictated this after a few years; but he continued to write for it, and in 1953 delivered an address to a large gathering of delegates to the Margate Conference of the Labour Party, which was published in *Fabian Journal*.[1] The *Essays* were edited, therefore, by R. H. S. Crossman, M.P., and Margaret Cole; the other contributors were Austen Albu, Anthony Crosland, Denis Healey, Roy Jenkins, Ian Mikardo and John Strachey, all members of Parliament.[2]

The *Essays* had a wide sale, and attracted much attention and discussion, and in competence and readability compare favourably with the original. But the times—and the world situation—had changed so much that neither the authors nor the Society could expect them to have the same effect as their predecessors of 1889. The editors, in their introduction, while repeating the statement in the first Preface that the Essayists claim to be 'no more than communicative learners', point out that

> the first Fabians took for granted both the shape of things past and the shape of things to come. We cannot write today without a much soberer consciousness of history, and a much more acute scepticism about the particular interpretation we give it. In fact, we do not claim either finality or comprehensiveness for *New Fabian Essays*. Even the three years during which they were composed have brought changes which defied our predictions and warned us against ready-made conclusions. These essays, for example, were written under a Labour Government, and revised in proof under a Tory Government. If they ask at least some of the new pertinent questions, their authors will be content.

[1] Towards the end of 1952 the newly elected President, when guest of honour at a Fabian dinner at the House of Commons held after the Annual General Meeting, discovered to his shocked amazement that a Loyal Toast was to be called, going contrary to his deep republican principles. To avert the disaster of the guest of honour immediately leaving the dinner table, John Parker, who was in the chair, called the toast in the words, 'All those who are not republicans will rise and drink the Loyal Toast'—and a number of those present retained their seats along with the President. On December 16th the Executive, having received a letter of admonition, meekly resolved never to repeat the offence.

[2] A copy was presented to Pease, then in his ninety-sixth year, and living happily, though stone-deaf, in retirement on Limpsfield Common in Surrey, home for over half a century of many 'advanced' persons.

This was true enough, and hardly had the first edition of the *Essays* sold out before 'new pertinent questions' began to show their faces. By the time of the Society's seventieth birthday, its new young director, W. T. Rodgers, General Secretary from 1953 to 1960, was already observing signs of change and the need for some new orientations. Stalin's death in 1953 and the subsequent gradual slackening of the cold war—the influence of which is so obvious in some of the *New Fabian Essays*; the increase in material production which some publicists, borrowing from the American Professor Galbraith, dignified with the name of 'The Affluent Age', and the realisation that 'affluence' did not connote equality, but was compatible with disgraceful conditions of life for a considerable minority of the population, with remarkable outbursts of brisk individual spending, and with a great unbalance of development as between social and other services; the discovery that 'nationalisation' had not solved either the economic problems of the nationalised industries nor the human problems of their administration;[1] the troubles of crowded, ugly and straphanging life for the moderately better-off—all these questions were coming up for solution, and solution, moreover, largely by a younger generation which would have to live with the results if a solution were not found. Accordingly, Rodgers and the Executive set out gradually to do two things; to promote fresh thinking, and to recruit younger members to make good those who had been lost during the years of disillusionment.

The second task proved more difficult than the first. The young *were* disillusioned—Kingsley Amis's Tract 304, *Socialism and the Intellectuals*, gives a vivid statement of the mood; they wanted something brighter, more positive, more startling, and quicker in its probable effects than Fabianism. *Mutatis mutandis*, the students of the 'fifties were looking for some cause comparable to the Spanish Civil War in the 'thirties, which would clearly align them on the Left which was right—and failing to find it. *The Universities and Left Review* (started in 1957) was only one of several strong competitors to Fabianism. But gradually headway was made, aided by patient recruiting campaigns, particularly in

[1] As far back as 1949 a research group of the Society had drawn attention to these problems in connection with the miners. Their findings (Research Series 134, *The Miners and the Board,* edited by Margaret Cole) earned them a smart slap from the Labour Minister of Fuel and Power.

the universities. Schools for 'under-thirties' proved an attraction, and, by the end of the decade, when Shirley Williams was succeeding Rodgers as General Secretary, it seemed that a new Young Fabian Group (shades of the Nursery!) might be coming into being.

Publications and research, partly because the tradition was strong and partly because they were not dependent on a large membership, were easier. As early as September 1953, Brian Abel-Smith, one of the ablest of young Fabians, had produced in *The Reform of Social Security*[1] the first strong criticism of the Welfare State as adapted by the classes in power. He was co-opted to the Executive in 1954, the first of a new generation to reach that body; and his pamphlet was followed (to cite only a few of the more important titles) by James MacColl's *Policy for Housing*, John Vaizey's *Cost of Social Services*, *New Pensions for the Old*, by Abel-Smith and Peter Townsend, *A Socialist Education Policy*, by H. D. Hughes, *Plan for Rented Houses*, by James MacColl, *The Child and the Social Services*, by David Donnison and Mary Stewart, *Policy for Mental Health*, by Kenneth Robinson, M.P., and finally Audrey Harvey's *Casualties of the Welfare State*, which caused something of a Press *furore* on the day of publication.[2] (The Labour Party's new plan for pensions and superannuation, which was generally acknowledged to be a Fabian product, was published by the Party, not the Society.)

This group of pamphlets began to add up to a new policy on social problems, looking forward to the 'sixties; Humphrey Cole's edition of *Facts for Socialists* (Research Series 184) pointed the moral by selecting—since selection was by now inevitable—facts about the wealth and income of the country compared with its expenditure on social services. On industry, the output was less coherent and more sporadic, partly owing to the difficulties already described of finding workers. Machine Tools, for example, was a subject for which an author was repeatedly sought in vain; but there was a *Plan for the Aircraft Industry*, a *Plan for Cotton* and a *Plan for Retail Distribution*, a *Plan for Shipbuilding*, and a pamphlet on the problem of the roads.[3] Under the

[1] Research Series 161.

[2] Research Series 164, 166, 171, 173, 192, 196, 200; Tract 321.

[3] Research Series 176, by Frank Beswick, M.P.; 181, by John Murray; 182, by 'a Fabian Group'; 198, by John Hughes; Tract 299, by John Willey; Research Series 206 by W. T. Rodgers. The Society bore no published

title *The Machinery of Economic Planning* (Research Series 168) the Cambridge economist Robin Marris produced a study of possible means to achieve Socialist planning which has yet to receive the attention it deserves. G. D. H. Cole gave the Society his last published pamphlet, *Capitalism in the Modern World* (Tract 310), in addition to stating in Tract 301 *What's Wrong with the Trade Unions*.

Other questions discussed in detail included New Towns, legal aid for the poor, prison reform, consumer research (before the arrival of journals dealing with that subject), tax reform, second chambers, commercial television and the theatre, the reform of House of Commons procedure.[1] Of the sixty-five research pamphlets and thirty Tracts published between January 1952 and February 1960, ten came from the Colonial (Commonwealth) Bureau, and sixteen from the International Bureau—making good the loss of its journal. There was one biography, Margaret Cole's *Sidney and Beatrice Webb* (Tract 297). At the very end of the period, just as this book was going to press, Professor Richard Titmuss, in *The Irresponsible Society* (Tract 323), opened an attack on 'the changing concentrations of economic and financial power' which was clearly going to go further.

Here, at the opening of the 'sixties, this record must come to an end, repeating the obvious reflection that it stops in the middle of a fast-running stream, and that many changes may have taken place before it sees the light of print. All that remains, by way of epilogue, is to try to sum up, with some appraisement, some reflections on what 'Fabian Socialism' has contributed to the social history of Britain over nearly four generations.

responsibility for the policy of acquisition of shares in private companies, as evolved in 1959.

[1] Research Series 172, by Norman Mackenzie; 191, by Peter Benensen; 203, by Howard Jones; 199, by C. D. Horbury; 190 (Evidence to Royal Commission). Tracts 305, by Anthony Wedgwood Benn; 317, by Richard Findlater; 318, by Christopher Mayhew; 319, by Bernard Crick.

CHAPTER XX

Epilogue—the Record of Fabianism

IN June 1905 the Fabian Executive requested Bernard Shaw to prepare for it a paper on 'The Results of the Society's Political Recommendations' over the twenty years of its existence. A month later, Shaw declined this offer in a Shavian reply indicating that though practically all that was good in British political development had come about through the Fabian Society, if you said so nobody would believe you; it was therefore 'impossible to be objective', and though a disappointed committee urged him to try again, nothing came of it.

Something of the same difficulty confronts anyone who would today attempt any such assessment, especially one who, like the present writer, has spent a lifetime in the service of the Socialist movement, and has watched the fulfilment or non-fulfilment of so many predictions from a Socialist angle. Yet 'Fabian Socialism' has meant something, or this book would not have been written at all, and there would be no Fabians to write about; and it should be possible, without assuming an objectivity which no one can possess, to try to assess the effect of Fabianism over the years, without underwriting Shaw's somewhat extravagant claim.

The task is not made easier, of course, by the absence of dogma and dogmatically prescribed principles of action which has been insisted upon by generation after generation of Fabians and Fabian leaders. No Fabian was ever compelled to obey any Fabian resolution or to act on any Fabian pronouncement or recommendation; if he did not do so, he faced nothing worse than the 'black looks' which Pericles found to be the supreme peril for dissenters in fifth-century Athens—or at most a pained letter from the General Secretary. Concerted political action, the action of a 'pressure group' like the Anti-Corn Law League or Mrs Pankhurst's Suffragettes, was therefore very rarely open to the Society. We have to fall back, then, on Sidney Webb's 'the work of individual Fabians', in so far as that can be discovered; but even where it can, who is to decide when an individual Fabian was acting politically as a Fabian, as a member of a Labour Party committee or a County Councillor, or just in his individual private capacity? For that matter, who is to say with confidence, when a non-Fabian makes proposals or suggestions which are very much in consonance with what Fabians have been saying for a very long time, that this was due to 'Fabian inspiration'? Mr Alan Bullock's recent biography of Ernest Bevin reprints, at length, some memoranda written by its subject, particularly in the 'thirties, which might, if unsigned, have easily been imputed to Fabian authorship; but one can hardly suppose, in the light of Bevin's known views about 'intellectuals', and some of the letters quoted in the same volume, that he would have been pleased to be regarded as a Fabian disciple or convert. Fabians, hoping by direct or indirect means to influence the 'climate of opinion' among the millions who were not and never would be Fabians, were unlikely to know in detail how far they had succeeded. Nevertheless, it is possible, looking over the social history of three-quarters of a century, to draw some tentative conclusions about the effects of Fabianism on Socialist discussion, on actual events, on proposals made for reform, and on the general attitude towards social problems—bearing in mind, of course, that for the whole of the period, allowing for occasional set-backs, the tide of opinion was in general setting in a Fabian direction. As Sidney Webb might have said, Fabians, while assisting the *Zeitgeist*, could hardly claim it as a recruit.

Pease, in the last chapter of his 1916 *History*, suggested that the first great achievement of Fabianism was 'to break the spell of Marx'. This reads rather oddly today; but what Pease was alluding to was, first, the practice of the Social-Democratic Federation of treating the actual words of Marx as a sacred text on which glosses only were to be permitted; and secondly, the belief, natural enough in the police States of Europe, that the State was an enemy to be destroyed, and in no wise an instrument which could be used in the interests of the working class. And thus far his claim was well-founded; once *Fabian Essays* had taught the intellectuals that it was possible to be a Socialist without mouthing jargon, British Socialism was freed from that disease; and the advances in social legislation secured from both

Tory and Liberal governments made nonsense of the conception of the State as no more than the policeman of the *bourgeoisie*. Even the Russian Revolution and the inter-war defeats, and the neo-Marxism of writers like Laski, Strachey, and to some extent Cole did not bring back the jargon or cause crude old-type Marxism to penetrate deep into Labour thought.

But it may well be argued that, in putting paid to Marxism and being content to rely, as *Fabian Essays* did, on reinterpretations of Mill, Jevons and Ricardo for their philosophy, the Fabians emptied the baby out with the bath-water, interpreted Tract 70 too rigidly, and while they saved themselves from Hobson's 'joyful hair-splitting' and from breaking-up over doctrinal disputes, left themselves without any discernible philosophy at all, and so discouraged some potential members—and the bulk of the British Labour movement—from discussion of fundamentals. Something of this impatience with what the Webbs certainly regarded as 'unprofitable talk'—Webb had no use for philosophy, and Beatrice regarded 'Abstract Economics' (see Tract 70) as sheer waste of time—accounts for the refusal to acknowledge any basis for the theoretical arguments of the Guild Socialists; it also goes some way towards explaining the failure of 'Fabianism' to take any deep root outside the British Isles. Mrs Webb's *Diary* shows that she appreciated Continental Socialists as more cultured and more intellectual—more interesting, in fact—than the leaders of the British Labour Party during its first twenty years; but it does not appear that she discussed political theory with them.

Pease, indeed, would have accepted the charge in full. 'None of the Fabians', he wrote, 'would claim to rank beside the great promulgators of new ideas such as Owen and Marx'—and broadly speaking this is true; whether this lack has proved a serious weakness must be matter of opinion. What the Fabians can claim, however—a claim which is not generally put forward on behalf of 'great promulgators of new ideas'—is to have established a standard of tolerant discussion within Socialist circles, to have insisted on laying a foundation of fact for all assertions, and to have exposed their proposals to the kind of criticism designed to prevent them from the imputation of utopian (or other) sillinesses.

On tolerance something has been said already; and it is not necessary to do more here than repeat that while no one would contend that no Fabian was ever arrogant, rude, overbearing or simply 'superior' to the point of exasperating those with whom he came in contact, this, when it occurred, was an individual failure and not a policy.[1] The Fabians did criticise their opponents without the personal abuse which has been the prerogative of so many enthusiasts from the Puritans onwards, and the leaders did try consistently to reach agreement with opposition within their own ranks, and to conciliate a defeated minority—if this minority were willing to be conciliated; to this is chiefly to be attributed the astonishing freedom of the Society from splits and the small number who in the course of its history resigned on a declared disagreement on Fabian policy. These words are carefully chosen; they do not imply that no Fabian ever left on a difference of opinion. Some Socialists 'grew out' of being Socialists at all—the late Leo Amery, M.P., like Lord Woolton, was once a Fabian; some decided that the Labour Party had ceased to be Socialist or worthy of even the indirect support of Fabian affiliation fees; some became Communists, others simply bored. But very few flung out, like Wells, in a passion of fury—or even wrote letters of condemnation to the Secretary.

'Laying a foundation of fact' was one of the most fundamental parts of the Fabian approach—exemplified by the issue of *Facts for Socialists* when the Society was only three years old. Damning capitalism out of its own records was not, of course, a Fabian invention—Marx and Engels, to mention no other names, had made furiously effective use of information obtained from official statistics. But to extend this to a demand for factual studies in general was comparatively new. *Facts for Socialists* came out two years before the first volume of Booth's *Life and Labour of the People of London* and fourteen years before Rowntree's study of poverty in York; and the flood of statistics and social enquiries which have since been presented to the world owes a very great deal to the Fabians' insistent demand for facts, and more facts, to the conviction that the facts would prove the Socialist case to the hilt and that, in any event, proposals for reform which were not supported by a solid basis of unchallengeable fact were not worth making at all. 'Measurement and Publicity' was a slogan coined by the Webbs in the early 'twenties; if the measurements have now reached a volume and complexity with which

[1] Except, perhaps, in the case of the Guild Socialists. Neither the 1914 War, nor the Bevanites, nor the post-1959 disputes, were reflected in the Society.

the individual modern Fabian finds it difficult to cope, and if publicity seems to have given too much scope to that recently invented functionary the Public Relations Officer, the modern Fabian has his forerunners to blame. It does not, however, prove that they were wrong.

On the third point, the sense and 'practicality' of Fabian proposals, only those who have time to read through the huge output of Fabian books and pamphlets can confidently pronounce. I can only say here that, so far as my information extends, no proposition was ever put out in the name of the Society without being submitted to searching criticism by those who might be expected to know what its effects would be; and suggest, further, that a quite infinitesimal proportion of the proposals so made can be shown to be really silly, when account is taken of their date and the conditions of the time at which they were made. It may perhaps be suggested that some of the silliest were advanced by the Society's great 'amanuensis'—but Shaw was *sui generis*, and did not produce his wildest propositions under the Fabian imprint.

These, then, being the Fabian methods, what can be said of the Fabian aims? What, lacking a theology, were they endeavouring to urge upon British opinion, and how far were they successful? To put it as simply as possible, the Fabians were answering the question asked in their first Tract, *Why Are the Many Poor?* with the assertion that they need not be, and that concerted action by society as a whole could prevent it. They began their propaganda at a time when it was the general opinion that poverty was an inescapable fact of society, destitution a reasonable consequence of a person's own faulty character, and unemployment, for the most part, a form of malingering which could be stopped if the penalties were made sufficiently deterrent. Today nobody—or hardly anybody—believes that any longer; and the disappearance of the belief can without hesitation be ascribed in great part to the persistent propaganda of Fabians over the years. It is, as Tawney said, the Acquisitive Society, and not the laws of nature, which prescribe poverty. But to diagnose evil is not to cure it; and the merit of Fabian reformers is that they went on to press for the abolition of great tracts of poverty by specific action—through a system of social security above all, but also through such lesser measures as provision of dinners and milk for schoolchildren and of public housing of reasonable standard, through reduction of hours of work and improvement of factory conditions, through wage regulation for the underpaid and fair wages clauses in local authority and government employment. All these today are commonplaces, and the phrase used by the Webbs to sum them up, 'A National Minimum of Civilised Life', seems sometimes to irritate young Socialists who feel (not unreasonably) that a society calling itself 'affluent' ought to have something rather more inspiring to offer as an end; nevertheless, that irritation is largely due to the change brought about in social consciousness, the belief that primary poverty—in Britain, at all events—need no longer exist, and a great reluctance to admit, on the evidence of eyes and ears, that it still does.

The Fabians argued that poverty was preventible, and most people now agree with them. They also argued, however, that it could not be prevented, finally, on a nation-wide scale, otherwise than through communal ownership and direction of productive resources. This part of their legacy to Britain is set out most clearly in *Labour and the New Social Order*; but long before that programme was formulated they had been pioneers of the municipal enterprise which was rather unhappily christened 'gas-and-water Socialism'. Unhappily, because it did not mean, as Chamberlain's programme in Birmingham had meant, running trading services at a profit in order to protect the pockets of ratepayers, but the administration of communal services at the lowest possible cost for the common good; and also because 'gas-and-water' was not at all an adequate description. The Fabian municipal programme envisaged a whole host of other services—transport and electricity, banks, bakeries, laundries, pawnshops, abattoirs, public houses, etc.[1] which could be advantageously run by local Councils; and in the realm of nationalisation proper, i.e. in industries and services where local administration was clearly not practicable, Fabian pamphlets advocating national ownership of land, mines and minerals, railways and insurance had been current well before they were specifically embodied in the programme of a major political party.

These general aims—the abolition of poverty by means of social enforced minima and social control of resources, including of course the method of progressive taxation—form the main

[1] See, in addition to the many Tracts mentioned earlier, Shaw's *Common sense of Municipal Trading* and R. B. Suthers's *Mind Your Own Business.*

contribution of the Fabian Society to the 'climate of opinion' in Britain of the twentieth century. It is not suggested that the Society was alone in the advocacy of any one of these aims, but that the steady and incessant propagation of all three in combination, backed up by a barrage of facts and arguments, created eventually a situation in which few were found to resist them. 'Fabianism', whether regarded as a merit or a crime, has long been recognised as a word carrying a definite meaning and having an effect attested by social historians of the calibre of G. M. Trevelyan, the most recent tribute to it being the formation in 1951 of the 'Bow Group' of the Conservative Party with the avowed purpose of 'Combating the influence of the Fabian Society'.[1] What remains to be done is to try to do what Shaw declined to do in 1904, to supply certain instances of particular as contrasted with general changes which can be attributed to Fabian efforts.

The first of these is without doubt the present system of public education. The essentials of modern state education, with its partnership between the Government, the local authorities and the churches, were laid down definitely in the Education Acts of 1902 and 1903, which succeeding Acts, circulars and memoranda have done no more than modify and amplify; and these Acts, as Chapter XI of this book has shown, were as near as no matter a translation into legislative terms of the proposals made in the Fabian Tract, *The Education Muddle and the Way Out*, published so shortly before the Bills themselves. Whatever may be thought of English public education, the line of responsibility for its shape is perfectly clear.

The second case is the modern Labour Party—not the original foundation, with which the Society's connection, as we have seen, was accidental, for long almost unnoticed and for a while regarded with very mixed feelings. But when the two Fabians, Webb and Henderson, combined in 1918 to provide the Party simultaneously with a constitution and a programme they created an organisation which endured for over forty years with far less modification than that undergone by the educational system. The constitution of the Party has scarcely been changed at all;

[1] The deletion of this particular clause in the Group's constitution was proposed in the spring of 1960. The change in the 'public image' of Conservative home policy over nine years, however, shows the flattery implied in the clause to have been both sincere and wise.

the lineaments of *Labour and the New Social Order* can be clearly seen to persist in policies and programmes, year by year, election after election; and notwithstanding the cursory paragraphs with which Mr R. McKenzie's study of *British Political Parties* dismisses the Fabian Society, it will scarcely be contended that the policy has been of less importance than the structure. It was not until 1959, in the aftermath of the election, that voices were heard suggesting that serious changes were required in both.

These two instances stand out particularly, because the results followed so quickly upon the first moves. In the third, which may be summarised as 'social security', the process was much slower, though the facts are no less well known. Beatrice Webb's *Minority Report* to the Poor Law Commission, which had been preceded, be it remembered, by earlier Fabian Tracts, was itself a fully worked out and cogently argued scheme of social security. It appeared in 1909. Two years later, Lloyd George appropriated a small piece of it in the first Insurance Acts; eighteen years after that, Neville Chamberlain took a further step by abolishing the Guardians of the Poor, though not the Poor Law; in the middle of the war, so long after the *Minority Report* that its very name had been all but forgotten, its proposals, with inevitable modifications, reappeared in the Beveridge Report; by 1948 the Poor Law had finally ceased to exist, and universal insurance and a national medical service were a reality. Sidney Webb, in a moment of pessimistic realism, said that it took the British public twenty or thirty years after a reform was first proposed to accept it; in the case of the *Minority Report* it took forty.

The suggestions made by Sir Ivor Jennings for the reform of Parliamentary procedure, brought into effect in 1945, have already been mentioned; so have the various proposals for nationalisation which, worked upon during the 'thirties by committees of the Labour Party in which Fabians participated, became law during the lifetime of the third Labour Government. Finally, and not by any means least in importance, comes the work of the Colonial (Commonwealth) Bureau in making suggestion after suggestion—far too numerous to be listed here—which were taken up in whole or in part by virtue of the close relationship of its officers and members with those who were to run the Colonial Office in the Labour Government—an influence which did not cease when the Labour Government fell. The changed attitude of the British upper classes to 'natives', displayed so unmistakably in the 1960 conference on Kenya, is largely due to the patient work of the Bureau, in its pamphlets, its conferences, and in the pages of *Venture*, showing that the leaders of freedom movements in the dependent territories were not merely 'brothers', as they had been proclaimed by all Socialist idealists, but responsible individuals who had their own problems, could be criticised as well as supported, so that it was possible to meet them in serious round-table discussions of practical proposals.[1]

The preceding paragraphs have concerned themselves with changes in which the influence of the Fabian Society, or part of it, acting as a group, is clear and traceable. It would be possible to lengthen this chapter almost indefinitely by including, or trying to include in it, 'the work of individual Fabians' in many other fields. The debt of London University to Sidney Webb, of Oxford and working-class education to Tawney, Lindsay and Cole, of the L.C.C. to Webb, Herbert Morrison and Emil Davies, and of leaders of 'emergent' countries, notably India, to university pupils of Cole and Laski[2]—to mention no other than prominent members of the Society—would almost make a book in itself; and there are many lesser cases which might be quoted, if the exercise were profitable. There are regions, of course, in which the Fabian contribution has been slight; on the broad issues of international policy, since the publication of *International Government* forty-five years ago, the Society has done little more than collect facts and proffer varying individual solutions; the same is on the whole true of industrial democracy. On 'municipal enterprise', so strongly urged by the Society in its youth, there is little success to record, as the Labour Party, ever since Morrison commandeered the L.C.C.'s trams for the London Passenger Transport Board, appears to have forgotten all about it; other proposals, such as the superannuation plan mentioned in the last chapter, have yet to make their impact, as have the dozens of suggestions put out in Fabian pamphlets from time to time. What the fate will be of these, or of others presently

[1] The importance of the Fabian role was emphasised, and the critics mentioned in Chapter XVIII largely answered, when newly independent Nigeria invited the Bureau to send representatives as its guests to the investiture of its first indigenous Governor-General. A case in which the strong representations of the Bureau were ignored—the setting up of the Central African Federation—might well be held to point the moral.

[2] And of the world to Bernard Shaw.

under discussion, no one but a prophet willing to risk his reputation at a moment in time particularly unfavourable to prophecy can venture to predict. All that can be said is that, whatever the mistakes which have been made, whatever the gaps and however wide, the legacy of the nine who on that January afternoon in Osnaburgh Street decided to work for improvement in society rather than perfection in themselves remains surely a remarkable one.

APPENDIX I

Rules and Basis of the Society

(a) *First Rules*

The Society, though chary of tampering with the Basis, had no such hesitation with regard to its Rules, which were continuously subject to proposed and actual alteration; in fact, almost up to the present time, rule-making might have been considered to be one of the favourite parlour-games of Fabian Annual Meetings. The first Rules are printed below; the order is rather odd, the Rule relating to officers preceding by several clauses that relating to membership. (Rule 4—*Want of Confidence*—was retained by the suspicious Society through a number of revisions.) The severe terms of Rule 8—*Elections*—will be noted, including the provision enabling the Executive to strike off the name of any member who failed for six months to put in an appearance at meetings. It is not surprising that membership remained small for some time; and after 1890, as with the influx of new members it became clear that the strict provisions were impracticable to enforce on members who did not live in or near London, a new Rule, embodying a milder procedure, was devised to meet their case. But that the intentions of the original Rule were serious is shown by a warning notice in *Fabian News* of June 1891, telling members to be more careful to make sure that the candidates they are proposing really understand the nature and purpose of the Society, and suggesting that they ought to have studied all the Tracts (23 by then, including some of 40 or 50 pages!) and possibly *Fabian Essays* as well. The previous issue of the *News* had announced that non-members might make application for tickets for forthcoming meetings '*valid for two meetings only*', and in the 'eighties it was not uncommon for a candidate to be rejected or to fall to the ground because his seconder did not turn up in person to the meeting.

Text of the Rules as adopted in 1886, including amendment of 1887, follows.

1. *Officers*. At the first meeting in April in each year the Society shall elect an Executive Committee which shall hold office for one year, unless removed by vote of the Society. The numbers of the Executive shall not be changed except by vote of the Society,

with due notice given. A Secretary and Treasurer shall be appointed at the same meeting.

2. *Executive Committee.* It is the duty of the Executive to conduct the General Business of the Society, to prepare pamphlets and Tracts, and to appoint delegates to represent the Society.

3. *Election of Committees.* Members nominated to serve on the Executive Committee must be proposed at the meeting next preceding that for their election. Nominations for other Committees must be sent to the Secretary 10 days before the election, and the names in both cases must be given on the notice convening the meeting.

4. *Want of Confidence.* Notice of motion to remove a member from any Committee must be given as provided in Rule 3 for election of Committees.

5. *Business.* Any resolution, the subject of which has been notified to the Secretary 10 days before any ordinary meeting shall be announced by him on the notice convening that meeting, and shall, together with any amendments thereof, take precedence of all other business. Notice of any proposal to issue a pamphlet must be sent to members 19 days before a vote can be taken.

6. *Urgency.* Any resolution not affecting the constitution of the Society may be declared urgent by a majority of $\frac{3}{4}$ of the members present in a meeting of not less than twelve members.

7. *Finance.* The Treasurer shall from time to time apply to the Society for such sums as are required.

8. *Elections.* Candidates must signify acceptance of the Basis of the Society, must attend two meetings as visitors, and must be proposed and seconded by members from personal knowledge. The names of candidates shall be sent to all members before each meeting. Candidates shall be elected by an unanimous vote of the Executive Committee. If a candidate be rejected his proposer shall have a right of appeal to the Society, in which case a ballot shall be taken, when one black ball in five shall exclude. The names of members who do not attend any meeting for six months may be struck off the list at the discretion of the Executive.

9. *Corresponding Members.* Residents in the provinces or abroad may be elected as corresponding members on the proposal of one member on personal acquaintance, the election proceeding as in the case of town members.

10. *Branches.* Branch Societies may be formed in accordance with such regulations as may be made from time to time.

(b) *Basis*, 1887–1919 (italicised words inserted in 1907)

The Fabian Society consists of Socialists.

It therefore aims at the reorganisation of Society by the emancipation of Land and Industrial Capital from individual and class ownership, and the vesting of them in the community for the general benefit. In this way only can the natural and acquired advantages of the country be equitably shared by the whole people.

The Society accordingly works for the extinction of private property in Land and of the consequent individual appropriation, in the form of Rent, of the price paid for permission to use the earth, as well as for the advantages of superior soils and sites.

The Society, further, works for the transfer to the community of the administration of such industrial Capital as can conveniently be managed socially. For, owing to the monopoly of the means of production in the past, industrial inventions and the transformation of surplus income into Capital have mainly enriched the proprietary class, the workers being now dependent on that class for leave to earn a living.

If these measures be carried out, without compensation (though not without such relief to expropriated individuals as may seem fit to the community), Rent and Interest will be added to the reward of labour, the idle class now living on the labour of others will necessarily disappear, and practical equality of opportunity will be maintained by the spontaneous action of economic forces with much less interference with personal liberty than the present system entails.

For the attainment of these ends the Fabian Society looks to the spread of Socialist opinions, and the social and political changes consequent thereon, *including the establishment of equal citizenship for men and women*. It seeks to achieve these ends by the general dissemination of knowledge as to the relation between the individual and society in its economic, ethical and political aspects.

Note. From time to time other passages about working methods, etc. were printed as part of the Basis, and these sometimes ran to a considerable length, but the paragraphs set out above are the operative ones.

Revision of 1919

The first two paragraphs stood unchanged. From the third paragraph onwards the Basis read:

The Society accordingly works for the extinction of private property in land, with equitable consideration of established expectations, and due provision for the tenure of the home and the homestead; for the transfer to the community, by constitutional methods, of all such industries as can be conducted socially; and for the establishment, as the governing consideration in the regulation of production, distribution and service, of the common good instead of private profit.

The Society is a constituent of the Labour Party and of the International Socialist Congress; but it takes part freely in all constitutional movements, social, economic and political, which can be guided to its own objects. Its direct business is (*a*) the propaganda of Socialism in its application to current problems; (*b*) investigation and discovery in social, industrial, political and economic relations; (*c*) the working out of Socialist principles in legislation and administrative reconstruction; (*d*) the publication of the results of its investigations and their political lessons.

The Society, believing in equal citizenship of men and women in the fullest sense, is open to persons irrespective of sex, race, or creed, who commit themselves to its aims and purposes as stated above, and undertake to promote its work.

(c) *Rules 1–8 of Fabian Society, as adopted 1939* (amendment of 1959 in square brackets).

1. The name of the Society shall be the Fabian Society.

2. The Society consists of Socialists. It therefore aims at the establishment of a society in which equality of opportunity will be assured and the economic power and privileges of individuals and classes abolished through the collective ownership and democratic control of the economic resources of the community. It seeks to secure these ends by the methods of political democracy.

The Society, believing in equal citizenship in the fullest sense, is open to persons irrespective of sex, race or creed, who commit themselves to its aims and purposes and undertake to promote its work.

The Society shall be affiliated to the Labour Party. Its activities shall be the furtherance of socialism and the education of the public on socialist lines by the holding of meetings, lectures, discussion groups, conferences and summer schools, the promotion of research into political, economic and social problems, national and international, the publication of books, pamphlets and periodicals, and by any other appropriate methods. [It also aims at the implementation of the Charter of the United Nations and the Universal Declaration of Human Rights. It seeks the creation of effective international institutions to uphold and enforce world peace.]

3. The Society as a whole shall have no collective policy beyond what is implied in Rule 2; its research shall be free and objective in its methods.

No resolution of a political character expressing an opinion or calling for action, other than in relation to the running of the Society itself, shall be put forward in the name of the Society. Delegates to conferences of the Labour Party, or to any other conference, shall be appointed by the Executive Committee without any mandatory instructions.

4. Full membership of the Society shall be open to those who are willing to accept the Rules and By-Laws of the Society. The acceptance of candidates is subject to confirmation by the Executive Committee.

The Executive Committee may, in special cases, elect Honorary Members of the Society.

Those who do not desire, or are ineligible for, full membership of the Society may become Associates, if in general sympathy with the objects of the Society. The acceptance of candidates is subject to confirmation by the Executive Committee. Associates shall have the same rights as full members in regard to the publications, schools, conferences and lecture meetings of the Society, but shall have no voting rights, shall not be eligible for membership of the Executive Committee and shall not be entitled to attend Annual and Special General Meetings of the Society. Federations of Labour Parties, Borough, Divisional and Local Labour Parties, Trade Unions and their branches, Co-operative organisations and other bodies may become subscribing bodies to the Society. The acceptance of candidates is subject to confirmation by the Executive Committee.

5. The Society shall be governed by an Annual General Meeting of members to be held at a time and place to be determined by the Executive Committee. Members shall be invited to submit resolutions. The resolutions shall be circulated and the members invited to submit amendments. The full agenda, including the resolutions and the amendments thereto, together with copies of the Annual Report, shall be circulated not less than a fortnight before the meeting. The Chairman of the meeting shall have the right to accept emergency resolutions and amendments with the consent of the meeting. All National members, fully paid up members of recognised local societies and the representative from each subscribing body shall have the right to attend and vote at the meetings.

6. The Executive Committee may at any time call a Special General Meeting to discuss any business of the Society.

If 5 per cent of all members entitled to vote in the election of the Executive Committee send to the General Secretary in writing a request for a Special General Meeting, the Executive Committee shall appoint for the meeting the earliest convenient date thereafter and shall circulate any resolutions submitted.

7. The Executive Committee may, and on a requisition signed by not less than 5 per cent of all members entitled to vote in the election of the Executive Committee shall, refer any question to the decision by Postal Ballot of all the members entitled to vote in the election of the Executive Committee.

8. The Rules may be revised by an Annual Meeting or by a Special General Meeting, provided the proposals have been circulated 14 days before the meeting, or by a Postal Ballot.

Any alterations of or addition to Rules 1–6 shall be adopted only if supported by *not less than three-quarters of the members present and voting* at the Annual or Special General Meeting or by a simple majority of those voting in a Postal Ballot.

APPENDIX II

Fabian Officers

President	None before 1939	
	1939–1941	Beatrice Webb
	1951–1952	Stafford Cripps, M.P.
	1952–1959	G. D. H. Cole*
Chairman	New Fabian Research Bureau	
	1931–1934	C. R. Attlee
	1934–1937	Lord Addison
	1937–1939	G. D. H .Cole
	Up till 1939 the Fabian Society had no Chairman; thereafter	
	1939–1946	G. D. H. Cole*
	1946–1948	Harold Laski
	1948–1950	G. D. H. Cole
	1950–1953	John Parker, M.P.
	1953–1954	Austen Albu, M.P.
	1954–1955	Harold Wilson, M.P.
	1955–1956	Margaret Cole
	1956–1957	Arthur Skeffington, M.P.
	1957–1958	Roy Jenkins, M.P.
	1958–1959	Eirene White, M.P.
	1959–1960	H. D. Hughes
	1960–1961	Lord Faringdon

* Also Honorary Secretary of Labour Research Department, 1916–1924.

Treasurer	1884–1911	Hubert Bland
	1911–1936	F. Lawson Dodd
	1936–1947	Emil Davies
	1947–1950	Ian Mikardo, M.P.
	1950–	John Diamond, M.P.

G. R. Mitchison was Treasurer of New Fabian Research Bureau, 1932–1938.

Honorary Secretary

New Fabian Research Bureau

1931–1935	G. D. H. Cole
1935–1939	Margaret Cole*

Fabian Society

1884–1885	Frederick Keddell
1885–1890	Sydney Olivier
1890–1891	E. R. Pease
1891–1915	None
1915–1939	E. R. Pease (Acting General Secretary 1915–1919)
1939–1953	Margaret Cole
1953–	John Parker, M.P.†

* Also Assistant Secretary (paid officer) of Labour Research Department, 1917–1925.

† Also joint Honorary Secretary with Margaret Cole.

General Secretary New Fabian Research Bureau

1931–1933	E. A. Radice
1933–1939	John Parker, M.P.

Fabian Society

Honorary Secretary only until 1891, thereafter

1891–1913	E. R. Pease
1913–1920	W. S. Sanders (in Army 1915–1919)
1920–1939	F. W. Galton (Joint Secretary with John Parker for first 6 months of 1939)
1939–1945	John Parker, M.P.
1946–1947	Bosworth Monck
1947–1949	Andrew Filson
1949–1953	Donald Chapman, M.P.
1953–1960	W. T. Rodgers
1960–	Shirley Williams

APPENDIX III

Distribution of Fabian Societies

(a) *Local Fabian Societies in 1893—nineteenth-century peak*

Ashton-under-Lyne, Aspatria (Cumberland), Bacup, Barrow-in-Furness, Batley, *Bedford*, *Belfast*, Berkshire, Birkenhead, *Birmingham*, Blackpool, *Bournemouth*, *Bradford*, *Cardiff*, Carlisle, Castleford (Yorks), Chester, *Clifton-with-Bristol*, Copley (Yorks), *Darlington*, Dewsbury, *Dublin*, Dukinfield, Dunfermline, *Edinburgh*, Failsworth, *Glasgow*, Gorton, Halifax, Hanley, Holmfirth (Yorks), Herfield (S. Wales), *Huddersfield*, *Hull*, *Hyde*, Jarrow, *Leeds*, Lincoln, *Liverpool*, Longton (Staffs), *Manchester* (2), Middleton, Neath, Newcastle upon Tyne, Newcastle under Lyme, *Northampton*, *Nottingham*, Oldham, Orllwyn Vale, Plymouth, *Preston*, Ramsbottom, Reddish (near Stockport), *Richmond* (Surrey), *Rochdale*, Rotherham, *Sheffield*, *Southampton*, South Shields, Sowerby Bridge, *Stafford*, Stalybridge, *St Helens*, Stockport, *Sunderland*, Tottington, Tyldesley, *Walthamstow*, Warrington, *Wolverhampton*, *York*.

Also Central London and ten other Groups in London area.

(b) *Local Fabian Societies in 1947–8—twentieth-century peak*

Aberdeen, Ashford, Barking, Barnsley, Barry, Bath, *Bedford*, *Belfast*, *Birmingham*, Bishop's Stortford, Blackburn, Blaenavon (Mon.), Bolton, Bootle, *Bournemouth*, *Bradford*, Braintree (Essex), Brighton, *Bristol*, Bromley, Bury St Edmunds, Canterbury, *Cardiff*, Cheadle, Chepstow, Chesterfield, Coventry (2), Colchester, Crewe, Crosby (Lancs), *Darlington*, Dartford, Derby, *Dublin*, Dudley, Durham, Eastbourne, *Edinburgh*, Enfield, Epsom, Exeter, Frome, *Glasgow*, Great Yarmouth, Guildford, Hartlepools, Haslemere, Holbeach (Lincs), *Huddersfield*, *Hull*, *Hyde*, Ipswich, King's Lynn, Kingston, Leamington, *Leeds*, Leicester, Leigh (Lancs), Luton, Maidstone, *Manchester*, *Merseyside*, Newport (Mon.), *Northampton*, Norwich, *Nottingham*, Oxford, Padiham (Lancs), Paisley, *Preston*, Rhondda, *Richmond* (Surrey), *Rochdale*, Romford, Rugby, *St Helens*, Scarborough, *Sheffield*, Slough, *Southampton*, S. Somerset, *Stafford*, Stratford-on-Avon, Stretford (Lancs), Stirlingshire, *Sunderland*, Swanage, Swansea, Tadworth, Tees-side,

Tenby, Tyneside, Wakefield, *Walthamstow*, Wellington (Salop), W. Somerset, Whitehaven, Wigan, *Wolverhampton*, *York*.

Also Central London and twenty-three other Societies or Groups in London area.

Note. The italicised Societies are those which appear in both lists; among the others, the number of industrial centres in the first list is noticeable, compared with that of home counties and residential areas in the second.

APPENDIX IV

Overseas Fabianism

The Fabian Society never founded branches of itself outside the British Isles. This was not by any means wholly due to the 'insularity' for which Shaw scolded the Society; for long before the Colonial and International Bureaux made definite efforts to attract non-British membership there were always a number of foreign names, some distinguished names, on the roll, and from the earliest days visiting foreigners of distinction were welcomed and entertained. Nor was the cause that Fabian 'gradualist' Socialism was in itself unacceptable outside; though there were a good many countries to which it could have carried no message (Tsarist Russia, notwithstanding Lenin's translation of the Webbs' *Industrial Democracy*, being one of them), there were others, particularly some of the Dominions, where the possibility of non-violent change to a socialised, social welfare economy would have been as welcome as it was to the Britain of 1889. It has even been suggested, though proof is lacking, that a good deal of European 'Revisionism' of Marxist doctrine and practice can be attributed to the discussion which Eduard Bernstein and other leading exiles had with early Fabians in London. But the main reason was, to some extent, the early association of Fabianism with 'gas-and-water', i.e. with the particular structure of English local government, but very much more, and as time went on, more important, its peculiar and unique connection with the historic institutions of the working class—the Trade Unions and the Labour Party. There was no federal Labour Party, with Socialists sitting with Trade Unionists on its executive *in their own right*, anywhere else than in Britain; there was no way, therefore, in which a Fabian Society, however 'Fabianly orthodox' it might be in heart and mind, could make itself an integral part of the Labour movement in its own country, as the British Society had done. However much it might set out to serve the Labour, Socialist, or Social-Democratic Party as the case might be, it could only be an association for research and discussion; it needed no 'self-denying ordinance', and that is why the Fabian Executive, while looking with a friendly eye on Societies which sprang up and called themselves Fabian, always refused to take any responsibility or commit itself to any form of official approval. It could not patent the Fabian name; sometimes, as we have seen in the case of Vienna, it was not even aware that a Fabian Society existed at all, and if it had known of them, it would not have felt inclined to underwrite anything it might do or say.[1]

The uniqueness of the Society was of course less marked in its early days, before the Labour Party had come into being, and some imitators did start up. The most notable of the originals was the American Fabian Society, which began in Boston under the auspices of one Rev. W. D. P. Bliss, of Boston, who was assisted by J. W. Martin, a member of the London Executive who emigrated; for several years it ran a journal, *The American Fabian*, in Boston and New York, and fathered Societies in Philadelphia and San Francisco; later there are recorded Societies in Chicago and at Yale; and across the forty-ninth parallel there turned up, at one time or another, Fabian Societies in Ottawa, Toronto, Montreal and Hamilton, Ontario. But in later years the attempt to form Fabian Societies on the American continent appears to have been given up;[2] and Fabian influence there, such as it is, has been exercised by contact with Dr Harry Laidler's League for Industrial Democracy in New York, and in Canada through the various groups of the Co-operative Commonwealth Federation.

After the Americas, the next to come were, naturally, the Dominions and the Empire. Australian Fabian Societies were mentioned in 1894; Societies at Dunedin and Christchurch before the first world war; later New Zealand, South Australia and New South Wales had strong groups which did research and published pamphlets. The Bombay Society recorded in 1892 seems to have faded away; but in 1921 there was news of a 'neo-Fabian' Society at Madras, which five years later blossomed into an impressive-sounding Fabian Society of India, with Annie Besant as President and N. M. Joshi, Secretary of the All-India Trades Union Congress, as secretary; it is sad that no more was ever heard of it. Even South Africa, in happier days, contributed—Johannesburg in 1916, Capetown in 1931 and again in 1942, Stellenburgh as late as 1945. In the mid-twenties there was a Fabian Society in Trinidad; the 1942 Nigerian Society has been mentioned in the body of the book, and there are one or two hints

[1] The Japanese Fabian Society, whose foundation was announced in 1925, did some very odd things before it had finished; it was also alleged that revolution in Burma had been partly inspired by a 'Burmese Fabian Society', but no confirmation was ever forthcoming.

[2] Unless a 'Sociedad Shawiana' in Buenos Aires be held to be an exception. Its existence was first announced in 1934, and it appeared in several successive Annual Reports, though Galton's habit of keeping Annual Reports paragraphs in standing type makes it uncertain that this proves anything.

of groups 'on Fabian lines' at Madrid, Copenhagen, Frankfurt, Budapest. All these developments, however, did not amount to much, as will be observed, and since the war have shrunk to almost nothing. Fabian Socialist thought has certainly had an impact outside its country of origin, as the many Fabians who have travelled and lectured overseas can testify, but Fabian organisation has had very little.

APPENDIX V

The Fabian Summer School

The Fabian Society did not invent summer schools, nor did it ever have a monopoly in that field. Long before the Society had ever thought of the idea religious gatherings like the famous Chautauqua Schools in the United States had made their name; and in the last fifty years many organisations, religious, political, educational, artistic, have come to maintain their summer schools almost as a matter of course. But in 1907, when the first Fabian School opened, the notion of voluntary residential study of politics seems to have been something of an innovation; and during two distinct periods of its life the School played a considerable part in Socialist political discussion, and had a certain notoriety of its own.

Its genesis was due mainly to the energy of a woman Fabian, Mabel Atkinson,[1] who was something of a stormy element in Edwardian Fabianism, a very truculent member of the Fabian Women's Group and a supporter of the Fabian Reform Committee described in Chapter XIII. She made the suggestion in January 1907, to a rather cagey Executive Committee; it was backed by Shaw and his wife and Lawson Dodd, and four months later was approved, the E.C. appointing Dodd and four others of its members to serve on the managing committee, of which Dodd was chairman. J. W. Shaw, a faithful Fabian, was made secretary at the opulent salary of £15 per annum, Miss Atkinson educational secretary, and Mary Hankinson, the square, blue-eyed Swedish gymnast and games mistress who subsequently became so monumental a Summer School character,[2] 'secretary for physical education'. A house was bought at Llanbedr, in North Wales, accommodating 39 persons—with outside lodgers the attendance at times reached 60—and arrangements were made for a six-weeks session. Courses were given on 'Lives of Great Socialists', 'Elementary Economic History', 'Present-day Problems', etc.; every morning there was a Swedish Drill Class, for which an extra 2*s.* 6*d.*

[1] She made an unfortunate marriage with a man named Palmer, emigrated to Natal and died at an advanced age in 1959.

[2] A poem to 'Hankey', by Dover Wilson the Shakespearian scholar, is preserved in the Summer School archives book for 1911.

per week was charged; open-air speeches (with Red Flag flying) were delivered on Barmouth Sands, and addresses—some in Welsh—given on Sunday evenings for the benefit of the villagers.

The chief attraction was undoubtedly Shaw, who was there almost the whole of the time—except for one evening when, having gone for a long mountain walk in the morning he failed to return, and the School embarked on a mass lantern search for its star, who was placidly sleeping in an hotel; but there were also marathon discussions on what Fabian policy ought to be, particularly with relation to the Labour Party—it will be remembered that the 'episode of Mr Wells' was then at its peak. Much of the housework was done voluntarily. 'This experiment', wrote *Fabian News* of November in a lyrical report on the School, 'was very successful. The School, which was rather unduly grey-headed, benefited greatly by the presence of eight or ten delightful young members (four at a time) who would not have been there had work not been found for them. To be waited on with so much friendliness and intelligence was a novel and pleasant experience . . . opens a new epoch in the history of the Society'—while the female grey-headed found the Swedish-drill costume 'so convenient' that they tended to 'adopt it as a uniform'.

The voluntary helper experiment proved not quite so epoch-making as this would suggest; the report of the manageress in the following summer complains of casualness and irregularity and proposes the charging of an additional fee (1*s*. a head!) to provide for paid service; and already there appeared signs of difficulties about 'house rules' and demands that committee members should attend the School, presumably for the purpose of helping to maintain order. But, by and large, it was certainly a success; the house filled up and was used for conferences at Easter and Whitsuntide as well. In 1909 the Webbs decided to try the School out as a vehicle for intensive education. They came down, not as residents of the School itself, but staying in the neighbourhood; Mrs Webb gave an inaugural address in which she 'laid down several rules of conduct', lectured on the National Minimum to audiences of over 80, and Sidney conducted classes in 'the Elements of Socialism' and appealed for donations for the National Committee for the Prevention of Destitution.

The Poor Law campaign, in effect, started at the School of 1909; and Beatrice was so taken with the possibilities that the Partnership took the step of offering to direct the entire School for the following year, hoping, *inter alia*, to bring in the new University Socialists and make them work and discuss along with Fabians of older standing. They did run the School for six weeks—a fairly formidable undertaking—but it was not wholly satisfactory. Beatrice began with a disagreement with 'Hankey' over the amount of personal service with which she was to be provided; she had no opinion at all of voluntaryism in that field, and an amusing and acrimonious correspondence preserved in the Webb Collection ends with the words, 'I am not going to pay for my board, and be sweated as Director, lecturer, and working-housekeeper with insufficient service!' [1]

On the running of the School itself she again disagreed. 'There are two conceptions', she wrote in her *Diary*,[2] 'which are really incompatible with each other—the Webbs' conception and that of the general manager, Miss Hankinson. She and Miss Atkinson desire a co-operative country holiday—made up, in the main, of organised games, excursions and evening entertainments—with a few lectures and discussions thrown in to give subjects of conversation. Our conception is that of an organised school. This involves getting at least one hundred to one hundred and twenty persons, and having a real bond of union based on a particular philosophy of life, with many specialised sections. . . .

'We must try to solve the question of a compromise between studiousness and a certain amount of carefully devised entertainment. It is *not* desirable [*sic*] to exclude games, exercise, music, but this must not be permitted to absorb the whole energies of any section of the company. Exercise, like walking, cycling, golf, bathing, tennis, etc., are all right, if they are taken when convenient. But regular lessons [she meant drill or dancing] or highly organised games, the learning of parts in plays, and the preparation of dresses and scenery, become an occupation in themselves and turn the mind for good and all from listening to lectures and quiet fireside discussion. . . .

'Points to be remembered . . .

'Fees for lectures should be separate, and the payment of it should constitute the qualification for residence. (When lectures are thrown in they are regarded as necessary evils and discipline, instead of being the main purpose.)

'The whole staff should be under one head, and should be inspired with the same purpose as the director. . . .

'The boarding arrangements should be differentiated with regard to *quiet* accommodation and extra luxuries, according to the diverse wishes of the guests. Of all the differentiations *quiet and freedom from noise* is the *most* important. Some people delight in noise. Would it be possible to exclude the more boisterous, larking entertainments, and substitute, or at any rate include, something of the nature of religious music or time for meditation?'

Finally, she found the response of the University Socialists disappointing. '"They won't come unless they know who they are going to meet", sums up Rupert Brooke (who came for a week with

[1] May 10th, 1910. (File copy in Sidney's writing.)
[2] September 4th, 1910.

some other Cambridge men). And I gather that, even if they *did* come, they would only talk together and to us. So that it would not be much use. They don't want to learn, they don't think they have anything to learn. The egotism of the young university man is colossal. Are they worth bothering about?'

When the Webbs next attended a Summer School, in 1912, by which time the Society itself had taken over the venture from the original committee,[1] and transferred the venue to Barrow House on Derwentwater, the young University men were attending in force and not from Cambridge only, and there was plenty of hard work and vigorous debate, even if neither 'quiet fireside discussion' nor 'religious music' were much in evidence. But Beatrice was not much better satisfied; though she could not call the Schools of 1913–14, at which Control of Industry, etc., was so hotly discussed, lazy or unintellectual, she could not prevent them playing games—or staying up to all hours making a great noise and breaking School regulations. 'Why must these young men be so *rude*?' she asked her *Diary* more than once.

The conflict described in the preceding paragraphs has been stated in Webbian terms, with which not all would agree in every respect; but it is none the less a real dilemma—or rather, two dilemmas—which beset generations of Schools. Was the main emphasis to be on work, or play? And what sort of compromise was to be reached between the natural—or wilful—anarchists and the necessity of some sort of order? The second question, which, it will be noticed, had arisen well before the 'manners of the Guild Socialists' threw spanners into the works, was a perennial headache. In 1914 the Executive (which always tried to keep out of Summer Schools disputes) was moved to 'ask Directors to state to members of the School that rules are made for practical reasons' [2]—while at the same time suggesting that rules need not be too inflexible; in 1919 Emil Davies had to preside over a lengthy and turbulent meeting on 'restrictions';[2] in 1930 we read of a Vigilance Committee being set up 'to help Director to maintain order'; and as late as the 'forties and early 'fifties directors and secretaries were always liable to meet trouble. Actual exclusions of members were, however, comparatively rare.

On the first question, though Mrs Webb's ideas were too ambitious to be achieved without an expenditure (on lecture fees, for example) which would have been too much for the Society's funds to bear, and

[1] By 1914 the Summer School Committee included representatives of all the main groups of the Society as well as of the Executive, and one member elected by the provincial Societies; after 1939 it was appointed by the Executive, but included outside members.

[2] Minutes, May 22nd, 1914. School records.

a restriction upon physical and other relaxation which would have been insupportable, there is no doubt that in the main she was right. After the Guild Socialist battles (resumed for one exciting week during the School of 1920), the School declined gradually into a gathering of Old Faithfuls, enjoying a holiday with lectures thrown in. There was an exception to this—also in 1920—when the Webbs staged an International Week, during which Kamenev and Krassin came to explain and defend the U.S.S.R. under the eyes of reformist Socialists from the Second International. The tremendous response which this received from the membership of the School should have pointed the moral; but the lesson seems not to have been learned, partly, perhaps, because the General Secretary took no interest—in 1928 the fact that he had honoured the School with a visit was specially noticed. 'Courses' of any kind ceased to be held, for lack of appeal to the (largely greying) patrons. Enthusiasts, in the 'twenties, patronised the Schools run by the I.L.P.

Ten years later began a new era. The amalgamation between N.F.R.B. and the Fabian Society was first openly discussed at the 1938 School, where it was enthusiastically received; and reference has already been made in the body of the book to the role of the School in policy discussions during and immediately after the war. For Dartington Hall, its home from 1938 onwards, the number of students multiplied three times; there were long waiting lists, and leading Socialists, soon to be members of a new Government, came down to discuss policy in public. It is true that the School did not, even then, quite live up to the standards of austerity suggested by Mrs Webb; it remained fairly noisy; it performed rehearsed revues; and some members adhered conscientiously to the traditions of country-dancing and nudist bathing and sunbathing preserved from the 'twenties. (One visitor to the School is reported to have fled without ado when, on a fine summer afternoon, he fell over Professor Joad wearing nothing but a hat.) But, by and large, going to the Fabian Summer School was then regarded, particularly by the University young, as an intellectual adventure. From 1947 onwards the School declined in importance, partly because Dartington was no longer available and no other places appeared to have the same appeal, partly because an increasing number of competitors, such as the official Labour Party School, appeared, partly because of the difficulty of accommodating young children, but mainly for the political reasons described on pp. 316–17. Summer Schools continued to be held in various places in England and on the Continent; but the interest and discussion of recent years have shifted to week-end schools of various kinds, of which something like half a dozen, some of limited and some of general appeal, such as the long New Year Schools, are regularly arranged during the year.

Index of Persons

General Index